Strategic Change and the Management Process

Corporate Strategy, Organization and Change

Series General Editor: *Andrew Pettigrew, University of Warwick*
Associate Editors: *Henry Mintzberg, McGill University*
             Peter Lorange, The Wharton School, University of
                 Pennsylvania

Published titles in the series

Management of Strategic Change
Edited by Andrew Pettigrew

Dynamics of Strategic Change
Christopher Hinings and Royston Greenwood

Managing Change for Competitive Success
Andrew Pettigrew and Richard Whipp

Forthcoming titles in the series include

Strategic Planning and Control
Edited by Peter Lorange

Organizational Learning: Lessons from Joint Ventures
Marjorie Lyles

Strategic Change and the Management Process

Gerry Johnson

Copyright © Gerry Johnson 1987

Extract on pages 288-9 from *The Changemasters* copyright © 1983 by Rosabeth Moss
Kanter reprinted by permission of Simon & Schuster Inc. and George Allen & Unwin
Publishers Ltd.

First published 1987
Reprinted 1989, 1992

Blackwell Publishers
108 Cowley Road, Oxford OX4 1JF, UK

Three Cambridge Center
Cambridge, Massachusetts 02142, USA

British Library Cataloguing in Publication Data
A CIP catalogue record of this book is available from the British Library.

Library of Congress Cataloging in Publication Data
Johnson, Gerry.
  Strategic change and the management process.

  Includes index.
  1. Strategic planning.   2. Foster Brothers—
  Management.   I. Title.
HD30.28.J65   1987   658.4′012   87–5152
ISBN 0–631–14717–9

Typeset in 10/12pt Times by Opus, Oxford
Printed in Great Britain by T J Press, Padstow

To the managers of Foster Brothers

Contents

Figures and Tables

Foreword

Strategic Change and the Management Process is the first volume to appear in the Basil Blackwell series on Corporate Strategy, Organization, and Change. Gerry Johnson's book combines a well-ordered but eclectic theoretical base, novel and important empirical findings and a critical reflection on the field of strategic management. As such this first contribution to the series begins to set the tone for other scholarly and research-based work which will appear over the next few years.

Among the many areas that focus on the nature of management in public and private organizations, there is one that is universally acknowledged to be in the greatest state of flux and most in need of creative development. This is the area variously referred to as corporate strategy, strategic management, and business policy. The primary objective of the Blackwell series is to provide a forum for scholars and researchers from a variety of disciplines to communicate new concepts and empirical findings in the areas of corporate strategy, organization, and change to students and informed practitioners.

As the title of the series suggests, the editors are seeking to publish innovative books on the strategic development of the firm. However, it is increasingly recognized that studies of firm level behaviour need to be understood in the context of sectoral, economic, social and political influences. Innovative work in the area of strategic management and change is likely to require analyses across and within levels of analysis which takes into account the context, content, and process of strategic change. The series will therefore publish volumes dealing with the firm, sector, industry and product market levels of analysis, and will draw on scholarly work now underway by researchers with backgrounds in business policy and strategy, business history, organization theory and development, industrial economics, manufacturing policy, and marketing.

Gerry Johnson's book is a welcome addition to the relatively small number of longitudinal and processual studies of strategic change in the firm. For many organizations in the European and North American context, the period since 1979 has been an era of environmentally driven radical change. The managerial responses to environmental pressure have included divestment, internationalization, structural and cultural change and a variety of strategic changes designed to promote the survival and regeneration of organizations. From a practical perspective these pressures for change have revealed the limited amount of information about the what, why, and how of managing strategic changes. This cry from managers and consultants for assistance in managing change has coincided with an increasingly visible trend amongst scholars and researchers in the strategy area to move beyond the linear and rational understanding of strategy formulation to begin to describe and understand how and why large scale changes are implemented in the firm. This book gives a considerable impetus to scholarly work uncovering the reality of managerial processes of strategic change.

Drawing on the experience of Fosters, a national clothing retailer in the UK, this book presents a thorough-going review and critique of some of the currently available process theories of strategic choice and change. This review teases out the overlaps and idiosyncrasies of rationalistic, incremental, and interpretative perspectives on strategic change and then juxtaposes these frameworks against a longitudinal study of the strategic development of Fosters.

Empirically the book contributes by adding to the still sparse collection of longitudinal cases which reveal the realities of how senior managers grapple with the prospect of major change. Here Johnson's account of the jointly political and cultural character of strategic change, his analytical and practical message that change can only be understood in the context of continuity, and his careful analysis of how organizational paradigms are challenged and changed all make notable additions to research on managerial processes of change.

Andrew M. Pettigrew
Director, Centre for Corporate
Strategy and Change
University of Warwick

Preface

The origins of this book and the research upon which it is based go back some years. When I left employment as a full-time executive and entered, somewhat later than is usual, into the teaching and the research of management, I was struck by one thing more than any other. Most of my reading on management that became my early guide was from books and papers that appeared to say very little about management as I had understood it. The theories and the techniques seemed sensible enough and I could identify that many were known and some employed by managers, but the authors neglected a whole raft of issues and problems that managers faced and that, at least in my experience, were central to the lives of managers and to decision-making. Such issues were concerned with the social and political fabric of the organizations in which I had been working and bore upon the difficulties of reaching agreements or implementing decisions. It was also some surprise to me that so few scholars seemed concerned to learn from the managers who were themselves in the process of managing. It seemed to me, as one who had relatively recently found the process of management fascinating and demanding, and had been faced with coping with the problems it raised, that trying to learn from the experience of managers was a legitimate and rather overdue task.

I was later to find that there were, indeed, writers and researchers who were concerned with such issues. It was just that, in the area in which I specialized at that time, their research and their views were not commonly understood and not commonly employed in the models and frameworks for writing and teaching. The fact was that the teaching of marketing and the teaching of strategy in the mid-1970s had inherited a theoretical basis strongly linked to that of economics and operational research rather than having any strong links with the disciplines of social enquiry. Moreover such moves as were taking place in research terms tended to be dominated by positivists who were anxious to develop laws or rules of strategic development that could somehow be shown to be proven and presumably used as more or less prescriptive guidelines for managers.

At the time there were very few books or papers about strategy and strategic management that started from the question of what managers actually did, the problems they faced and how they took decisions. It was therefore with some delight that I found eventually that there were indeed writers and researchers interested in such questions. My early discovery of the work of Henry Mintzberg and, later, Andrew Pettigrew was encouraging. It was developed by an exposure to the work of, and later friendship with, J–C Spender, to whose ideas the origins of this research can be traced. It was also developed by reading about the work of many of the researchers whose studies are summarized in this book.

This book has grown out of the simple aim of trying to relate the emerging body of research findings and theory about the nature of strategic management to the practical problems of managing strategic change in organizations. I chose to do this by means of a detailed examination of such change processes over time primarily in one organization. The book therefore takes the form of an investigation of the relevance of models of strategic management to an extensive and detailed case study of strategic change as understood by the managers in that organization. It must therefore be obvious that such contribution as this book may make to the literature on the subject is thanks very largely to the managers in that organization.

The company concerned is Foster Brothers, a national clothing retailer in the UK, traditionally and primarily concerned with menswear retailing. This book is dedicated to the managers in that company who were not only prepared to invite me into the organization over a period of some six years, but were prepared to talk frankly about not only their success, but also about problems they faced and the mistakes they thought they had made. Moreover, they were prepared to accept – indeed encouraged – the publication of the findings of the work in the belief that it would prove useful for others who might be faced with managing strategic change. I would like to record my thanks to, and my admiration for, those executives. In particular I am indebted to Barry Davison who as Chairman of Foster Brothers agreed to the research being undertaken in the company.

The developing ideas in the book have also taken shape as a result of many discussions with colleagues interested in similar problems concerned with the process of strategic management. In particular I would like to record my thanks to J–C Spender for his early inspiration and to Professors John Child and Ray Loveridge at Aston University, Professor Andrew Pettigrew at Warwick University, Professor Howard Thomas at the University of Illinois at Urbana–Champaign and my colleagues when I was at Aston University, Ken Clarke and especially Martyn Pitt. I would like to thank them for their helpful comments and stimulating ideas, whilst taking full responsibility for the content of the analysis and the conclusions arrived at in the text.

Others too have helped. In particular I would like to thank Christine Dunn at Aston University and Christine Guest at Manchester Business School for their patience in preparing the text, Tom Grocock for his assistance in indexing and Tony Sweeney at Blackwells, not only for waiting for this work, but also for encouraging its production.

Gerry Johnson
Manchester Business School
November 1986

Part I

A Background to the Study of the Management of Strategic Change

1
Introduction

This book is about how managers manage strategic change in organizations. It discusses the question by reviewing existing concepts and theories that help in our understanding of the problem, and also by means of a detailed examination of how managers in one organization attempted, over a period of some ten years, to adjust the strategy of their company as the market in which they were operating changed considerably. The analysis and discussion is rooted in the belief that existing approaches in the management literature as to how strategy should be managed are rather limited and are based on a view of managers as essentially scientific in their approach to problem identification and resolution. This study, on the other hand, is based on the conviction that we need to understand management as a social, political and cultural activity. One aim of the book, therefore, is to consider the extent to which existing concepts and theory explain the phenomena of strategic decision-making and change as observed. A second is to develop explanations for the processes of managing strategic change that arise from an analysis of the in-company study. In particular, the focus is on the way in which managers make sense of the competitive environment in which they operate and how this, in turn, contributes to the development of strategies in the political and cultural milieux we know as organizations.

This introductory chapter sets the scene in a number of ways. It discusses briefly what is meant by 'strategy' and 'strategic management' in this book, and what distinguishes the management of strategy from other management tasks. It also introduces the reader to the sorts of ideas employed by those who have researched and written about strategy in the past. It then goes on to describe in a little more detail what this book aims to achieve and how it sets out to do it.

THE CONCEPTS OF STRATEGY AND STRATEGIC MANAGEMENT

We will start with the question of what strategy is and from this, move to the question of how it is managed. There is a good deal of disagreement about how 'strategy' should be defined in terms of what should or should not be included in any definition. Hofer and Schendel (1978), for example, review 13 different approaches. Rather than attempting to provide a watertight definition here, the idea of strategy will be explained by discussing briefly the sorts of characteristics commonly employed by authors when they discuss what sorts of decisions in organizations are of a strategic nature (e.g., see Johnson and Scholes, 1984).

Strategic decisions are likely to be concerned with some of the following.

(1) The *long-term direction* of the organization: strategic decisions are likely to be concerned with time horizons of a different order from day-to-day operational matters. Time horizons will, of course, vary by organization: managers in a major oil company might be considering the future of their business on a ten- or twenty-year timescale whereas a small localized service company is likely to be concerned with much shorter time horizons. Managers in both sorts of companies know, however, that they need to have some idea of where they are going rather than manage only where they are currently.

(2) The *scope* of an organization's activities: for example what markets should be served by what products or services and in which geographical area? This, then, is to do with the boundaries the organization places upon itself.

(3) The *matching* of *organizational activities to the environment* in which it operates. A fundamental notion is that organizations need to respond to a variety of external forces – economic, social, political, technological and so on – and need to take decisions that maintain and develop activities to cope with that environment.

(4) The *matching of the organization's activities to its resource capability:* the extent to which an organization is able to respond to environmental forces must, necessarily, take into account its resource capabilities. So current resources – for example, people and their skills, technology and finance – are likely to constrain what might be done in the future; and also intentions for the future may well lead to the need to change resource capability.

(5) This leads to the next point. Strategic decisions are likely to have *major resource implications* for an organization. It is unlikely that current resources will be suitable if significant changes in the scope of activities are to occur; it may, for example, be that large amounts of capital are required – while new operations through acquisition or significant divestment may be necessary.

(6) The *expectations and values* of stakeholders in the organization. An organization is not just responsive to its environment or its resource

constraints: how it develops is also likely to be influenced by what people involved with that organization want. Traditionally this has been thought of in terms of organizational goals or objectives, perhaps set by senior management in terms of the expectations of others – the government or shareholders for example. Such goals and objectives might well be important; but so too will be the values and expectations, often less explicit, of those active in the organization – for example the managers.

It is also clear that strategy can exist at a number of different levels in an organization. To take the example of a major business corporation, corporate strategy will be concerned primarily with decisions about the allocation of large-scale resources between businesses within that corporation or about how it might be organized so as to manage the range of its interests, perhaps throughout many countries. Business strategy will be concerned with how a particular business unit competes against its rivals and will, therefore, be concerned with what markets are best served with what sorts of products or services so as to provide some advantage over competition. Also strategy, as a concept, is relevant at an operational level, particularly in terms of the functional translation of business strategies into action so as to effect and maintain competitive positioning.

Thus the concept of strategy embraces many characteristics at different levels of managerial activity. What then is strategic management, and what distinguishes strategic management from any other aspect of management in a firm? There is no attempt here to suggest that the management of strategy is somehow distinct in terms of managerial activity from the management of anything else in an organization; managers do not compartmentalize their working lives so that at one time they are 'managing strategy' and at other times doing something else (Mintzberg 1973a). However, what can be said is that the issues that have to be dealt with in managing the strategy of an organization are of a different nature from many of the day-to-day activities of managing. First, they are likely to involve a higher degree of *uncertainty*. They are usually to do with decisions and action that demands that some view of the future be taken. It cannot be that managers are able to 'know' what the future will be like; yet they must take a view about it on some basis. Clearly these sorts of decisions must be much less certain than the day-to-day management of the operations of the business.

Second, such decisions are likely to demand an *integrated* approach to managing the organization. We are not likely to find that such decisions can be managed within any one function, or area of expertise, within the organizations. Thus a strategic decision and the implementation of strategy are likely to involve managers in crossing boundaries within the firm and in negotiating and coming to agreements with managers in different parts of the organization who, inevitably, are likely to have different interests and perhaps different priorities.

Third, strategic decisions are likely to be decisions concerned with _change_. It is unlikely that managers will foresee a future in which there is no change and therefore they will have to consider how their organization should adjust to such change. Implementing strategic decisions is therefore also likely to involve the persuasion and organization of people to change from what they are used to doing. Moreover the expectation may be that they change towards something that is ill defined, uncertain and unfamiliar. Not surprisingly the management of strategic change in organizations can be highly problematic.

Pulling all this together, what we can say is that, whereas strategic management should not and cannot be regarded as separated from other forms of management, it is likely to be distinguished b† _complexity_ than the operational tasks that management face on a day-to-day basis. It is this area of complexity that we will return to time and again in this book; complexity that arises from the management of uncertainty and change of a high order of magnitude in a political environment. The issue that is raised in this book is how managers cope with managing the complexity of strategy, how they cope with formulating strategies and how they cope with implementing the change that is usually necessary to effect those strategies.

APPROACHES TO UNDERSTANDING STRATEGIC MANAGEMENT

There is no dearth of literature on the subject of strategic management. More so than in most areas of management, numbers of books and papers on this subject appear to be growing exponentially. A review of such literature is provided in chapter 2 in so far as it relates to the theme of this study, but it is worthwhile, at this stage, to summarise the nature of the developing debate about strategic management, simply because it helps provide an explanation of why there should be yet another book.

The study of management in the twentieth century, at least, has its roots in an essentially scientific view of management. It is a view that holds that, faced with the problems of managing organizations, the primary task is to establish the facts about any problem so that it can be defined and, once defined, an objective assessment can be made of what possible solutions might contribute to dealing with the problem. Given such a definition of the problem, the assumption is that managers behave 'rationally'. They will evaluate possible courses of action against explicit goals, and identify a solution that is likely to achieve these goals and can be put into effect. It is a view of management that is essentially driven by the notion that the complexity we have here identified can be reduced through analysis so as to provide an understanding that is susceptible to the objective identification of rational solutions. If the volumes of literature written on strategy since the 1940s are examined, it is this sort of approach that predominates.

However, there is another body of literature, more recent and rooted in a more empirical research tradition, that shows that, rational and scientific as such approaches might be, they do not describe well the activities of managers in managing such complexity. Researchers who have looked at what managers actually do in dealing with strategic issues argue that it is difficult, if not impossible, for managers to 'know the facts' about the future, or about the ramifications across the organization of decisions of a strategic nature; moreover, it is unrealistic to assume that the supposed objectivity and rationality of one manager will be appreciated, let alone agreed upon, by another; rationality, in this sense, simply does not take account of the political or cognitive realities of organizations.

There has, then, grown up a significant question about the management of this higher order of organizational issues we call strategy. It is essentially this: if, faced with the complexity of strategy, the scientific models of management can at best offer partial guidance on what to do, and if managers appear not to manage in such ways, how then do we advance our understanding of what, almost by definition, must be the most important aspects of managing? Broadly speaking, there appear to be two options. We simply argue that managers really should be rational and scientific in their approaches and we had better educate them to be so; or that, given such complexity, rational scientific models, partial as they may be, are the best we can do. Alternatively we can argue that the task of the researcher is to understand better what managers actually do in managing such complexity, and to start to build some explanatory models for this, from which some better or at least fuller guidelines might emerge.

Unashamedly this book takes the latter approach. It is a book about the problems of managing the sorts of decisions we have described as strategic. It seeks to understand the processes of management as they occur, warts and all. It does not start from the premise that managers are rational and scientific in their approach, nor does it start from the premise that managers are unable to cope with complexity and uncertainty. It starts from the premise that it is the role of the researcher to understand how intelligent, well informed managers working in a political and social environment cope with the sort of complexity we have described. Any models that are built, whether they may be descriptive or prescriptive, derive from this understanding.

THE BASIS OF THE STUDY

The overall aim of the book is then to improve our understanding of strategic management and, in particular, the problems of managing strategic change. It does this by examining and building upon such research on the process of strategic management as does exist by means of a detailed study of the management of strategic change in a company and, through this, by refining and developing models that might provide useful guidelines to managers and theorists alike. In this sense the book is strongly in sympathy with the views of Henry Mintzberg when he writes that his aim is to:

> . . . present theory that is 'grounded' – that is rooted in data, that grows inductively out of systematic investigation of how organisations behave. I am firmly convinced that the best route to more effective policy making is better knowledge in the mind of the practitioner of the world he or she actually faces. This means that I take my role as researcher and writer to be the generation and dissemination of the best *descriptive* theory possible. I believe it is the job of the practitioner – line manager, staff analyst, consultant (including myself when in that role) – to prescribe, to find better approaches to policy making. In other words, I believe that the best description comes from the application of conceptual knowledge about a phenomenon *in a specific and familiar context*. To me, good descriptive theory in the right hands is a prescriptive tool, perhaps the most powerful one we have. (Mintzberg, 1979a, p. vi)

Surprisingly there are relatively few studies that have attempted to study how managers actually manage strategy. How this is done here is described in some detail in chapter 3 but the characteristics of the study can be summarized very briefly. First, it concentrates on one firm primarily. It does this because the aim was to get as close to understanding how managers coped with their situation as possible. This was done in the main by letting the managers talk at length at different periods of time about the problems they faced and how they were coping with them. Thus the study was able to piece together the elements of change that had taken place and were taking place in the business over time and check this against how different managers understood them and explained them. This, supplemented by extensive secondary data search, in order to set out the chronology of change in the organization, provided a rich basis on which to understand and describe the processes of management. It is not claimed that the picture is perfect; however, it is claimed that it gives a great deal fuller an understanding of the processes of management over many years in a company than might be obtained by casual observation or by survey techniques scanning necessarily more superficially across many organizations.

It is not suggested that this one organization, or the managers in it, are representative of all organizations or all managers. Indeed the nature of the context of the study and the limitations this places on the generalizability of the data are explicitly discussed in Part III of the book. Rather, the aims of the study are, first, to examine in as live and real a situation as possible the relevance of our existing understanding of the processes of strategic management. In this sense the study is concerned with understanding the relevance of existing theory. A second aim is to generate some theoretical propositions that advance theory, and that others might critically examine, develop, test or simply find useful. There is no attempt to suggest that the study 'proves' anything as such; it is essentially concerned with theory-building. In reading the book, the reader should be aware, then, of the nature of the argument it advances. Whilst rooted in many well-established ideas, the propositions put forward are essentially hypothetical and are for others interested in the subject – managers, researchers and students – to examine, criticize and hopefully develop.

The original research upon which this book is based did include a longitudinal examination of strategic management in two other companies within the same industry sector as the one discussed here. It would also have been possible perhaps to have undertaken still more comparative work. However, although there is some discussion throughout the book, and in the final chapter, of comparisons with other organizational studies of change, this is deliberately limited. The reasons for this are twofold. First, it would have been impossible to provide the sort of detailed descriptive account of strategic management processes as is provided here for a number of companies without the book becoming excessively long. Second, comparative work is most useful in examining the extent to which the propositions and patterns that emerge from the stages of the research discussed above are generalizable. In this sense comparative studies are to do with the confirmation of propositions. This is, of course, important and – in the sense that this book does examine the relevance of existing concepts to the explanation of the observed process – the study provides a basis for discussing confirming evidence from the data. Moreover there is a discussion in the final chapter of the extent to which the findings of the study and the propositions arising from it are generalizable; but this is not the main purpose of the research and this book. The primary aim is to build on existing theory so as to develop further explanatory propositions about strategic management that, hypothetical though they may be, help develop our understanding of a complex area of management. It is hoped other researchers will critically examine the sorts of propositions put forward here in the context of their own studies of the processes in other organizations. In other words, the comparative element of the study is dependent, not on the effort of just one researcher, but on the efforts of many, interested in similar fields.

The Context of the Study

The organization that provides the context for the discussion of strategic management is Foster Brothers, a national clothing retailer in the UK. Its main activity was the retailing of men's clothing, but it also had other retailing interests, particularly in children's clothes and, variously in the period studied, in womenswear, camping and leisure goods and drugstores.

A detailed description of the problems facing the business and the changes that took place in the company, primarily in the period 1970–84, are given in chapters 4 and 5 of the book. However, it might be in order to set out briefly why the company was so attractive as a basis for discussion of the sort of problems dealt with in the book. Fosters was faced in the 1960s and the 1970s with major changes in its business environment. It was always primarily a retailer of men's clothing and in those two decades the changes that took place in the sort of clothes that men were prepared to wear were dramatic. Moreover, the way in which the businesses competing with Fosters responded to those changes was varied: many of the competitors hardly changed at all, others changed very rapidly, still others died and others were born. So the competitive market situation that Fosters faced, and with which their managers had to cope, was one of turmoil. The pattern of strategies followed by the business, given such turmoil, is particularly interesting for this sort of study. Throughout the 1970s the company attempted to adjust to the changes it faced. It is clear that the managers were aware of the changes and tried to adjust the historical strategy of Fosters in line with them. As with so many businesses, they thought, at the time, this was being done successfully and effectively and for much of the 1970s their beliefs were borne out by the financial performance of the company. Yet in 1981 the company suffered a severe financial downturn. By 1983 an attempt was being made to reconfigure substantially the strategy of the business and by 1984 the managers believed that this was well under way. In fact, looking back on it, many of them were to argue that even the fairly fundamental changes made in that period were insufficient. The company was eventually taken over in 1985. In short, Fosters provides a context in which many of the key issues concerning the management of strategic change can be examined. How do managers conceive of the problems they face in strategic terms? How do they reconcile these views amongst themselves? How do they go about adjusting the strategy of their businesses when they recognize the need for change? What contribution do analytical techniques make to this? Why is strategic change so problematic? Why do the changes made by management often appear to be too little too late? And how do managers deal with more fundamental change?

These are the sort of questions raised in the study of Foster Brothers and dealt with in the rest of this book.

THE STRUCTURE OF THE BOOK

The book is in three parts. This first part of the book introduces the subject for study and, in chapter 2, reviews some of the main strands of research on strategic management. This is done by considering three broadly different approaches to the subjects. First, the rational, scientific management approach is discussed. Second, the idea is developed of strategy as evolving in organizations – as a product of the history of the organization and the political activity and compromises in the organization. The idea of the manager consciously managing this incremental process is also introduced here. Third, the view that strategy needs to be conceived of as a product of the managers' understanding and perception of the organizational world is discussed. Here strategy is seen as a product of management cognition, so the nature of cognition in an organizational setting is discussed.

Chapter 3 deals more specifically with the way in which the research for this study was conducted. It is provided for those who are interested in the problems of what must be largely qualitative research work. As such some readers may wish to skip over this. However, it does contain some specific acknowledgements of the problems of undertaking such studies and some suggestions as to how future work of this kind can be undertaken.

Part II of the book presents the context of the study. Chapter 4 outlines the changes that occurred in the retail market for menswear clothing, a market that changed dramatically prior to and during the period of this study. Chapter 5 is a detailed account of the way in which Fosters' managers tried to cope with these changes from 1970 to 1985, although the focus is mainly on the period 1975–84. This case study of strategic change is presented, as far as possible, through the words of the managers themselves. It is an attempt to provide as full an account as possible of how managers who were actively involved understood solutions as they developed, the responses of their colleagues, and their own and others actions.

Part III of the book then seeks to understand the processes observed in the case study. It begins in chapter 6 with an examination of the extent to which rationalistic models of strategic management explain the phenomena observed and, broadly, concludes that they do not. It then goes on in chapter 7 to re-examine the notion of strategic management in cultural terms, that is as a product of the taken-for-granted assumptions, beliefs and routines of managers. The conclusion is that the processes observed in Fosters are better explained in these ways. Chapter 8 then utilizes the Fosters material more specifically to examine how such a cultural and interpretative approach to strategic management can aid our understanding of the processes in practical terms. In so doing propositions about interpretative approaches to strategic management are advanced and examined in the light of examples of adaptive and also more fundamental modes of strategic change described in the Fosters case study. Finally, in chapter 9, the wider implications of the themes developed in the book are considered in terms of comparisons with other organizational contexts and the extent to which they are of practical use to those involved in the management of the strategic change in organizations. It may be that those who approach the book primarily from an interest in the practical application of the themes developed would do well to read chapter 9 out of sequence, since it does provide both a summary of key propositions and a discussion of their relevance to the practice of management. Such readers may care to follow this introductory chapter and perhaps chapter 2 with chapters 4 and 5 and then chapter 9, before referring to chapters 6, 7 and 8 for more detailed explanation and illustration of the arguments.

2
The Process of Strategic Management – Some Theoretical Perspectives

We began by stating that this book is about the process of strategic management, but so far the question of what is meant by 'process' had not been addressed. So what is meant by 'process' in the management of strategy? The purpose of this chapter is to clarify this by describing the ways in which 'process' has been handled as an issue by researchers and writers on strategy. It is not the purpose of this chapter to examine the work of all writers on process in detail but rather to illustrate different perspectives on the question so as to develop a 'language' of explanation with which to discuss the observations made in the case study of Fosters and its analysis in part III of the book.

In explaining and illustrating the different ways in which the process issue has been addressed, it is convenient to conceive of a number of different models found in the literature, models that bear some comparison to those discussed by, for example, Mintzberg (1973b) and Chaffee (1985). Three broad approaches can be discerned, as detailed below.

(1) A *'rationalistic'* view of strategic management in which strategy is seen as the outcome of a sequential, planned search for optimal solutions to definable problems, with strategic action as the consequent implementation of decisions made about such problems. This approach has also been called 'linear' (Chaffee, 1985,), the 'planning mode' (Mintzberg, 1973b), 'rational' (Peters and Waterman, 1982) and 'synoptic' (Frederickson, 1983).

(2) An adaptive or *incremental* view of strategic management in which strategy is seen as the outcome of the managerial action of corporate life. Strategy here is seen as a matter of evolution and needs to be understood in terms of the activities managers undertake to cope with an uncertain and complex external environment, and a work context characterized by social and political considerations and action.

(3) An *interpretative* view in which strategy is seen as the product of individual, or collective, sense-making about the organization and the environment in which it operates. Here the emphasis is not so much on rational analytic interpretation of complexity as on the cognitive and symbolic bases of interpretation that characterize the lived world of managers.

These three approaches overlap to some extent and, indeed, it would be possible to characterize schools of thought by re-drawing definitional boundaries somewhat and coming up with different headings. However, these categorizations will serve for discussing the significance and implications of different approaches to be found in the literature.

A RATIONALISTIC PERSPECTIVE

If strategic management is seen as the management of complexity and uncertainty, then the underlying principle of rationalistic models of strategic management is that the clearer the understanding of that complexity, the more likely it is that sensible decisions can be taken. This clarity can be obtained through an analytical approach to understanding the environment and the organization's position in it, and by planning the response to that environment through a series of steps that are clear and likely to provide a basis for rational, objective choice and well considered action. It is a view of complexity reduction through scientific management and is traceable back to the concepts of the early management writers of the twentieth century such as Taylor and Fayol. Indeed Donald Schön has argued that the appeal of such rationalistic notions has much deeper and more long-standing origins:

> Since the Reformation, the history of the West has been shaped by the rise of science and technology and by the industrial movement which was both cause and consequence of the increasingly powerful scientific world view. As the scientific world view gained dominance, so did the ideas that human progress would be achieved by harnessing science to create technology for the achievement of human ends. This Technological Program, which was first vividly expressed in the writings of Bacon and Hobbes, became a major theme for the Philosophers of the Enlightenment in the 18th Century and by the late 19th Century had been firmly established as a pillar of conventional wisdom. (Schön, 1983, p.31)

Whether writers of management texts on strategy, who have employed essentially rationalistic models, would recognize themselves as in direct line from Hobbes and Bacon is less pertinent than the point that Schön makes, that an essentially scientific, essentially rationalistic approach to strategic management has deep roots; it is not surprising that it should be regarded as accepted wisdom by many writers, students and managers. Indeed virtually every book published since 1980 that includes the words 'strategic management' in the title (e.g. Wheelan and Hunger, 1983; Harvey, 1982; Glueck, 1980; Pearce and Robinson, 1982; Rowe et al., 1982) adopts a similar approach on the subject – it is dealt with by using an essentially normative model with the focus on the rational formulation of strategies. In doing this a model comprising elements summarized below and illustrated as figure 2.1 is used.

(1) Often seen as a first step is the establishment of strategic *objectives* at an appropriate level of generality. For example, objectives at a corporate strategy level might be to do with some measure of financial return, whereas objectives at a business unit level might be to do with market share, levels of profitability and operating efficiency. The idea is that without clear objectives it is very difficult to make a sensible strategic decision since there is no yardstick against which to evaluate strategic options. It is also assumed that if these objectives are known throughout the organization a more unitary approach to decision-making and implementation of strategy is likely.

(2) It is through a process of *analysis* that an understanding of the strategic situation of the organization can be obtained. Such an analysis might consider, for example, what changes have occurred and are likely to occur in the environment and how they will affect the organization. The analysis would also deal with assessing the resource strength of the organization in the context of these changes. Does the organization have the physical, financial and management capabilities to deal with the sorts of changes that are occurring? There are tools and techniques recommended for such analysis: methods of examining environmental trends, projecting future environmental changes, resource audit checklists, methods of financial analysis and so on. In these ways analysis can be thorough and systematic and would be expected to deal with substantial amounts of data so as to give a view of the key influences on the organization in terms of the cause and effect on the organization's performance.

(3) Strategic decisions should not be taken without consideration of a range of relevant *strategic options*. Here the concern is with generating conceivable strategies that might be followed. It is assumed that the

strategist can and should be aware of the possible benefits and consequences of such options.

(4) Such options are capable of *evaluation*. Faced with a set of options, the management is able to assess them in terms of the analysed strategic position of business, and evaluate which strategy or combination of

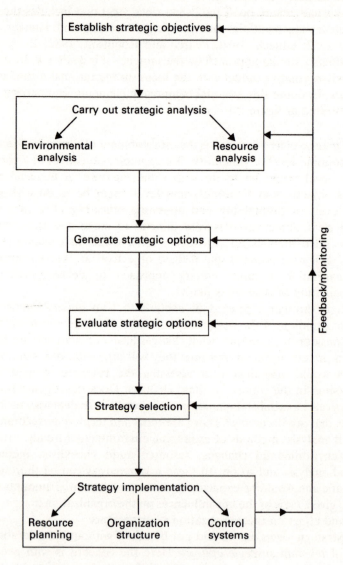

FIGURE 2.1   A normative model of strategic management

strategies would be likely to achieve the business or corporate objectives in the context of known strengths, weaknesses and threats. In addition other criteria of evaluation such as degree of risk and feasibility might be employed. Such evaluation thus provides the basis for a rational selection of strategy.

(5) The chosen strategy or strategies must then be implemented. *Implementation* would involve developing what may be generalized decisions into specific plans. Management will need to consider the resources needed: it will also be necessary to consider how the company as a whole should be organized and what systems of control would be needed to manage the new strategy and provide the means of monitoring its progress.

(6) Implicit within such a model are other properties. For example that strategic decision-making is the property of *'top managers'*; other managers implement strategy, or 'service' such decisions through their role in corporate planning or management information departments. Indeed, the process of strategic management is seen as a *planning* activity with planning systems (eg see Argenti, 1968, 1974; Ansoff, 1968; Steiner, 1979). The concern of strategists is seen as the *long-term development* of the organization as such strategic management is concerned with long time horizons.

It is a model that has much to commend it. It is neat, rational, understandable and provides managers and students of management with a clear approach to taking strategic decisions. Underlying the approach is a number of assumptions: that the management of strategy can and should be conceived of as essentially rational and analytical; that rational analysis and evaluation will yield sensible strategies; that analysed environmental change will galvanize a rational search for strategies to cope with such changes; that rational choice of strategy will lead to changes in strategy. There is also the implication that strategies will be grounded in analysis that questions and tests existing assumptions and in so doing takes nothing for granted.

The position taken here is that such a model of strategic management, whilst of value as a logical model in structuring debate, is not representative of what strategic management is in actuality. Whilst it might provide a useful means of considering strategic problems and planning their solutions, it says little about the problem of management. Specifically it does not address such issues as the limitations on analytical and rational behaviour, the interaction of managers and stakeholders in the location and definition of strategic problems or the exercise of choice and the management of strategic change at an inter-personal level. In short it is a de-personalized model of management, which equates management with analysis and rationality. Its weaknesses and limitations have been discussed thoroughly by other writers, notably Schön (1983) in the context of management in the professions, Allison (1971) in the field of defence strategy and governmental decision-making, using the Cuba Missile Crisis as a case study, and Peters and Waterman (1982) in '*In Search of Excellence*'. Indeed Peters and Waterman go further. Whilst accepting that such an approach is seen as conventional management wisdom and recognizing that it has a part to play in management thinking, they argue that managers who see the job of management in such a way share beliefs and operate in ways that actually have negative influences on the business. Amongst the dangers they list as the outcome of an over rationalistic approach are:

- a bias towards conservative, or maintenance management with a fixation on control;
- the analysis of information and events that are available rather than the search for and understanding of uncertainty;
- a de-humanized approach to management where efficiency, productivity and data become overbearing concerns;
- a propensity for saying 'no', since it is easier to develop negative arguments; and the de-valuing of experimentation because of the risk of making mistakes;
- over-formulization of planning systems and controls and the consequent dampening of managerial flair;
- the diminution of the role of corporate values at the expense of hard objectives and analysis;
- concentration on the analysis of competition external to the business but the fear of competition or conflict within the organization.

The argument that Peters and Waterman put forward is not that analysis and rationality are unimportant; rather that such an approach to management can become dominant and supplant a concern for the *activity* of managing. They argue that managers need to understand more, and consider how they can improve, *managing*. The view is that an analytical approach to strategic management may well be necessary but, as a description of strategic management or as a guide to managers on how to manage strategy, it is insufficient.

A critique of the descriptive validity of the rationalistic model is contained within the review of other schools of thought, and the empirical evidence supporting them, which follows.

An Incremental Perspective

The rationalistic model of strategic management implies that strategic decisions are made on the basis of a knowledge of the strategic position of the organization, and then strategy is implemented. This view has received an increasing amount of criticism, largely from researchers who have sought empirical evidence on the process of managing strategy in organizations. It is also a model that does not square with the evidence that, as Kolb has it, managers are 'distinguished by very strong active experimentation skills and are very weak on reflective observation skills' (Kolb, 1974, p. 33). Managers do not tend to consider in abstract, intellectual form the responses to perceived problems; rather, they seek to enter active stages of problem resolution and implementation.

This section briefly examines the findings of a number of researchers whose evidence and arguments indicate that strategy can, in the words of Henry Mintzberg (1978), better be viewed as a 'pattern in a stream of decisions'. In other words it makes more sense to think of strategy as the outcome of management processes.

However, it would be over-simplistic to suggest that an incremental view of strategy making can be explained as a single model. It cannot. In this section an explanation is therefore attempted that distinguishes the observed patterns of strategy-making in organizations, then moves on to different accounts of why such patterns occur. It will be seen that the explanations vary considerably, from that of writers who hold that incremental strategic decision-making is quite logical – and in this sense they provide an alternative rationalistic model – to that of those who see organizations as essentially social and political theatres of action and incremental change as an outcome of social and political processes.

Patterns in Strategic Decision-Making

Miller and Friesen (1980) characterize the development of strategy in organizations as a tendency towards '*momentum*'; that is, a state in which reversals in the direction of change in variables of strategy and structure are relatively rare. Such changes do take place but they are infrequent and may be of a dramatic nature. It is an observation for which they provide empirical evidence of a statistical kind and that bears out the observations of others – for example Chandler (1962), Greiner (1972), Mintzberg (1978) and Tushman and Romanelli (1986). Mintzberg's research, in particular, provides a good deal of illumination on the patterns of strategic development in organizations. His research consisted of 'intensive historical studies of single organizations over periods of decades', so strategies were seen in a historical and action context: strategy was not taken to mean what was said by managers but what was carried out by organizations. From these historically observed strategies, Mintzberg deduced that strategies changed in different ways. Some periods of change he described as *incremental*, during which new strategies formed gradually; other periods were characterized by *piecemeal* change, during which some strategies changed while others remained constant; and still others were *global*, during which many strategies changed quickly and in unison. He also identified periods of *continuity* during which established patterns remained unchanged; periods of *limbo*, during which the organization hesitated to make decisions; and periods of *flux*, during which no important patterns seemed evident in the decision streams. Whilst the labels he gives to the observed patterns may be somewhat elaborate the observations themselves do suggest that strategic change is not always a continual gradual process but is intermittent and that global changes, though not typical, may occur. Mintzberg also distinguished between different means by which strategies might come about (or be realized). He identified (a) 'deliberate' strategies as those intended by management that get realized; (b) 'unrealized' strategies as those that do not get realized; and (c) 'emergent' strategies as those not really intended at all but arising through a flow of decisions taking place in organizations. He also argued that it is possible to perceive deliberately set '*gestalt*' strategies, characterized by being unique and integrated, in the sense of their elements being 'complementary or synergistic'. However, if we concern ourselves less with his descriptive typologies and concentrate on the findings about overall problems in the development of strategies in organizations, the picture emerges of changes in strategy typically being the product of the apparent tendency of organizations to 'feel their way' through the uncertainty and compelexity of their environment with gradual or 'trial and error' changes. It is this idea of the developments by strategy in action that has increasingly been termed 'incrementalism'.

More can be learned about patterns in the strategic decision-making process by looking at research carried out within organizations that has analysed decision routines themselves – that is, how particular strategic decisions are made. Such studies are still rather few in number and vary in the extent of their detail. The richest studies are those carried out by Pettigrew (1973; 1985b) on a major computer decision for a retailer and the strategic development of ICI, and by Bower (1972) on resource planning and strategic decision-making in four manufacturing firms, although a number of business histories have concentrated on decision-making processes in some depth (e.g. Grinyer and Spender, 1979b; Boswell, 1983).

These researchers have shown that the complex area of strategy-making is coped with by management in anything but the linear fashion promoted by the rationalistic models discussed earlier. Strategic decisions are characterized by the political hurly-burly of organizational life with a high incidence of bargaining, a trading off of costs and benefits of one interest group against another, all within organizational context with a notable lack of clarity in terms of environmental influences or objectives.

Discernible patterns in the routines of strategic decision-making have, however, been mapped out and some generalizations can be made, if tentatively, on the basis of empirical work.

Research by Mintzberg et al. (1976), Lyles (1981) and a research team at Bradford University in the UK (Hickson et al., 1986) has focused on routines of problem formulation and selection. These pieces of research traced a large number of individual decisions through the stages of organizational processing either by reference to secondary data or by interviews with participating managers. Their findings show that strategic decisions do not tend to come about in neat, patterned ways:

> Strategic decision process is characterised by novelty, complexity and open-endedness, the fact that the organisation usually begins with little understanding of the decision situation it faces or the root to its solution, and only a vague idea of what that solution might be and how it will be evaluated when it is developed. Only by groping through a recursive, discontinuous process involving many difficult steps and a host of dynamic factors over a considerable period of time, is a final choice made. It is not the decision making under uncertainty of the textbook, where alternatives are given, even if their consequences are not, but a decision under ambiguity, where almost nothing is given or easily determined. (Mintzberg et al., 1976. pp. 250–1)

David Hickson and co-workers (Hickson et al., 1986) bear this out: their study of 150 decisions in 30 different organizations in the UK identified numerous delays and impediments to decision-making and varying degrees of formality, cooperation and interaction in the process. They were, however, able to identify three broad types of decision-making processes characterized according to the degree of discontinuity in the processes and the dispersion of influences on the decision (see figure 2.2).

Sporadic processes of decision-making are characterized by a high level of delays and impediments and, typically, a variability of sources of influence and information impacting on that decision. Decisions are likely to be the result of often protracted personal interaction and negotiation of an informal nature and culminate in reference to a higher management level for authorization. *Fluid* processes are characterized by less discontinuity: there are less delays and impediments in the process, fewer sources of influence and information, more formal channels of decision-making and, in consequence, rather less time taken over them. Even so, decisions here are also likely to be referred upwards to a higher level for authorization. *Constricted* processes are not characterized so much by the sort of delays and impediments characteristic of multiple-information-source situations, but here the information is usually more readily available, perhaps of a specialist kind, and is handled by more restricted groups of managers, who take decisions without reference to higher levels, and without so much reference to committees and working groups. Such processes might, for example, be found most often within specialist groups such as research organizations or within a business with a dominant chief executive or senior team.

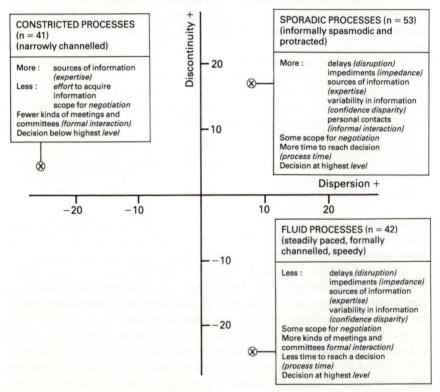

FIGURE 2.2   Three ways of making decisions.

Source: D.J. Hickson et al., *Top Decisions: Strategic Decision Making in Organisations,* Basil Blackwell, 1986.

David Hickson and his colleagues point out that in most of the organizations they studied, all three types of process were to be found in the different decisions they observed. However, there did tend to be some bias towards sporadic decision-making in manufacturing industries in which decision-making tended to be more de-centralized and subject to more conflicting interests than in service industries, which were characterized rather more by fluid processes and did 'not so often face this level of complexity and politically' (Hickson et al., 1986, p. 204). They also noted that public ownership tended to result in more sporadic decision processes largely because of committee procedures, external intervention and the prevalence of the seeking for a negotiated consensus.

They also reported that the strategic decisions observed typically took place over a period of about a year, though this varied from one month to two years. However, Mintzberg and his colleagues reported that, of the 25 decision processes they examined, nine lasted from one to four years and six for more than four years; eight decisions took less than a year.

The research by Mintzberg and his research team and by Lyles, when examined jointly, do provide an image – inevitably simplified – of the sorts of processual patterns at work in strategic decision-making. There emerge from their analyses four generalizable stages that can be recognized in the decision process. These are:

- *problem awareness*: the recognition that 'something is amiss', that a state of affairs exists that needs remedying;
- *problem diagnosis*: the collection of information about, and examination of, the circumstances of the problem and the definition of the problem;
- the *development of solutions*: the generation of possible solutions to the problem;
- the *selection of a solution*: the means by which a decision about what is to be done is reached.

We should be careful to regard these stages only as a convenient means of describing what is in fact anything but clear and precise. Indeed, in passing it can be noted that the descriptive stages employed by the researchers themselves bear a striking resemblance to some of the stages described in essentially rationalistic approaches to decision-making – which is perhaps indicative of its powerful influence. None the less they do provide a useful framework on which to discuss some of the characteristics of strategic decision-making. These stages are now amplified and also represented in figure 2.3.

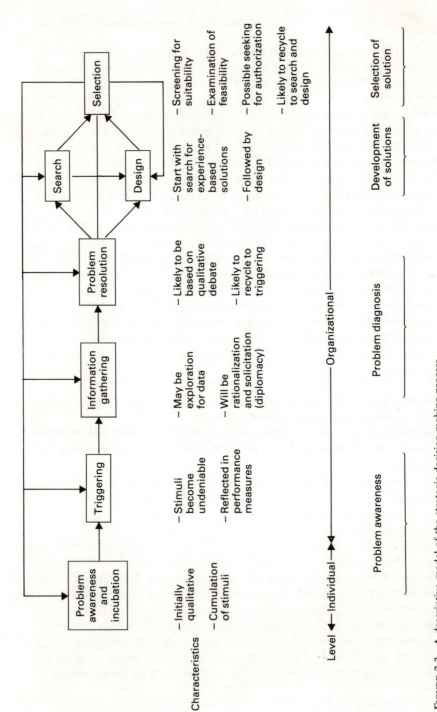

FIGURE 2.3   A descriptive model of the strategic decision-making process.

Source: G. Johnson and J. Scholes, *Exploring Corporate Strategy*, Prentice-Hall, 1984.

Stage 1: Problem Awareness

The awareness of a strategic problem usually occurs at an individual level. It is individual managers who are likely to get a 'gut feeling' that something is wrong. This awareness is likely to develop through a period of what Lyles calls 'incubation' and others call 'observation and reflection' (Kolb, 1974) or 'intermediate buffers' (Hunt, 1971). In this period of incubation, managers sense various sorts of stimuli that confirm and define a developing picture of the problem. Such stimuli may well be of a 'low amplitude . . . collected, cumulated and stored over a period of years' (Mintzberg et al., 1976, p. 253). These stimuli are what Norburn and Grinyer (1973/74 call 'signals' or 'ear twitchers' and seem to be primarily of three sorts: there are internal performance measurements such as levels of turnover or profit performance; there is customer reaction particularly to the quality and price of services or products; and there are changes in the environment, particularly in terms of competitive action and technological change (Norburn and Grinyer; 1973/74) and economic conditions (Glueck, 1980). Together they create a picture of the extent to which an organization's circumstances deviate from what is 'normally' to be expected. This deviation may not be from a specified set of performance criteria such as profit measures, but could well be a perceived divergence from a normal trading pattern or a change from a typical customer response to some marketing activity for example. These stimuli seem to have two different roles. External information, on the whole, has the role of awakening interest to a greater extent than internal information which feeds more directly into strategic decisions, mainly in the form of financial and volume performance indicators.

This accumulation of stimuli eventually reaches a point at which the amount of evidence is such that the presence of a problem cannot be ignored at an organizational level. This 'triggering point' may well be reached when the formal information systems of the organization begin to highlight the problem; perhaps the variance against budget becomes undeniable or a number of sales areas consistently report dropping sales. Mintzberg and his colleagues hypothesize that such triggering is most likely in conditions where 'quick re-inforcement of one stimulus by another magnifies their perceived combined amplitudes' (Mintzberg et al., 1976, p. 253). It is at this triggering point that organizational activity takes over from individual consideration of the problem.

Digressing slightly, it is worth underlining the significance of this first stage of the individual's role in problem recognition. There is evidence to suggest that successful business performance is associated with management's capability in sensing their environment (Norburn and Grinyer,

1973/4; Quinn, 1980; Miller and Friesen, 1978). This does not mean that such businesses necessarily have a complex or sophisticated means of achieving this sensitivity but rather that managers respond to or take into account a wide range of influences and have an internally consistent view of these influences.

Stage 2: Problem Diagnosis

At the organizational level two aspects of problem diagnosis can be discerned. The first is information-gathering and the second is problem resolution, or definition.

Information-gathering can take the form of (a) exploration for information to determine more clearly the facts of the problem; (b) the rationalization of information and stimuli to do with the problem so as to clarify the picture of the problem; and (c) diplomacy and solicitation to establish what those with power in the organization think about the problem and gather political support for individuals' views of the problem.

As far as information gathering is concerned, this is usually on a verbal and informal basis (Norburn and Grinyer, 1973/74; Mintzberg et al., 1976; Aguilar, 1967) and this appears to be the more so the more senior the management in the organization. Managers are, in effect, building up and refining a picture of the situation facing them by seeking for qualitative evidence. There is little empirical evidence to support the notion that systematic environmental analysis is the norm of that there is extensive use of management information systems for the purposes of strategic analysis and decision making (Hall, 1973; Aguilar, 1967). Indeed it appears that, whilst much information may be collected in organizations, much of it is not used and, as Feldman and March (1981) argue, may be 'subject to strategic misrepresentation' and collected to 'symbolize a commitment to rational choice' (p. 182).

By problem resolution is meant the clarification of the problem through an attempt to get some sort of organizational view or consensus on it. This is likely to be attempted through debate and discussion and, since there may be many different views, it is likely to give rise to disagreement. Indeed, it is quite likely that some organizations may find difficulty in proceeding beyond this stage and continually refer back the problem to the information-gathering or triggering stages of the process. Lyles (1981) in common with other researchers (Huse and Bowditch, 1977; Soelberg, 1967) found this to be a time-absorbing and complex activity for managers. In fact Lyles found that there is considerable re-cycling within the process anyway. The most common re-cycling, in 70 per cent of the cases she investigated, was from the problem resolution stage back to triggering; the attempt to resolve what a problem was about at an organizational level triggered different conceptions of the problem at an individual level. Both Lyles and Mintzberg, in their studies of the process of strategic decision-making, also point out that the diagnosis stage may be missed out altogether; Mintzberg and his colleagues found diagnostic routines in only 14 of the 25 decision processes examined. Managers may proceed directly from problem recognition to the choice of solutions.

The dominance of inter-personal, qualitative approaches to problem definition is, arguably, to be expected and beneficial in a management context. The process of solicitation of views is not simply concerned with clarification of the problem. Quinn (1980) sees it as a means of reconciling disparate perceptions of the problem to achieve the greater degree of consensus necessary for decision-making. Quinn is pointing out that we must see the management of strategy as concerned with management action, not just analysis.

Bower's work on problem identification and definition within resource allocation processes (Bower 1972) adds to the understanding of the dynamics of this stage. He found that both problem identification and definition tended to take place within lower levels of management, primarily amongst functional managers within operating divisions. Discussions on problem definition were problematic for a number of reasons. There was little integration of the particular nature of the problem with business level or corporate level strategy, because the managers involved did not have such understanding and more senior managers were often not involved. Also the more junior management rarely questioned the assumptions upon which conclusions were based. For example, bases of costings or sales projections might be accepted uncritically. Moreover the development of a definition of a problem tended to drag on until more senior management got involved.

Stage 3: The Development of Solutions

If the decision-making process proceeds to the development of solutions, then this phase can also be time-consuming and resource-demanding.

Managers will first search for ready-made solutions to the problems that have been triggered. The indications are that this will first occur through 'memory search', in which the manager seeks for known, existing or tried solutions, or 'passive search' in which he or she will wait for possible solutions to be thrown up. It is only if these are unsuccessful that the manager will move onto more active searches for possible solutions. The manager starts with what he or she has experienced and moves from there. It is likely that there will be a number of these 'searches' amongst the known, tried and familiar before any attempt is made to move to the next step which is the 'design' of a solution. 'Design' is where 'custom-made' solutions specific to the problem at hand are constructed. Here it is not a matter of looking for what is familiar, what has been done before, for example, but rather of originating a solution. Whether the search routine or design practice is employed, the process of choice is iterative, beginning with a vague notion of what is desired and gradually being refined by recycling through selection routines, back into problem identification or through further development routines: 'a solution crystallises as the designers grope along, building their solution brick by brick without really knowing what it will look like until it is completed' (Mintzberg et al., 1976, p. 256).

Certainly there is no evidence to suggest that this stage of strategic decision-making is well structured. Far from managers having a clear set of options that they can evaluate, it is likely that there will be a lack of clarity between managers as to what options exist, how to analyse them and what criteria to apply (Fahey, 1981).

Stage 4: The Selection of a Solution

It is perhaps misleading in some respects to suggest that selection is a different part of the process from the development of a solution. Solution development, taking place, as it does, as a series of iterations that develop towards a limited number of solutions, in effect means that selection is taking place as development occurs. Certainly the selection routines bear little resemblance to the neat logical patterns that might be expected from rationalistic ideas on strategic choice. What can be explained, however, is the basis upon which the selection might take place within the development processes.

Screening takes place throughout the development stage, particularly where there are more possible solutions than can sensibly be accommodated by the organization. Screening is 'a superficial routine, more concerned with eliminating what is infeasible than with determining what is appropriate' (Mintzberg et al., 1976, p. 257). In effect managers assess the 'feasibility' of a possible solution – that is, whether or not it is likely to work. However, what is significant here is that the predominant criterion is judgemental feasibility, as distinct from evaluative suitability of a possible solution in terms of any analysed strategic position of the organization. In short, managers are concerned with what they think will work, what is operable, rather than analytic evaluation.

Indeed Mintzberg's work showed that, in so far as managers exercise choice between options, the most common basis of choice is judgement, followed by bargaining and, last of all, analysis. By judgement is meant the personalized, individualized choice of a manager based on previous experience, which he or she may not be able to verbalize. By bargaining is meant the process by which the conflicting aims or aspirations of competing sub-groups are resolved through an essentially political process. And by analysis is meant the generation of factual bases upon which managerial choice can be made. There is little evidence in the literature that analysis plays a large part in the process, although Mintzberg hints that analytical bases for choice may well be post-rationalized following the arrival at solutions through processes of judgement and bargaining.

An alternative way of selecting between possibilities might be to refer the choice to a more senior level of management – to seek *authorization*. It should be remembered that this whole process is incremental in nature and therefore is taking place below the most senior levels of management; so referring possible solutions to some higher hierarchical level may be required anyway. Typically, though not always, authorization is sought for a completed solution after steps of screening and evaluation have taken place. Such referral raises the question of whether or not it is sensible to view this referral as a sort of checking of an incrementally generated strategic solution against some overall strategy. It would certainly be in line with Bower's and Mintzberg's view that, whilst most strategic decisions emanate from a stream of decisions from within the management sub-systems, the role of leadership is to maintain some sort of general direction. If this view is taken then the process of authorization might be thought of as the matching of one strategic decision against an overall, more generalized strategy of the organization.

Strategy-Making as a Political Process

Researchers consistently point out that in the process of strategic decision-making there is a much greater reliance on managerial judgement and past experience than the evaluative techniques of the management scientist would suggest. If evaluation does take place it is likely to be qualitative in nature, perhaps taking the form of a discussion of problems or options amongst the managers. What becomes clear is that the selection of strategy is primarily by means of management judgement and is likely to be bound up in a process of bargaining within the organization. Solutions are not so much likely to be adopted because they are shown to be better on the basis of some sort of objective yardstick, but because they are acceptable to those who influence the decision or have to implement it. The process of bargaining and negotiation taking place arises because different groups within the organization pursue different aims and seek to exercise control over a finite set of resources. It is a process that is essentially political in so far as 'political behaviour is defined as behaviour by individuals or – in collective terms – subgroupings within an organisation that makes a claim against the resource sharing system of the organisation' (Pettigrew, 1977, p. 81). This political view of organizational decision-making received impetus in the management literature by the work of Cyert and March (1963) who saw an organization as comprising coalitions that indulged in a process of bargaining with each other to achieve their own ends, and through which the goals and strategies of the firm emerged. Such coalitions may be formed on the basis of specialization within an organization as a result of size or complexity. They might also exist as informal coalitions where shared interests and loyalties arise for reasons other than performing specialist tasks (Reed and Palmer, 1972). The central point is that these coalitions are likely to be interdependent within the organization, so the interests and fortunes of one are to a greater or lesser extent dependent on another. A conflict of interests, will, therefore, inevitably arise as the coalitions bid for the resources of the organization. Strategic decision-making can therefore be explained as a political process and the observed incremental or adaptive pattern of strategy development explained as the working through of the conflicts of interest through bargaining processes within the routines and systems that predominate in an organization (Harvey and Mills, 1970). In terms of analysis and the production of strategic decisions in organizations, it can therefore be argued that a key requirement is to understand why power lies in the hands of certain individuals or groupings in the organization, who they are and why one party is able to exercise that power over another (Johnson and Scholes, 1984)

Fahey points to the importance of powerful advocacy within the context of competing coalitions. Without such advocacy, and given the uncertainty of the problem, and the criteria for choice: '. . . . organisational decision making procedures provide many avenues for delaying (a project's) development into a fully documented proposal' (Fahey, 1981, p. 55). Power, however, may not correspond to formal lines of authority, as pointed out by Dalton (1959). Pettigrew (1973; 1975) conceives of power being endowed upon individuals or groups according to their possession, control or use of power resources; these might include control over information and systems, access to higher authority, group support, assessed structure, or specialist expertise. Others (Hickson et al., 1971; Thompson, 1967; Hambrick, 1981) have emphasized that power is derived from an individual or group responsible for activities that reduce uncertainty facing the organization. To be more specific: '1) The degree to which a sub-unit copes with uncertainty for other sub-units, and 2) The extent to which a sub-unit's coping activities are substitutable' (Hickson et al., 1971, p. 218). It is here that we discern a fundamental link between power and strategic decision-making processes: 'Organisations . . . are at one and the same time instruments which serve collective purposes, and coalitions which respond to localised pressures and interests' (Hickson et al., 1981, p. 152). As such the greatest power will devolve upon those who can be seen to secure perceived collective purposes despite an uncertain environment. In such a context, the management of strategy is, by its very nature, likely to be highly politicized.

Incremental Strategic Management – Muddling Through or Purposive Logic

Under the general heading of 'incrementalism' patterns of change have been described that are characterized by gradual developments of the overall strategies of organizations as the product of internal organizational bargaining and iterative decision routines. Such a description begs the question of whether or not such a process can be described as strategic *management*: is the process actually being managed at all? Clearly the processes described are quite different from those within the rationalistic model, but are they just a muddle in which the politics and dramas of organizational life throw up decisions that, over time and collectively, can be discerned by the observer as 'strategies'? Such a view would argue that strategies are, at best, rather random, or that they can more accurately be thought of as a construct of outside observation.

There are, however, management writers and researchers who admit to an adherence to models of strategy formulation as an incremental process, and argue that the phenomenon can and should be explained in managerial terms. Managers *manage* incrementally according to such writers.

The main proposal of Lindblom (1959) and Lindblom and Braybrooke (1963) is that not only do rationalistic decision processes not occur but that, if they did, they would lead to poor decisions. Instead, what Lindblom calls 'successive limited comparisons' build strategy. Choice is not made on the basis of evaluation of possible options against set objectives; rather, possible options are compared with each other to decide which seems to give the best outcome. Thus objectives are not set initially but arise as alternatives are compared. Managers do not have the cognitive ability to rank all options against objectives, particularly as, often, the objectives are in conflict and have to be traded off against each other. Added to this is the problem that decision-making is usually a group activity, and the group is unlikely to agree on the relative value of objectives. Lindblom argues that the importance of any objective will depend on how well it is already being achieved prior to this decision being taken. Thus an objective that is well achieved at present will be of less value than one that is poorly achieved at the moment. However, there is no practical way to state marginal objectives or values except in terms of particular policies and each decision is likely to change the value of an objective anyway.

Lindblom argues that 'decision making is a succession of decisions approximating to some desired objectives in which the objectives themselves continue to change under reconsideration'. The reason for this is that it is difficult to predict the outcome of previous decisions to determine what will occur for the present alternatives being considered. Hence only alternatives similar to past decisions are considered to enable experience of these to be used. Each decision becomes a trial that can be tested before moving onto the next one. This also reduces risk as each decision is similar to the last and, being only an incremental step, can easily be remedied if wrong.

This process occurs within the political context of the organization, in which different groups, with different aims, have different degrees of power. Each will use this power to influence decisions taken, to ensure they, at least to some extent, satisfy their aims. Thus, assuming the present situation is a satisfying one to most individuals or groups, only incremental changes from it are likely, unless one group gains a lot of power; and, unless one group is very powerful, decisions reached will be a compromise.

Lindblom's position is, in many respects, similar to that of Quinn (1980) who has argued that managers are well aware of the complexities and uncertainties of the environment and the politics of organizational life, and that they manage strategy through a process of 'logical incrementalism' precisely because of this. His research consisted of studying nine large ('multiple billion dollar') companies with different technologies, time horizons and national and international dimensions. The study was carried out via a survey of secondary-source data and interviews of at least ten people in each company involved in recent important strategy changes. It might be noted that this was not a historical study looking at strategic change over a period of time, but the examination of a single change in each company. Also Quinn was primarily concerned with managers accounts of how they managed strategy. Quinn's findings can be summarized as follows.

(1) Logical incrementalism is manifested as evolutionary but purposive strategic development in an organization. Strategy is formed by managers ensuring the success and evolution of a strong, secure but flexible core business but continually experimenting with 'side-bet' strategic trials.

(2) The process is managed by managers accepting the ambiguities and uncertainty of their environment and therefore being sensitive to environmental signals through constant environmental scanning; but also managing that uncertainty by testing changes in strategy in small-scale steps. There is also a reluctance to specify categoric objectives too early as this might stifle ideas and prevent the sort of experimentation that is desired. Indeed there is a recognition that such experiments do, and should, arise from the sub-systems of the organization: they cannot be expected to be the sole responsibility of top management.

(3) Such a process is seen by managers to have significant benefits. Continual testing provides improved quality of information for decision-making and enables the better sequencing of the elements of major decisions. There is also a stimulation of managerial flexibility and creativity and, since change is always likely to be gradual, it is more likely to be possible to create and develop a commitment to change throughout the organization. Such processes also take account of the political nature of organizational life since smaller changes are less likely to face the same extent of political resistance as more major changes, and it is more possible to accommodate the variety of resource demands and political ambitions of different coalitions.

Another implication of an incrementalist view of the development of strategy is that the idea of the implementation of strategy following on from the choice of strategy in a sequential way does not hold good. It is not the case that strategy is first decided and then implemented, but rather that strategy is, to a much greater extent, worked out through being put into operation. It is this choice through action that persuades Pondy (1983) that incrementalism is the unity of rational and intuitive models of strategy-making – that incrementalism is 'unfolding rationality'.

It is also possible to see the phenomenon of incremental strategic change in terms of programmatic decision-making in organizations. March and Simon argued:

> When a stimulus is of a kind that has been experienced repeatedly in the past, the response will ordinarily be highly routinised. The stimulus will evoke, with the minimum of problem solving or other computational activity, a well structured definition of the situation that will include a repertory of response programmes . . . .When a stimulus is relatively novel it will evoke problem solving activity aimed initially at constructing a definition of the situation and then at developing one or more appropriate performance programmes. (1958, p. 140)

Managers, they argue, act within the 'bounded rationality' that characterizes the organization and that copes with the complexity of organizational existence. It would be wrong to conceptualize the manager as re-constructing anew the 'reality' of the task every time a problem or opportunity arises. Rather managers will lean on the programmes that evolve in the organization. It is a view that has more recently been put forward and examined in terms of its impact on microeconomics by Nelson and Winter (1982). They too see as centrally important the evolution of 'routines' at many levels in the organization:

> . . . from well specified technical routines for producing things, through procedures for hiring and firing, ordering new inventory, or stepping up production of items in high demand, to policies regarding investment, r and d or advertising, and business stategies about product diversification and overseas investment. (1982, p.14)

These routines are 'a persistent feature of the organism and determine its future behaviour' (p. 14). As Teece summarises Nelson and Winter's views:

> What emerges is a conception of the firm with a limited range of capabilities based on its available routines and physical assets. There is no 'shelf of technologies' external to the firm and available to all industry participants. A firm's capabilities are degined very much by where it has been in the past and what it has done. (Teece, 1985, p. 60)

Such a view could lead the reader to conceive of the organization as purely reactive to situations, responding to stimuli through a series of 'knee-jerks'. This does not necessarily follow. Such organizational routines can be seen as forming what amounts to a distinctive competence and experience in particular markets – what Pumpin (1983) refers to as the 'strategic success position' of the firm – and which provides capabilities and tacit knowledge that it would be difficult for other firms to replicate – the 'uncertain imitability' that Lippman and Rumelt (1982) see as a very real barrier to entry into uncertain markets.

A 'garbage can' model of organizational choice is proposed by Cohen et al. (1972). They too see the dominant affect of routines and programmes but argue it is these

> . . . sets of procedures through which participants arrive at an interpretation of what they are doing and what they have done while in the process of doing it. From this point of view, an organisation is a collection of choices looking for problems, issues and feelings looking for decision situations in which they might be aired, solutions looking for issues to which they might be the answer, and the decision makers looking for work. (Cohen et al., 1972, p. 2)

Here we have a pro-active view of the effect of organizational routines. It is also possible to argue for more negative outcomes. The collection of routines that define the responses of organizations can become so fixed a basis for organizational interpretation and action that there may be immense resistance to their change.

> Managers demand a large potential benefit before they are willing to destroy the order and complementarity of elements inherent in the old gestalt and begin to construct a new one. The price paid for this is sluggish responsiveness to the need for reversals in evolutionary trends, and occasional revolutionary periods with all of their turmoil, expense and confusion. (Miller and Friesen, 1980, pp. 612–3)

The two views are not, of course, incompatible. What may be an essential, indeed valuable, set of guiding principles and procedures for an organization may well over time become a conservative set of constraints.

Rationalistic Processes and Incremental Strategic Decision-Making

If the processes described in this section and the last are typical of ones that occur in organizations, what then of some of the more traditional views of strategy formulation that are advocated, which are rooted in the notion of rationality?

Central to the arguments of these writers is that strategy is evaluated against clear *objectives*; as Chang and Campo-Flores (1980, p. 76) argue: 'Without realistically established business objectives, strategy is impossible to formulate and thus is totally ineffective'. However, there is little empirical evidence to suggest that objectives perform this role. Rather, they are often ill defined, very diverse and not agreed upon (Norburn and Grinyer, 1973/4), post-rationalized (Mintzberg et al., 1976), unstated, not explicit or very generalized (Quinn, 1980). Quite simply, they do not appear to have the central role that a traditional strategic decision-making model would claim for them. Organizations certainly have objectives. Norburn and Grinyer (1973/74) for example found that the companies they studied had many objectives and that managers almost always agreed that one was to increase profits. They also found that there were many other objectives managers perceived to exist, and that managers thought there should be more of them. However, there was a low level of agreement in the firms about what the objectives were.

The second question is whether or not objectives are or should be stated in clear and precise terms. It is received management wisdom that they should: after all, Drucker (1968) argued that 'if objectives are only good intentions, they are worthless'. Yet the fact is that there is evidence to show that many successful companies do not have precise, explicit objectives, and what is more their senior executives do not think they should have. Quinn found that successful executives "announced" relatively few goals to their organization. These were frequently broad and general, and only rarely were they quantitative or measurably precise'. They tended not to be announced for three main reasons. First, because the effect would be to over-centralize the organization, to '. . . tell subordinates that certain issues are closed and that their thoughts about alternatives are irrelevant'. Second, announced objectives could be very difficult to change; there is a fear of creating rigidity and an out-of-date or inappropriate stance. And finally, and most obvious, because of the fear of lack of security: there is the danger that competitors will get to know too much about what the intentions of the firm are.

Quinn and Fahey (1981) found that the use of objectives in organizations was rather more tactical: there were times when it was seen as appropriate to have general objectives, and other times when it was seen to be more appropriate to have specific objectives. General objectives were seen by senior executives as being useful in achieving what Quinn called 'cohesion, identity and clan'. By ignoring specificities, which would create disagreement, and concentrating on broad, generally accepted directions or intentions, a general consensus could be reached. Furthermore, if objectives were broad enough, it allowed managers the latitude to develop their own areas of discretion within them. What emerges is that broad, non-specific objectives are another way of managing the coalition existing in the firm. However, it also became clear to Quinn that there were times when specific objectives were required. These were times when immediate or urgent action was required, such as a crisis of some sort, or at times of major, usually strategic, transitions. Here the role of objectives was to focus the attention of management onto a limited number of essential requirements.

And what of '*planning*'. The words 'strategy' and 'planning' have become so inextricably associated that it becomes necessary to define the role and forms of planning clearly. This necessity stems from a common confusion between 'planning' in the context of strategic decision-making and 'corporate planning' as a function often incorporated into a department with an organization. There is little evidence to support the idea that corporate planning as a specialist activity or corporate planners as managers in organizations are actually responsible for strategic decisions being taken (Quinn, 1980; Fahey, 1981; Mintzberg et al., 1976; Hall, 1973). Rather, the role of corporate planning appears to be to contribute to the strategic management process in other ways (Bahrami, 1981; Mintzberg, 1981).

(1) By assisting in the adaptation of the organization to its environment by means of monitoring changes in the environment, formulating environmental and strategic scenarios and acting in a consultancy capacity to parts of the organization that wish to examine the implications of environmental change. In this sense corporate planning is carrying out a strategic analysis function.
(2) By providing an integration role in an organization in the sense of acting as a communication channel between, for example, a corporate head office and its divisions.
(3) In programming the detailed resource allocation necessitated by a strategic decision. This, then, is the planning of strategy implementation.
(4) By providing a control mechanism to monitor the performance of parts of the organization (e.g. divisions) in implementing strategies.

The picture emerges of corporate planning as an aid to strategic analysis or strategy implementation rather than as the means of strategy formulation. Quinn also discussed the role of formal planning systems in the strategy formulation process. All firms in his study had some form of such a system despite the fact that he found that strategy was formulated in an incremental fashion. He argued that these formal systems 'rarely formulated a corporations central strategy'. However, he added that what a corporate planning system may well provide is a mechanism for verification of earlier decisions made by or arising from sub-systems within the organization.

At a more general level on rationalistic processes, Gladstein and Quinn (1985) suggest that it is useful to distinguish between conditions when action rationality (by which they mean incrementalism) and decision rationality (by which they mean what has here been called rationalistic decision processes) are likely to pertain. Their assertion is that action rationality is the norm in organizations but that it may lead to insularity and the organization becoming 'uncoupled from its competitive environment'. In such circumstances the organization will need to reorientate its strategic direction. Gladstein and Quinn suggest that it is at this point that the organization is likely to switch to an emphasis on decision rationality – that is rationalistic decision processes. In other words strategy is typically formed incrementally but, faced with major problems, and the need for more fundamental strategic change, organizations will change their decision-making mechanisms to rationalistic modes. It is an argument that is not supported by Mintzberg and Waters (1983) whose observations suggest that an organization faced with the need for major change, even one that might be described as operating as a machine bureaucracy, will revert to a simple structure with highly centralized management around a dominant leader.

AN INTERPRETATIVE PERSPECTIVE

An important difference between the two models of strategy formulation reviewed so far is that the rationalistic approach sees managers taking action on the basis of environmental stimuli, which they analyse in order that they might 'know about' them. In this sense an objectively understood environment drives strategy formulation. The incrementalist's view is that it is the organizational systems that are imposed on the environmental stimuli to cope with them. It is a fundamental difference, which we can take further by exploring more carefully just how the complexity of the organization's environment is made sense of by managers. It is here that we move into our third model of strategy formulation, which can be termed 'interpretative' and which sees strategy as the product of the sense-making of managers.

An underlying argument has been that a key property of strategic problems facing organizations is their complexity. The interest in studying how managers formulate strategy arises very largely because it is the study of management at this higher order of complexity. The discussion so far within the section on the incrementalist model has argued that this complexity is coped with in action through the systems of the organization. It can also be argued that complexity is coped with at a cognitive and ideological level. The significance of this in terms of strategic management, and its relationship to incremental schools of thought, will now be discussed.

The two hemispheres of the brain have different functions. The left hemisphere is concerned with conscious thought processes that can be articulated. The right hemisphere with the more subconscious and esoteric. There is little research to inform us of the nature of the workings of the right hemisphere but it seems likely that, whilst there is a great deal of 'knowledge' within it, the processes of retrieval in an explicit, intellectual form are limited. The ordered consciousness of the left cannot bring to bear and process the vast array of information of the right, which is likely to take outward shape in intuitive, creative behaviour. It is a view similar to that of Hyman and Anderson (1974) who argue that the brain's capacity to store information vastly exceeds its capacity to process that information. The result is that there is a need for some sort of patterning – Hyman and Anderson talk about 'chunking' – of the information into larger units so that it can be managed. Moreover, when faced with new situations the individuals seek to allocate that experience to an existing pattern or 'chunk'. There is not a search amongst the vast store of latent information, at least not at a conscious level, to relate all possible previous experience and knowledge to the new experience. This is a view of problem-solving deriving its arguments from clinical psychology but that comes to conclusions that closely resemble those of other psychologists and management theorists who have addressed the problem or observed how complex patterns of information are retained and the consequences of such retention.

The construct theory of Kelly (1955) and the 'field expectations' of Tolman (1949) within the field of cognitive psychology are both models of cognition that argue that individuals have a coded perception of their world to which they relate new experiences. These ideas are similar to the idea of the 'script', as a 'hypothesised cognitive structure that, when activated, organises comprehension of event-based situations' (Abelson, 1981, p. 717). The script performs the functions of enabling one to understand situations and also providing a guide to behaviour appropriate to those situations (Gioia and Poole, 1984). Abelson (1973) separately argues that there exist what amounts to a hierarchy of scripts, from those that address the particular to 'master scripts' which are concerned with generalized world views. He also points to script properties of boundedness and admissibility; that is, the script defines the boundaries within which an individual will be likely to act and outside which events and stimuli are likely to be disregarded or discounted. It would then be quite mistaken, at a cognitive level, to regard individuals as simply responding to or reacting to outside stimuli; rather, the inidividual imposes a construction of his or her reality on the outside world.

Similar cognitive mechanisms are at work in the processes of management. In *The Social Psychology of Organising*, Weick argues that the members of an organization

see what they are attuned to see and these 'perceptual sets' [elsewhere he refers to a similar phenomenon as 'causal maps' (Weick, 1977)] are regarded as stable characteristics constituted on the basis of past experience. The perceptual sets are ready-made explanations that the actor carries from situation to situation. (Weick, 1979a, p. 38)

He goes on to suggest that 'the human actor does not react to an environment, he enacts it' (1979, p. 67); that is he creates meaning from environmental stimuli on the basis of attention to what has already occurred, and that, in turn, what he understands by what is occurring currently affects his perception of past occurrences. There is then this notion of present decisions being taken on the basis of past experience, and past experience being confirmed by present action. In this way the uncertainty and ambiguity – Weick calls it 'equivocality' – is reduced and becomes manageable. Schön argues in similar vein that such 'perceptual sets' or 'causal maps' provide the manager with 'a repertoire of examples, images, understandings and actions [so when he] makes sense of a situation he perceives to be unique, he *sees* it as something already present in his repertoire' (Schön, 1983, p. 138).

The emphasis on past experience and the inclination to build new decisions on past understanding through that experience is also demonstrated by Argyris and Schön (1974; 1978). Central to their argument is that, whilst managers may possess 'theories of action' – that is, espoused theories of how they would behave in a situation – they tend not to act according to those theories but according to discernible 'theories in use'. Decisions are typically made by individuals seeking to relate new experience to such theories in use; in effect by interpreting new experience according to pre-determined patterns. Moreover these 'theories in use' that guide action are, demonstrably, very difficult to change. Even when 'owners' of these 'theories' are able to spell them out and recognize the need for changing them, it is still very difficult for them to do so. Individuals seek, rather, to confirm and reinforce their theories in use by searching for solutions to problems or behaving in ways that are in line with them. Argyris and Schön show how managers respond to changes in the internal and external environments of an organization by detecting errors that can be defined in terms of their existing 'theories'; these errors can then be corrected so as to maintain the central features of organizational theory in use. It is this recycling of a problem within the bounds of the existing theory in use that they call 'single loop learning'.

This argument is quite different from those embedded in notions of scientific decision-making built on the premise that thought processes and stimuli are quite separate. Changes in the environment or decisions that ought to be taken to deal with them are conceived of as separate from the cognitive processes by which they are handled. This may be conceptually convenient for the analyst standing apart from the stimuli and the decision – as might an academic economist – but the evidence is that, for the decision maker, a precise distinction between stimuli, action and cognition is misplaced. As Karl Weick has argued:

> While the categories external/internal or outside/inside exist logically, they do not exist empirically. There is no methodological process by which we can

confirm the existence of an object independent of the confirmatory process involving oneself'. (1977, p. 273)

Schön (1983) also argues that it is a mistake to think of managerial thought and managerial action as separable. He argues that the process of management is characterized by thought or 'reflection in action', the continual interweaving of cognition and action. As Weick (1983, p. 223) argues: 'when managers act, their thinking occurs concurrently'; there is a 'presumption of logic' in meeting a situation, so action is natural and the thinking (in action) in turn endows the action itself with greater meaning.

Environments are, for Weick, enactments by managers of the world in which they live; their 'reality' in terms of management action is to be understood not as empirical reality but as a function of management cognition. It is an argument that is at first difficult to grasp; yet it is clear in our everyday lives that what one person perceives and makes sense of is different from what another sees even given apparently identical data. A simplified example would be the crowd at a soccer match. The data are exactly the same – 22 players playing to a set of rules – yet the game will be seen quite differently at least by opposing sets of fans. Weick argues that for the manager, the data that managers act upon are not to be thought of as separate from their processes of understanding it. Management action is rooted in perception and cognition.

However, the discussion so far has been at an individual level. Strategies are not typically the property or product of one individual but of groupings of individuals, of parts of, or of whole organizations. Do the arguments advanced here have relevance at an organizational level?

Beyer argues that there exist organizational ideologies that 'can be defined as relatively coherent sets of beliefs that bind some people together and that explain their worlds in terms of cause and effect relations' (Beyer 1981, p. 166). Hedberg and Jönsson (1977) use the word 'myth' to describe the same sort of phenomenon – an organizational view of the world that helps interpret the changes the organization and the individuals within it meet. Other writers refer to similar organizational sets of beliefs as 'paradigms' (Sheldon, 1980; Pfeffer, 1981a; Dighton, 1980), 'interpretative schemes' (Bartunek, 1984) and, if we follow Schein (1985) and Sathe (1985), then we are here referring to 'ideational culture' or the 'set of important assumptions (often unstated) that members of a community share in common' and that 'govern communications, justifications and behaviour' (Sathe, 1985). Such ideologies, as bonding and interpretative mechanisms, appear to be particularly important where there is a degree of ambiguity or uncertainty in the organization, where formal structures and bureaucratic procedures cope less well (Beyer, 1981; Ouchi, 1980) and where there are less formal, more organic structures but long-serving and stable membership (Wilkins and Ouchi, 1983).

Others (Spender, 1980; Grinyer and Spender, 1979a, b; Huff, 1982) have argued that such ideologies exist at an industry level; that is managers within the same industry tend to subscribe to a similar set of beliefs and assumptions. What Grinyer and Spender term the 'recipe' performs a similar function to other interpretative schemes, however; it is 'an accepted set of beliefs about what is consistent, realistic and which outcomes will follow the commitment of resources to specified actions' (Grinyer and Spender, 1979b, p. 83).

Whilst researchers have noted such phenomena, there is little explanation of just what beliefs and assumptions actually constitute management ideologies at an industry, organization or individual level. Spender's work attempted to isolate 'constructs' of the 'recipes' he identified and found that they embraced both assumptions and beliefs about the nature of the business environment, and, in particular, constructs at a more operational level that were much more to do with how to compete in the industry. What is, however, clearer from the work of such researchers is the effects of management ideologies and some of the 'mechanisms' associated with them that help explain how organizations work, and in consequence how strategy is formulated.

Ideology and Strategic Change

Those researchers who have examined the role of ideology in mangement decision-making all observe that ideologies are of particular importance, not least because they are resistant to change even in the face of potentially disconfirming evidence. Managers will cycle problems through routines of interpretation and adjustment variously called 'first-order change' (Watzlawick et al., 1974) or 'single loop learning' (Argyris and Schön, 1974); but the cycling of problems is, here, taking place within the set of assumptions and beliefs that predominate in the organization. Grinyer and Spender (1974a, b), employing their term 'the recipe', demonstrate how, faced with the need for change, managers will seek to deal with the situation in ways that protect the recipe from challenge. Figure 2.4 characterizes how this might occur. Faced with a stimulus for action, in this case declining performance, management are first likely to seek means of improving the implementation of existing strategy; this could be through tightening of controls for example. If this is not effective, then the management will consider a change of the strategy, but still a change in the strategy that is in line with the existing recipe. There has been no change to the recipe itself and Grinyer and Spender argue that there is not likely to

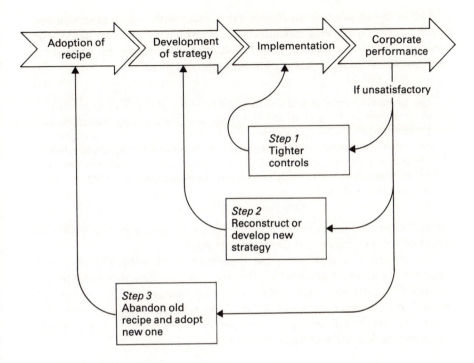

FIGURE 2.4 Dynamics of recipe change.

Source: P.H. Grinyer and J.C. Spender, *Turnaround: Managerial Recipes for Strategic Success,* Associated Business Press, 1979, p. 203.

be one until this attempt to reconstruct strategy in the image of the familiar and an attempt to avoid or reduce uncertainty or ambiguity, which manifests itself as a threat to the recipe.

Janis, too, observes the central and highly resistant role of organizational ideology. He observes:

> a concurrence-seeking tendency among moderately or highly cohesive groups. When this tendency is dominant, the members use their collective cognitive resources to develop rationalisations in line with shared illusions about the invulnerability of their organisation . . . (1985, p. 169)

He points out the value of what he terms 'groupthink' in so far as it reduces internal dissonance and can speed implementation of decisions, but also shows how such imposition of taken-for-granted assumptions in interpreting forces acting on the organization can lead to misinterpretation and decision-making 'fiascos' (Janis, 1982).

This is not to say that no change takes place within such organizations. Ouchi (1980) describes organizations in which commonly held belief systems and values hold together potential divergences of interests or ambiguities of goals as 'clans'. He separately argues:

> The necessarily general and abstract nature of the clan paradigm seems to allow members to use it to deal with the considerable variation in organisational conditions. Further the loyalty produced by assumptions about goal congruence provides tremendous energy and willingness to adapt. The change problems come organisational conditions are so radically altered that clan members must clearly violate their basic assumptions. (Wilkins and Ouchi, 1983, p. 479)

In such organizations, change may take place readily, but only within the limits of the prevailing and dominant ideology.

The evidence is that given the complexity and ambiguity of organizational situations, managers 'need' a pattern of beliefs through which to interpret occurrences and within which to manage. These beliefs are rooted in past experience and are likely to be held relatively commonly. They are preserved through a number of mechanisms – for example, according to Kiesler and Sproull (1982) by

- overestimating facilitating reasons to utilize the ideology and diminishing inhibiting reasons (see also Tversky and Kahneman, 1975);
- discounting disconfirming evidence and focusing on powerful facilitating reasons to support current practice (see also Kozielecki, 1981);
- 'perceiving or inferring events as correlated due to their fortuitous associative pairing of their mutual infrequent occurrence' (Kiesler and Sproull, 1982, p. 553);
- the false inference of causality.

They go on to point out that since the relevance of any evidence of events is likely to be defined in terms of the patterns of beliefs that exist, it is not likely that such patterns will be easily changed since disconfirming evidence is likely to be deemed irrelevant, a finding also supported by Herden and Lyles (1981). It is also likely that, since previous decisions are based on or associated with dominant ideologies, resources have already been committed to decisions that bolster the ideology. There is evidence that 'sunk' resources are likely to mean that further resources will follow and evidence disconfirming the dominant ideology will be ignored or 'misconstrued' (Staw, 1981; Fox and Staw, 1979; Staw and Ross, 1978).

Overall, then, it is likely that managers will resist views or actions from others that diverge from current norms. The power of the dominant ideology exists because it provides the basis for organizational action; it is thus socialized. New ways of doing things that move outside such established ways of doing things will therefore also affect social systems and working relationships and therefore will give rise to resistance. Such change will be percieved as threatening to present power groupings (Pettigrew, 1973) and may well give rise to greater group solidarity and organizational mechanisms to protect current norms. Such protective mechanisms might include the denial of the competence of the protagonists of new ideas, the withholding of information, the control of recruitment (Pettigrew, 1973) and, according to O'Day (1974) and Schein (1974), the regularisation of such divergent individuals to organizational acceptability.

These writers have then pointed to the tendency for ideologies to dominate organizations in a relatively conservative way. They and others also emphasize that strategic change in organizations may well require that ideologies be changed. Sheldon, who employs the word 'paradigm' by which he means 'some idealised way of working that is cherished' (1980, p. 62), argues that organizations may enter a 'paradigmatic state' in which they cease to adapt in their environment, or may simply adjust marginally within that paradigm. In such circumstances a 'paradigmatic shift' will be required at some stage. A similar argument is given by other writers, though the terminology may be different: organizations may need to move from 'first-order change' to 'second-order change' (Watzlawick et al., 1974), or adopt new recipes (Grinyer and Spender, 1979a, b). Lewin (1952) has shown that such changes will be resisted. Argyris and Schon (1974; 1978) have demonstrated the difficulty that managers find in moving from 'single-loop learning', where they are making responses within their present cognitive frameworks, to 'double-loop learning', where they are prepared to internalize divergent views that do not correspond to such frameworks. Whilst there have been studies of change processes of the fundamental kind, they have been primarily at an individual level; there have been few studies that have observed how organizations achieve – or fail to achieve – such shifts.

The underlying notions about the bases for managing change refer us back to the work of Kelman (1958) and Etzioni (1961). An amalgamation of their arguments on the management of compliance is summarized in the list below, which provides a typology with which to conceive a basis upon which individuals or groups might change their ways of operating. The greater the extent to which change can be achieved through internalization or identification – both of which imply a ready acceptance of, or voluntary compliance with change – the more likely it is that that change will take place smoothly. However, the implication of our previous discussion is that the more major the change, the more it shifts from current ways of operating and challenges current scripts or ideologies, the more it is likely that identification or internalization will not take place. Pfeffer (1981a) argues that the use of persuasive and manipulative acts of a symbolic kind appears to be associated with more rapid compliance than the use of more explicit coercive power. However, the extent to which the mechanisms concerned with strategic change have been studied in the context of such a typology is limited.

(1) 'Coercion' – that is, the threat or application of physical, financial or psychological sanctions to induce pain, discomfort or material loss in the event of negative behaviour
(2) 'Remuneration' – that is, reward for positive behaviour via the provision of financial or fringe benefits.
(3) 'Persuasion/manipulation' – that is, the conscious use of symbolic activity, rewards or deprivations (Etzioni calls this 'normative').
(4) 'Identification' – that is, the voluntary compliance of individuals because of their identification with others who are complying.
(5) 'Internalization' – that is, compliance because of commitment to change because it is 'believed in'. The power of compliance lies within the change itself rather than being external to that change.

Grinyer and Spender (1979a, b) argue that such major change is likely to need the impetus of an actual or perceived organizational crisis and also support the assertion made by Dalton (1970) that such change must build on existing, if latent, impetus. There is then a need for some intrinsic motivation for change, but what are the processes and conditions that are likely to promote change?

Biggart (1977) studied such changes in the US Post Office and noted the 'destructive' mechanism at a symbolic and political level that were involved in the change process; existing systems, he argued, needed to be broken down before new approaches could be accepted. Sheldon (1980) observed processes of fundamental change in hospitals and concluded that there has to be acknowledged evidence of the existing 'paradigm' dying. Bartunek (1984) studied such changes in a religious order and found that 'second order change in interpretative schemes occurs through a dialectical process in which old and new interpretative schemes interact, resulting in a synthesis' (Bartunek, 1984, p. 356). She observed that such interaction typically began with a perceived crisis, which challenged the validity of existing interpretative schemes, and proceeded as a conflict-ridden dialectic between existing and divergent views, in which 'the resolution of the process will depend in part on the comparative power of these different groups to have their perspective heard' (Bartunek, 1984, p. 365). The process is stressful, supporting the view of Lewin (1952) that such changes are likely to involve an 'emotional stir up' and involve 'pain' (as noted by Schein, 1973) as individuals find themselves questioning the assumptions upon which they may have operated for many years. Grinyer and Spender (1979b) in their study of change in an engineering company observed that 'recipe' change was associated with the advent of new top senior management or take-over. The study by Pettigrew (1985b) of the changes over time in ICI is the richest terms of organizational and managerial context. It shows the relative failure of institutionalized Organizational Development mechanisms for change and the potentially powerful influence of new top management with alternative cognitive frameworks. It also demonstrates the role of perceived crises in facilitating change, the essentially political nature of change processes and the way in which organizational action, for example in administrative mechanisms, was important in building 'energy and commitment around particular problems and their solution' (Pettigrew, 1985, b, p. 458) and thus creating a dynamic for change. It is an observation similar to that of Kotter (1982), who showed how the general managers that he researched 'achieved much of their more direct influence by using symbolic methods. That is they used meetings, architecture, language, stories about the organization, time and space as symbols' (p. 74). At the meetings at which these general managers were attempting to initiate change they rarely gave orders; the meetings were characterized by a great deal of joking and cajoling and appeared to deal with relatively small-scale administrative issues. The emphasis of their approach was on the informal and indirect – what Pfeffer (1981b) would regard as symbolic.

Culture, Ideology and a Symbolic View of Organizational Life

In considering the way in which managerial beliefs affect organizational behaviour we move inevitably into a consideration of organizational culture. Although an elusive concept, culture is typically conceived of in terms of the sorts of beliefs and assumptions held by members of a committee relatively commonly. The elusive nature of the concept arises from the extent to which it is something of a catch-all in its implications. As Schein points out, ideas on culture have embraced observed behavioural regularities and norms of behaviour of working groups, and espoused dominant values, guiding philosophies, 'the rules of the game' in organizations and the feeling or climate of an organization. Schein himself is a good deal more specific:

The term culture should be reserved for the deeper level of basic *assumptions and beliefs* that are shared by members of an organisation, that operate unconsciously and define in a basic 'taken for granted' fashion an organisation's view of itself and its environment. These assumptions and beliefs are *learned* responses to a group's problems of *survival* in its external environment and its problem of *internal integration*. They come to be taken for granted because they solve those problems repeatedly and reliably. This deeper level of assumptions is to be distinguished from the artifacts and values that are manifestations or surface levels of this culture but not the essence of the culture. (1985, p. 6)

It may be argued that, if culture as a concept is at risk of being a catch-all, Schein's definition is somewhat confined, in that it focuses only on beliefs and assumptions rather than activities or systems – a point we will return to later. However, Schein's approach does have the merit of differentiating between different aspects of fundamental beliefs in organizations. He distinguishes between very broad beliefs about the relationship of the organization to its total environment – beliefs about 'mission' – through to beliefs about the extent to which the organization can control its environment or is subject to its forces, to beliefs about the 'right' way to behave in the organization. He makes the point that it is configurations of beliefs that cross these categories and are compatible and consistent one with another that go to form developed cultural 'paradigms'. It is a point somewhat similar to that made by Davis (1984) who distinguishes 'guiding beliefs' from 'daily beliefs' in organizational cultures and argues that, where these are out of line one with another, there are likely to be problems. For example, strategy may be intellectually compatible with guiding beliefs but its implementation baulked by a conflict with daily beliefs.

Schein's emphasis is therefore on 'ideational culture'; he recognizes that other organizational artefacts such as structures, systems, stories and activities are observable cultural phenomena but argues that such artefacts, in themselves, are of value only in so far as they may help signify what is important in the belief systems of members of the organization: in this sense, their value lies in their symbolic significance. However, such organizational artefacts are important in explaining the strategies followed by organizations. Alan Meyer has argued that 'organisational ideologies are manifested and sustained by beliefs, stories, languages and ceremonial acts' (1982, p. 45). As such he is arguing that the ideology of organizations can be discerned within what the 'cultural adaptationist' (Keesing, 1974) would view as culture; that is, the patterns of activity, speech and use of material objects 'where significance lies in their relationship with human behaviour' (Lindesmith et al., 1977). Meyer's research identified the verbal images used by managers in a number of American hospitals about their environments and organizations, compared these with more conventional structural variables, and found that 'ideologies exert strong forces guiding organizational responses, whereas structures exert weak constraints' (Meyer, 1982, p. 59).

Other researchers have also pointed to the significance of symbolic aspects of organizations. Stories, or myths, have been shown to be important in organizations, not least because they are easily recalled (Wilkins, 1983; Martin and Powers, 1983). There is evidence that stories also help to link current situations with the past and thus experiences of previous situations (Schrank and Abelson, 1977). Wilkins (1983) also argues that people tend to believe more readily things that are enshrined in myth; thus, within organizations, myths encourage commitment to the values of that organization. Trice and Beyer (1984) and Meyer and Rowan (1977) have also shown the importance of organizational rituals and ceremonies in binding individuals in organizational action. Dandridge et al. (1980) suggested three basic roles for such symbolic mechanisms: they might be descriptive – that is, providing an expression of the organization to its members; they may be energy-controlling, reducing tension; and they may have a systems maintenance role – that is, providing coherence to the organization. Certainly myths and symbols seem to perform several functions; Wilkins (1983) argues that organizational stories are 'vehicles for conception', embracing within them complex explanations and thus providing 'cognitive short cuts'; but more than this they may also communicate the 'vision of the organisation's mission or role'.

Both Daft (1983) and Abravanel (1983) point to different levels of symbols in organizations. Daft points to 'instrumental' symbols as serving 'a rational purpose, to convey information or meaning that will achieve some rational need for the organisation' (Daft, 1983, p. 202) and which are likely to 'pertain to well understood organizational phenomena' (p. 204). Abravanel (1983) uses the term 'operational' to describe the same phenomona. Whichever term is used the implication is similar; they are symbolic systems of the organization, which can be identified as the more formal aspects of control; they include organization charts, reward systems and procedural systems. They are the mechanisms of the organization for which managers might find the words cultural and 'symbolic' as descriptors rather unusual: but they are used deliberately. Just as anthropologists write about kinship systems or witchcraft as cultural systems in a society, so control systems of organization can be regarded as a feature of the culture of that organization in so far as 'the idea of a culture rests on the premise that the full meaning of things is not given a *priori* in the things themselves. Instead meaning results from interpretation' (Louis, 1983, p. 41). It is not the control systems *per se* that are significant but the fact that they are 'symbols' – they 'express much more than their intrinsic content' (Morgan et al., 1983).

Daft also identifies what he calls 'expressive' symbols (Abravanel calls them 'fundamental'). These 'pertain to underlying feelings and emotional needs' (Daft 1983, p. 202) or pertain to the 'moral principles' (Abravanel, 1983, p. 274) of the organization. They are less capable of being routinized because they are to do with the way in which the organization is managed, with organizational ethos or with the social commitment of the organisation. They are what Perrow has called 'third order control' systems (Perrow, 1979) and are to do with the identification and preservation of the nature of the organization, not in terms of what it does, but what it is. Abravanel goes on to suggest that myths play an important role because they mediate between likely contradictions and conflicts between the more fundamental aspects of ideology in the organization, which may be divergent between individuals or groupings, and also between what the organization sees itself as (or wishes to be) and what it has to do to operate. The role of myths is therefore to maintain legitimacy and 'help us get on with our work' (Abravanel, 1983, p. 286). They are particularly prevalent in 'clannish' organizations with long-serving stable staff and where loyalty and long service are highly valued (Wilkins, 1983; Wilkins and Ouchi, 1983) and where there is a congruence of general organizational goals but ambiguity in performance criteria (Ouchi, 1980).

In explaining the role of myths in organizations it is worth quoting fairly extensively from a paper by Boje, Fedor and Rowland. They see organizational culture as including the language of organizations, their symbols and metaphors, and myths that are peculiar to that organization, and argue that the understanding of myths and the intervention by managers and consultants at a symbolic level in organizational change is powerful yet poorly understood. They go on:

> These particular components of culture facilitate the feelings of rational action in the midst of otherwise overpowering uncertainty and political manoeuvering. Myth making is an adaptive mechanism whereby groups in an organisation maintain logic frameworks within which to attribute meaning to activities and events. The meanings that organise past activities and events into a system of logic then become the basis for legitimising present and future behaviours. A myth making system is evident to some degree in every organization. Without such an adaptive system the technological and administrative structure would lack sufficient shared meaning to serve as a basis for co-ordinated behaviour in the face of excessive uncertainty.
>
> For those who become socialised into an organisation, myths constitute a factual and highly objective reality. They are a major part of the taken for

granted assumptions and common sense theories of organisational experience. In general we hold myths to be social attempts to 'manage' certain problematic aspects of modern organisations, through definitions of truths and rational purpose. This process of 'management' results in a composite of standard operating procedures and organisational characteristics such as acceptable practices concerning treatment of subordinates and procedures for their placement, transfer and promotion. A myth is constructed to exemplify why the given practices and procedures are 'the only way' the organisation can function effectively . . . . Myths are a form of 'bounding' permitting meaningul organisational behaviour to occur, while glossing over excessive complexity, turbulence or ambiguity. (Boje et al., 1982, p. 18)

Here we have the link between the importance of symbolic action in organizations and management cognition. Symbolic action endows organizational action with meaning. Widening it to the issue of organizational culture, Tichy argues that the 'cultural system glues the organization together because it 1) provides members with cognitive maps with which to understand and influence behaviour in the organization and 2) it provides a social justification for what people are doing' (Tichy, 1983, pp. 253–4). There is, then, this inherited and powerful cultural system which must fundamentally influence the organization's strategy. Proponents of this view would argue that it is not sensible to try to understand organizational decisions about strategy, structure or methods of control out of this essentially cultural context. Pfeffer goes further and argues that 'the task of management [is] to provide explanations, rationalisations, and legitimation for the activities undertaken in the organisation' (Pfeffer, 1981b, p. 4) and that in doing so 'management control [is] derived from language and symbolic action' (p. 7). In effect he argues that managers manage symbols to create meaning at an organizational level – that management is symbolic action.

Ideology and the Strategies of Organization

The links between ideology, culture and symbolic acts, and strategy become clearer when it is remembered that the typical patterns of strategic development in organizations are incremental, or adaptive. Myths, rituals and other symbolic aspect of organizations do not merely endow and encapsulate meaning on a transitory basis; they are enduring and resistant to change, as interventionists in organizations have found (see e.g. Pettigrew, 1985b; Marshall and McLean, 1985). In effect they are an important mechanism in preserving the assumptions and beliefs in which strategy is rooted.

Shrivastava and Mitroff (1983) have demonstrated the importance of understanding the differing cultures and ideologies of organizations. They describe different 'managerial frames of reference' which take the form of internally consonant systems, beliefs and ways of operating that are quite different from each other. For example they identify the following four frames of reference (FORs).

(1) An 'entrepreneurial' FOR characterized by a largely individualistic way of operating, heavily reliant on anecdotal and informal information bases, largely experience-based and heavily dependent on managerial intuition. Here formal analysis is limited and time horizons short with a heavy emphasis on operational issues. Managerial assumptions are generally unstated but there is an underlying emphasis on growth, action and aggression. The language used is also aggressive and often militaristic: however, the aggression is not limited to the language; the mannerisms and attitude of managers here are also likely to be aggressive.

(2) The 'bureaucratic' FOR has a bias towards objective verifiable information usually gleaned from 'hard' data sources. Objectives are explicit and managers here tend to work within well defined organizational rules and systems. In such situations the language used tends to be essentially economic with much reference to formal measures of performance and bases of evaluation.

(3) The 'professional' FOR emphasizes the explicit sharing of organizational assumptions and means of analysis, the analysis itself utilizing both subjective and analytical information to arrive at a unitary view of situations. There is a heavy emphasis on planning and analysis with relatively long time horizons and a concentration on external 'reality'. Managers here tend to have a high degree of professional training and this is reflected in their language, which is that of science and research with 'a generous use of theoretical concepts, technical words and managerial jargon' (Shrivastava and Mitroff, 1983, p. 176).

(4) The 'political' FOR is, on the other hand, characterized by an orientation around sub-groups rather than any organizational unity. Loyalties of managers are to these sub-groups and information collection largely provides a basis for bargaining between such sub-groups for obtaining resources. The reality for managers here is essentially internal to the organization and behaviour is such as to preserve and enhance the sub-group and, although language appears to be analytical and evaluative, it is largely used as a shield to justify the essentially political aims of sub-groupings.

What Shrivastava and Mitroff are demonstrating here is that organizations may well show a degree of cultural unity that is pervasive and enduring. It would, for example, be a mistake to assume that a similar set of environmental stimuli would result in the same strategic output from an organization that is essentially 'political' as compared with one that is essentially 'bureaucratic'. In this sense strategy is the product of the ideology and culture of the organization rather than the environment.

A good example of this is given in the work of Miles and Snow (1978) in collaboration with Meyer. Far from strategies being the rational responses to environmental stimuli, strategies were explained as a matter of strategic choice by managers (Child, 1972) in which managers enacted their environments (Weick, 1979a) on the basis of the meaning systems of the organization. They showed that strategy and culture were intimately intertwined and demonstrated this within four generic strategic groupings of organizations – 'defenders', 'prospectors', 'analysers' and 'reactors'. As a means of illustrating their research and arguments, we will take two of these groupings, 'defenders' and 'prospectors' as exemplary extremes.

The defender-type organization is one that typically tries to 'seal off' a part of a market in order to create a stable environment in which it can operate with minimal disruption. It will tend to organise itself so as to be as efficient and low cost as possible within that market and will offer much the same products or services with little change but with a high emphasis on service. The problem for them is one of control for efficiency: the most powerful executives tend to be from financial or production functions; there is relatively little environmental sensing but much attention to internal systems; promotions are from within the organizations which themselves are defined internally through clear (usually) functional structures and mechanistic procedures. This then is a relationship between strategy and structure: but the work of Meyer (1982) also measured more symbolic aspects of such organizations, including the language used and the stories told. For example managers in defender organizations tend to tell stories that enshrined stability and that stress consensus in the organization; moreover there is a tendency towards the use of anthropomorphic imagery by managers in describing their organizations.

Prospector organizations are quite different. They see their role as achieving growth by seeking out new market opportunities through continual environmental sensing and fostering change in the industry. The emphasis is on strategies of product and market development. There is a low commitment to the maintenance of current technologies or systems. The problem of administering the organization becomes that of managing deliberate diversity: in such circumstances there is a tendency for marketing and research and development specialists to achieve the most powerful office, for coalitions within the organization to be transitory and for planning to be action-oriented within an essentially organic system of control, emphasizing high degrees of autonomy. Prospectors are also characterized by, in effect, having much looser, less rigid ideologies, except in so far as they have an ideology of change and experimentation. Meyer found such organizations have quite different organizational stories, emphasizing re-orientation and organizational dissent and the imagery of language tends to be much more to do with business operations or machines.

Three main points arise from this allusion to Miles and Snow's (and Meyer's) work. First the linking pattern between strategy, structure and symbolism becomes clearer. We need to conceive of strategy, not as something standing apart from the organization, as separately capable of analysis, but as part of the wider culture of the organization. In order to understand organizational strategies we therefore need to understand organizational cultures (Pettigrew, 1979; Tichy, 1983). The second point is perhaps more fundamental: if we take the example of 'defenders' and 'prospectors', Miles and Snow argue that the strategies followed by these different types of organizations are the product of their cultures. The argument here is, as with Pettigrew, who broadens it to political processes too, that strategy 'is ultimately the product of a legitimisation process shaped by political/cultural considerations, and expressed in rational/analytic terms' (Pettigrew, 1985b, p. 46). Third, it is possible to argue that the reason one organization is more likely to adopt strategies more divergent from its previous strategies than another organization is because it has less homogeneity of ideology within it; 'defenders' are characterized by homogeneous ideologies and 'prospectors' by a greater heterogeneity of ideology. It is a view supported by Friedlander (1983) and Hedberg et al. (1976) who also argue that organizational learning in a reconstructive (or fundamental) rather than adaptive mode takes place more readily where there is such heterogeneity. Here is a view of strategy that is quite opposed to that taken in rationalistic models. It sees the organization as an arena, in which the political and cultural systems are to do with the legitimization of that organization, through the creation of meaning, by those within the organization for themselves and their stakeholders. The mechanisms for this are cultural, symbolic and political. Organizational strategies result from this. They may be post-rationalized and given the support of analytical exercises – but these are justifications of, not reasons for, strategy.

Strategic Management and the Management of Organizational Culture

The argument within what has here been termed the 'interpretative' model is, then, that central to the process of formulating strategy are the meaning systems of those parties to the process – most typically management. Managers possess cognitive maps through which they make sense of a complex and uncertain organizational world; they impose such maps on that world and, in this sense, strategy is the organizational enactment of managerial meaning. It is not the environment in any objective sense that drives strategy, but managers' conception of their organizational world within that environment that forms strategy. Strategy, in this sense, is the product of managerial ideology. The set of organizationally relevant meanings that forms ideology is, in effect, the 'reality' of organizational life; and it is a reality that is preserved in the symbols of organizational life – in the stories that are told and the rituals that are performed. Moreover, managers more or less consciously manipulate these symbols to reinforce or adjust the meaning of organizations for others internal and those external to the organization. Since strategic change is likely to involve the change of meaning systems it can be argued that the management of strategy is close to the management of culture. It is this that is at the root of the growing and influencial literature that argues that managers must pay special heed to the cultural fabric of their organizations. When Peters and Waterman write 'an effective leader must be the master at two ends of the spectrum: ideas at the highest level of abstraction and actions at the most mundane level of detail' (Peters and Waterman, 1982, p. 287), then they are advocating the management of the everyday aspects of organizational life that represent organizational culture. As Peters pointed out some years earlier '. . . the mundane tools that involve the creation and manipulation of symbols over time have impact to the extent that they reshape beliefs and expectations' (Peters, 1978, p. 11). Smircich (1983b), observing this growing advocacy of the management of culture, cites Quinn (1980), Schwartz and Davis (1981), Tichy (1983) and Salmans (1983) as contributing the view that: 'organisation culture may be another critical lever or key by which strategic managers can influence or direct the course of their organisations . . . . The task awaiting individual managers is to find ways to use stories, legends and other forms of symbolism in their unique situations, for their own particular ends' (Smircich, 1983b, p. 346).

EXPLAINING STRATEGIC MANAGEMENT IN CONTEXT

Table 2.1 is a summary of the central characteristics of the three models of strategic management discussed so far. However, this review of these three different schools of thought did commence by stating that the three generic

TABLE 2.1 *Characteristics of different models of strategic decision-making*

A rationalistic model	An incremental model	An interpretative model
Strategy is formed through the analysis of an uncertain environment and the evaluation of the extent to which organizational resources can be utilized to take advantage of environmental opportunities so identified.	*Strategy is the outcome of the action of corporate life: it is therefore the product of social and political activity, and the routines of the organization.*	*Strategy is the product of the ideologies of individuals or groups in the organization.*
* Uncertainty and complexity can be reduced through comprehensive analysis.	* Strategy develops typically through small, serial steps resulting in an evolutionary, if intermittent, pattern.	* Managers possess 'scripts', 'causal maps' or 'ideologies' which – act to make sense of situations and guide appropriate behaviour; – are presumed logical; – are difficult to change.
* Such analysis will yield explanations of cause and effect in terms of organizational performance.	* Organizations, in effect, 'feel' their way through the uncertainty of their environments.	* In the context of decision-making, environments are enacted: they are a function of management cognition.
* Clear objectives can be established that: – permit measured evaluation of strategic options; – create organizational unity in decision-making and implementation.	* More global change occurs infrequently and may be accompanied by dramatic internal changes within the organization.	* Stimuli that do not accord with dominant cognitive maps will be ignored, or over-ridden by facilitating reasons for ultilizing existing maps.
	* Problem awareness is likely to be at an individual and qualitative level initially. Organizational action is likely only after an organizationally relevant 'trigger' – e.g. a performance downturn.	* Fundamental strategic change is characterized by and requires a shift in organizational ideology.
	* Diagnosis of problems is typically informal and verbal, iterative and characterized by solicitation and bargaining.	* Such shifts are infrequent and problematic.
	* There is a propensity for managers to draw on past events and experience in identifying problems and developing solutions.	

* Strategic decisions are taken in the light of the consideration of a range of strategic options.

* Strategic options can be evaluated against the 'facts' established through analysis and the explicit objectives of the organization.

* The implementation of strategy follows the choice of strategey.

* Strategy-making is a step-by-step linear process.

* Strategic decisions are the property of 'top management'. Other managers either 'service' such decisions or implement them.

* Strategic decisions are decisions with long time horizons.

* Typically problem identification and definition takes place at the level of functional/operational management. Senior management are more likely to be involved in selecting (or authorizing) strategies, or resolving stalemate situations.

* Adopted strategies are likely to be dependent on the locus of power.

* Strategies can be viewed as compromises designed to accommodate conflicting power groups, competing for organizational resources.

* Objectives are likely to be unclear, absent or post-rationalized.

* Incrementalism may thus be seen as:
  – purposive, experimental and logical, with active environmental scanning and partial implementation securing commitment; or
  – the manifestation of routinized organizational behaviour; or
  – a 'muddle' of (partial) decision-making arising from the politics and day-to-day operation of organizational life.

* Ideologies are preserved in the symbols, rituals and myths of organizational culture.

* The more homogeneous the ideology in an organization, the more unlikely will be changes in strategy except within the parameters of that ideology.

* Symbolic action thus endows organizational action with meaning relevant to that organization.

* Managers manipulate organizational symbols to reinforce or adjust organizational meaning.

* The manipulation of organizational symbols is an important means of managing strategic change.

* Strategy is not separate from, but part of, or the outcome of, ideology and culture of organizations.

models used here are somewhat artificial divisions used for the convenience of description. There is indeed a very considerable difference between the idea of strategic management as an essentially analytically driven process in which rational managers optimize performance by establishing facts about a knowable environment, and evaluate options against clear objectives; and the idea of managers manipulating organizational symbols in the enactment of organizational ideologies. Whilst such extremes are most certainly different, it is less clear that what Quinn (1980) would call 'logical incrementalism' is that much different from many aspects of the rationalistic models: and it might also be argued that we need to understand political aspects of incrementalism very much in terms of the reconciliation of managerial groups operating with competing or conflicting ideologies.

In short it is perhaps more helpful to conceive of different models of strategic management, not as watertight explanations, but as a continuum of description, within which there is supportive explanatory power. Figure 2.5 represents such a continuum. It is the overlapping relevance of the perspectives that provide additional insights into the idea of strategic management.

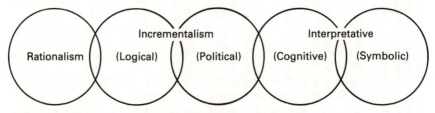

FIGURE 2.5   A continuum of strategic management models

If, as has been demonstrated, strategic management in practice cannot be equated with the linear and optimizing models we have called 'rationalistic', that does not mean that managers do not behave in a rational way when dealing with the complexity and uncertainty that characterize strategic decisions. The idea of 'logical incrementalism' bridges the apparent divide between the rational search for strategies within an inevitably ambiguous external context and an essentially political organizational arena. The apparent confusion of the political arena of organizational life in which competing groups bid and bargain for resources can be understood not merely as self-interest but as competing or resisting ideological camps enacting their constructs of reality in an uncertain environment. If we wished to complete a circle of overlapping schools of thought we can even conceive of the corporate planning systems and strategy committees of corporate life, not so much as the processes characterizing the rationalistic approach to strategy formulation but as the symbols and rituals of post-rationalization in action.

In short, there is no simple explanatory model of strategic management: the level of complexity with which we are concerned cannot be reduced to one model. What does emerge, however, is that it is artificial to remove 'strategic management' from the dramas of organizational life and endow it with a meaning and significance all of its own. The process of managing strategy needs to be examined and understood within the richness of management in organization. This study is one contribution to that task. What the models so far described provide is a set of questions and issues worthy of clarification by such studies as these. They are not issues that can be resolved by any one study but are likely to be understood better as more about the context of strategic management is explored.

The aims of this study were to seek to understand how, if at all, existing theories illuminate observed processes and, out of this, to generate further explanatory propositions about strategic management. The review of existing theories carried out so far, in itself generates a set of issues with a potential for clarification: these are listed below.

(1) At the most general level, in what ways and to what extent do the models of strategic management discussed here help explain and have a relevance to the business context studied? In this sense this research is an exercise, if not in verification, then in the testing of theory and propositions about the processes of strategic management.

(2) How do the different models of strategic management interrelate – if indeed they do? We have suggested that the models, in so far as they explain managerial processes, shade into each other. This implies a relevance to each other, which needs clearer explanation.

(3) It is perhaps surprising that within a developing body of research, which points to strategy as evolving from the interplay of individuals, there are so few systematic studies of the way in which the interaction of individuals contributes to strategic decision-making. There is still a scant empirical basis for examining the relationships between the observed characteristics of strategic decision-making modes and routines and the more detailed characteristics of interaction at a personal level. This research begins at the level of interaction and seeks to understand process specifically from this point of view.

(4) The notion of incrementalism as a descriptor of strategic change is becoming well established: it is generally accepted that it does help describe strategy development rather better than other less empirically rooted notions. There are 'however' some problems. It is arguable that Quinn (1980) for example has built normative guidelines on management

on the basis of an analysis of what managers say without a sufficient study of the context of how incremental processes work. He suggests that managers consciously manage, and manage effectively, incrementally. Is this the case? If they do, what benefits and what dangers might be seen to be within the approaches to strategic management that Quinn character-ised as 'logical incrementalism'?

(5) The idea of strategy as the resolution of environmental forces and resource opportunities and constraints remains central in the literature on strategic management. Do such forces have the primacy that is argued for them in the development of strategy? On the other hand is the notion of 'enactment' more powerful an explanation of managers' and organizations' relationships to their environment?

(6) Another area in which research into the process of strategy formulation is lacking arises from the aggregate nature of the interaction of individuals in an organization context. It is clear that strategic decisions have outcomes that infer some sort of reconciliation of divergent views and beliefs, or conversely that organizations must exist in a perpetual state of 'ideological turmoil'. This research examines the way in which divergent managerial beliefs are reconciled sufficiently to allow for the formulation of strategy; in particular this is examined both within the context of the incremental processes of change that typify strategic change and within the context of more fundamental shifts in strategy.

(7) What are the links, if any, between strategy, ideology and symbolic aspects of organizations? Are cognitive structures so resistant to change; and, if they are, what are the change mechanisms? Do managers 'manage symbolically' (Pfeffer, 1981b); and if they do, what, in practice does it mean in terms of the management of strategic change?

(8) There is an apparent paradox in the literature on strategy and culture. Peters and Waterman (1982), Deal and Kennedy (1982), Ouchi (1980) and Wilkins and Ouchi (1983) emphasize the importance of 'rich cultures' where there is close identification with dominant corporate values. Yet others warn that 'a strong sense of identity involves investment, commitment, momentum – and paradoxically, rigidity. These will preclude learning because their existence depends on limiting knowledge to that which will re-inforce and applaud investment in . . . the established mission' (Friedlander, 1983, p. 210). There are, then, apparent dangers of an uncritical acceptance of group ideals and assumptions, which can lead to 'groupthink' (Janis, 1972) and an inability to respond to the need for change. Is this the paradox it seems to be; and if so, how does it relate to processes of the management of change in organizations?

This is a substantial agenda of issues. How it has been tackled will be discussed in the next chapter. However, it is important to point out at this stage that, wide as the scope of the work is, its width is necessary if a more holistic conception of the management of strategy and particularly of strategic change is to be developed. It is a central argument here that an approach to the study of process by attempting to isolate parts of processes is of limited value. Essentially the management of strategic change needs to be studied in its cultural context, and culture infers both an integrated and an historical perspective. The scope of the work is, then, wide in order to handle one central issue – the problems of managing strategic change.

3
The Research Programme

This chapter provides a fairly brief explanation of how the research was carried out. It is concerned with clarifying (a) what the epistemological basis of the research is, (b) why the research was primarily focused on one company and (c) how the research was carried out in terms of the choice of company context, and the collection and analysis of what was highly qualitative data. Throughout there is discussion on the benefits and also limitations of the research approach employed.

The choice of research method arises from the aims of the research, which were to examine the management processes of strategic change in the light of existing theory and research findings with a view to advancing our understanding of such processes. Overall the research chosen to achieve this is built around an approach to social investigation to be found in the quite different field of social anthropology. As long ago as 1951 Evans–Pritchard (1951) described the stages in anthropological research, as he saw them, as follows:

> As I understand the matter, what the social anthropologist does can be divided into three phases. In the first phase, as ethnographer, he goes to live among a primitive people and learns their way of life. He learns to speak their language, to think in their concepts, and to feel in their values. He then lives the experience over again critically and interpretatively in the conceptual categories and values of his own culture *and in terms of the general body of knowledge of his discipline.* In other words, he translates from one culture to another.
>
> In the second phase of his work, and still within a single ethnographic study of a particular primitive society, he tries to go beyond this literary and impressionistic stage *and to discover the structural order of the society,* so that it is intelligible not merely at the level of consciousness and action, as it is to one of its members or to the foreigner who has learnt its mores and participates in its life, but also at the level of sociological analysis. . . . The social anthropologist is not content merely to observe and describe the social life of a primitive people but seeks to reveal its underlying structural order, the pattern of which, once established, enables him to see it as a whole, as a set of interrelated abstractions. (pp. 61–2)

There is of course no intention here to suggest that Foster Brothers is the literal equivalent of a primitive society, but the principles remain the same. The italics in the extract above are mine and attempt to indicate two key steps employed in this study. The first is to become familiar enough with the social system and history of the company studied to be able to relate the processes observed to the 'general body of knowledge' of the literature on strategic management processes. The second is to go beyond that and 'discover the structural order', if any, that can be observed in those processes. The first stage is, then, essentially to do with description and a reconciliation of that description with the studies undertaken by others. The second stage is essentially concerned with theory generation. The third phase that Evans–Pritchard goes on to describe is essentially comparative, in which researchers examine the patterns they observe in their own studies with that in other societies. His third phase of investigation is not central to this study. There is some discussion throughout of comparative material and a specific discussion in the last chapter of the extent to which findings and propositions here bear general comparison with other contextual studies; but the view is taken that this research is one of the still few rich organizational studies, and that the primary task is to explore this context to the full.

THE RESEARCH PERSPECTIVE

On several occasions during the fieldwork for this research, I was asked by managers, on first meeting them, to explain why I was doing it. The explanation I gave also serves as an introduction here. I explained that, by career background, I had been a manager in industry who had switched to an academic career; and that one of the things that had struck me was that in all the reading I had done about theories of management, there was remarkably little I had read that was based on what managers saw themselves doing. My intention was to add to the little that did exist. This was not only a true statement of my aim, but it also served as a good way of getting into the interview because it properly placed the manager as the focus of the interview with the prime status. It also serves as a means of now introducing the logic and method of the research.

Burrell and Morgan (1979) have shown that approaches to research and the understanding of social phenomena will inevitably differ according to the ontological and epistemological stance of the researcher. They argue that different stances usefully yield different interpretations of the same phenomena. It is therefore important to be clear as to which stance is being taken here. However, it should be stressed that in so doing it is not being suggested that there is no value in other perspectives. On the contrary, the view here is that different perspectives by others on the data in Part II are to be welcomed.

Underlying the research were doubts about 'rational' models of strategic decision-making: specifically that such rational models assume that decision-making is an essentially analytical process in which a 'real' environment can be understood in terms of an objective view of organizational resource, so that the 'organization' can and does make decisions designed to achieve some more or less explicit aim. This model, or variations of it, has been shown to have many weaknesses, most of which are dealt with in the account of different schools of thought on processes of strategic management reviewed in the previous chapter. A number of points arising from that review do, however, bear emphasis in clarifying the methodology employed here.

First, what is meant by the 'environment' has to be considered as problematic as far as decision-making is concerned. There is no denial here that actual events occur. For example, in the context of this research, there is no denying that in the late 1960s there was an increasing proportion of imported menswear into the UK and that this trend continued for much of the 1970s. This, and similar phenomena, are regarded as empirical facts. What is more problematic is that as 'raw data' (Weick, 1977) such facts are of questionable consequence in terms of management decision-making. What is more important is what is understood by such facts or, indeed, if they are recognized or not. In this sense rational models of decision-making are weak in so far as they undervalue interpretative and subjective interpretations of events, and minimize the role of cognition.

Second is the idea of 'the organization': that decisions are made for or by an organization. This has not so far been addressed. The difficulty is that there is little explanation of what an organization is when it comes to rational models of decision-making. Again in this work there is no attempt to deny that organizations exist in the sense that they have a public face and, it is argued here, a reality unto themselves: they have systems and institutions which identify them as operating and cultural units and endow them with meaning for the individuals associated with them and interacting within them. It is the very centrality of such systems, and of individuals' roles within such systems that is the starting point for this research. It is important, in terms of examining decision-making, to understand the relevance of the dynamics of organizational structures, beliefs, norms, history and so on, as they contribute to those decisions. Implicit within this view of the organization is that it is not defined or bounded by one or even a set of explicit aims but, rather, is conceived of, not only by the researcher, but also by stakeholders as a vehicle for fulfilling many and therefore potentially conflicting goals. In this sense the organization is an essentially cultural and political arena, and decisions are the outcome of social and verbal interaction within such arenas.

Bittner argues that it is important to examine organizational activity, not simply by understanding it through the eyes of the chief executive or a power elite, but to accept that the perceptions of one individual or group may be different from those of another and differ again according to events or problems. Given this complexity, the danger is that simplified notions of strategy, or structure, or organization will be implanted on the analysis. The attempt in this research, however, was to start from what Bittner calls a 'common-sense' view of organization, to attempt to avoid 'a refined and purified version of the actors' theorising' (1965, p. 245) that he suggests is a danger inherent within notions of bureaucracy, in which the organization 'as a notion is reified'. In studying an organization he argues it is important 'to decide that the meaning of the concept, and of all the terms and determinations that are subsumed under it, must be discovered by studying their use in real scenes of action . . .' (p. 246).

This is not, then, the study of an organization so much as a study of the interplay between the beliefs and actions of individuals over a period of years, and through a series of events. The organization is not seen as the subject of study so much as an output of the processes under investigation. In this sense the notion of 'the organization' is mainly a convenient device by which to bound the study. 'The organization' is conceived in much the same way as Beattie describes his view of 'society' for the social anthropologist:

> It is a concept, an abstraction from people's observed behaviour; and it exists only in the minds of the people who are concerned with it. . . . It is simply a number of people who are related to one another and to their environment in innumerable ways. . . . Simmel put this point in a different way when he said that society is not a substance but an event – or, we might add, series of events. (1964, p. 56)

It is these events that take form in the public face of 'the organization', which this research seeks to explore and understand.

An alternative approach that might have been taken is to have studied process as 'public' output – that is, in the context of management studies, by assuming that, because 'firm *x*' acts in such a way, it is possible to infer how it came to behave in that way. This is an assumption underlying most of the work of business analysis and managerial economists. The flow of rationalistic logic from which the assumption is derived is that, if an act can be discerned to be relevant to an environmental (or some other) dynamic, then the act must have taken place as a response to that. It is a logic that imputes causality because of effect. Those who would defend such an approach argue that this sort of statement trivializes such analysis which is, in fact, a good deal more rigorous. Yet the roots of the criticism are not trivial. The first is, to return to the discussion above, that 'an organization' as a unity cannot respond to anything: it is individuals who respond within a cultural context. Second, if this is so, then it cannot be assumed that individuals will interpret, or respond to, environmental dynamics uniformly. Individuals respond according to how they interpret events. Within any management group, output will be a function of the interplay of different perceptions of reality. The possibility of potentially significant divergence of perceptions must be considered. Bittner's views argue for a methodology that takes as problematic the mechanisms by which an individual or individuals make sense of their context by starting with the individual and not a notion called an organization. Blumer argues that: 'Human beings interpret or define each other's actions instead of merely reacting to each other's actions. Their 'response' is not made directly to the actions of one another but instead is based on the meaning which they attach to such actions' (1967, p. 139).

Action thus arises out of the interaction and inter-perception of individuals and must be understood in these terms. This research attempts to understand processes of strategy formulation and change by examining in a social and cultural context, the way in which individuals make sense of the actions and views of, for example, their customers, their competitors and colleagues; it is, in this way, within a symbolic interactionist tradition of social study. The emphasis is on how 'human beings construct their realities in a process of interaction with other human beings' (Meltzer et al., 1975). Such an approach requires an understanding of events and social process as the subjects of investigation perceive and interpret them (Van Maanen, 1979).

This brief review of doubts about rationalistic views of decision-making and positivistic approaches to research should serve to fix one view of the perspective adopted in this research. It is essentially subjective in nature. It seeks to explore the complexity of strategic decision-making by understanding the ways in which those involved in it make sense of it. In this sense it is important to understand that the nature of the findings and, in particular, the explanation of decision processes, are essentially hypothetical.

In terms of the Burrell and Morgan (1979) model, there is, however, no difficulty in locating this work within the field of the sociology of regulation. The perspective is that the sorts of belief systems that form a core of the findings do contribute to regulation and conformity, and it will be argued later that, within this, organizations as cultural phenomena can be thought of as devices for regulating potentially divergent perception and action. It follows that the stance taken here is defined as essentially 'interpretative'. However, it is important to comment on the extent to which limitations are therefore accepted here as to the findings of the study. Certainly there is no attempt in this research to enter into debate on the wider sociological aspects of organizational theory that change theorists (in Burrell and Morgan's terminology) would quite properly be concerned with. The data presented and some of the findings might lend themselves to such interpretation, but this is not the focus adopted here. Nor is it the aim to build overly prescriptive models of organizational change which the positivist might claim were possible given his or her approach to a study with this theme. It is accepted that this study cannot be over-ambitious in terms of claims of generality. None the less it is asserted that the findings do have a relevance outside the particular confines of the situation studied and allow generalization. The findings illuminate processes of decision-making and can be seen to support and advance a good deal of other research, as well as being compatible with processes observed in other organizational contexts.

An additional concern is the notion, implicit within the classificatory scheme given by Burrell and Morgan (1979), of the polarization of 'objectivity' and 'subjectivity'. The concern here is that it is a fundamentally artificial distinction. It leads to questions about the 'factual' nature of observations which can be misleading. It is recognized that an important problem is the legitimacy of reconstructing events when examining processes of change, on the basis of interviews with managers – one of the bases of data collection employed here. After all, are such discussions not merely their verbal *post hoc* accounts of events, mere personalized rationalizations? There are two points to make here. The first is that such accounts play a part in the analysis used to reconstruct events in the same way as individuals' accounts might be employed in any historical analysis. The utility of such data is, however, valuable from a historical point of view, in so far as it may be cross-checked against the accounts of others and against secondary data (see the discussions on 'triangulation' later). The second point, however, is that relativity must be accepted as inevitable. There is no means of obtaining an objective account of process. What can be established virtually factually may be the date when a new shop opened in a particular town, for example; but that tells us nothing about the process of how the decision was taken. An examination of the minutes of meetings, where they do exist, would yield no more than a cryptic interpretation of a formalized part of the process. Participant observation does not provide objectivity in terms of the contribution of the beliefs of managers, because they may not be made explicit and, as are the events observed, a matter of the subjective interpretation and account by the observer. The point is that when it comes to the study of process, there is no such thing as objectivity. In the context of this research the distinction between subjectivity and objectivity has little practical relevance as far as managerial processes are concerned.

THE FOCUS ON ONE CASE

It has been said that the research is not conceived as a study of one organization so much as a study of how strategy is managed by many managers through a series of events. None the less, the issue as to why the focus of research is on one 'case' rather than a number does warrant explanation. First, it should be made clear that there is no claim here that this one company, or these managers, are somehow representative of all companies or all managers. Nor was it the view that by carrying out the research in a few more organizations, the data would somehow become representative of all organizations. Comparative research was, indeed, carried out in other clothing retailers, both large and small (and some details are given later), but this was done not to 'prove' the total generalizability of the findings so much as to provide a basis upon which the developing theoretical propositions could be challenged and thus clarified. To conceive of one case as being a methodological problem is to slip back into positivistic notions of 'the organization', of eliciting social facts for proof and so on.

This research was not designed to provide 'proof' as much as to illustrate and examine a complex and problematic issue. We saw in the previous chapter how many different ways there are of conceiving of the idea of the process of strategic management. Yet most are essentially theoretical in nature: there are still few studies that have examined such processes in action, that have set out to understand the complexity of strategic management. If complex situations are to be examined and understood, there are two fundamental research alternatives. The method of research either needs to accommodate the complexity or reduce it so that the research task is simplified. There is value in the reduction of complexity for research purposes by concentrating on particular phenomena and adopting methods that, for example, examine identified hypotheses relating to these. The value of such an approach is recognized in that it provides useful insights into the complexity it seeks to reduce. For example the work of those who have studied the relationship between strategy and structure of companies (e.g. Wrigley, 1970; Rumelt, 1974; Channon, 1973; 1978; Grinyer et al, 1980; Donaldson, 1982) have raised valuable questions about companies' strategic development, appropriate structures for strategic response, determinism between strategy, structure and performance and so on. These are all issues related to process; but such research does not – indeed cannot – deal with the process of how strategic decisions are actually made.

The position is taken here that complexity-reduction strategies of research can only be of use if there is a context in which to place them; and that context must be the study of the complexity itself: this view has certain implications for the research approach. As Scott argued over 20 years ago:

> As organisational theory develops, the researcher should be less and less inclined to think in terms of one or more hypotheses guiding his inquiry and begin to work with theoretical models which generate numerous implications each of which becomes a proposition guiding field observations. To the extent that the models developed focus on social processes the most important contribution of field research in the future may be the collection of detailed descriptive information. (1965, p. 269)

Mintzberg has been more directly condemnatory of complexity-reduction research approaches:

> As soon as the researcher insists on forcing the organization into abstract categories – into his terms instead of its own – he is reduced to using perceptual measures which often distort the reality. The researcher intent on generating a direct measure of amount of control or of complexity of environment can only ask people what they believe on seven point scales or the like. He gets answers alright, ready for the computer; what he does not get is any idea what he has measured . . . . The result is sterile description, of organizations as categories of abstract variables instead of flesh and blood processes. (1979, p. 586)

If this is a somewhat over-dismissive attitude to positivistic research, it does none the less, point to very real dangers of such an approach that were taken into account in the design of this research. The logic of Mintzberg's views, as expressed elsewhere, is that complex problems must be understood by the generation of more 'descriptive theory':

> . . . to present theory that is 'grounded' – that is rooted in data, that grows inductively out of systematic investigation of how organizations behave. I am fairly convinced that the best route to more effective policy making is better

knowledge in the head of the practitioner of the world he or she actually faces. This means that I take my role as researcher and writer to be the generation and dissemination of the best *descriptive* theory possible . . . . In other words, I believe that the best prescription comes from the application of conceptual knowledge about a phenomenon in a *specific and familiar context*. (1979a, p. vi)

Mintzberg is here arguing both that the complexity of organizational studies needs a greater emphasis on the description of context, and also that such description, used to explore the utility of existing theory and concepts, is useful not only in theoretical terms but to the practical world of managers. By such means are managers, as well as students of managers, able to examine the relevance of managerial theories. This is precisely the position taken in this research. The aim of the study is to provide a rich contextualist (Pettigrew, 1985a) study within which notions of strategic management processes might be examined. This does not mean that what is shown to be the case here will in all respects be the same in all other organizations; rather, the aim is to employ a rich case study, as suggested by Yin (1984) for the purposes of (a) *describing* complex events in some detail, (b) *exploring* and analysing the relevance of different models of strategic management and thus, (c) providing an *explanation* of such complexity. In this way the case study approach is able to provide both a basis for examining the validity of existing propositions and also the development of new propositions that build on them and that, in turn, may be tested out in future studies.

THE RESEARCH STRATEGY

As with Turner (1971), the underlying aim of the research strategy was 'to get under the skin of an organization'. This section gives a summary of what has been involved in trying to achieve this, and why the work was carried out in the way that it was.

Foster Brothers Limited – Selection and Approach

The company on which the research has been based – Foster Brothers Limited – is a clothing retailer with a head office in Solihull in the West Midlands. Its operations and the market in which it operated are described fully in part II of the book. It will become clear from reading that that the company was of particular interest as a research subject for this study for two main reasons. First, because it was of a size and structure that permitted a reasonably grasp of the influences on its strategy. Second, because in the years covered by the study the company experienced an extended period of relatively uninterrupted profitable growth, followed by a sharp downturn in performance and then an energetic attempt at strategy re-formulation: within one company there were, thus, different contexts for examining processes of strategic change. Here it is sufficient to set down one or two points concerning the way in which the research was conducted within the company.

The first point to make is the extent to which the research was dependent on, and benefited greatly from, the remarkable openness of the managers themselves. Constraints on the use, and publication, of the research were not placed upon the researcher by the company, so much as suggested to the company. They took the form of an undertaking that all information of a strategic nature that might be considered useful to competitors or in any way harmful to the company would not be made 'public' without the agreement of the Chief Executive; on the undertaking to individuals that the confidentiality of their statements would be observed; that in any published material every effort would be made to preserve anonymity; and that in the case of the naming of any individuals, permission would be sought for attribution of statements. The practical consequence of this relationship was that part II of the book has been made available to those who took part in the study and permission for its use obtained. However, the company and the managers at no time requested any editorial or censorial powers over the interpretation of the findings.

During the research programme in Fosters, entry was obtained into other retailers within the same retail sector. Similar sorts of research work were undertaken as far as those organizations were concerned with the same sort of cooperation. However, this book does not include as explicit a use of these data as for the Fosters material. Some of the findings of the other work are drawn upon in part III of the book for comparative purposes but the richness of data upon which the book is built is from the study of Fosters.

The basis of the research took the form of extended, rather discursive, interviews with a large number of managers over a number of years, together with the search for secondary data both within and outside the organization. The research was longitudinal in nature – that is, it sought to understand processes of change over a fairly lengthy period of time. In this, the aim was to surface and understand: 'a sequence of dramas [that] allows varying readings to be taken of the development of the organization, of the impact of one drama on successive and even consequent dramas, and of the trend of mechanisms that lead to, accentuate and regulate the impact of each drama' (Pettigrew, 1979, p. 571). The focus in this study was mainly on the period 1975 through to 1985, although there was reference made to the history prior to 1975. The timing of the research work within the company was as follows:

- A first round of interviews carried out with 21 managers took place in September through to November 1980. These interviews took place in the year following the announcement of record profits and after their many years of profitable growth.
- In 1981 a second interview took place with the Chief Executive of the company.
- From April through to November 1983 a second round of interviews with 17 of the managers and an external company consultant took place. These interviews took place during the attempts to overcome the deviation in company fortunes that had taken place.
- In May 1984 a third round of interviews took place with three senior executives of the company.

In the intervening periods contact was also made by letter and telephone with the managers.

Throughout 1985 and 1986 further interviews were carried out with executives individually and in groups within the business and with three who had, by then, left. Since, a draft case study, similar to that in part II, had been prepared by the end of 1985 and sent to managers previously interviewed, a number of these interviews and discussions were concerned with gaining managers' feedback on their views on the accuracy of that case or omissions from it.

The Collection and Preparation of Data

The interviews with managers usually took place in their office and were tape-recorded. The interviews themselves were discursive in nature rather than highly structured and usually commenced by my asking the managers to recount something of their career background. Interviews then hinged on a number of general issues, which might be raised by myself explicitly or, more usually, which managers touched on in conversation and which I followed up or promoted for discussion. These issues were:

- Managers' attitudes to past strategy and performance in terms the benefits to and interests of stakeholders.
- The discussion of how a number (usually two) of important company events within about the last five years (i.e. from 1975) had come about;

managers were encouraged to select these events themselves, but it became clear there were a limited number that almost all managers saw as particularly significant.

- Managers' views on future strategy.
- If and why they thought the company was successful. (It must be remembered that in 1980 the company had experienced a decade of virtually uninterrupted growing profits.)

In the second round of interviews in 1983, the introduction to the discussion was achieved simply by asking managers their views about what had taken place since we last talked. This they did with some feeling since the company had experienced a substantial downturn in performance and was in the midst of what they saw as major change.

Again a checklist of issues was used for this second round of interviews. First the managers were shown a chronological listing of main events up to 1980 in Fosters' history as derived from the 1980 interviews with them and documentary sources, and they were asked if they thought anything should be added or deleted. They were then asked what they thought were the most significant events (good or bad) and why they thought they were particularly significant. These events were then taken as the basis for discussion of the process of how they came about and how decisions relating to them were taken. In this way managers not only covered the events that were, according to them, of most importance particularly during the period 1970 to 1980, but also the historical data collected in 1980 were cross-checked.

Managers were then asked to update the story – that is, to explain what had happened in the company from 1980 to 1983 and explain why the events described had taken place. Their accounts covered both external events and internal decisions; and they were encouraged to 're-live' the experience of the events of that time they considered to be most important. They were also asked what Fosters should do from 1983 onwards.

Throughout the interview, but particularly towards the end, the opportunity was taken to encourage the managers to explain what they saw as 'lessons' from the events of the past. In fact, managers often did this without any prompting, but if prompting was necessary, the sort of question asked was that of why Fosters had done so well in the 1970s and, relatively, so poorly more recently.

A year after the second round of interviews, and following further analysis of the data, the further three interviews with Fosters personnel were conducted to check certain facts that were confusing about the company's chronology and trace through certain decisions that had been pending or unclear in 1983. Thereafter interviews with individuals or groups took place periodically to clarify events and issues raised by a draft of the case study in Part II and to continue to update events.

The tape recording of interviews as a means of data collection deserves some comment. The fear was that it might be a disincentive to open discussion. Certainly there was no evidence that it limited the quantity of data collected. On several occasions managers who had explained that they 'only had a spare half-hour' were still talking an hour and a half later having postponed a meeting. On one occasion, aware that a director had missed an appointment as a result of our discussion, I felt I should close the interview. When I suggested this he replied 'Haven't you got any more tapes? Put another tape on'.

Also the device of encouraging managers to begin by discussing their own career seemed to help in creating a relaxed atmosphere. There were some signs that more junior managers were reluctant to 'open-up' to the full about their relationships with senior executives but this was, probably, not so much affected by the tape recording as by the potentially sensitive issues they were discussing with an outsider. It was also noticeable that, as the relationship built up with the company over the years, managers became more and more open about the issues they were discussing.

The benefits of the tape recording of discussions were considerable. Even if some restriction on freedom of discussion did occur – and there was little evidence of this – the richness and complexity of the material that resulted was such that it could not possibly have been handled in any other way. Quite simply my initial recollections, notes or impressions of a discussion were so inferior to, or out of line with, its actuality, that I seriously doubt the possibility of making use of in-depth discussions of this sort without the facility of taping them.

The interview programme was supplemented by an extensive secondary data search. Secondary data had the particular role of providing a means of cross-checking chronological events and thus contributing to the understanding of the nature of the firm. The secondary data used were helpful in the following ways, for example:

(1) Over 250 articles from the financial press and newspapers for the period were referred to as were over 30 articles in trade journals. These were useful in building up a history of the industry and of particular companies from a perspective different from those of the managers.
(2) Certain specialist reports were obtained: notable amongst these was published research on the market by market research companies.
(3) As simple a datum as the published organizational chart was useful in understanding the formally stated responsibilities of the directors of

the company and also comparing formal lines of authority with the power relationships described in the interviews.

(4) Annual reports not only provided a basis for checking performance, but the public statements contained therein also provided a means of checking the chronology of events and comparing explanations of events with current versions by managers.

(5) The company newspaper to employees was useful in so far as it reflected the 'corporate' attitude to trading conditions and policy.

(6) Three research students also undertook separate secondary-data-based studies of the industry and the companies in it.

(7) In addition reports from within Fosters itself were made available. These included internal market and attitude research reports that managers referred to in the interviews, briefing documents for meetings and to the design consultant, minutes of meetings relating to some of the key events discussed by the managers and a 'data history' of the company drawn up by the Financial Director. All of these were valuable because, again, they provided a means of relating verbal reports by managers of past events to data current at the time of the events.

However, it has to be said that since this research was less about the factual reconstruction of historical events than about managerial perceptions and interpretations of events, the secondary data, whilst important and interesting, have more a contextual than a substantive role. It was therefore the interviews with managers that formed the core of the data.

Indeed, it was clear that there was no one 'right way of collecting and preparing data. It was recognized that there were dangers inherent in the employment of in-depth interviews and personal documents as a basis of the research. These include the danger of an over-intrusive approach of the researcher to the discussions and, as anthropologists have found, that interviewees 'have a tendency to tell you either what they think you want to know, or what they can most easily explain' (Cohen et al., 1973). These were not risks that could be entirely overcome, but the relaxed relationship built up between interviewer and interviewee and the ability to check with verbatim data did mean that they could be recognized.

The interviews were transcribed verbatim as 'personal documents' (Bogdan and Taylor, 1975). The employment of the personal document, or what Denzin (1978) calls the 'life history method', provided a number of benefits, as argued by Denzin. First: 'A central assumption of the life history is that human conduct is to be studied and understood from the perspective of the persons involved. . . . Clearly this is a case for taking the role of the "acting other" and actively sharing in the subject's experiences and perspectives' (1978, p. 216). It is an approach that allows the researcher to plumb the views, beliefs and interpretations of events and relationships of individuals as explained by those subjects in their own way. The danger of other methods, such as surveys, is that they require the subjects to express themselves in the way the researcher requires, which may be convenient for the researcher but inevitably constrains and bounds the expression of the subjects. So the method does permit a relatively greater degree of free expression than some other methods.

Denzin also argues that research using this method 'will be concerned with relating the perspective elicited to definitions and meanings that are lodged in social relationships and social groups.' In the context of this study, the aim was not just be to elicit individual views and interpretations of process, but also to build an understanding of the interrelationships and interconnectedness of these views and interpretations. Since the individuals were engaged in social interpretation as a means of managing, it is necessary to understand how management processes work as a social and interpretative process. The use of personal documents allowed this, not least because it was found that managers were very keen to talk about it.

Denzin's third point is that: 'Concern will be directed to recording the unfolding history of one person's, one group's or one organization's experiences. This feature becomes a hallmark of the life history – the capturing of events over time. The sociologist employing the method becomes a historian of social life, be it the life on one person or the life of many persons similarly situated' (1978, p. 216). The method is likely to be useful, therefore, in understanding interpretative processes in their perceived historical context; that is, in trying to get an understanding of history as the managers taking part in the complexity of social relationships we call the management process see its relevance to decision-making and decision implementation.

Denzin's final argument for the 'life history method' reinforces the first. It is that: '. . . because the life history presents a person's experiences as he or she defines them, the objectivity of the person's interpretations provides central data for the final report'. The use of personal documents provides the opportunity to use the subject's own intepretations as data, with perhaps less interpretative interference than in any other method – and this is done as far as possible in part II of the book.

The Analysis of Data

In the context of this study there were three difficulties with analysis. The first was how it might be possible to get a sensible view of the historical development of a business. The second was how to understand the dynamic processes at work within an organization throughout that history. The third was that the data were unstructured, which required that the analysis should be structured enough to accommodate them. The analysis of qualitative data is, as Miles (1979) has it, 'an attractive nuisance' largely because methods of analysis are not as explicitly developed as for quantitative data. The nature of the data, as well as the research aims themselves, do not lend themselves to the formality of hypothesis generation and testing; rather there is the search for patterns from within the data and between data and current understanding yielded by existing research and theory. At the most basic level, the approach to analysis was as described by Dalton: it was 'to frame questions about specific events in the disorder visible behind the official calm and to fill out partial answers I thought I had. This was a kind of implicit hypothesising . . . (Dalton, 1964, p. 63). The result is quite different from more positivistic analytical research structures. As Hammersley and Atkinson point out in their discussion of ethnographic principles:

> Research has a characteristic 'funnel' structure, being progressively focussed over its course. . . . First over time the research problem is developed or transformed, and eventually its scope is clarified and delimited and its internal structure explored. In this sense, it is frequently only over the course of the research that one discovers what the research is really 'about'. . . . Progressive focussing many also involve a gradual shift from a concern with describing social events and processes to developing and testing explanations. (1983, p. 175)

Notwithstanding the difficulties of handling such data and the relative lack of pre-ordained research structure, there were some quite formalized systems of analysis that were employed.

One fundamental feature of the analysis was the deliberate and extensive use of triangulation (Denzin, 1978; Jick, 1979). Triangulation is the employment of different methods of analysis to observe the same data base. In this case the main bases of triangulation were as listed below.

(1) Data triangulation, which is the use of different data sources to examine the same phenomena – in this case by collecting data from different sources and at different times and from different people.
(2) Theory triangulation – that is, the examination of the data from the point of view of multiple perspectives. Here the data were examined in terms of the different schools of thought that were reviewed in the previous chapter.

From the kind of data collected, it was therefore possible to cross-check personal documents against each other and against secondary data in a large number of ways.

Specifically:

- by examining individuals' views of events as at 1980;
- similarly, by examining individuals' views of events as at 1983;
- by comparing the extent to which an individuals' views were similar or different between 1980 and 1983;
- by examining similarities and differences in interpretations of history between individuals as at 1980;
- similarly by examining similarities and differences between individuals as at 1983;
- by examining any differences and similarities at a collective level between 1980 and 1983;
- as far as chronological history is concerned by comparing the sequence of events discovered through secondary data searches with the sequence derived by other researchers (e.g. research students);
- finally by examining the extent to which either individual or group interpretations of history were similar to or differenced from chronological accounts of historical events.

These data and this system of cross-referencing and cross-checking provided the basis for the reconstruction of the strategic developments of the companies as 'history'. As significant, however, is the fact that the data provided a basis for the analysis of the perceptions and understanding by managers of the situations, decisions and events within this history, and their reasons for them. Moreover it was possible to examine and attempt to explain to what extent and why managers' accounts differed. In this way, events and perceptions of events were usefully illuminated through the very differences between the accounts. As Hammersley and Atkinson say of triangulation: '[it] is very time consuming but, besides providing a validity check, it also gives added depth to the description of the social meanings involved in a setting' (1983, p. 198).

The second activity of analysis was what Denzin (1978) calls 'abduction', that is to 'ask how it is that the persons in question go about producing orderly patterns of interaction and meaning'. What occurs is a matching of the reasoning of the managers with the understanding of the researcher as guided by the concepts and theory with which he or she is familiar. The result is a greater understanding of what the managers think and do, and also the identification of gaps in understanding that the theory does not account for. In this way the theory helps make sense of the data, but the data also inform and provide a critique of the theory.

As the analysis progressed there was an increasing level of analytic induction as 'the investigator is forced to systematically define critical concepts and inspect multiple instances of the behaviour in question' (Denzin, 1978). There is thus the systematic building of propositions which, as Lindesmith (1947) explains, are continually tested (a) by the extent to which they explain the data and (b) by the extent to which negative cases cannot be found to invalidate the proposition. In the event of negative evidence, then the proposition has to be scrapped or, more likely, re-formulated. Furthermore, the search for a fit between propositions and the 'reality' of the data continues and is increasingly generalized until theory is developed that accounts for the phenomena being studied in a universalistic rather than purely piecemeal fashion. The approach used in both these steps was that of grounded theory (Glaser and Strauss, 1968; Schatzman and Strauss, 1973; Turner, 1981) which provided a structured approach to the analysis of the qualitative data.

As Homans states, 'theory is nothing if it is not explanation' (1964, p. 952); and in this context the task was to generate propositions to explain the data, in which the building blocks of theory are re-ordered and tentatively built into explanations only to be knocked down by counter-evidence or by their own explanatory insufficiency, and rebuilt again, until an order emerges that does account for the phenomena being observed. Thus, throughout the whole process, the analyst returns to the data to provide supporting or challenging evidence. Moreover there is also the challenge of existing research and theory, which must be taken into consideration; it is the recognition that 'in large part, knowledge and theory can be profitably conceived as the outcome of a dialectical interplay between relatively autonomous and prior, theoretical knowledge about the objective features of social life . . . and the relevatory activities of field research' (Laynder, 1982, p. 112).

It was through this interaction of different data – those gleaned from different individuals within a common context, and those from secondary sources – with existing theory and research, that an understanding of management processes was built up. The result is inevitably simplified; it cannot be claimed that the complexity of organizational decision-making on strategic issues can be captured in its entirety. The claim is not that this research approach yields perfect understanding but that it does advance understanding.

Part II

A Context for Examining the Management of Strategic Change

This second part of the book provides the contextual data for the analysis of the management processes, which will be discussed in Part III.

Chapter 4 is a brief outline of the main changes that took place in the market for men's clothing from 1970 onwards. It shows the degree of change in the market in terms of styles of clothing worn, the increase in imported goods and the types of retailers accounting for clothing sales. It provides, then, an understanding of the sort of changes that the managers of Fosters had to deal with during the years studied.

Chapter 5 is an extensive case study of the management of strategic change in Fosters and, as such, is a representation of the transcribed interviews that are the main body of data on which the analysis, findings and theory generation are based. The case study takes the form of a more or less chronological account of the development of Fosters as described and explained as far as possible by the managers themselves, particularly for the period 1975–85. It should be borne in mind that these verbatim extracts of the transcripts are minimally edited and therefore represent conversational and not written language: allowance should therefore be made for relatively unstructured expression of ideas and argument in some of those extracts. However, with well over 70 hours of taped interviews, it has been impossible to provide total transcripts of all interviews and therefore some ordering of the data has been necessary; it is hoped that this has been done in such a way that it fairly provides an understanding of events based on what the managers themselves had to say. The aim has been to avoid theoretical interpretation of the data in part II of the book: in as much as this occurs, it is left to the managers themselves as far as possible. The author's comments are limited mainly to descriptive linkages of the accounts of the managers, an indication of the extent to which the verbatim extracts represent what other managers had to say, and an explanation of occurrences or views that were difficult to make clear by the use of verbatim material.

Apart from providing a context for the more theoretical discussion in part III, this part of the book, and chapter 5 in particular, is important because it provides the most direct evidence of what the managers themselves experienced and learned from the events in and around Fosters. To the greatest extent possible, it represents their account of events.

4
The Menswear Retail Market: 1970–1985

'All is well and the outlook is good' concluded Geoffrey High, the Chairman of Foster Brothers at the end of the company's 1971 annual report. It was a sentiment that, to a great extent, was reflected in most of the major menswear retailers of the time. Hepworths had been able to report record profits for two consecutive years; United Drapery Stores (UDS) were continuing their expansion plans and trading from over 600 menswear outlets fed by 13 factories, and Fosters themselves had just acquired Bradleys, a Northern men's outfitter with 160 branches to take their total number of menswear shops to nearly 450. Even for Burtons, who had spent several years trying to overcome management succession problems, prospects seemed exciting: in 1969 they had appointed Ladislas Rice as their first Chairman from outside the family and were embarking on a programme of reorganization and expansion for the decade ahead. In fact the next 12 years was to see the takeover of UDS, the near collapse of Burtons and its eventual total strategic re-positioning, severe profit downturns for all the companies in the industry, a revolution in retailing methods and product mix and a determined attempt by the major companies to diversify away from their menswear base, as menswear retailing's share of consumer spending slumped in the late 1970s.

The structure of the menswear retailing industry in 1970 comprised three main sectors. There were the multiple tailors who concentrated on the sale of suits and other outerwear – jackets and overcoats for example. Traditionally the service they offered was a tailoring service – that is, the making of garments to the individual measurement of the customer. The retailer measured the customer and assisted in the choice of material and the fitting of the garment; and the companies' factories cut and assembled the product. This was the business that Hepworths, Burtons and the menswear chains of UDS (John Collier, Alexandre's and Claude Alexander) were in; it was also a sector that included such companies as Weaver and Wearer, Hector Powe and Willerby's, part of Great Universal Stores, Moss Brothers, Austin Reed and many smaller independent companies. The sector was, however, dominated by the large, vertically integrated multiples such as Burtons. In the 1930s these companies had expanded their manufacturing capacity when the retail demand for suits had outstripped production capacity. Since the end of the Second World War, during which most had concentrated on the production of uniforms, they had found that capacity exceeded demand and had opened or acquired more and more retail outlets to provide the throughput needed for their factories. Indeed, for most of them, manufacturing was the central focus of the business; their shops provided a retail distribution point for that manufacturing capacity. It was an emphasis that was to impede the response of the multiple tailors to the market changes that were to occur.

The second sector comprised the outfitters. These were companies such as Foster Brothers, Harry Fenton and Ray Alan, smaller than the multiple tailors, and selling shirts, ties and knitwear as well as jackets and trousers, usually read to wear. Some of these companies had their own manufacturing capacity but to a much more limited extent than the tailors. It was in this sector that the great majority of the 14000 independent menswear retailers were to be found. Many of these retailers, without the impediment of manufacturing, were to make the most rapid adjustments throughout the 1970s.

The third sector comprised companies who were not menswear specialists at all; these were the departmental stores and variety chains which sold menswear products as part of their overall range. In 1970 the menswear merchandise focus for these companies was mainly the sort of products sold by the outfitters and, in particular, they had a high proportion of sales of underwear, ties and the socks. However they were to take an increasingly large percentage of menswear sales over the next 15 years; and Marks and Spencers, in particular, was to become a major force in the retailing of men's outerwear.

There is no precise record of the number of menswear retailers in the UK. The Business Monitor/Retail Inquiry of 1984 estimated that there were 9930 specialist men's and boys' outfitters in 1982, compared with 10,451 in 1980, 14,339 in 1971 and over 15,000 in 1967, so overall numbers declined over the period. However, as the multiples divested themselves of smaller units from the mid-1970s onwards, these shops were acquired by small independent chains, or individuals, giving rise to a growth in the number of independents as a proportion of all menswear shops. By 1980, although the total number of menswear shops was less, 75 per cent were independent compared with 63 per cent in 1971.

PATTERNS OF RETAIL EXPENDITURE ON MEN'S CLOTHING

Table 4.1 shows consumer spending for the years 1972–84 in the menswear and womenswear market sectors. Overall the picture is one of a relatively depressed market: sales of men's and boys' clothing rose less than women's and girls' clothing, less than total clothing and a good deal less than overall consumer expenditure. Indeed, if expenditure on mens clothing is compared with other items of consumer expenditure, it becomes clear that it showed less growth than almost all items of consumer spending in the 1970s: only expenditure on tobacco grew less in the period. If the expenditure pattern on clothing is studied more closely it becomes clear that the differences in growth between the different sectors did not in fact become evident until the mid-1970s. Until 1977 expenditure on men's and boys' clothing was roughly in line with the total clothing market. It was in the period 1979–81, in particular, that the growth rate of clothing in general, and menswear and boyswear in particular, dropped. From 1982 onwards there were signs of recovery and menswear sales began, again, to grow at a rate comparable with that for womenswear. Figure 4.1 shows this graphically.

TABLE 4.1   *Menswear and womenswear sales, 1972–1984*

	1972	1973	1974	1975	1976	1977	1978	1979	1980	1981	1982	1983	1984
Sales (£m) Menswear	977	1150	1364	1569	1723	1916	2231	2589	2702	2749	2932	3270	3579
Index	100	118	140	161	176	196	228	264	277	281	300	335	366
Sales (£m) Womenswear	1834	2069	2409	2769	3111	3604	4257	4966	5401	5569	5922	6512	7040
Index	100	113	131	151	170	197	232	271	294	304	323	355	384
Sales (£m) Total clothing	2811	3219	3773	4338	4834	5520	6488	7555	8103	8318	8854	9782	10619
Index	100	115	134	154	172	196	231	269	288	296	315	348	378
Consumer expenditure index	100	112	132	162	188	215	248	294	341	379	415	453	484

Source: United Kingdom National Accounts, 1985 Central Statistical Office

An examination of the Chairman's statements in the annual reports of the major menswear companies yields some explanations for variations in expenditure patterns. Specific influences on clothing expenditure such as the effects of weather are mentioned: for example, it was claimed that the

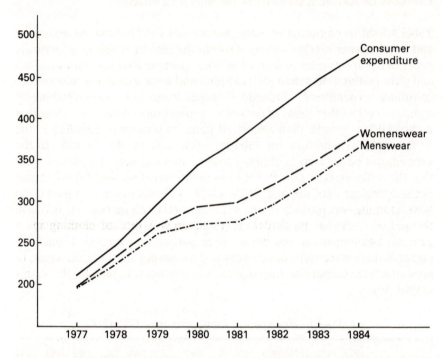

FIGURE 4.1   Index of clothing sales and consumer expenditure 1977–1984 (index 100 = 1972)

long hot summer of 1975 and 1976 depressed sales as did the mild winter of 1975. Increases in VAT (e.g. in 1979) are said to have depressed sales of suits and the decline in the tourist trade in 1980 to have reduced sales of menswear particularly in London. However, it is the annual reports for the years 1979 to 1981 especially that assert that the major reason for the decline in sales was that, given the growing recession and reduced buying power, particularly amongst the unemployed or low-wage earners, menswear purchases were delayed or shelved. It is a claim borne out in consumer research undertaken for one of the major retailers at the time: the research report found that clothes were a low priority for most men; many fathers, in particular, bought clothes as a last resort, especially if the family was short of money. Also the economic situation was forcing many men to make their clothes last longer than was the case earlier in the decade.

If the evidence of the Chairmen's statements is to be accepted, then this relatively low priority given to men's clothing expenditure is also borne out in the context of alternative purchasing decisions throughout the 1970s. For example, in 1971 Everard Chadwick, the Chairman of Hepworths, reported that sales 'moderated . . . immediately following Mr Barber's [the Chancellor of the Exchequer] stimulation of consumer durable sales and purchase tax charges'. And again in 1975 he reported:

> Wages and salaries rose faster than prices, and fears of price increases persuaded customers to buy without delay. In anticipation of large increases in VAT this rush became concentrated on consumer durables prior to the budget, and the month's delay between announcement and imposition of the increase fed the flames. Spending was thus diverted from men's clothes, and when the bonanza ended in durables, the public was in no financial condition to return to its former buying habits.

His view was that, given competition for the family expenditure, menswear will take second place. This analysis of the problem was also suggested by the financial press. In 1972 the Financial Times reported that Department of Trade and Industry figures for menswear multiples: 'show a sub-inflation 6% sales value increase on the second half of 1971, and the way growth tailed away sharply in August tends to confirm the theory that diversion of spending on durables after the abolition of credit controls in July was one explanation' (13 May 1972). The depressed nature of the market for menswear in the period is further illustrated in table 4.2. Not only did expenditure on menswear fall below that of other clothing, but the growth in value of expenditure disguised a drop in volume purchases. Table 4.2 compares total expenditure on men's outerwear with the price index for men's outerwear. Between 1974 and 1981 average prices rose by 133 per cent but expenditure by only 116 per cent. Growth in expenditure was therefore disguising a much flatter pattern of volume sales. Moreover, if

TABLE 4.2 *Price indices and retail performance for men's outerwear*

Year	Price index	Expenditure ($m)	Index
1974	100	810	100
1976	146	1000	123
1979	208	1600	197.5
1981	233	1750	216
1983	236	n/a	n/a

Sources: Retail Business/EIU: Reports on Clothing and Footwear Shops nos 227 (January 1977), 275 (January 1981), 299 (January 1983) and 311 (January 1984) and Mintel: 'Consumer Spending': 1982

we examine the relative performance of the specialist menswear and boyswear retailers we see that, whilst expenditure on men's clothing as a whole was depressed, the sales of men's clothing through specialist retailers was even lower. Table 4.3 provides a detailed examination of trends by outlet type from 1976 to 1983, at the time of greatest depression in menswear clothing sales. Although there are some signs that this decline in menswear sales through specialist shops was beginning to bottom out by 1984, the overall picture is that sales of menswear in specialist retailers fell well below total menswear sales and show virtually no growth at all in 1977–8 and 1980–1. Sales of menswear were therefore taking place increasingly in outlets other than the specialist menswear retailers: by 1984 menswear sales by distribution channel were as shown in table 4.4. It should, however, be borne in mind that Marks and Spencers, alone, accounted for around half of all menswear sales in variety stores. This shift in spending pattern corresponds to a move by consumers towards a greater proportion of expenditure on casual and leisure wear. The overall picture is quite dramatic, with sales expenditure in menswear and boyswear shops rising just 60 per cent from 1976 to 1983 compared with an estimated 90 per cent for all expenditure on men's and boys' clothing.

Table 4.3 also shows that, in the womenswear sector, the specialist womenswear retailers did not perform to the level of their sector but the lag is much less marked than for menswear. It is perhaps not surprising that in increasingly difficult times many of the menswear retailers turned, with varying degrees of success, to womenswear retailing.

TABLE 4.3   *Comparative performance of specialist clothing shops*

Year	Total clothing	Men's/boys' clothes	Men's/boys' clothing shops	Women's/girls' clothes	Womenswear shops
1976	100	100	100	100	100
1977	114	111	111	115	110
1978	134	129	112	137	135
1979	156	150	129	160	155
1980	166	157	134	174	168
1981	172	160	136	179	177
1982	183	170	141	190	185
1983	202	190	160	209	206

Source: C.S.O. and Retail Business EIEU Reports on Clothing and Footwear Shops Np. 311 (January 1984)

TABLE 4.4 *Menswear market shares by distribution channel*

	1984 market share (%)
Variety Stores	25
Independent menswear specialist	21
Multiple menswear specialist	19
Mail order	10
Department stores	6
Other	19
	100

Source: Manchester Business School, Centre for Business Research, 1985

SALES OF MEN'S CLOTHING BY PRODUCT TYPE

The 1960s witnessed something of a men's fashion revolution during which the younger man in particular expressed his changing social attitudes in wearing more casual clothes. It was a change that, throughout the 1970s spread throughout age groups and socio-economic groups.

The change in the mix of sales from the 1960s to the 1980s is particularly marked in terms of certain products. In value terms the market was dominated by suits in the 1960s which, in the main, were made to measure. By 1982 there had been a dramatic decline in suit sales and, significantly, a marked switch from made-to-measure suits to ready-to-wear suits. The period also saw a substantial rise in sales of jeans, both denim and cord casual trousers, of the share of the market taken by jackets, and of the casual knitwear market, particularly tee-shirts and sweatshirts. Table 4.5 shows the volume of the market by product type in this period of major change from 1975 to 1984.

TABLE 4.5 *Menswear product sales (million units)*

	1975	1980	1982	1984
Shirts	69.6	84.6	80.9	92.7
Trousers/jeans	47.3	66.3	60.0	72.0
Jackets/blazers	8.1[a]	6.4	4.7	4.6
Suits	7.4	4.6	3.7	4.4
Knitwear	n/a	47.0[b]	65.0	n/a

[a] Includes waistcoats.
[b] 1979.
Sources: Market Research GB 1975, 1985 and Retail Business/EIU Reports 1980 and 1983

Prior to 1979 there were no separate records of sales of trousers and jeans. It is clear, however, that the growth in sales of trousers in the mid-1970s came mainly from the increased demand for jeans. From combined sales of around 50 million pairs in 1975, by the late 1970s jeans sales alone were approaching 30 million. This trend did not continue into the early 1980s as sales of jeans plateaued and sales of trousers marginally declined in the recession which affected menswear sales so badly. However, there were signs in 1983 and 1984 that sales of trousers were rising again both in volume terms and, through trading up, in value terms too (see table 4.5).

As with fashion wear generally, so with trousers – the younger age groups were the most important customer type as these changes took place. Almost half of all purchases were made by the under-35 age group, the 15–25 group being the largest and accounting for nearly 30 per cent. This younger age group spent up to 25 per cent more per item and their average number purchased, at 2.5 articles, was greater than the overall average of 2 per annum. Jeans remained the province of the younger man with the under-25 age group accounting for more than 50 per cent of the jeans sold and purchasing about three pairs of jeans a year compared to two or less by members of other age groups. Price rises in jeans between 1974 and 1979 are significant. The average retail price for jeans in 1974 was £4.00 but by 1979 it had increased by three times to £12.00, whilst during the same period retail prices for men's outerwear went up by only 82 per cent.

Volume sales of suits remained relatively stable at around four million in the early 1980s (see table 4.5). However, this represented a decline of over 50 per cent from the early 1970s. The main cause of the volume fall-off was the increased popularity of more casual wear. The demand for suits had been growing by about 2.5 per cent per annum up to 1974, in which year volume demand grew by 1.5 per cent. Up to 1974 the main change in the market for suits was the switch from made-to-measure suits to ready-to-wear suits. With a volume share of 75 per cent up to the mid-1960s, made-to-measure suits dominated the suit market; indeed by 1968 they still had a two-thirds share of it. By 1974 made-to-measure suits had declined to a 40 per cent share of the volume of the suit market, by 1979 20 per cent and by 1982 just 10 per cent. Because of the price premium, however, this 10 per cent volume share in 1982 represented a 25 per cent share in value.

There are several reasons for this change that took place from made-to-measure to ready-to-wear suits. New technology in cutting, initially from Europe and particularly Italy, meant that ready-to-wear suits were more likely to give a better fit, and improved flow line production processes led to reduced costs. Both provided the customers with a more acceptable product. Whilst in the UK most of the men's tailors were slow to invest in the improved techniques, European manufacturers, who had little commitment to made-to-measure manufacturing, more quickly converted to the new processes and began importing into the UK. The availability of the new products helped promote the growth of the menswear boutiques of the mid- and late 1960s, retailers that were not vertically integrated into manufacturing and thus and no reason not to promote the new merchandise. In some respects this single change in menswear fashion had repercussions that were felt throughout the whole of the 1970s. It spurred the growth in more fashionable menswear merchandise, since the boutiques offered wider and more colourful ranges of menswear. It forced the menswear multiples to think of themselves as retailers and required them to meet the needs of a more fashion-conscious customer, rather than continue their traditional manufacturing orientation.

The customer purchasing pattern for suits shows that the most important group is the 25–44-year-old age group which account for 40 per cent of all purchases, and there is a bias towards purchasing by a higher socio-economic group, with AB socio-economic groups making 20 per cent of all purchases. The 45–55 age group accounts for nearly 30 per cent of purchases of made-to-measure suits.

There was some evidence of a growth in volume in the 1970s of jackets and blazers, perhaps beneficiaries of the trend towards casual wear. Volume sales since 1979 have however steadied (see table 4.5). Casual jackets are more popular among the under-25 age group who account for up to 50 per cent of all purchases. The appeal of tailored jackets by comparison is more evenly spread. The anorak sub-market, which expanded very rapidly between 1975 and 1977, shrunk to under 5 million garments in 1979 from a peak of 5.5 million garments in 1977 and held its volume up to 1982.

The shirt market represents the single largest volume sector of the menswear market: by 1984 it was estimated to be about 93 million garments and had shown significant volume fluctuations over the years. There has been a gradual trading up in this sector of the market, particularly in the 1980s. Between 25–30 per cent of the shirt market is accounted for by 'leisure casual' shirts. (This excludes 'sweater shirts' and 'tee-shirts' which are included in knitwear as they are made of knitted fabric.) The average annual purchase of shirts per man is around 4.25 with purchasing frequency declining with age. The under-24 age group buys between five and six shirts a year compared with one and two among the elderly. Similarly, higher socio-economic groups are estimated to buy twice as many as lower socio-economic groups.

The volume of the men's knitwear market was estimated as 497 million in 1982 with a volume of 65 million garments. This represented an increase over 1979 of 38 per cent in volume. In 1979, 60 per cent comprised conventional jumpers and sweaters, 20 per cent cardigans and the remainder (20 per cent), knitted casual shirts (i.e. tee-shirts and sweater shirts). Knitwear weathered the post-1975 recession better than most other sectors and was quite buoyant in 1977 and 1978. In 1979, though, in volume terms it was static. The major growth since 1979 was in casual knitwear, particularly tee-shirts and sweatshirts, which accounted for 38 per cent of volume by 1982. Sales of sweatshirts, in fact, fluctuated throughout the 1970s. Prior to their growth post-1979, in the period 1976–7 they went rather out of favour, with sales down by more than 50 per cent to under four million in 1979 from a peak eight million garments in 1976. On average, about 2.25 knitwear articles are purchased every year but the purchasing frequency varies significantly among the different types of knitted garments and for the various age groups. For example, the 15–24 age group, the most important group overall, purchases between 2 and 2.5 jumpers each year, 40 per cent more than the next group, whereas in the cardigan sector this age group is on a par with most others and substantially lower for sweatshirts. By contrast, the 'tee-shirt', which is very much young-menswear, is heavily dominated by the under-24 age group.

The Growth of Imported Goods

The importing of ready-made clothing into the UK began to play an increasingly important role in the menswear sector of the United Kingdom clothing industry from the late 1960s onwards. Manufacturers were continually threatened by increased competition from imported textiles from countries with low-fuel-cost policies and from the Far-Eastern countries with low labour costs, in comparison with increasing wage rates at home. This threat of imported goods multiplied with the increase in popularity of casual clothes, so many of which were manufactured from cotton. Because of low labour costs abroad, the traditionally strong cotton areas in this country, particularly Lancashire and Yorkshire found they could no longer compete with the increasingly cheap goods arriving from Hong Kong, Singapore, Korea, Spain and Portugal. Although of a recognizably lower quality, the shift to casual clothing meant that quality was less significant a purchasing consideration. The extent of impact of importing is illustrated in table 4.6, which shows the volume of imports by menswear products. The high import penetration for trousers (over 50 per cent) and suits (48 per cent) had been established prior to 1979. The main growth in importing later was in knitwear and in particular in casual shirts and ties and sweatshirts. By 1982, 60 per cent of the UK sales of knitted shirts and pullovers were from overseas sources.

TABLE 4.6   *Share of menswear product sales by volume of imported goods 1979–1982*
(shares of the total product sector are given in brackets for 1979 and 1982)

	millions of units sold		
Product	1979	1982	1984
Trousers/jeans	37.9 (54)	34.9 (52)	40.4
Suits	2.6 (43)	2.4 (48)	2.9
Jackets/blazers	4.8 (44)	2.8 (25)	3.2
Shirts – woven	49.0 (58)	48.1 (60)	57.1
– knitted	14.6 ⎫ (31)	13.2 ⎫ (60)	(n/a)
Pullovers/jumpers	— ⎭	26.1 ⎭	

Source: Business Monitor/Overseas Trade Statistics

These levels of import created major problems for UK manufacturers of menswear. In all categories apart from jumpers/pullovers, tee-shirts and sweatshirts, and jeans, UK manufacturers' output dropped as capacity was reduced in the face of overseas competition, though there has been some recovery from 1982 onwards in shirts and trousers. A major problem faced by manufacturers was their capability to create any brand loyalty or much brand awareness. Apart from the branding of jeans, customers appeared to identify increasingly with the retailer rather than the merchandise, a development that the retailers were happy to develop and build upon increasingly in the late 1970s and 1980s.

RETAIL DEVELOPMENTS

A number of significant shifts in purchase patterns of products by source of purchase took place from 1970 onwards. It has to be remembered that prior to 1974 the multiple tailors were, in the main, specialists in made-to-measure garments. However, the 42 per cent share of the suit market they held in 1974 still represented a decline in share from the 1960s, since within the category of 'independent men's shops' were the boutiques, which had built up their sales of ready-to-wear suits. This decline in the share of the suit market held by the multiple tailors continued and by 1982 they held only 18 per cent of that share, partly because by then they had adopted a deliberate policy of widening their range and moving away from a reliance on suits. However, another major impact in the suit market was the entry into it of Marks and Spencers, followed by other variety chains, in the early 1970s. By 1975 Marks and Spencers alone were reported as selling 300,000 suits a year or 3 per cent of the total market at that time and a share that has increased since then. By 1982 their share of the suit market was equal to that of all the multiple tailors. This demise in the demand for suits and the switch in purchasing patterns from specialist shops to variety chains meant that multiple tailors had to face a major change in merchandise mix. In effect by the early 1980s, the expression 'multiple tailors' was misplaced since the distinction between them and other menswear chains was largely historical. In 1974 this was not so. At that time the menswear independents and outfitters were predominantly concerned with ready-to-wear jackets and trousers, with the boutiques and traditional small independent tailors, rather than the outfitters, accounting for a 30 per cent share of the suit market. By the early 1980s the traditional demarcations in the retail clothing trade, based as they were on merchandise types, were no longer appropriate. In terms of any general classification of merchandise, most specialist menswear shops were selling much the same. What had changed dramatically was the extent to which, by the early 1980s certainly, the more successful multiples such as Burtons had re-orientated their total retail offering to provide differentiated focussed retail chains, such as Top Shop, to cater for the stylistic needs of particular consumer groups. It was a trend that was to develop further in the 1980s, with the advent of what became known as 'life-style' retailing in which companies set out to provide a total package of retail image, merchandise and service to suit precisely targeted consumer groups. Until the mid-1970s the menswear chains which, like Fosters, regarded themselves as 'outfitters', had themselves enjoyed a relatively differentiated merchandise offering in the high street. Tailors had been reliant on suits, and variety chains on shirts, knitwear, underclothes and so on. Moreover as men's fashion tastes changed towards more casual wear in the 1970s, as reflected in the changes in product volumes discussed above, the 'outfitters' benefited initially. It was they who, traditionally, sold such merchandise, and many attempted to 'become more fashionable' to appeal to changing customer tastes. This changed markedly in the late 1970s and increasingly in the 1980s. The 'outfitters' became squeezed between the switch by the traditional tailors, and Burtons in particular, to casual wear and the variety chains' increasing sales of outerwear.

By 1984 the changes that had occurred in the retail market had led to a market share configuration as shown in table 4.7. Marks and Spencers had almost twice as much share of menswear sales as its next rival, the Burton Group, and three (C & A, British Home Stores, and Littlewoods) of the next five highest shares were held by variety chains. Fosters was ranked fourth with a share of 2.8 per cent. Whilst the retail market for menswear in particular and clothing in general was not as concentrated as, for example, grocery retailing, buying power was becoming more and more centralized on the multiples. It was estimated that by 1980 60 per cent of trousers, 55 per cent of suits, 40 per cent of jackets and 30 per cent of jeans were purchased through 30 buying points. However, there still remained a large number (over 7000) of menswear shops with less than 10 branches that accounted for 35 per cent of the trouser market, 40 per cent of the jeans market, 35 per cent of the suit market and 29 per cent of the jacket market in 1982; and the shares in all these cases had increased since 1974 apparently at the expense of the multiple tailors. This was largely because the number of independent menswear shops increased from the mid-1970s onwards.

TABLE 4.7   *Retailer market shares of menswear 1984, by value*

			Percentage of total menswear and boyswear sales
Marks and Spencers			14.8
Burton Group	– Burton/Top Man	6.0	
	Collier	1.0	7.4
	Fenton/Studio	0.4	
C & A			4.5
Fosters			2.8
British Home Stores			2.5
J Hepworth	– Next M/Hepworth	1.8	2.2
	Lord John/Detroit	0.4	
Littlewoods			2.2

Source: Manchester Business School, Centre for Business Research estimates

In a decade and a half the structure of the retail market for men's clothes had changed fundamentally. Fosters began the 1970s as the dominant chain of outfitters in a retail market with clearly different retail types defined primarily in terms of different merchandise offerings. However, the fashion changes of the 1970s, the demise of the tailors, the successful re-positioning of companies such as Burtons and the growing power of Marks and Spencers, threw this market into turmoil. Fosters was faced with the erosion of its dominance and the challenge of adjusting its strategy to compete effectively as the market changes took place. Chapter 6, which follows, looks in detail at how the managers attempted this.

5
Foster Brothers: A Case Study of Management and Strategic Change

The data in the main body of the research take the form of historical accounts of the strategic development of Foster Brothers. Much of this is presented through the words of the managers themselves and is concerned with the interaction between them. It is therefore useful to know something about those involved. This brief section gives job titles at the time of the interview programmes, some brief background on those named within the case and, additionally, some descriptions of managers interviewed, but who remain anonymous in the case itself.

BARRY DAVISON: In 1983 Chairman and Joint Managing Director of the Group; and in 1980 Managing Director of Menswear. After leaving school at 16 he became articled to a firm of accountants and worked with a number of retail clients. He qualified as a chartered accountant with that firm. After National Service in 1960 he joined Foster Brothers as Assistant Company Secretary. His initial involvement was with accounting and property and he was also intimately concerned with the development in the 1960s of computerized stock control and distribution. He became Joint Managing Director of Menswear in 1973 and sole Managing Director a year later. In 1976 he was appointed Deputy Chairman and Managing Director of the Group and took over the chair on the retirement of Geoffrey High in 1979. He left the company in 1985.

MIKE ADAMS: In 1983 Joint Managing Director of the Group, Chairman and Managing Director of Adams Childrenswear and a member of the Menswear Board. In 1985, on the departure of Barry Davison, he became Managing Director of Foster Brothers. After public school he worked in textile manufacturing and, during this time, took a Diploma course in Business Management at Nottingham University. After two years in the Army and a short spell back with his previous employer, he joined a manufacturer and wholesaler of childrenswear in 1954 as a trainee manager. In 1960 he then joined the Adams family business which was a retailer of baby linen. Under his direction they grew to five shops by 1973 when Fosters offered to buy the business and give him a service contract. He remained as Chairman and Managing Director of Adams and later joined the Group and Menswear boards too, as well as the boards of all the trading subsidiaries.

BRIAN WOOD: In 1980 Deputy Managing Director and Sales Director of Menswear; by 1983, Managing Director of Menswear. After leaving school at 13 he joined Hepworths as a 'boy' (a junior assistant in a branch), becoming a shop manager at the age of 21. After working with a number of other menswear retailers he joined Fosters as an Assistant Shop Manager. His career with Fosters included area management and general management of Jessops with their seventeen shops and factory for three years. In 1974 he came to head office to help install the centralized distribution system. In 1975 he became Retail Operations Manager, Sales Director in 1976, and also Assistant Managing Director in 1979. In 1983 he was made Menswear Managing Director and appointed to the Group board.

JOHN FALLON: Financial Director of the Group. After school he joined a local firm of accountants in Sheffield with whom he qualified as a chartered accountant. In 1971 he then joined a small subsidiary of Wigfalls, the electrical retailer, as company accountant. On that company's absorption into Wigfalls, he progressed through several jobs on the finance side of the business until he became Financial Director of Wigfalls. In 1979 he left to become Financial Controller of Burtons Retail (i.e. the division responsible for the Burtons menswear shops) reporting to the division's Financial Director. In 1981 he was 'head-hunted' to join Foster Brothers.

NORMAN PHILLIPS: Merchandise Director of Menswear in 1980 who resigned in 1983. He joined Fosters from school at the age of 16 and worked his way up through the buying side. Initially in the 1950s this was when buying performed a 'wholsaling' function for the retailers who had buying discretion. As centralization of buying and stock distribution progressed in the 1960s he headed up various merchandise departments. In 1972 he took over as Assistant Merchandise Director and in 1978 as Merchandise Director. In 1983 he was appointed to the Main Board but resigned later in the year.

RICHARD HAYNES: Marketing Director. In the early 1980s he was the only university graduate in senior management, having read economics and law at Cambridge. After leaving university in 1964 he joined Massey-Ferguson as a marketing trainee and also spent a year as personal assistant to the managing director. After three years he and two colleagues set up their own marketing consultancy. He then spent three years as marketing director of a building products firm before setting up the

Birmingham office of Harrison Cowley, the advertising agency. After six years he became managing director of the Birmingham agency and Group Development Manager. The agency handled the Foster Brothers account. In 1979 he was approached by Barry Davison to join Fosters, which he did in January 1980. In 1980 he was responsible for a small department handling market research, communications and advertising and marketing planning. During 1982 and 1983 he was responsible for coordinating the development of 'new image' branches for the company. He resigned in 1985 and returned to advertising as Chief Executive of the Rex Stewart Group.

MELVYN TAYLOR: Financial Director of Menswear in 1985. He joined Peat, Marwick, Mitchell from school and did five years' articles, qualifying as a chartered accountant. After a further year he joined Foster Brothers in 1970 as an accountant and became Chief Accountant in 1973. He was appointed Financial Director of Menswear in January 1980, with his main role as the provision of management accounts and information. By 1983 he was becoming more involved in the management and administration of the branch network.

TONY GRAY: In 1983 Special Projects Manager for Menswear and, by 1985, Sales Director of Menswear. Related to the owners of a company acquired by Fosters, he worked in retailing and buying in that company until the takeover and in 1970 became a buyer with Fosters. In 1971 he became managing director/general manager of Mr Christopher, a boutique operation within the group. Mr Christopher was absorbed into another subsidiary and he joined that board with responsibility for buying, in 1978 becoming Assistant Managing Director. In 1979 he was appointed Managing Director of Blue Movers, a new venture business, which closed in 1982. He then became Special Projects Manager for Menswear, initially responsible for merchandise coordination for new style branches being developed, but later for the coordination of the whole branch development programme.

Interviews were also carried out with the following who are not named in the case study.

The Group Company Secretary who had been Assistant Group Secretary under Barry Davison and took over from him when he vacated the position as Company Secretary.

The Personnel Director of menswear who had been in menswear retailing since the age of sixteen, mainly in retail management. He was appointed Personnel Manager for menswear in 1978 and Director in 1980.

The Assistant Merchandise Director of menswear who joined the company in 1952 and who had uncles and cousins in the clothing retail business. In 1980, reporting to Norman Phillips, he was a Director of the three factories that the company owned, in which capacity he coordinated buying and manufacturing. By 1983 he was the acting head of the merchandise department and was appointed Merchandise Director in 1985.

The Regional Sales Director of menswear who had been with Hepworths since 1948 and joined Fosters in 1963, progressing through from shop salesman to Area Manager, to Divisional Manager, to General Sales Manager and, in 1980, as Regional Sales Director with two Divisional Managers reporting to him and a responsibility for half of the company's geographical area.

The two Merchandise Managers for menswear responsible for the buying and merchandise of the ranges. Both had joined Fosters in the 1960s and both had clothing retail experience before that data. Both had been appointed Merchandise Managers in 1979 in which position each was responsible for buyers managing the merchandise range of the company.

A Divisional Sales Manager who reported to the Regional Sales Director. He had joined Fosters in the 1960s and progressed through shop management to take over as divisional manager in 1975 in which position he controlled 130 shops. By 1983 the company retail structure had been reorganized, the position of Regional Sales Director disbanded and two Divisional Managers each responsible for half the company's shops appointed. This manager was, by this time, one of those Divisional Managers.

The Sales Promotion and Advertising Manager whose father had been a shop manager with Fosters and who, as a child, had lived above a Fosters shop. He joined the company from school at the age of 16 in 1955 and had progressed through the display management side of the business eventually becoming Display Manager and, in 1980, Sales Promotion Manager.

The Display Manager, reporting to the Sales Promotion Manager who had gained mainly display experience with Hepworths and Fosters before his appointment as Display Manager in 1979.

The Head of the Accounts Department who, after experience with a firm of accountants had joined Fosters in 1954 and taken over as Head of the Accounts Department in 1960. The main responsibility of the job was dealing with payments and processing of branch sales information within a department of 40 personnel.

A Divisional Display Manager who had joined Fosters in 1964 from Hepworths as a window dresser and had progressed through display management to become Divisional Display Manager for the Northern Division, in 1976.

The Stock Distribution Manager who had joined Fosters in 1970 from GEC where he had been a computer operator. His expertise was in the computer control side of stock distribution and he reported through the retail operation side of the business.

The Training Manager who had joined Hepworths at the age of 14, and progressed through shop management until 1957 when he joined Fosters. He became involved with the training of shop staff in the 1960s and was appointed a full-time Training Officer in 1968 and eventually Training Manager for the company in 1972.

BASES FOR PROFITABLE GROWTH

To understand Fosters it is important to understand something of their history, which shows that, certainly up to the early 1970s, and arguably until the early 1980s, they were a very different menswear retailer from what they were in the mid 1980s or indeed from other retailers of those times. If 1970 is taken as a convenient point at which to make this comparison, then there are perhaps five differences that need to be emphasized. First, Fosters was smaller than Burtons, John Collier or Hepworths in terms of turnover; it had a turnover of around £10 million compared with Burtons' £70 million or even that of Hepworths, small compared with Burtons, who had a turnover of £17 million. Second, it was a different sort of menswear retailer – it was an outfitter with minimal commitment to manufacturing. Third, it had built up a property portfolio of some 450 shops which were, in the main, small outlets staffed by two or three, often in smaller towns than those in which the larger tailors were sited or in shopping precincts that did not warrant a Burtons or Hepworths. Fourth its customers profile had always been at the lower end of the market. Traditionally it was the shop older men went to for clothes they wore to work, or to which mothers took their children in order to buy school clothes. Finally, they were much bigger in terms of number of shops and turnover than any other retail outfitting company; they were, indeed, the one national retail outfitter in the 1970s.

William Foster, the founder of the Company, opened his first shop in Pontefract in 1876. He sold a variety of cheap, ready-made clothing for men and boys – workwear, hats, ties, shirts and coats. Eight years later he moved to set up shop in Coventry Road, Birmingham, with Mr W T Webster, who joined him from John Shannon, a Walsall clothes manufacturers. Together they built up Fosters, by the time of the Great War, into a chain of more than 80 shops, with its own clothes factories. From then until 1966, William's widow, his son Harry, and Mr Webster's son successively guided the Company as Chairman or Managing Director.

The emphasis on workwear began at this early stage: the aim was to provide good-value clothing at prices that would attract the working man and his family. Company growth was steady and by 1945 there were 140 shops, situated chiefly in the Midlands area. The company finally went public on the 20th January 1951.

Figure 5.1 shows two advertisements for Foster Brothers that are 50 years apart. They not only illustrate the product range over this period but also show how the emphasis remained primarily on utility clothing for men combined with low prices.

During the 1960s, however, changes had begun to occur that had important consequences for Foster Brothers. First the Company began to alter its product range and image, moving, under the guidance of their Merchandise Director, Tom Jacks, towards a greater emphasis on menswear jackets and trousers in particular. Second, from 1962 onwards the company began to speed up its acquisition of new shops.

Throughout the 1960s and into the 1970s there was an emphasis on growth through the acquisition of new shops: as Barry Davison, the Chairman and Chief Executive from 1979 to 1985, explained:

> Retail companies are very much property companies. In those days we were very much a branch acquisition business, more than a retailer, I think. The business was run by people who looked after the property, rather than people who were traders. We were always very entrepreneurial about our property decisions; we made quick decisions which gave us a big advantage over companies that take a long time to make decisions.

During the 1960s growth also occurred through the acquisition of companies. The first was that of 'Dormie Menswear', a Scottish-based firm involved in the sale and hire of men's clothing. Both areas of the business were expanded after the acquisition, particularly the hire side. The product range was aimed at the top end of the market and was a definite move on the part of Foster Brothers to expand their product/market mix.

The next acquisition of note was Jessops, in 1967, a traditional bespoke tailor business, producing a range of made-to-measure suits, with 16 shops and one factory. This was a move away from the ready-made menswear image Foster Brothers were cultivating. One executive explained: 'It was an attempt to compete with the multiples in a very small way, simply as a means of providing extra turnover. As a venture, it was never more than a sideline.'

This growth in the 1960s meant that the Head Office, then in Central Birmingham, became increasingly cramped. As a result, in 1968, the company moved to Solihull, with a Head Office and a large warehouse.

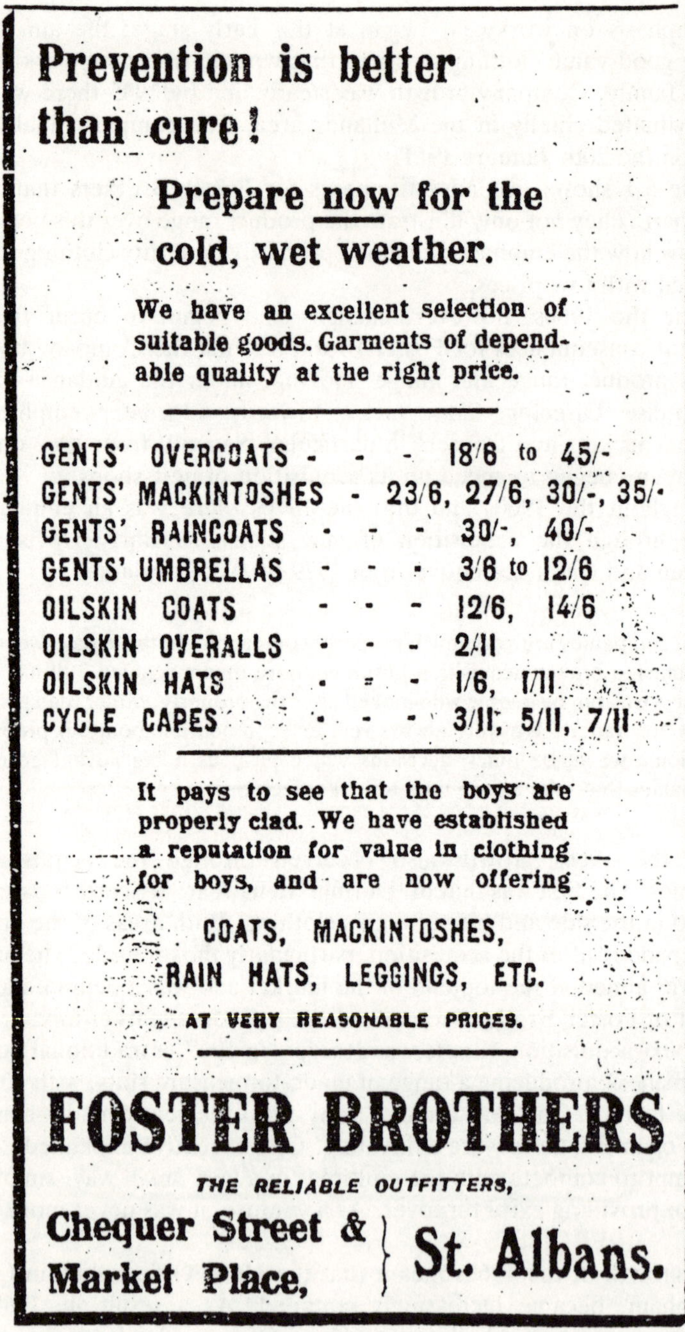

FIGURE 5.1 Fosters advertisements in 1917 and 1967

Reproduced by kind permission of Foster Brothers

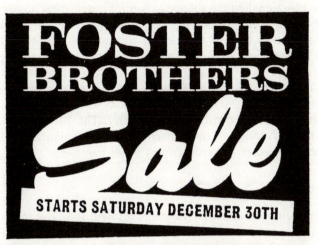

FOSTER BROTHERS
Sale
STARTS SATURDAY DECEMBER 30TH

MEN'S CORD JACKETS	99/6	MEN'S SHIRTS for Casual Wear	19/11
MEN'S GREY TROUSERS	29/6	MEN'S SHIRTS WHITE POPLIN	17/9
MEN'S TROUSERS (Terylene/Worsted)	55/-	MEN'S PYJAMAS	17/9
MEN'S TWEED CAR COATS	from £6·6s	Coopers Y Front Underwear (Slightly Imperfect)	5/-

These are just a few of the sensational lines Foster Brothers are offering in their SALE. Don't miss your chance to get full value for your money—hundreds of bargains in every Branch, and everything is reduced.

BARGAINS IN BOYS' WEAR

SCHOOL GREY SHORTS (Terylene/Sarille)	18/6	PYJAMAS (Brushed Cotton)	15/9
		CHARCOAL GREY TROUSERS (Terylene/Worsted)	35/9

'Back to school' at Sale prices including school uniforms — EVERYTHING reduced

OVERCOATS All stocks must be cleared— sweeping reductions.

CARCOATS All carcoats reduced to clear.

FOSTER BROTHERS

Bargains for all—come early for best selections

This move also signalled the change to central distribution of merchandise, the warehouse providing stock to every branch in England and Wales, by the company's own fleet of vehicles. It was a move that virtually all the managers saw as central to the success of the company throughout the 1970s.

The company entered the 1960s as one of the largest men's outfitters in the country with some 290 shops and a capacity for growth in terms of both financial resources and distribution capability. The 1970s were to see the company take advantage of this capacity and demonstrate a rate of growth in turnover and profits in excess of any other menswear retailer.

The Bradleys Acquisition

The senior managers at Foster Brothers all held the view that the single most significant strategic move made by the company occurred in 1970. That year saw the acquisition of Bradleys, a Chester-based menswear outfitter with 160 shops; the number of branches of the company was virtually doubled at a stroke. The perceived benefits were largely to do with size and distribution of branches. The earlier move to the Solihull headquarters meant that the company already had the central warehousing and distribution facilities to cope with the increased numbers of shops; the buying capacity of the company was also increased; and since there had existed a tacit agreement between the two companies to avoid trading in each other's areas, the acquisition provided almost entirely new geographical locations for Fosters.

The acquisition was not problem-free, however: in 1970 the Chairman, Mr Geoffrey High, had predicted it would take at least two years before Bradleys would be enhancing the Group's performance. In 1971 he reported the closure of 20 of their branches and in 1972 he revised his two-year forecast to three years explaining that many of the smaller, often rural, branches were 'responding more slowly than we have anticipated'. The initial impact of the Bradleys takeover was reported in the press as affecting the 1970/1 company performance by doubling stocks, reducing stockturn to 3.75 a year from 5.75 and requiring a £451,000 write-off of reserves.

1970 and 1971 also saw the acquisition of 53 new Fosters branches, including the first branches in Scotland and the beginnings of in-store concessions with Woolco as a means of expanding turnover. This was accompanied by a cut-back on some smaller, loss-making outlets and a closure of one of the factories at Tamworth, further reducing the already low commitment to manufacturing.

Merchandise Policy

This period also saw the consolidation of a second major decision. Earlier in the 1960s buying of merchandise was the responsibility of shop managers. A policy later seen to have its weaknesses:

> The managers were allowed to buy their own merchandise. Reps came round and we were allowed to buy merchandise. The profit margins were bloody awful. The reps used to say 'if you can't get rid of it, offer it to Fosters and the silly so and sos will take it.'

The desire to improve the efficiency and profitability of the operation led to the move to centralized control and purchase of stock. This, together with the increasing proportion of merchandise bought abroad, increased the influence and importance of the merchandising function. These moves coincided with a change in merchandising director. Barry Davison explained.

> He (Mr Jacks) was a very different personality. He had a very big influence on the type of merchandise that should be sold, basically because my predecessor (Mr High) was very much a property man and was not so interested in the buying side. Although he (Mr High) controlled the company on what the performance of branches was, he really did not want to get down to what we should be doing with our merchandise and image mix.

The new merchandise director was Tom Jacks and it was under his direction that the importing of Far-Eastern merchandise grew. His approach to buying dovetailed in with the move to centralized control; it consisted of buying in large quantities outfitting for the working man. At the time, the policy was seen as competitively necessary, as well as providing special benefits to a group of Fosters' size, particularly after the acquisition of Bradleys.

> Up to 10 or 12 years ago, we were a comparatively small company sourcing all our requirements in the UK. Independent of the factories, tied to the major multiples, the supply sources were fairly small. So manufacturing sources allied to our turnover were more or less compatible. You get the situation where overseas markets develop – principally Hong Kong and South Korea. In order to survive in a highly competitive market we had to tap those sources of supply, otherwise we would have been outpriced and our market would have disappeared to the people who were sourcing overseas. When you move into overseas markets you are dealing with an entirely different approach to clothing manufacture. They are very much bigger

units, geared to supplying world markets. In South Korea the production resources are vast. You have got to be of a certain size before you can even attempt to purchase from them. If you go with your quantities below their minimums they just won't entertain making for you at all. So in order to compete you have got to have buying power.

It was buying power that, by 1971, Fosters had achieved by acquisition and centralized merchandise control. In that year the decision was taken to switch to direct importing rather than acting through an agent as they had done before. It was a decision that further widened the margins but carried with it the requirement to concentrate on high-volume, long-production-run items. It consolidated Tom Jacks' approach to buying which became known in the company as the 'pile it high and sell it cheap' approach. In marketing terms it also consolidated the company's position with regard to competition. Fosters had deliberately aimed their merchandise at the lower end of the market; this became the more important as the buying quantities required volume sales of merchandise.

Despite the fact that the group had its own factories, these produced only 13 per cent of turnover, so a great deal of buying from outside the company had always taken place. In 1968 Foster Brothers bought 80 per cent of its merchandise from within the United Kingdom. By 1973 this figure had gone down to below 45 per cent, as the company began to buy further afield – for example from Portugal, Hong Kong, Taiwan, Rumania and Yugoslavia. By 1975 the company was reported to be the single biggest importer of clothing from Hong Kong.

Faced with rising prices at home and a conviction of Tom Jacks that Fosters must be able to demonstrate low prices to attract their customers, the proportion of imported merchandise grew throughout the 1970s. The effect was felt throughout the 1970s. Fosters were the first of the large menswear companies to import in quantity so they got the benefit of bulk buying, together with the ability to price below competition whilst achieving margins greater than competition. It was a decision that underpinned much of their success in the years to come, and was central to the reasons given by managers for the success of the company in the 1970s.

In political terms the status and influence of the merchandising department and the merchandise director, Tom Jacks, in particular rose as the importance, first of centralized buying control and then of overseas buying, rose.

The emphasis was very much on the buying side of the company dominating the selling side of the company. Tom was a very strong personality. He felt he had to dominate the selling side although he was merchandise director because the volume he was purchasing in the Far East had to be sold and therefore he had to have a strong influence on retail. There was a period of several years when the retail side was very much the poor relation. It was a very successful period in financial terms. They had sales promotions; and if you went downstairs to the display room it would be Tom Jacks who would be saying what went where and why (in the windows). It wouldn't be the retailers saying this is how we're going to do it. Discipline in his buying department was also extremely good. Discipline in terms of attention to detail that is.

The decisions of the late 1960s and early 1970s also had a major impact upon the personnel in the company. The rapid branch growth necessitated the influx of many new people into the company. During the 1960s a large intake of retail personnel from Hepworths took place, through the inducement of higher salaries and the potential for promotion. With the branch acquisition programme there was a particular need to bring in, or train, shop managers to run the branches. The company began to take school-leavers, with the intention of preparing them for branch management by the age of 20. This stands in stark contrast to the period prior to 1965 when managerial positions were rarely open to anyone under the age of 30. At one stage the Group was looking for a new manager every nine days.

The Bradleys acquisition did, however, depress company performance in 1971 (see table 5.1). Margins were reduced and return on capital employed fell from 12 to 10 per cent on the increased capital base. The financial press was concerned that there were 'too many factors . . . playing against the company, including continued problems of the integration of Bradleys, economic pressure on young families and growing unemployment in the Midlands in which area the company was still mostly concentrated'. They were comments about threats to the company that may have seemed very real at the time; but Fosters was to face more severe threats in the next few years and demonstrate a capacity to out-perform competition.

GROWTH AND DIVERSIFICATION

From 1972 to 1974 the emphasis for Foster Menswear was on branch development. From the base of 385 Foster Menswear branches in 1971 the company grew to 448 by 1974 mainly through the acquisition of sites in areas of the country in which the company was poorly represented. These

TABLE 5.1   *A summary of the financial performance 1970–1975 (a) and a summary of key financial ratios (b)*

	1969/70	1970/1	1971/2	1972/3	1973/4	1974/5
(a)						
Turnover: retail sales (£m)	11.1	17.3	18.6	21.8	27.8	34.4
Trading profit (£m)	1.3	1.8	2.0	2.9	3.3	3.1
Surplus on sale of properties (£m)	—	—	—	—	—	0.1
Less interest (£m)	0.1	0.3	0.3	0.1	—	—
Profit before taxation (£m)	1.2	1.5	1.7	2.8	2.3	3.3
(b)						
Growth in turnover (%)	n/a	+56	+8	+17	+28	+24
Growth in trading (%)	n/a	+38	+11	+45	+14	−7
Trading profit as percentage of sales	12	10	11	13	12	9
Profit before tax as percentage of capital employed	25	18	22	31	26	23

Source: Foster Brothers Annual Reports

acquisitions were accompanied by the refitting programme, begun in 1971, and by the closure of some of the very small branches. In these years it was this growing chain of shops that profited from the high-margin, low-priced merchandise imported mainly from the Far East.

However, 1972 also saw the first move by the company into areas other than menswear with the purchase of D. P. Adams, a small retailer of children's wear. The agreement was reached largely due to personal contacts between Mike Adams, the owner of the company, and Barry Davison, who as the company secretary at that time saw the growth of the Mothercare chain as an indicator of an opportunity for a similar Foster Group venture. The Chairman, Geoffrey High, described his plans for the company in 1973:

> This privately owned concern previously operated through five shops and specializes in children's wear for both boys and girls covering the age range from birth to the brink of teenage years. We think it is fortunate that we have been able to purchase the Adams business and with it the acumen and enterprise of its Chairman and Managing Director, Mr Michael P. Adams, who has entered into a service contract for several years ahead. We intend to expand the business fairly quickly.

Adams Childrenswear was expanded from the initial five shops to thirty within twelve months.

In 1973, with the acquisition of Adams and the growing number of properties, the decision was taken to re-structure the Group. Geoffrey High described this as follows:

The considerable growth of your company during the past few years makes it virtually essential for the parent company to act in the role of a holding company so that each retail activity within the organization has clearly defined responsibilities which are reported upon, at regular intervals, to the main Board. This is a natural step and the adoption of this new structure will make for greater management and administrative efficiency.

The main trading concerns operating within this structure were, in 1973, Foster Menswear, with 427 shops; Mr Christopher Boutiques, with 7 shops; Dormie Menswear, with 42 shops; and Adams Childrenswear with 30 shops. In addition there were the remaining manufacturing concerns operating outside Jessops and, newly established, a property company Marshall Lake properties – and the distribution service – Foster Brothers (Group Services).

By the beginning of 1973 sales had virtually doubled – to £21.8 million – since 1969/70 and trading profit stood at £2.9 million, giving a return on capital employed of 31 per cent, far in excess of that achieved by any of the major companies in the industry. Cash in the business, in the form of short-term deposits, stood at £1.75 million and had risen to this figure from just £6191 the previous year through the rise in profits, a tightening of controls on stock and rising margins. The decision was taken to use the cash to diversify further.

Stone-Dri was a chain of 118 shops selling cheaper women's and men's clothing to meet the same sort of market profile as Foster Menswear. It was acquired in 1973 with a view to developing an interest in the womenswear market in a market sector in demographic terms that Fosters saw themselves as used to dealing with. Davison recalled that, at that time, the benefits to the company were discussed, not in terms of market opportunities, but in terms of how the existing ways of operating could be applied to Stone-Dri:

> Our philosophy in those days was that we had a very good buying arrangement in the Far East where we could buy very cheaply compared with other people and that will give us better margins. We had very good systems to operate and if we impose those on other businesses we will have a bigger profit return than they are getting. That was the philosophy that we worked on, rather than strategically talking about what merchandise profiles we were in. And giving us a hundred more outlets overnight. The merchandise people were for it because they were going through a period of such confidence, they were saying that we are so much better than these amateurs who are running this business we can give you another three or four per cent margin on what they are doing.

Again the view was taken that it would take at least two years to sort out the merchandise and stock situation. It was not to prove a profitable venture, however, and by 1975 branches were being closed or converted to selling men's or children's clothes.

Managers in 1983 recognized that the attempts to move into womenswear in the 1970s failed largely because it had been assumed that the perceived excellence of Foster Menswear buyers was applicable to womenswear.

> Fosters put their own managers into those companies with the hope that their expertise from clothing would bear fruit on the other side.

A senior retail manager explained why this was not appropriate:

> I know very little about women's fashion but I would guess it's more fickle even than men's fashion; so if they adapted the same methods to Stone-Dri as they did for Menswear, such as buying in bulk in massive quantities, they would get their fingers burnt because women do not buy like that. They do not want the same dress as the lady next door they want fashion that is more individual. So it has to be bought in smaller quantities.

By the end of 1974 the Group was trading through 670 shops with a turnover of £34.4 million. However, in common with most retailers the company found 1974 a difficult year with rising inflation, the disruption in the early part of the year through a reduced working week, and the later imposition of price controls. The company reported half-year trading profits down by £400,000 in the autumn, together with declining margins and a cutback on the expansion plans for the branches. Profit decline for the full year was held to £225,000 but margins had been reduced substantially to 9 per cent from the previous year's 12 per cent and the company, for the first time in the 1970s, declared a surplus on disposals of property. Despite what was for Fosters a poor year, the return on capital employed still stood at 23 per cent on a property revaluation at the beginning of 1974 which had raised the fixed assets by some £5.3 million to £14.4 million. Whilst there had been a drain on the cash resources of the business, short-term borrowings and overdrafts had been substantially reduced and the stock levels reduced despite the sales increase. It was a pattern that was repeated through the history of the business: in times of hardship the company was able to tighten its controls so as to minimize the effects on profitability and cash flow.

Important changes occurred in 1973 and 1974 at the top of the company. For the first three years of the 1970s the company's senior management had been Geoffrey High as Chairman and Joint Managing Director with John Foster, the last of the Foster family, as the other Joint Managing Director.

In 1973, Barry Davison, who was Company Secretary, and an accountant by background, was appointed Joint Managing Director with John Foster; Mr High became Chairman.

A CHANGE IN MERCHANDISE POLICY – THE 'FASHIONPOINT' VENTURE

The evolving merchandise policy of low-cost merchandise imported from the Far East allowing highly competitive prices seemed to benefit the company. Fosters were, in 1975, out-performing competition and doing relatively better in the more difficult trading conditions of 1976 in which year about half the sales were from imported goods.

Up to 1975 Foster menswear had retained its traditional target market, concentrating namely on satisfying the older man's market, the 35–50 age range. However, 1975, saw the beginnings of a shift away from This traditional stance. It was a change that was to involve adjustment in merchandise over a five-year period but its origins may be traced further back.

Political Alliances and Merchandise Policy

When in 1973 Barry Davison was appointed Joint Managing Director with John Foster, nominally it was John Foster who was made responsible for merchandise and selling with Tom Jacks reporting to him. In fact at board level the policy on merchandising was dominated by Tom Jacks:

> Mr High had a lot of time for Tom and, therefore, any merchandise decision he wanted Mr High went along with.

Moreover Barry Davison also had his own views on Merchandise Policy and there were some differences of opinion between Jacks, John Foster and Davison. John Foster argued that the reliance on cheap importing for the bottom end of the market was unwise. He advocated a move further up the market, to provide outfitting merchandise for higher-income groups. Davison, on the other hand, was more concerned that the emergence of the supermarket home and wear departments could be a threat to the market position occupied by Fosters:

> I felt we had set off on a road with Mr High and Tom Jacks which put us on a collision course with the growing dominance of the large supermarket groups whose move into cheap clothing was just starting. I felt at that time that the

low-overhead structure that they had would enable them to devastate our
price structure and that would take a substantial part of our turnover away.

The basis of this concern was, then, that the supermarket threat could
undermine Fosters main strength. Fosters would have to compete, in
supply terms, head-on with the supermarkets who were developing their
clothing sales for the lower end of the market. Given their ability to offset
overheads against a wider merchandise range and higher retail productivity, Davison was concerned that Fosters would not be able to compete.
His personal view was that Fosters needed to differentiate themselves from
the supermarkets by selling a greater proportion of fashion merchandise,
but not moving to a more up-market target group as John Foster
advocated:

> What I was saying was let's buy cheap fashion crap. That is where the
> difference was with Tom Jacks. Tom said we can't sell fashion in our shops.

One executive, at that time working under Tom Jacks, explained his
stance:

> His ideas were very firm. He had the approach that if the price is right and
> you stack it high enough, you will sell it in the working lads' market. You
> would have to say he closed his eyes to areas beyond that.

There ensued a period of policy adjustment: Davison explained:

> I had a period with Jacks when we attempted to reduce the cost of operation
> of the business. My first attempt to do something with it was to say if we are
> going to go up against Tesco we have to reduce the cost of operations, so we
> tried to cheapen our operation down – not with the cooperation of John
> Foster who was against it, and who in the end was right.

He also added:

> We were being so successful doing what we were that I was having a job in
> pursuading myself that I needed to take the step we needed to take.

And in any case there was also a political dimension to the action. Jacks
and High represented the major power base in the company at that time
and, as Davison said:

I wasn't really getting senior management support in the area.

John Foster disagreed with his views too and, in any case, Davison and Foster were rivals for political status as joint Managing Directors.

In tandem with the debates and alliances at board level, there was activity within lower management levels of the company. The more junior managers in both retail and buying were aware that sales were being lost in the shops because the company was not providing the more fashionable clothes that their traditional customers were now looking for. The activity that took place is recounted by many of the managers involved at the time. It took various forms.

One Divisional Sales Manager of the time explained:

> I had been on the shop floor and witnessed the amount of business we were losing through not having fashionable merchandise. . . . I had my Area Managers lobbying me and I was lobbying my boss.

Since a small amount of merchandise that was more fashionable was made available to some branches, there might also be the chance of an Area Manager obtaining some of that:

> There was little that you could do; of the stock that was available to you, you might be able to obtain a little more than your share.

Brian Wood recalled that this process of lobbying and 'infiltration' of merchandise had been going on since the late 1960s:

> I was manager of Exeter branch and pioneered merchandise I bought myself. The move into fashion merchandise started with people like me who were buying merchandise that was fashionable at the time; and when I say fashionable I don't mean high fashion but ordinary everyday fashionable merchandise for the working-class guy. I bought this merchandise and, they said why are you so successful at Exeter and other people aren't. I said it's a combination of what you supply me and what I buy myself. Other areas were doing this. And the times I sat at meetings and had it thrown out and thrown out until one day Barry said we have to look at this and we started at various things and slowly worked up to what we call Fashionpoint.

The younger buyers were also promoting gradual change at the same time.

> I looked at the range and wasn't entirely happy with the philosophy of buy cheap and never mind anything else. It seemed to me inevitable that people would get more sophisticated and demand higher quality so we ought to have

more eye to design and colour whilst still retaining a nucleus of more traditional merchandise. This was coming from my end of the corridor and coincided with what those in the market knew, that there was a younger market. We were trying to influence decisions upwards by saying 'look at this, isn't this the way we should be going?': one does this softly, softly when working upwards: it might come down as tablets of stone.

This early piecemeal infiltration of merchandise produced little success. 1974 saw a downturn in profits for the company:

> Because our merchandise was better value than anyone else, we ran on that for a while and then we came to a standstill and we didn't get any further. The problem was we were buying cheap rather than value, so we got to be known as a cheap-jack operation. We could get cheap goods but not always what you wanted. . . . We were losing sales to Levi's and more fashionable merchandise. 'Come on you have got to give us this merchandise'. Mr Jacks at that time said we buy big and we sell it big. Stick to the things we know: that is where our business lies; it took a long time to get over that.

It was not simply a closed mind that argued against change; there were very real practical dangers in changing from what was seen as a proven approach to buying:

> When you have such lead times abroad . . . if you make a mistake, God you make one hell of a mistake.

There were also other blockages to change; particularly older managers and directors wedded to the outfitting tradition of the firm:

> The resistance was there from the older supervisors and Area Sales Managers who were not modern in their outlook right to the Board, who hadn't, other than Mr Davison, got a young person on there.

Resolution – Incrementally

The accounts of how the issue was resolved vary in detail but agree on a general level that it was a step-by-step approach called by some 'experimental'. In 1975 John Foster decided to take early retirement and Barry Davison assumed the role of sole Managing Director of Foster Menswear. He began more actively to promote the idea of buying more fashionable merchandise, and was not as easily put off as others had been. He also appears to have prevailed to some extent over the reluctant Tom Jacks in trying somewhat more fashionable merchandise:

I had been asking Tom to try and do it before, in experimental ways with young people's merchandise and it hadn't been successful but I was still sure that it would be successful. I was absolutely convinced that we had to be in that area.

Initially these 'experiments' were of limited success:

We bought some fashion lines and they didn't sell; and the reason we couldn't sell them is that we didn't buy good ones.

The first signs of success came with experiments with three-piece suits, a move that found more support with Tom Jacks than a wholesale widening of the range. Davison claims that the further widening of the range resulted from his seeing a published market research report on menswear retailing that showed a higher proportion of younger men shopping at Fosters than he believed to be the case. It appears to have been a discovery that consolidated his alignment with the perceptions of the retail management and decided him that 'we ought to widen the range of merchandise to utilize the pedestrian traffic flow we were getting through the business in a better way'.

Others however, were quite clear of the main reason for the wider expansion of the range:

That decision came about by the retirement at about that time of the Merchandise Director [Jacks].

And there were suggestions of more overt political dimension to that event:

John Foster retired and Tom Jacks came against BGD. BGD was seeing the changes. Others had caught up on our big margins and to some extent on the distribution system. The general public were demanding better quality and BGD wished to have an influence on the merchandise side. And with Tom there it was nigh impossible. Then Tom was ill and BGD seized his opportunity and Tom decided to retire.

To what extent the range extension resulted from argument and discussion between Davison and Jacks and other older members of the Board or from the retirement of Jacks after a 'political coup' by Davison, or simply as a result of a series of small-scale experiments that built a momentum for change, is not clear. What is more clear is the manner of the range of extension which eventually became known as 'Fashionpoint'.

The beginnings were the experiments with three-piece suits:

> We bought two or three ranges in the year [1975] which were moderately successful but not as successful as we wished to be. The following year we went in a bit further. We controlled it very carefully.

By the second year (1976) the range was being widened slightly from three-piece suits: more general fashionable merchandise was being tried in 20 experimental shops. Gradually between 1976 and 1980 the range and number of shops was increased. By 1978 the project had acquired the title 'Fashionpoint'.

The following accounts give some idea of the nature and organization of the venture as it progressed:

> We tried to appeal to the younger factory worker. . . . We went into this but we didn't lose sight of our foothold with the older market. It wasn't a case of doing a Burtons' 'Top Man' sort of thing.

> We decided to hold what we had but attract new customers. The existing, conventional staid range remained.

These moves were not without critics:

> There was coolness in certain directions for historical reasons. Its going to utilize space, are we utilizing space we've already got, and what about the stocks we've already got; its more investment and unknown territory.

There is evidence then, that doubts and some resistance remained. It appears that these were largely overcome by moving slowly and making relatively low levels of buying commitment. There was to be little risk-taking. The branches were selected on the basis of proven suitability to range extension, and ranges introduced so as not to offend existing customers.

> Branches were selected if they had a demand which was somewhat more fashionable. Regional sales directors called for information from the computer about how branches sold these lines. Displays were dressed a little bit more fashionably: an area of the branch was set aside for this merchandise and it was pointed out with overhead signs.

SHIRT
Crisp and very fashionable
short collar style shirts.
Colour woven fabric in a
multitude
of designs. £5.99

V NECK PULLOVER
A really fashi nable
pullover with patterned
front in lots of great colours.
Real easy to care for too,
£6.99

LOPEZ CORD JEANS
Easy on the pocket, tight on
the hips western style cord
jeans, in a wide range of
colours.
Take 'em straight or with
flare. £10.50

Also a great range of
heavyweight denim jeans
from only £9.95

"Real style for real men"

Ask about Fashionplan and get the
CREDIT for making the most of our low.
low prices.
For the address of your local Foster
Menswear shop, ring 021-745-3163
between 9a.m. and 5p.m.
Monday—Friday

FOSTER
MENSWEAR
**Britain's Biggest Value
in 500 shops nationwide.**

*Subject to availability

FIGURE 5.2 An illustration of the Fashionpoint range

Reproduced by kind permission of Foster Brothers

Sourcing for the merchandise change remained mainly overseas 'however' and pricing policy remained keen. In addition there was very little branded merchandise bought. Gradually some branches received greater proportions of 'Fashionpoint' merchandise and more conventional merchandise was phased out. By 1979 there were 250 branches carrying 'Fashionpoint' to a greater or lesser extent.

It was in fact in the Annual Report of February 1977 that the Chairman announced the move to the shareholders:

> We are widening our range of merchandise so as to appeal more markedly to the younger generation whose spending power is probably more virile than that of families who are encountering ever-increasing pressure on their disposable incomes.

By the following year he was able to say:

> A number of factors contributed to greater buoyancy in our turnover figures but probably the most important single factor was the decision to place greater marketing emphasis towards younger and more fashionable clothes.

In effect the company had moved over four years from an almost exclusively older man's shop to providing merchandise for a wider age grouping, although still primarily within what was seen as the traditional market target – "the C2DE socio-economic group". Figure 5.2 is an advertisement from this period and illustrates the sort of merchandise introduced and the continued emphasis on price.

These merchandise moves were taken within the growing commitment to overseas buying. In 1976 factories producing their own clothes in Bolton and Salford were closed down. Throughout the period there was also a progressive conversion to and opening of larger retail outlets, search for sites in the towns and cities in which the company was unrepresented and the closure of some of the smaller, less profitable shops. From the 458 Foster Menswear shops in 1975 the number rose to about 500 by 1977 and then remained static as a total number of shops but continued to grow in terms of square footage.

DIVERSIFICATION AND NEW VENTURES

Despite a disappointment with the Stone-Dri acquisition, the commitment to the desirability of entering the womenswear market remained. In 1975 a number of shops were converted to a womenswear 'Fosters equivalent' called "Crowds". Initially four shops were opened with the expectation that this number would be increased by both site purchases and transfers from other businesses within the Group. By late 1976 the importance of this trial for the future of womenswear within the Group was heightened by the demise of Stone-Dri. Geoffrey High announced in the 1977 annual report:

> We purchased Stone-Dri in 1973 when retail conditions were far more buoyant than has been the case throughout the past 12 months. In consequence of severely escalating costs in virtually every direction, a number of the Stone-Dri shops earning profits at the time of acquisition are no longer commercially viable. We have therefore decided to carry out a radical programme of reorganization. Approximately 30 units will operate under the 'Crowds' banner – keenly priced ladies' fashion to the 18–35-years age group.

Initially some of the Stone-Dri branches were left as they were – the more profitable ones – whilst the remainder became either Foster Menswear or Adams Childrenswear stores. The Crowds initiative 'however' fared no better than the Stone-Dri acquisition. Within twelve months of the announcement of the rundown of Stone-Dri, Crowds was also disconti-nued. Geoffrey High explained it as follows at that time:

> It is a fiercely competitive and sophisticated field which lost no time in showing us our weaknesses and our lack of flair.

The decision to pull out of the venture was taken in Autumn 1977 and the Crowds shops closed early in 1978.

By 1977 the company's strategy in the menswear sector at least seemed to be proving successful. Group turnover was in excess of £50 million, trading profits over £5 million and total borrowings were limited to an overdraft of £500,000 against a cash position in excess of £1 million. Return on capital employed was running at 28 per cent, and virtually all of this was the result of the menswear business. With cash to spend and a commitment at the most senior levels to the need for diversification, further attempts were to be expected. Barry Davison had seen the growth of cut-price drug and cosmetic stores in the USA and the beginnings of a similar operation – 'Superdrug' – in the UK. He had also agreed with Mr High that the Group should be seeking for ventures outside menswear retailing. In August 1977, the Group acquired 'Discount for Beauty', a cut-piece retailer of toiletries and cosmetics with 18 shops mainly in Yorkshire and the North East.

Within 12 months the number of branches had risen to 35. Despite initial growth, this business did not remain free from problems either. In the annual report two years later, 1980, it was stated that:

> Turnover in drugstore businesses has been depressed during the year and Discount for Beauty did not emerge unscathed. The three directors who were incumbent when we acquired this company have since resigned by mutual agreement. During this year we have reviewed the trading and management control policies of the business and new management systems have been installed.

During 1978 Foster Brothers developed the cosmetics business further when they acquired over 95 per cent of the ordinary shares in Staff Facilities (Holdings) Limited. Once again they were retailing cosmetics, toiletries and perfumery but, unlike Discount for Beauty, not through the traditional retail outlet – the shop. Instead, representatives sold these items, again at discount prices, to people in their place of work – the factory or office. The venture appeared to be successful and was immediately expanded with six new depots opened in the space of twelve months. In 1979 the venture was taken a stage further when a pilot operation along the lines of Staff Facilities Limited was tested in the United States. In addition, in 1979, an experiment was carried out into the scale of discounted cosmetic lines direct to the public through the medium of magazine advertising. By the end of 1979 it was, however, becoming clear that neither Discount for Beauty nor Staff Facilities were providing the sort of returns that Fosters were looking for. Both companies entered 1980 making losses.

During 1978 the company also acquired Millets of Bristol Limited which consisted of a chain of 50 shops specializing in camping equipment, casual wear, leisurewear and menswear to a limited extent. The aim here was to apply the successful management and control procedures in operation at Fosters to improve the profitability of Millets. Part of the Millets operation was Henderson Sports; Hendersons had both their own shops, as part of the Millets chain, and also traded from departments within Millets branches. In 1979 the possibility of this latter type of trading was examined in other sectors within the Fosters Group with a view to utilizing as much space within the stores as possible, without substantially raising overheads in the stores.

The search for growth outside the traditional menswear business also took place from the base of existing Group activities. In 1978 a decision was taken to expand the Adams Childrenswear business further. The 1979 annual report stated:

A five year growth plan and profit projection for the Group clearly demonstrates that we will have run out of space in less than two years' time. We have, therefore, taken a decision to build an additional warehouse and administrative block primarily to house this important subsidiary.

In 1979 a new head office and warehouse complex in Nuneaton was built to house the Adams operation. There were also plans developed for the operation of a mail-order service in the childrens' field. With this planned extension in mind a market research exercise was carried out in 1980, in order to identify possible areas for development of the business and a design consultant was engaged to create a new design concept for Adams shops. By the beginning of 1981 there were 82 Adams Childrenswear stores throughout the United Kingdom.

For each of these diversified business operations Barry Davison adopted a similar approach to its management. He assumed a position on their board, usually as Chairman, and appointed Foster Menswear managers to senior positions. Typically this took the form of appointing a buyer as Merchandise Director and an Area Sales Manager as Sales Director or General Manager, although attempts were made at both Discount for Beauty and Millets to retain senior executives in the posts they were in before the takeover.

Blue Movers – Internal Diversification and Development

The year 1979 also saw an extension of the retailing of fashion goods within the Group, with the opening of a limited number of shops retailing jeans and denim goods, under the name 'Blue Movers'. The annual report of February 1980 described the venture:

This year has also seen the opening of nine specialist shops selling jeans and casual clothes aimed especially to appeal to people of both sexes in their teens and early twenties. These shops operate as a division of Foster Menswear and if the present encouraging trend continues there are great hopes for the rapid expansion of this side of the business.

Fosters had operated two menswear boutiques, Wise Guys and Mr Christopher (which had been part of Bradleys). By the late 1970s these operations were not making profits, partly because of the rise at the time of specialist jean shops which were taking sales from the boutiques.

One Director explained the situation, as the management saw it, at the end of the 1970s:

We were already joint leaders in jean sales with M&S and we felt that if these specialists in jeans can succeed, and if the market is still fairly small in relation to the USA and Europe, there is a lot of potential growth and that maybe we should be in there attacking it.

More specific to the Blue Movers venture was that by the end of the 1970s Fosters were faced with a problem of what to do with the residual shops from the Stone-Dri operation. Many of the shops that had been part of that chain had been re-allocated to Foster Menswear or Adams but there were some remaining that had not been re-allocated because they were in poor sites or duplicated existing Foster sites. Many of these were being used as what the managers called 'junk shops' – shops used to dispose of redundant stock and that were trading under the name 'Bargains Galore'. The company had begun to experiment with some of these as specialist jean shops in 1979 which 'were trading under all sorts of funny names'. Some of these were called 'Blue Movers', some as 'Mean Jeans' and yet others as 'Jean's Jeans'. One senior retail manager who had been involved in setting them up explained the early developments:

In Liverpool we had a really run-down Stone-Dri shop still trading as Stone-Dri clearing out old stock in Church Street which is a good shopping area, although it was at the wrong end. Mr Davison said to me 'try a fashion operation – I'll give you carte blanche'. So I did a fairly garish exercise. Mr Davison said call it 'Blue Movers'. We didn't spend money on the shop – only £3000. We tripled the turnover overnight so we decided to do one or two more. I suppose it was the figures that prompted Mr Davison.

According to Tony Gray, at about the same time:

We actually had in the late seventies a small retail committee. On that were the chief executives of six of the smaller activities. Our specific brief was to look at the viability of a jeans concern. We sat for about six months and we decided at the end of the day it did not work. We felt that the shops and locations available were not appropriate. They were too small and in secondary sites.

The recommendations of the committee were overruled, and the decision to go ahead with a chain of jeans shops was taken. There was no market research undertaken into the market potential for specialist jean shops, or particular shop designs, or names, and no discussion of the matter at the Group Board. Most of the managers in 1980 were quite clear that the major reason for the initial go-ahead was Barry Davison's view. He decided that some of the 'Bargains Galore' shops should be used as an experiment using the name 'Blue Movers', operating within the Menswear division.

> We came out with some research on the profitability of other operators in this field. We didn't want to do it by acquisition because at that time we would have had to pay a lot when we had sites and expertise. If we are one of the leading jean sellers we must have some knowledge. We launched the thing in July 1980. We had these shops not doing anything – they were not selling jeans properly. They weren't making profit. We can't get rid of the sites unless people want to buy them. There is no point in sitting there with them empty. The positive way was to find something to do with them. The initial suggestion came from the Chairman. We had a Marketing man who was keen, but he may have been keen to have something to hang his hat on. The buyers were keen because they buy a lot of jeans anyway. They felt they could just as easily buy branded jeans as own-brand jeans. We felt we had a good brand name of our own and we were trying to give it an image of being a branded line like Levi's. We felt it could be a useful way of expanding that name. We had personnel available because we were closing down another operation so we had to find another role for those people or they had to leave. It was felt that we could afford to experiment in a reasonably substantial way. We looked at the profit potential of the branches we had short-listed. We had various people estimate what the turnovers were they felt they could achieve. We know what the costs of running the branches were and we could estimate the gross margin. It showed a breakeven position in the first year. Everybody was keen on it.

There was, in fact, not quite the total agreement suggested here. The buyers were wary of the need for branded jeans and the lower margins they entailed: 'Could we survive if we only sold branded jeans with their limited mark-up?' However, this problems was resolved by the decision to use the introduction of branded jeans so that 'we would introduce our own brand merchandise to give us the added profitability'.

Also, at least one senior board member, Mike Adams, was entirely against the idea; in 1980 he stated:

> Totally wrong, emotional, chasing a pot of gold, looking over your shoulder, moving into a market late in. It will be a non-existing business within 18 months. Barry is very anxious to be aggressive. What are other people doing? We must be doing that. He looks at Foster Menswear figures and sees a sizable proportion in jeans. He sees Jeans Junction, Jean Machine and so on and says we ought to be in that field. It was very much his decision. He said what do you think and I said just what I said to you. He said you are too 'fuddy duddy', etc. We come back to the clash of two personalities. But as far

as £10 million profits [the Group profit figure in 1979] is concerned, it is incidental. Go ahead. But it will be a disaster.

The initial trial of Blue Movers was run on six shops, Fosters' property company, Marshall Lake Properties, undertaking the shop design, and Brian Wood coordinating the operations from within the Menswear company. The results of the experiment were seen to offer sufficient promise to go ahead with an extension of the number of shops. It was decided to add the shops from the Mr Christopher chain and two Dormie (Scotland) branches to the Blue Movers operation, making 18 shops in total. Decisions then had to be taken as to how to operate the chain.

It was also decided that Blue Movers should be a division of Foster Menswear rather than a separate operation with the Group. The selection of the general manager for Blue Movers was described as follows:

> You have a situation in Dormie of being slightly heavy on management so Tony Gray is found from there to go to Blue Movers instead of choosing a man specifically with experience of jeans and modern clothing.

Tony Gray was Assistant Managing Director of Dormie and had sat on the review committee that recommended against the pursuit of a jeans operation. He none the less accepted the position in the hope that a successful venture might be helpful to his career prospects.

A young trainee buyer in the Menswear company was given the job of buyer because he 'moved in the same circles as potential customers'. When Tony Gray took over as General Manager he had different ideas:

> Blue Movers was envisaged from day one as a business where we would be selling more products to ladies than men, and we were in fact – about 60:40. I saw the need for a ladies' fashion buyer as a central need in the operation. The board disagreed and decided that a caretaker buyer, a man who had started it before I was involved, when there were two or three shops, should be allowed to grow with it. It was very commendable but a thoroughly bad decision. He did not have the experience to buy ladies' fashion casual wear. It's a very specialized business.

Gray had argued for the employment of an experienced senior ladies' buyer. This was not agreed. Blue Movers recruited a female assistant buyer straight from college. It was in line with the Fosters practice of always promoting within – a policy that was seen as a means of maintaining and generating morale as well as being less expensive than recruiting expensive outsiders.

Whilst the general management and buying for Blue Movers was set up specially, the sales and display organization was not; this was retained by the Menswear retail team. Tony Gray supported this step:

> We had a sales team in Menswear that we regarded as very competent.

Disenchantment and the Decline of Blue Movers

By 1980 Blue Movers had developed into a separate business within the Menswear Division. The first test shops had been set up in the image of those who ran the existing shops; display managers had designed windows and area managers had laid out the shops. The Blue Movers shops as they evolved, however, were not what these managers had originally envisaged. Outside shop designers had done away with windows with backs in and demanded that they have little merchandise in them. They had designed a shop interior that was open and uncluttered. The shop staff were expected to wear jeans and look casual. Moreover it was found that branded merchandise had to be sold in order for the shop to be credible and represented an important share of sales. By 1980 there was concern by those that had to manage the operation that it was not really for them:

> I don't think I have the necessary experience in what is a specialist field.

and:

> Our company is middle-of-the-road, not highly fashion-oriented. Blue Movers is moving up-market as far as I am concerned to the more stylish lad who would not come in to Fosters. The company policy is to deliberately disassociate it from Fosters for that reason. I am not sure that it is the right decision; I would rather have seen the money spent on refitting my shops or more shops of the type I have got. If we had bought up a chain of jean shops I would agree that that is the way to go about it, but we are doing it on the cheap. We are making mistakes. It is not a successful operation. I think we would have been better to get expertise rather than do it ourselves.

and:

> I hear Area Sales Managers talking. I think as far as Blue Movers is concerned it should be taken off altogether with the amount of shops that they have now got. I am supposed to be responsible for their windows but I'll be honest with you; I just do not have the time. I haven't seen one for ages. I think it should be a separate company altogether.

Others within the company at middle-management level expressed similar concerns. One of the Merchandise Managers commented:

> I expressed the view that the management team should be totally divorced from Menswear. It's an entirely different animal. It's more akin to the Oxford Street type of trading. Fosters is good, strong, provincial retailer. On Oxford Street we would fall flat. I am keen: the image is great but we want a sales management team that can give the jean specialists a bit of a chase. They have to be more of a leader . . . . You would do alright in very select sites.

Blue Movers was originally given a trial life of 18 months. In fact it lasted until Spring 1982. Tony Gray later accounted for its demise as follows:

> The managers in the Menswear Group were not receptive to other ways of doing things. Remember, Fosters was so successful that there was genuine belief that what they were doing and the way they did things was right. It never performed to its target requirement. In the last six months I was aware that the concept was under the microscope by the Chairman and his colleagues.

If the Blue Movers venture failed the company as a whole none the less remained profitable and, on the public face of it, successful. From a turnover base in 1975 of £41.9 million and trading profits of £4 million, turnover and trading profit reported in the 1979/80 Annual Report had risen to £89.8 million and £10.5 million respectively. Return on capital employed rose throughout the late 1970s to a peak of 39 per cent in 1978/9, in which year margins stood at 14 per cent of sales. Throughout the whole of this time the growth of the business was achieved with minimal borrowings – indeed with a net inflow of interest on short-term deposits. The number of shops, however, remained fairly static at 700 for the Group and settled at around 500 for Foster Menswear. By any financial measures of success, Foster Brothers had shown five years of successful growth (see table 5.2).

A SUBCULTURE IN TRANSITION

In 1970 Burtons was a close company under family control. Hepworths retained significant influence from the family on the board. Fosters too had many characteristics that would be associated with a family business. In some ways the decade that was to follow can be thought of as the demise of the company as a family business. Until the mid 1970s John Foster was an

TABLE 5.2   *A summary of the financial performance 1976–1980 (a) and a summary of key financial ratios (b)*

	1975/6	1976/7	1977/8	1978/9	1979/80
(a)					
Turnover: retail sales (£m)	41.9	44.1	50.2	67.8	89.8
Trading profit (£m)	4.0	4.0	5.1	9.5	10.5
Surplus on sale of properties (£m)	0.1	0.1	0.2	0.3	0.2
Less interest (£m)	—	—	—	—	—
Profit before taxation (£m)	4.1	4.1	5.3	9.8	10.7
(b)					
Growth in turnover (%)	+22	+5	+14	+35	+32
Growth in trading profit (%)	+29	—	+27	+86	+11
Trading profit as percentage of sales	10	9	10	14	12
Profit before tax as percentage of capital employed	25	24	28	39	36

Source: Foster Brothers Annual Reports

executive board member. In the late 1970s the company was still manifesting signs of its family traditions, and the associated paternalism. It was still discernible in 1980: one director explained that:

> retailing is not like, for instance, engineering where you have well defined roads to go down and professional qualifications. In retailing it's so grey you have to depend on personalities, on understanding, and love.

It was a view that to an extent had pervaded the attitude to management throughout the company. Much emphasis was placed on loyalty and caring for the well being of staff. As one retailer manager explained:

> We don't overstretch anybody. We don't put anybody's job on the line by over-promoting people. And you know that if you fail at that particular thing you are not going to get fired. You may move sideways. Nobody is forced into any position if they do not want to take it.

The loyalty was also personalized around the senior management and in particular the Chairman. Geoffrey High, the Chairman for most of the 1970s, was described by those who worked for him as 'a gentleman' and many of the managers had stories to tell about how he had personal advice to offer about their career development or courses to attend, or how they felt he listened to their views and comments. The sort of comments made can be illustrated by the following:

The leadership we have had over the past 20 years, initially by Mr High and now our present Chairman, the leadership is there. Our Chairmen have worked in different ways; our previous Chairman was different to our present one, but they both have qualities which inspire loyalty. And the loyalty which applied to Mr High was absolutely tremendous. The feeling was unique. You could have said 15 or 20 years ago Mr High wants something and they would have fallen over themselves to do it, not because of fear, but because they wanted to, and being part of a dynamic team.

The same sort of personalization of loyalty was expressed in 1980 as far as Barry Davison was concerned. For example, when one retail manager talked in 1980 about the rewards for a good trading performance, it was not the company but the Chairman himself that was seen to be magnanimous:

At Christmas he might say, 'Buy yourself a bottle of brandy and put it on your expenses'. He sends you hampers at Christmas. A couple of years ago he took all the ASMs to Athens with their wives. The luxury was unbelievable.

Within this essentially paternalistic situation, relationships between managers remained hierarchical: for example, outsiders coming into the company were struck by the way in which board members called the Chairman 'Sir' in formal meetings. Nevertheless, middle managers felt that in the 1970s, certainly, there existed a direct, if personalized and informal line of communication with senior management. By 1980, however, there was the feeling of many in the company that this family ethos was breaking down, largely because the company was becoming too large for it to continue. One manager traced it back to the growth of the late 1960s and early 1970s:

I wouldn't like to describe it as an us-and-them situation, but when this company decided it was going to be a large multiple, in the Bradley takeover days, it tried to move from the family concern to an aggressive multiple. This was when the wedge started being driven in. They introduced very dictatorial policies. The management training side became a management factory: it had to train two managers a week for two years. It was training a type of manager that whether he had the type of skills as his predecessor didn't really matter.

Others described the situation in terms of their feeling more 'like numbers' than they used to, or to a 'distance' growing between senior and more junior management over the decade. Regret it as many did, it was generally felt that it was inevitable:

We all realise it isn't as small as it used to be. It used to be a family business: it is slowly losing that; whether that is good or bad I don't know. You get this family business and it can sometimes be a bit false anyway.

Whilst the nature of the business was changing, many of the historical characteristics remained. The management of the company was highly centralized in strategic terms; virtually all decisions of strategic consequence were taken or routed through the Chairman. He saw himself and was seen by others as having a legitimate interest in and involvement with all facets of the business. Managers were expected to manage the operations of their functions with independence and drive, but they could expect Barry Davison to get involved at any time.

The management team itself in the 1970s was characterized by being almost exclusively 'home-grown', senior managers having normally joined the company after leaving school at 14 or 15 and working themselves up through the retail or buying side. Typical of this sort of progression was Brian Wood who in 1980 was Sales Director and Assistant Managing Director of Foster Menswear. He left school at 13, started as a 'boy' with Hepworths, and became a shop manager with them at the age of 21. He then worked for two other menswear retailers before joining Fosters and working his way up the retail sales management side of the business, took over the management of one of the factories together with 17 retail Jessops shops, and eventually became Sales Director.

The links between the centralized nature of management decision-making and the speed of decision-making are evident. One story told illustrates the situation well. Foster had acquired Jessops, a small tailor, in the 1960s. It had its own factory making made-to-measure suits.

By the mid 1970s with the steady decline of made-to-measure trade, our factory was becoming unviable. . . . The decision was made to close that factory and we had got to the point of issuing redundancy notices and it was publicized on Yorkshire Television as a news item. On the day after that appeared on television, there was a sudden imposition of import quotas from Taiwan where we obtained all our boys' school blazers. This was 1976 and the quantity we were shifting that year was in excess of the total quota. We can't just lose all that turnover. I was called up to Mr Davison's office that morning because I had some inclination that this might happen and was already thinking of alternative sources in the UK. Four of us sat down with Mr. Davison. . . . The decision had to be made if we could transform the Jessops factory into a ready-made blazer factory. We took that decision in the space of three quarters of an hour. Yes we would rescind the redundancy notices and put the investment in.

It was a style of management described by a retail manager in 1980:

It's Monday morning management – what's the policy this week – we need to be this, that and the other to dovetail with the present trading conditions. In other words I think we have a slick operation. In other companies by the time they have taken a decision it's too late.

What was certain is that Davison would be involved in any decision of strategic consequences: he, and other managers, saw him as the decision maker in such issues. The situation was illustrated by Davison himself:

OK, I use other people's ideas; everyone does. They started that decision, OK they all started it; but they all start all sorts of other decisions which I never take. In any business there are loads of people giving ideas; it's a matter of whether the person who is running the business can pick the best or the right ideas. I make the most God Almighty number of errors in decision-making, but you get enough good ones that produce the goodies.

This process of feeding of ideas which are sifted by the chief executive did not extend to direct involvement by junior management. They saw their role not as influences of policy but as implementers of policy:

It isn't policy to go against policy. I do my best to make it work. Because the leadership we get in our company is right and if you work for a company which pays your salary, you should be loyal to that company. My job is not to make policy decisions but to implement them.

The central role of Davison was generally regarded as a benefit to the company. He was seen in 1980 as a main reason for the company's advances in the past decade. As Brian Wood stated:

Why the sudden growth? I will tell you in a nutshell – it's Barry Davison. I think he has made a major contribution to the progress of the company because he has pushed and pioneered schemes – not all right – but what he has done has been positive and made us move forward. He tightened up the costings as Company Secretary and generally put some boot behind people.

And another:

The Chairman epitomizes success and sets the pace for everyone: he can put his finger on any button in the organization.

It was a centrality that Davison himself acknowledged and also saw dangers in:

I think there is a very big difference between Chairman and Managing Director. I don't think they ought to be combined but there isn't anybody else here that could deal with the Managing Director's job yet. As Chairman I consider my responsibilities are to deal with the outside world, in the way of the City, and to try internally to plan where we ought to be going for the future, and checking that the companies in the Group are doing what they said they would. The Managing Director's job as I see it is a day-to-day managerial job seeing that the day-to-day problems that exist are dealt with. I would find it very difficult to disassociate Chairman and Group Managing Director. I don't really see that it is possible to be a Managing Director of the major retailing company which is Foster Menswear and do the Group Chief Executive job combined.

Later, however, he argued differently:

I believe that it is possible to be Chairman and Managing Director. I'm not sure that it needs to be a twofold thing. I tend to look upon myself rightly or wrongly as Fosters and believe that I generate inside and outside the business the identity of the Company. I do believe that it is possible to have a personality cult within a fairly large Company. There are very large organizations in this country – larger than ours – where they do revolve around one person. I think without doubt to the outside world the impression I give as to what goes on in the business affects what they feel about Fosters. As far as the City are concerned they are bound to think to a certain degree, when they think about the company, of me. It's not something I consciously try to put over. I would consciously seek to avoid it to some degree because it would indicate some weakness in the business if they felt that there is quite as much of a personality cult as there is in the company. It might be worried that in the event of something happening to me it could affect their long-term investment projects. Therefore, it would not be a good thing if they realized quite how many of the decisions wait until I generate them. I do believe that in the long term I have got to try and change it.

Whilst all within the company applauded the energy and drive of Davison, there were those who had reservations: Brian Wood was concerned that decisions could become disjointed:

We do have a Chairman who has his finger in every pie. That does restrict one slightly. If I were running Menswear, I would do it differently, I would get together more with people. At the moment it's disjointed because the Chairman can't be everywhere. He will see one person at one time. It is very difficult to tie it together.

He, along with others, also had reservations about the management style of the Chairman:

> . . . There is a shop full of staff and he says: 'Who the bloody hell did this; I'm not having that; that's coming down'. I said 'You can't do that here' and I left him for half an hour. In the car I explained that they had been up till three in the morning to get the shop right. I explained that they came to me and asked if the Chairman wasn't happy with it. He said 'I'm sorry I didn't mean to!' but I said 'You do'!

And Mike Adams was also concerned:

> The danger is the structure. I disagree with the structure. I don't think you can have a company of £100 million turnover with a Chairman like Barry also Managing Director and Managing Director of the major subsidiary, and also Chairman and virtually Managing Director of other subsidiaries. It is just not as an ongoing situation correct. It cannot survive. The man cannot stomach the workload. He comes under pressure, becomes irrational, paranoiac, whatever. Secondly, there is no financial director on the Main Board. So in effect Barry is Financial Director of the Group. He is also Chairman of the Property Company. So in practical terms if you want anything done you either do it yourself and get your head shot off by Barry or you don't ask him.

There were few such reservations stated by more junior management who, clearly, admired what they saw as a driving force. However, one manager who had been with the company for many years and had at one time worked with Davison did see problems:

> I worked for Mr Davison for some time and he knows his own mind and has a good financial brain. I have got a lot of faith in him; but I think whoever you are dealing with if you don't agree with something you should say so, even if it's only to stimulate conversation. I am not sure that some of the people that surround him do that. He is a bit of a bull at a gate, but I don't think people stand up to him. I think one of the non-executive directors might stand up to him but I wouldn't say any of the others would really, but he would have done in his day – stand up to anybody – and I think he respects people standing up to him.

Of the managers interviewed at Fosters who had been with the company before 1980, only the accountants had any real experience of other industries or any professional qualifications or experience of higher education. There had been a history of deliberate 'culturization' of managers who joined the company; the managers who joined in the 1960s, most of whom had been shop managers or area managers with Hepworths, were given positions as salesmen or assistant shop managers with Fosters so that they could 'learn how Fosters did things'. Indeed there was evidence of the resentment to resistance to 'outsiders' throughout the 1970s. On the recruitment of senior management from outside the firm, Brian Wood said:

> [The Chairman] once said to me that we had had a number of people in that had gone the way of all flesh and that it was my retail mafia that had got them. And I said 'Are you saying I am a godfather I suppose?'

Richard Haynes claimed that, as a newcomer at board level who was known to differ on some points of policy, he often felt deliberately excluded:

> I was not allowed to go to the display department or a shop without permission from Brian Wood. It was the same in buying: I wasn't allowed to ask buyers questions without Norman knowing. There was gentle ridicule at meetings: not being familiar with everything – you might use the wrong nomenclature and this would be used in public to show you didn't know anything about retail.

He and others did not believe that this sort of behaviour was unusual:

> If you look on the Menswear side it does not have a record of importing people. To bring in someone at the top on the Menswear side could be very dispiriting. Well the Mafia would kill him, as the Mafia has killed various importations – Brian Wood, Norman Phillips, the Mafia.

It was a phenomenon that extended to other areas of the business. For example, the Personnel Director, had 'brought in a modern O and M man who I had to get rid of because he upset everyone around the building with his modern methods'.

Fosters was a closed management system, recruiting from within and priding itself on the longevity of its managers and their record of promoting from within. It was a record that most managers saw as admirable. In particular the retail managers saw it as a means of motivation since most senior executives could point to their past as shop managers:

> Last week I gave a talk at Malvern School and I had all the stuff in the back of the car. I was assisted in taking this to the car by some junior retail staff on a training course at head office. One boy from Wallsend said 'What a super Rover, can I sit in it?'. He got in, sat in there and drooled over it and said

'You've earned it, haven't you'. He did not begrudge it. He was part of that success. I said to him 'If you work at your job well you can have the same'.

It was not too surprising, then, that there were few differences in opinion about the way the company managed its affairs. One critic was Mike Adams who, apart from being the most critical of Barry Davison's approach, also saw it as a structural problem. Some of his views have already been stated. Perhaps significantly, he offered the view that the reason for his different views was that he was the only person with a different background, having run his own business.

In 1980 there was one other and more recent 'outsider': Richard Haynes had only just joined the company. His views in 1980 were also less in line with the mainstream Fosters approach:

> There are two things that can happen in retailing. One is natural drift; in other words you just drift along updating your merchandise as the years go by. The other is to be much more positive about it and actually make sure you are making positive steps to reposition your business on a gradual basis; otherwise you have to do what Burtons did which was radically reposition. Amazingly Fosters have been as successful as they have without any of the sophisticated tools. I am not a through and through retailer; I do not pontificate about how to serve customers or how to lay out shops; I leave that to the experts – but I do think I can help in trying to get us to see how other people see us. If you are not being perceived as you want to be perceived, then you are wasting your time. If you think people see you as something and they still see you as that cut-price shabby menswear chain that sells working men's jackets and trousers – if that is how you are seen then you have got to do something about it.

In fact one of Haynes's first acts on appointment was to commission market research: research that was to show that the view customers had of Fosters was very different from what managers believed they had: it was research that was to play a significant part in changes that were to follow.

THE POSITION IN 1980

In July 1979 Geoffrey High retired as Chairman of the Board and was replaced by Barry Davison. He and Mike Adams became joint Managing Directors. Barry Davison was now Group Chairman and Joint Managing Director as well as Chairman of most of the subsidiary companies. Figure 5.3 is a diagrammatic representation of the company structure as it was in

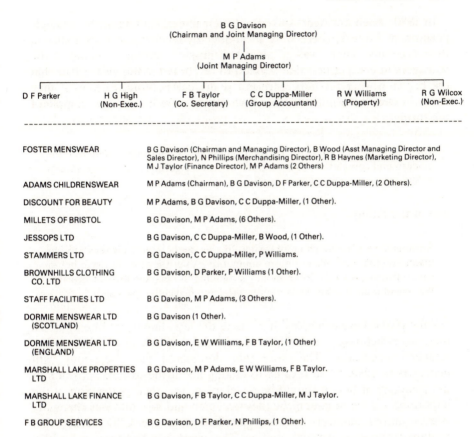

FIGURE 5.3   Foster Brothers' group structure in 1980

1980. There was a Group board with a number of subsidaries reporting to that board. However, a large proportion of subsidiary board membership consisted of Group directors, which meant that decisions taken at company board level would almost automatically be ratified by the Group board since the same individuals were involved at both levels. Similary Group directors' views, and particularly those of Barry Davison, were a direct and powerful influence on the strategic decisions of the subsidiaries.

On taking over as Chairman, however, Davison did make organization changes: Brian Wood, the Foster Menswear Sales Director, was appointed Assistant Managing Director of the Menswear company. Also in 1979 Richard Haynes, who was head of the company's advertising agency in Birmingham, was recruited as Marketing Director with Group-wide responsibilities. Later, in 1981, John Fallon, a financial manager from Burtons, was also recruited, as Financial Director.

In 1980, when managers talked out their understanding of the strategic position of Fosters, there were a number of recurring characteristics in their accounts. There was an almost dismissive attitude of many of the managers to competition that seemed to be rooted in the view either that the big menswear retailers were not really competitors, or that, if they were, Fosters were much better at what they were doing. An example of the former:

> There has been a contraction on the High Street. John Colliers went into the modern end completely, as have Burtons; we are getting quite a nice slice of it. There's only us and Dunns really.

and of the latter:

> Burtons have gone much more casual, like us, and I would say they are our major competitors. We are more competitive than they are and give better value. Burtons spend a lot of money swamping the market with advertising. We spend a lot less but have a more effective marketing package.

Having given these examples, it is, none the less, important to emphasize that, overwhelmingly in 1980, managers did not talk much about other retailers specifically. The issue that dominated the discussions with managers in 1980, when it came to talking about the strategic position of the company or how it should be developing, was their perception of the importance of the market niche they occupied and how that was changing. Almost all the managers interviewed talked about the 'C2D market' that Fosters deliberately concentrated on. The expression had become by 1980 a sort of code for their traditional working man's market segment. It was typically expressed as 'We believe we are servicing the majority of the population in the C2D market'. It was a market position that had been built up over years and had its roots in the company's provision of basic outfitting for the working man. The recent Fashionpoint exercise was seen as a widening of that base to a different age group but not to a different social group:

> We all accept that we should pursue the image of the younger factory worker yet still retaining the older factory worker.

and:

> We have never gone outside our social group because we have other shops in the set-up – Dormie and so on – so we should stick to what we know, at the

same time keeping our finger on what that social group wants and adapting to that.

In merchandise terms the market position, then, translated itself into the continued provision of outfitting plus the relatively new addition of what some of the management team called 'Yob's uniforms'. It was not a position that managers saw as different from what they had been doing for years.

We have kept our feet on the ground whereas others have flown off in various directions. You see, so many have gone off into fashion and come completely unstuck. The next time you read of them they are into voluntary liquidation. We have kept our feet on the ground. We know our market thoroughly.

It was a position that most of the managers insisted was non-controversial. In fact, there was some disagreement about the precise interpretation of the market position in 1980 and about how it should develop. One senior manager believed that the company had 'completely changed [its] image: we are much more fashionable now and are appealing to a wider market'. Another saw the company developing, if gradually, more fashionable merchandise to meet the needs of the new customers they were seeking:

If the Cs are becoming more educated and more sophisticated and are demanding these things – quality – for which they will pay a slightly higher price, then we ought to move up and get that. I see it as an extension.

The most radical position was taken by Brian Wood:

I do see change but I am the only one. I think the C2 market we have we should retain; but we have a lot of big stores and I have a feeling we ought to edge into the market of Hepworth at the lower end – and pinch some of their C1 trade. . . . But the Chairman says that we are in a C2 market and this is where we are staying; but oddly enough when we do produce something – we now have a simulated suede coat at £50 and it's selling quite well – it's incongruous that we can do that sort of thing. Again the Chairman says you cannot sell to the young fashionable market when there are kids buying school uniforms. Now every logic tells me that is correct, but I'm the best retailer in this business and I know that in these shops you can, provided you offer them the merchandise. My views are slowly prevailing now because we have gone into other sorts of merchandise. We are selling Tootal shirts and these suede coats; we do get setbacks when we buy more expensive trousers and they don't sell and they say 'I told you so'. Slowly we are evolving, I think.

It was an issue that had reached the level of boardroom discussion:

> There are one or two who would like to widen the range and attack a wider range of people. It comes up at board meetings. It is not terribly well organized as a discussion: it tends to just develop. Unfortunately people are not terribly equal at these meetings. We have a very dominant character in the Chairman and he has very strong views and in the past has been very firm in shouting down, maybe to protect his opinion. That is changing at the moment. He is part of this gradual change. There is only one who is advocating attacking another market. Mr Davison is saying we should stay where we are.

The picture emerges of a management team, dominated by the Chairman, largely committed to a traditional down-market posture but trying to reconcile itself to its relatively recent adjustments to marginally different merchandise and target market. It was a reconciliation that, individually, they expressed somewhat differently: some as a major move, others as no move at all, Wood as merely a beginning of a process of incremental change. Others thought there was real risk of confusing the customer:

> We are confusing the public trying to stay in the area we are in as to what we are and who we are trying to service. If we try to attack a new sector of the market they will get even more confused.

However, on both the sales side and buying there was little difference over how the divergences on perceptions of market position would be resolved. It would be through the gradual evolution of the merchandise mix within the bounds of what Fosters were good at doing:

> You never stand still with merchandise – it evolves. What you sell today you don't necessarily tomorrow, but the merchandise quality or our expertise with merchandise and our knowledge of our customers' requirements is important. I am not discounting the fact that there will be changes. In the next few years we might sell more suits and less jackets or no tailored jackets at all.

Norman Phillips translated this into market positioning terms:

> We need to strengthen our present market position. There is still a large central market. We need to find compatible means of attracting the younger more fashion-oriented person as well as Mr Average Conventional.

Compatible, that is, with what the managers saw the company was doing at the time successfully.

The mechanics of the process of fitting the evolution of merchandise to the target market was described by one buyer as follows:

> Different merchandise would not just drift into shops; there would be no aimless drift because the disciplining process would stop it.

He saw this 'discipline' working as follows:

> A policy will come downwards and merchandise will flow upwards.

The precise interpretation of merchandise mix, which is what the managers saw as defining their target market, was primarily in the hands of the senior management team, within the bounds of general policy guidelines from above. As a senior buyer explained:

> The market the company pitch at is pre-determined. We are told we are a C2 market: that's where we are at. Therefore if a buyer produced a range which was construed to appeal to a B1 socio-economic group he would have it thrown out. My job would be to hold that down.

It was a system of evolution through adaptive buying that the newcomer, in 1980, Richard Haynes, also observed:

> A lot of what happens here . . . the decisions are taken based on history. The selection of next year's merchandise is made largely by looking at this year's and seeing there are certain ongoing lines which go on year after year. All you do is change the width of the lapels or the trouser bottoms. So to that extent the buyer's job is not speculative. We are trend-followers not trend-setters. Now there are areas where they do take risks which are more in casual clothes where they gamble on a colour or a particular garment. They have just gambled on a suit which everyone said would sweep the board and it hadn't and no one is sure why. Generally speaking we are following trends through.

Advocated Strategies for the 1980s

Not surprisingly, perhaps, there was considerable unity amongst managers as to what strategies should be followed in subsequent years for Menswear. Almost every manager advocated a consolidation strategy for Menswear. This, most typically, took the form of 'doing what we do well' but increasing representation in towns and cities without Fosters shops, closing smaller shops to open bigger ones and widening the product range to include shoes and, perhaps, sportswear. The logic for such a strategy was, typically as put by Davison himself:

> Menswear is in a difficult situation. We have already got a very substantial portion of the menswear market and I don't see currently how we can substantially increase our share, not to achieve the sort of growth pattern that we have had over the last 20 years. We have got certain areas of the country where we are poorly represented and our plan is to increase the depth of our representation. The other thing we are trying to do is to attempt to enlarge the size of the shop operation. So we can widen the scope of our merchandise appeal still wider and thus take a bigger share of the market; but there must be a limit to how much one can get. And unfortunately in a stagnant economy like we have in the UK that is a problem. We have no plan, yet, and I don't see any likelihood of it moving Menswear into selling other sorts of merchandise. We have looked at selling shoes and we have a lot of successful branches selling boyswear, but I don't see any movement into ladieswear at all. So the growth aspect has to be much slower than it has been in the past.

There were different emphases placed on this by some managers. Some talked more specifically of concentrating on cost-cutting and improved efficiency given a threatening economy. Others, mainly buyers, felt merchandise quality should be improved. Others, mainly retail managers, suggested that there should be greater investment in improving shop premises.

The other main strategy advocated was that of diversifying into other retail activities. It was advocated by most of the Menswear Board but by few managers below that level. The logic for diversification was in effect an extension of that for consolidation; Davison again:

> It is obviously going to be more and more difficult to get worthwhile expansion. That is the reason why I am trying to move into other businesses but we are not having as much success there as we would like. There is no reason why because you have been successful as a menswear business you should be successful in others.

Only Adams and Wood raised objections to the attempts to diversify. Wood's view was that the company had made a number of mistakes with acquisitions, taking the company away from the problems of the mainstream business. Adams was not against diversifying, as such, but against the manner in which some of the ventures were managed and he linked this with the way in which the company was structured.

The Main Board have got to digest that they are a small holding company rather than a Menswear business with the odd incidental company. If it can grasp that and structure the company correctly and give the individual subsidiary a certain amount of autonomy within a Main Board Group Policy the world is its oyster. If it fails to grapple with that it will struggle and remain in Menswear with subsidiary companies starting up with ambition and then being folded up. That has been its history. I am not against these other things happening providing you recognize yourself as a holding company and say that all these other things are totally different operations. Don't try to implant the things in Foster Menswear into that subsidiary because you will kill it.

It was a view about the diversification programme that was held more widely outside the board room. Typically diversification took effect in the implantation of Fosters personnel and control systems as with Discount for Beauty, Staff Facilities and Millets and the presence on the board of the subsidiary of Davison and a number of other Main Board directors. Davison and other Board members believed that the evident success and experience of Fosters could be used to improve the companies they took over. It was not a view shared by middle managers in Fosters Menswear who did not see that their skills were necessarily transferable.

> I think growth should always be in areas with which managers are familiar. I think to diversify into areas with which the managers are not familiar is not a very good thing.

And there was some resentment that money was being 'wasted' on new business that was needed for the refurbishment of the Menswear shops:

> I am not sure that it is the right decision; I would rather have seen the money spent on investing in my shops or more shops of the type I have got.

A Market Research Perspective on the 1980 Strategic Position

Still largely dependent on menswear, Fosters entered the 1980s as the major multiple traditional menswear outfitter : 39 per cent of its sales were in jackets, trousers and suits; 18 per cent in knitwear, sweatshirts and tee-shirts; 15 per cent in shirts; 16 per cent in jeans; and 4 per cent in boyswear. There was a deliberate policy of not selling, or at least not emphasizing, branded goods, with a preference for promoting the merchandise bought specially for Fosters at the higher margins achieved initially from importing. Their retail sites were mainly in prime shopping areas with about one-fifth in major cities or large towns, about 130 in medium-sized towns (such as Maidenhead and Long Eaton), another 100 in small towns (e.g. Henley and Cirencester), about 70 in city suburbs and another 110 in country towns and seaside resorts. The selling area of the shops varied from as little as 500 square feet to 4000 square feet with the number of larger branches growing but still being much less than that of smaller branches of around 1000 square feet. Many of the older branches had little maintenance over the previous years and some were in a poor state of repair. Although traditionally involved more in casual clothes than their competitors and never really strongly involved in the suit market, the large multiples such as Burtons and Hepworths, and the variety chains such as Marks and Spencers and C & A, were, by then, much more directly competing with similar merchandise.

There also existed some quite specific evidence of a mismatch with market expectations by 1980. The market research that Richard Haynes commissioned in 1980 was available in June of that year. Some of its most telling findings were expressed as follows in these extracts from the reports:

Fosters featured relatively prominently as a source of purchase of schoolwear, but did not seem to appeal much to boys for casual wear.

Quite a number of the younger men in the sample were alienated from Fosters by memories of having been dragged there for schoolwear.

The Foster shops in older tattier shopping centres were generally spoken of more favourably than those in more modern shopping environments.

The research suggested strongly that Foster shops are suburban in appearance, mood and trading methods. They are acceptable (to women especially) in a suburban environment, but they are out of place in city centres because they do not relate to how people like to shop in that environment.

Respondents were much less favourably disposed towards Fosters than the nature of the sample would have led us to expect. Most of the young and quite a few of the older men were certainly not well disposed towards Fosters. The women were generally more positive about Fosters than the men but this was certainly not universal. Furthermore it was quite often because of their purchasing of boyswear rather than menswear.

Fosters was generally regarded very much more highly by the Ds than by the C1s. Fosters is not very relevant to the needs of C1 men.

Fosters' prices were often described as 'cheap'/'reasonable'. For some this meant low prices, acceptable quality, and good value. A more general view was that the prices were low and the quality matched the prices.

Many respondents talked of a lack of style.

Some respondents felt that Fosters' merchandise did not measure up to their standards.

In most cases when respondents described what they regarded as a typical Foster shopper they were talking about people with whom they did not identify. In other words they did not see themselves as the sort of people who were Foster shoppers.

Although a few respondents like the crowded windows, the vast majority found them unattractive and offputting. One complaint was that they were so cluttered that it was impossible to focus on anything in particular. Specific criticism was made of the 'dummies'.

Many respondents held a negative view of the merchandise. This seemed often to have been evoked more by the windows and the mood and style of the shop than by actual experience of the clothes.

Only a very few respondents felt that the styles and fashions sold by Fosters were very up-to-date. Quite a number thought that they were rather middle-aged, or a bit behind the times. Some regarded them as archaic.

Quite a few respondents of both sexes thought the quality of Fosters' merchandise was poor.

An element contributing to the impression that Fosters does not sell first-class merchandise is the frequency and manner with which sales and special offers are announced in the windows.

Many young men claimed not to shop at Fosters because they wanted to buy brands, notably of jeans, which Fosters did not stock.

Some of the verbatim comments from the group interviews were particularly galling to the managers, for example:

One of the things is the fact, that it's such an old firm . . . older firms tend to get mentally left behind in young people's minds . . . they sort of think, well I won't go in there because it's an old firm, they won't have come up to date.

From looking in the window I didn't fancy going inside.

It looks a bit grim from outside.

It's got a touch of the Oxfam shop about it.

From the outside . . . it gives the impression of being a cheap shop . . . it's not the sort of place I'd go to buy a suit, I'd feel embarrassed to walk in there. It's got a reputation like Woolworths or Tesco . . . you say 'Oh I don't want to go in there, its a cheap shop'.

Hall tests research pinpointed other problems. In particular it became clear that:

(1) Fosters appealed more to women buying for men than men buying for themselves;
(2) the shops were biased even more down-market than they thought; and
(3) even more towards older men (aged over 45) than they thought.

The hall tests also supported the group interview findings that Fosters was seen as unattractive in terms of shops, poor in terms of merchandise and rather old-fashioned. The report concluded:

In our view the present Fosters market, described demographically, provides the potential for a perfectly adequate customer base. The key problem which this research has demonstrated, however, is that the shops themselves are not currently sufficiently attractive to draw in enough customers from within these demographic groups. Furthermore Fosters' method of trading fails to meet the widespread desire for self-selection.

The findings showed a striking difference between the perception the managers themselves had of Fosters and the perceptions and behaviour of the customers. In particular, although Fosters' managers considered that the market focus was and should be down-market, they did not see the company as the rather cheap and nasty, old-fashioned retailer that the customers did; nor did they believe that the age profile was as skewed towards the older male as it was. The research also, most significantly, attacked some of the most firmly held beliefs about the company's basis for success. Merchandise was seen to be out-dated and of rather poor quality and what was seen by the managers as a shop presentation and staff attitude geared to the expectations of their customers was indicated as confused, tatty and aggressive. The research also showed that the customer was at least as concerned about the shop environment as the merchandise.

The managers, faced with the report, could not accept its wider implications; how could such an indictment be so when the company had just had years of uninterrupted growth culminating in record profits? According to Haynes the initial response was to 'rubbish' the research.

At one of the group interviews, which someone attended, there were two people in the group who were not really representative of Fosters customers. After that the follow-up groups were rubbished as unrepresentative.

And, according to Haynes, when the reports were presented, the executive from the research agency making the presentation

. . . pronounced fascia with a k: well how could he know anything about retailing!

The response to the research was to address some of the more admissable findings: it was argued that the move to a younger market was already under way and would be continued; window design was re-examined to cut down the clutter and deal with shop appearance; display cards were re-designed to make them less garish and there were some changes in merchandise layout.

DECLINE AND CHANGE

The 1980 half-year figures to August showed sales up but pre-tax profits down from £4.54 million for the 1979 first half to £3.12 million. The *Financial Times* reported Barry Davison as blaming unemployment and short-term working on the decline and saying that 'as soon as the public returns to normal spending levels upward growth in profits will resume'.

The decline continued throughout 1980: the year ended with Group turnover up just 5 per cent and trading profits down by 26 per cent. Pre-tax profits were boosted to £9 million by sales of properties of £1.2 million, far greater than ever before. The annual report for 1980/1 provides the company's public explanations for the downturn:

On menswear . . . Government policies have affected more adversely our traditional working class customer than any other section of the public. It has always seemed to be the case in a recession that men's clothes are one of the inessential items in the family budget. . . .

On Blue Movers, with 17 outlets in 1980:

The jean market has been highly competitive . . . with substantial price reductions on branded jeans necessary to stay competitive and this has had its effect on profitability.

On Millets:

> . . . price cutting which has taken place has made it necessary to reduce margins to maintain market share.

Staff Facilities selling cosmetics to people in their places of work:

> has been badly affected by factory closures and redundancies.

Adams Childrenswear was also suffering, not only from a decline in trading results but also from the disruption of its move to Nuneaton. The few signs of improvement were for Dormie and, with some reduction in its losses, Discount for Beauty.

Undoubtedly economic influences had an impact on Fosters' sales. However, there was the uncomfortable fact that Burtons, who had moved decisively into the market that Fosters had regarded as theirs, were doing exceptionally well by 1981 compared with their previous performance and the performance of Fosters. The financial press carried articles applauding the Burtons recovery and highlighted the role of Ralph Halpern, Burtons' chief executive. The articles that appeared on Fosters were brief and drew unfavourable comparisons with the Burtons performance. It was a comparison to which Barry Davison was sensitive both personally and in terms of confidence in the City. Managers talked of the way in which Davison took the situation personally:

> Suddenly he had a group on his hands which was a relative failure and his arch rival Ralph Halpern was riding the crest of a wave paying himself £150,000: and Barry was only getting £50,000. He is a very vain man and very concerned about his own image. And he was intelligent enough to realize that he had been wrong. Ever since he had taken over as Chairman the figures had gone down.

or

> Barry wants to win. He had a period as the best Chairman – £10 million profit. To come shooting down to three is a dramatic thing for a man with his chemistry. You've got to be able to see how you can come out of that valley, and he couldn't, and with the chemistry of the man he couldn't accept that. He was desperate and he did say 'I don't know what to do'. It really has got to be personal, because he is an egotist and selfish, with an incredible capacity for work; but the little thing that was grinding him was having been patted on the back with £10 million profit. He just didn't know what to do and he was not prepared to lose. He had to have something for the coming AGM.

The Response to Decline

The position within the company was described by one director as:

> Floating around like a ship without a rudder: no one knew where we were going.

Initially the emphasis was on traditional tightening of controls. The business had always been 'good at cost control' in the view of the executive. As Richard Haynes observed:

> It is an accountant-dominated company. As I jokingly say 'you open a door and they have cloned another one'. It has been very significant; when times were tough it kept our heads above water.

Managers talked of 'doing better what we do best' for example:

> When your figures start dropping you look at things purely on an area basis if you're honest. That's what you are really concerned about your 22 shops, when they start to go down. . . . When things go wrong you tend to stick to the rules much more rigidly. Had I got the stock right? Were the staff right? At the time we were nothing to do with profitability – our brief was turnover. Had we got the windows packed? You spent your time chasing around the branches asking the managers if they were doing everything right.

At Board level the decision was taken to embark in 1980 on an even more aggressive pricing policy. Fosters carried a sale for a large part of 1981 and increased advertising expenditure to promote the price-led strategy. To support this effort 1981 became designated 'The Year of the Salesman' with incentives at branch level for increased sales.

Sales and profits continued to decline so costs were further cut back. However, the major variable cost was retail wages and attempts to cut these had been resisted by the Area Sales Managers:

> Our wage costs were out of line with other people as far as we could tell. We had no system of control other than through our Area Manager and no matter how far down the line we went with disciplines on that it never seemed to have any effect because they said they needed the staff.

It was resistance that was understandable enough. The retail managers had come to believe that Fosters 'looked after' its staff; and the Area Managers claimed that the 'team spirit' and loyalty of staff was a major motivating force.

At this time the company were approached by Metra Proudfoot, consultants specializing in productivity programmes, who suggested 'they could save us a million pounds'. The board saw it as an opportunity to overcome the problems of retail resistance:

> We said we are taking it away from the ASMs [Area Sales Managers]. There was no way you could decentralize that as you wouldn't be able to implement it, and in fact we implemented it from here. We made decisions on each branch from head office. There was a group of people nominated to do that working alongside Metra Proudfoot.

A team of retail managers was formed to work alongside the consultants.

> They studied every branch and they were surprised to find how many customers we served in a day. We didn't know how much money we took off customers; we didn't know how many items we sold to our customers. So they built in a system which revolved around how many customers you could serve in one man hour and how many staff you actually needed.

They recommended that the staff levels could be changed to save costs by reducing staff at slack periods and staffing up at busier times. In addition they recommended a system of shop-based control which allowed the shop managers a greater ability to regulate their own direct costs. Some £1 million in savings were estimated to have been saved by this exercise, which involved 400 redundancies – a programme unprecedented in the company.

The trading decline continued, however. In 1982 turnover dropped to £91.2 million and trading profit to £3.7 million: in 1982 the figures were £82.5 million and £3.5 million. By 1981 the financial press were regretting the sales and profit decline but commenting on the impressive financial management of the Group which had mitigated the affects of the situation through the low borrowings, cost reduction and strict cash management.

An Impetus for Change

There had already been a recognition that Fosters shops needed updating. In the late 1970s the company had commissioned the shop designers Fitch, who had worked on Burtons' new-shop design, to design a Fosters refit and since that time there had been a gradual changeover to what became known as the 'Fitch image' shops. There was some evidence of an increase in sales after shops had been refitted but only of the order of 10 per cent. Barry Davison said:

I was not happy with our return on capital expenditure but I was told [by Fosters' retail management] that we had to spend just to stand still. As an accountant I was not happy about spending money on which I was not getting a return.

It was in 1981 that Davison recruited as Group Financial Director John Fallon, who had been with Burtons. Fallon was able to confirm the comparatively poor performance of Fosters and described the affect on Davison:

People like myself came in and told him [Davison] that Burtons had made something like 40 per cent out of a refit and he came back and questioned us about that, and he said that he had been prepared to accept 5 or 10 per cent as a benchmark as that's what they have been telling me I should expect, but I'm not satisfied with that any longer – I want something that is going to provide me with 40 per cent.

Fallon's arrival also appeared to be something of a catalyst in other business areas. As already indicated, there was growing disillusionment about some of the recent acquisitions. It was shortly after Fallon's arrival that both Discount for Beauty and Staff Facilities were disposed of, recovering some £258,000. The two subsidiaries had been making losses for most of their time with the group and John Fallon explained that 'the weight of opinion from those in the business was that we had to get rid of these subsidiaries'. However, the decision was not actually taken. John Fallon commented:

There is a principle within the trade which is sunk cost, which means we have spent so much we can't get out now. I don't subscribe to that view. So when I arrived I just said 'we've got to get rid of these subsidiaries', and suddenly the decision was taken. I didn't take the decision. I was like the matchstick on the top of the pile. It just needed my opinion to help the decision to get taken.

There remained the major problem, however, of improving the performance of Menswear.

The Stratford Meeting

Barry Davison decided to convene a management meeting over the weekend of 12 – 14 June 1981 at the Hilton Hotel in Stratford. The briefing document for the weekend shows that Friday afternoon and evening were to be spent reviewing the existing situation and the rest of the weekend attempting to resolve future 'objectives' which included 'market position', and more detailed plans of action. The meeting started as planned. The Friday was a review of the position, with each of the executives making a presentation about their own area of responsibility. The meeting began with a presentation by Melvyn Taylor on the financial position:

> I presented some projections of what would happen if we continued to decline at the rate we were doing.

Others recall that initial presentation as a good deal more dramatic:

> Melvyn had extrapolated that if the trends we were experiencing carried on then he forecast the demise of the business.

and

> Taylor had projected a rate of decline that would send them into a loss within months.

There then followed a discussion of the market position of the company led by Richard Haynes. Haynes based his presentation on the market research into customers perceptions of Fosters he had commissioned on his arrival in 1980. The report had been available since June 1980 and had already been discussed by Board members. As already seen, it amounted to an indictment that the company's trading image was out-of-date and no longer appealed to the market business was supposed to be aiming for. By 1983 managers in the company liked to recall that the research report led to their changing of the policies of the company, but the fact was that it had been available to managers for a year before its findings began to be considered.

Haynes's presentation was not simply a statement of the research findings. It also interpreted these as he saw them affecting operations and requiring action. He advocated the company building on its reputation amongst older men for casual clothes but remedying the negative perceptions of customers and potential customers. In particular his proposed strategy document argued:

> Our prices and discounting policies make the merchandise sound cheap to our non-customers. Non-customers see Fosters as a traditional old-fashioned organization, selling poor quality at cheap prices. Except at sale times, customers ask 'How do I look?' before 'How much is it?' All our promotion concentrates on price and price-cutting before style.

He went on to question the company's market and competitive position, advocating the need for greater market segmentation and arguing that Fosters could not hope to relate to the younger 18–25 age group. In effect this was arguing that the gradual changes to more fashionable clothes over the previous six years had been strategically unsuccessful. His recommendations included the following:

- Redefine our target as C2D, married women and men over 25.
- Develop our trading image to meet the aspirations of our target market.

The argument was that Fosters had allowed itself to drift into a market position that was ill defined. The business had not set about selecting a target market so much as sold merchandise of a particular sort and picked up customers as it was able. His advocated position was asking the company to accept that it could not really cater for the younger, really fashion-conscious man of whatever socio-economic group, and was asking managers to accept explicitly that women were important customers as buyers of clothes for men. His strategy paper went on to propose operational changes he regarded as necessary to achieve this re-positioning.

As the Friday meeting proceeded each of the functional heads also presented their views. Managers recalled how defensive this was:

> This was where you saw the fragmentation. The senior people were not so much saying what we can do together but tending to defend their own territory. I include myself in all this saying 'it's not us, it's you lot.'

and:

> We went through everyone's area in the country and no one admitted they had a problem. Buyers would say it's the shops, and the shops would say it's nothing to do with us, it's the crap you send us; and there's nothing wrong with the distribution and nothing wrong with the salesmen.

Mike Adams explained Barry Davison's role in this:

> BGD was trying hard to sit back and let things evolve around him. And learn and listen. He was looking and saying what was happening to other retailers: we were behind the times, they are doing this, haven't you seen Burtons; Ralph Halpern this and Ralph Halpern that. He was seeing outside and searching very hard to find what he should be doing inside Foster Menswear. The buyers were challenging him. They were saying 'Come out and go to

Burtons at Stratford and you find a garment and I will find an equally good
one at Fosters. It's the environment we are trying to stock them in.'

By Saturday the meeting had become not only defensive but began to get
heated. In particular the attacks were becoming focused on the shop
environment and on shop management. Brian Wood's recollection was
that

> It went fairly amicably to dinner. I remember walking through to dinner with
> Barry; we were having a discussion about arrangements for lunch at HQ –
> who should be able to eat in the executive dining room – but there was wine
> drunk at dinner.

After dinner, when the meeting re-convened it became more aggressive.
One story, in particular, was told by a number of the managers:

> The retail guys took a lot of flak during Saturday. Brian (Wood) was being
> fairly vociferous in the discussion and he kept being told we have these other
> points of view and we're all having our two-penn'orth: and the Chairman
> jumped on Brian.

Brian Wood recalled:

> Barry said 'If you don't like it you can go'. My reply was 'You surely don't
> mean that sir', but he said 'Go'. I went to bed. Norman Phillips came to see
> me and eventually persuaded me to come down. I stayed drinking with BGD
> till three. He said I shouldn't have got up and walked out. I said 'But at least I
> stand up to you', but I should have shut up and bit my tongue. You can't beat
> him.

By the end of the Saturday night little progress had been made on resolving
what could be done. The general view had developed, however, that the
retail shop environment was a major problem.
    Richard Haynes believed that Sunday morning was a turning point.

> On the Sunday morning we all had terrible hangovers, as the Saturday night
> we had all stayed up chewing the cud and drinking. I can remember distinctly
> saying on Sunday morning 'Chairman all that anybody had been talking
> about here is tweaking. In my opinion if we ignore his piece of research and
> don't do some of the things it has suggested then it will all disappear with us
> all losing our positions. In my view we have got to radically reposition this
> business'. This is where without Barry Davison the thing would have gone
> under because he said 'Put your money where your mouth is: you can chair a

strategic planning committee and we will not appoint people who are entrenched members of this board'.

Others present remember the meeting as resolving nothing much at all but rather as a sort of 'blood-letting', or giving rise to fragmentation publicly that was then resolved more privately:

> Having put up the smokescreen publicly, each facet would then privately come back and examine their own consciences but they would not change radically.

Looking back on it most managers in Fosters in 1983 said they did not think a great deal was achieved at Stratford and a good deal of bad feeling was caused. Certainly the minutes of the meeting, the short-list of conclusions and the action points show little in the way of major decisions. There was a recognition that 'our styles and values are not perceived by too many of our potential C2D customers' and that this was made worse by the quality of the display and promotional material which 'tended to degenerate the merchandise'. The main problem on merchandise was seen as a gradual rise in price when competitors were becoming more price-aggressive; it was felt that this might be the result of a 'preoccupation with margins'. As far as the shops were concerned the view was that there was little uniformity of image and that sales staff over-emphasized 'approaching customers, thus dissuading them from browsing'. On the personnel side it was agreed that the company had an 'urgent need for management development'.

The Chairman's summary at the foot of the minutes was as follows:

1. In the light of the current trading climate, would better results be achieved from new lower prices rather than from discounts?
2. The severe economic climate hits our traditional lowly-paid customers hardest.

As for action, there was the decision to set up the Strategic Planning Committee, but the main decision was to 'establish leading value lines at new lower prices in each department' and 'market this concept'. In short, to do rather better what they had been doing before. Whilst managers thought the meeting was frustrating, in that it decided little, some regarded it as significant:

> We were like a rudderless tanker without any firm direction. By late 1980, early 1981, we knew that we needed a new direction. We knew that this

direction would lead us to disaster. The conference in Stratford was the turning point.

The meeting had no immediate impact on financial performance, however. Summer results were poor and October's were particularly disappointing. As a result, the advertising budget was raised: 'by December we were breaking even but having to spend £100,000 a month to do it'.

The Strategic Planning Committee

The Strategic Planning Committee was set up by Barry Davison and chaired by Richard Haynes. It consisted of most of the middle management at head office from the merchandise, retail and distribution functions – and some field managers as well as two junior directors. Quite deliberately, Barry Davison ommitted Brian Wood and Norman Phillips; he argued that they were over-committed to past practice and therefore likely to be too defensive. Wood and Phillips resented the omission. Brian Wood was particularly bitter:

> Barry said we had our chance and needed young fresher people to have a look at it. I still [in 1983] don't agree with that. The reason I did not agree with it was because, although I had gone along with the Fitch image, my merchandise views were not adopted. [He is here talking about his advocacy of change in 1980.] Norman Phillips accepted it much better than me. I didn't accept it at all.

Later he was to add:

> When you have lobbied for change as much as I had and then get the situation reversed on you, it is a little hard to take. I would accept I did not adapt as much as I possibly could: my defensive mechanisms coming into play. The criticism from the Strategic Planning Committee perhaps was a good thing for me; it was a kick in the backside. It also gave me time to re-think the whole situation, but I was still confident that my merchandise views could be proven correct in the end.

Norman Phillips made his opposition known to Davison and the rest of the management. Mike Adams explained that:

> Sales people and Buyers were dragged out of their departments to sit on the Committee: and Norman Phillips would come up and say 'how the hell do you expect me to run the buying department like this?', but Barry backed Richard.

The first meeting of the Committee on 24 June 1981 opened with a presentation from Haynes of the current situation facing the company and was followed by a discussion of the market research. The minutes record the 'key points' that were made in the discussion; they are replicated in full below.

1. *Colour Blocking*
   It was felt that colour blocking at point of sale would enhance displays and merchandise appeal.

2. *Managerial Flexibility*
   Although the need for centralisation in a company the size of Foster Menswear was recognised, it is felt that there is also scope for giving greater flexibility to encourage initiative amongst our better Branch Managers.

3. *Flexibility of Opening Hours*
   A more flexible policy to opening hours and hours worked by staff was thought to be beneficial in capturing customers who may be around outside normal shop hours, e.g. on nights of late opening by supermarkets.

4. *Windows*
   Where there is space to browse within a shop, the window should convey an image of how the customer will look if he buys our clothes.

5. *Space Utilisation*
   It was felt that many of our windows would produce a better return if much of the space was used as a sales area.

6. *Rentals*
   It was pointed out that for a standard size shop measuring 20' wide × 60' deep that the first 20' of depth would account for 50% of the rental.

7. *Window Dressing*
   It was felt that windows are currently dressed primarily because they happen to be there. There would appear to be no difference between the performance of shops with large windows and those with small windows.

8. *Customer Complaints*
   There is a need for separate recording of customer complaints even though the merchandise is not returned to Head Office. It was felt that this could be achieved within existing systems.

9. *Sizing*
   The non-standardisation of sizing within and across our merchandise ranges is seen as a drawback and an unnecessary complication.

10. *Pricing*
    Whilst discussing the fact that our pricing edge has been eroded, it was pointed out that where prices are similar, people will tend to shop where the quality is thought to be better.

11. *Suits*
There was major criticism of the suit range because of its poor quality, cut and value.

12. *Current Promotions*
Current promotions were criticised because they did not appear to be increasing customer traffic, but they do appear to be an aid to the salesman in increasing the value of individual sales.

13. *Sales Staff Approach to Customers*
Whilst acknowledging the apparent desire of most customers to browse before being approached, the need was recognised to teach a flexibility of selling approach to our staff.

14. *Group Service Companies*
The service which Marshall Lake Properties and their Group Service Companies can give is limited because of shortage of staff.

15. *Clothing Technician*
In order to improve the quality of cut and fit of many of the garments from our own factories, there is an urgent requirement to employ a clothing technician.

16. *Training Adviser*
As shops are refitted in line with the new branch environment, there will be a need to retrain staff. It is felt that this need can be filled by the use of an itinerant training adviser.

17. *Price Changes*
Concern was felt at the fact that prices on current lines could be affected by changes in the rates of exchange and margin requirements and not by the market forces which help to fix the prices in the first place. This is a deterrent to garments being priced in the factories where they are made.

18. *Initiative*
It was felt that a centralisation of the business and a somewhat old-fashioned attitude to staff tends to dampen initiative which could otherwise be harnessed to the benefit of the company.

The most striking observations are:

- the highly operational level of discussions; there was much criticism of the way the business was run but little of it addressed issues such as market positioning or competitors' action at a strategic level;
- there was almost no criticism of the merchandise or the merchandise management except as regards suits; the basic traditional ranges were not criticized;
- the time horizons of comments were short: most of the comments were geared to action that could be taken quickly.

This discussion was followed by another on the objectives for the future and the proposal by Haynes that design consultants should be briefed to 'submit ideas which will encourage customer flow and turnover within our branches'. This was agreed though there is no record of extensive discussion of it; Haynes was designated as responsible for drawing up a design brief.

The next meeting of the Strategic Planning Committee was on 7 July. The first part of the meeting reviewed progress on some of the operational improvements discussed at the first meeting. There then followed the submission of a design brief prepared by Haynes; there is no record in the minutes of discussion on this. The meeting went on to discuss the request by Davison that it should take responsibility for the trial re-merchandising of two branches at Chester and Cardiff. The remaining three meetings of the Strategic Planning Committee in July, August and September were solely concerned with the activities at Chester and Cardiff.

There are two entirely different views about the committee's activities by Fosters' managers, even amongst those who sat on it. One view is that it was of very little use and achieved nothing; that it was something of a waste of time:

> It was frustrating as the Committee did not produce anything. There were specialists from far too many fields for what were broad meetings that we were having. The meeting was convened, for the sake of argument, to discuss Chester. The end result as far as I was concerned was to know what the branch was going to be stocking and when the opening date was, and everything to do with distribution. The meeting itself was concerned with the branch not distribution. Someone would suggest something, say the labels that the staff were wearing, and all these specialists sitting around, including me with my distribution hat on, and for the first hour they would be discussing what size the labels should be. There would be groups sitting around who would not be interested in the subject of labels. I was sitting there thinking 'I could be working now'. It would have been better to call different meetings for the different specialists. The initial intention was to propose to Foster Menswear Board how we could provide for a successful new image and to prove it by refitting two branches. One of the funny things about it was that you came away from the meeting not clear as to what decisions you had made to contribute to the new image. Behind the scenes something would happen. Those decisions came about as a result of certain people getting together whether it be the Marketing Director or whoever.

One of the directors believed that, in any case, those on the committee would have been unable to face the magnitude of discussions of wholesale strategic change:

They tried very hard to look into the future but they could not look far enough into the future. They would not be aware of the financial investment required. If you quoted some of the figures to them they would be frightened. They produced in Chester and Cardiff what they thought the customer wanted based on their own experience.

If the results of the Chester and Cardiff exercise are considered, then certainly such views are well founded. There was only a marginal sales increase in the two shops. Some managers were critical of the pricing policy attempted in which net prices rather than discounted prices were shown on goods: Haynes had the view that a continual emphasis on price reductions created a bad image. Others, including Brian Wood, argued that there was no room, then, to show any mark-down at all if it became necessary. The pricing policy introduced at Chester and Cardiff was, according to Wood, not succesful:

> It went national from those branches and it really was a failure: it didn't generate anything.

Haynes, however, interpreted the Chester and Cardiff experiments as important in so far as

> We re-merchandised with absolutely pristine merchandise, and above all else what that showed was that if you only change one element in the retail equation you will not have a success.

However, Haynes was equally convinced that the re-merchandising of the shops was not the major achievement of the Committee. Rather, the two main achievements were first to endorse the view he had already arrived at, that the company had to undertake a much more fundamental change than anyone was discussing or was capable of implementing.

> It was a growing realization that tinkering with things was not going to solve anything, and the figures, and the success of the Burton group – the fact that they had taken a radical step.

There are, however, no records on the minutes of recollections by other members of the Committee that the idea or consequences of 'radical repositioning' were ever discussed explicitly, nor do other members of the Committee recall that it was. Nor was it a view held widely by other members of the board. There was a view, as expressed by Norman Phillips, that:

We needed to have an identity, rather than just be another high-street shop – rather than a conglomerate of bits and pieces.

However, this did not necessarily mean 'radical repositioning': there was a historical position to be built on and developed.

What appears to be clearer is that Haynes saw the Committee as a political vehicle for advancing and legitimizing his ideas:

The only way I could get my views listened to was to have 60 people behind me. [The sixty being the committee members and their associates, for example in other retail areas.]

And he also saw it as a forum for canvassing his own approach;

When you got into discussion you all felt the same anyway. They just hadn't had it put this way before.

Or as one retail manager explained of the way Haynes guided the deliberations:

Richard Haynes had got it in his mind, a sort of overall image he wanted to portray and he wanted us to achieve.

According to Haynes, the second and most positive outcome of this committee was the decision to brief new design consultants. However, from the evidence of the minutes of that meeting, there appears to have been very little discussion within the committee of such a brief before it was drawn up and no detailed discussion in the committee when it was drawn up. It appears that the impetus for the brief itself came from Haynes. It was also drafted by Haynes and, whilst discussed with other members of the board, including Brian Wood and Barry Davison, it was progressed by Haynes. As Davison said: 'He was the one who was pulling it all together.'

Intervention and Resistance

Four design consultants were briefed to present to the company. The design brief, including much of the same marketing background as had been presented at Stratford, asked the designers to return with presentations to meet the following objectives for Foster Menswear:

a) to improve market share profitability in the C2D market.
b) to be recognised as the leading retailer of modern mens clothes offering up to date styles at the best value for the C2D market.
c) to create a retail environment where our target market feel comfortable to shop and browse.

The brief required the presentations to concentrate on the following:

a. Corporate image
b. Exterior appearance of our shops
c. Window displays
d. Interior design, furnishing and fixturing
e. Merchandise presentation – ticketing and signing
f. Customer promotions
g. The removal of physical or mental barriers to people coming into our shops.

It was essentially a brief to do with the physical appearance of the shops: it did not specify that the designers should address themselves to merchandise mix or staff. None the less, the brief contained sufficient indication that Fosters were being 'left behind' in the high street and clearly stated that customers regarded Fosters as 'selling poor quality at cheaper prices'. Set against this, the emphasis on style indicated a requirement for a substantial change in retail image.

The designers made presentations to the Board and the full Strategic Planning Committee, some 40 people in all. It came down to two possibilities: the Peters organization which had already done work for Adams Childrenswear, and David Saunders Design. Richard Haynes was in hospital at the time and had to see videos of the presentations. He described the developments as he saw them:

Before the presentations were made I knew who I wanted to work with; but Barry Davison was very impressed by Peters who did the original Adams Stores. Barry and I had a meeting at the hospital and we agreed we should appoint the two companies and give them two shops each. I wrote to these two companies saying 'you're going to get two shops each'; and Barry Davison came back and said he had changed his mind: he was going to pay Saunders to do two shops, but Peters did not agree with my marketing approach, and Barry was going to pay him to do a study to come up with his own brief from which he would do a design. It is the only time I have ever put my job on the line and we decided to appoint one consultant. I stood up to Barry – I knew what I wanted and stuck out for it.

To Haynes, the commitment was to the marketing brief. It was a commitment that, evidently, Davison did not share as totally. His idea was that Peters should be allowed to consider if the repositioning inherent within the Haynes brief was wise or necessary. The expression of reserve by Peters on this was apparently enough to raise significant doubts in Davison's mind. The 'radical repositioning' proposed by Haynes was more difficult for Davison to accept and many of the ideas continued to be difficult for others – notably Norman Phillips – to accept and comprehend.

David Saunders took a central part in the events that were to follow. His work was not simply constrained by his brief on design: he conceived of his task as one of persuading the managers to adopt a different approach to the menswear business and that involved him in the politics of change. He explained:

> The first thing I did was to call the Chairman by his first name: I happened to be an equal and he's got to listen to me – that's what he's paying me for.

He detected in his initial discussions with managers that the company had reached a point where they recognized the need for change; the problem was that they did not know how to change:

> It was great: they had already had their culture shock. Barry Davison had already done his 'it's not true' bit. With Fosters it was great because it was not someone planting me in: they were desparate to get someone and suck them into them to learn all they could.

In particular he found a momentum for change amongst the retailers:

> I gave Richard Haynes a programme and said 'I would like half a day with your Sales Director, half a day with an Area Manager and half a day with a Shop Manager, so I could get three different views from three different levels and find out how far down the line does this long-felt want go? And of course what we found was that at manager level there was total frustration. For years they had wanted to change; they had lost heart; they thought it was dirty and tatty. . . . What we have done is create the pivot which they can relate to, and the fantastic thing is that the retailer has been waiting for it for years. In most towns they looked worse than the local traders so they grabbed it with open arms. When I met Brian Wood we had rapport because he was an ex-Hepworth man. It gave him confidence that I knew something about retail – about men's multiple retailing. When I first met him he was giving me his version about the shock as a result of this report. And I think the biggest shock must have been for the Chairman. He was handed the Chair at a peak and it started going down. He had to show profits and

everything was geared to making money; so Barry Davison would not spend any money on any maintenance. He had shops where a third of the shop couldn't be used. They were absolutely disgusting shops. The retail side knew that. They said we are trying to sell nice clothes out of garbage tips.

His concept of repositioning of Fosters was based on the need to attract what he saw as a missing age group:

In the research it comes out quite clearly that they had a big back-to-school department; that when people got to 14, although they were spending Mum's money, they had a say in it, and the last place they wanted to go back to was Fosters: they wanted to go somewhere else. So Fosters lost them until they were 25 when they were married with two children and had a hole in the seat of their pants and wanted distress purchase of a pair of trousers.

His designs, in this sense, did not address themselves to the brief: his view was that the under-25 age group could not and should not be ignored, but that the shops did not have to be exclusively for them. He argued that:

The major change that has taken place in mens retailing is linked to mental change expectations. People are living longer and therefore don't perceive themselves as being middle-aged until much later. Also much younger children see themselves as being adolescent much earlier. Effectively this means that the 8/10 to 35/40 age groups are now buying similar sorts of products.

His argument not only ran counter to the creative brief, but was contrary to the perceived wisdom in the industry, where Burtons by this time had led the way in building their business on age segmentation. However, the managers in Fosters did not talk about the activities of Saunders in terms of this shift of emphasis, but rather in terms of the designs he showed them; designs for shop interiors, windows, posters and facias, which were seen as excitingly new and colourful.

Saunders began in 1982 by testing his proposed shop design in a new store acquired in Peterborough. His initial presentation to the Board and the Strategic Planning Committee, and his implementation of it at Peterborough envisaged, not just shop design, but a change in all aspects of the shopping environment. For example:

One of the pivotal things we did for them was to insist that it should not be price-orientated shop. In the past shops had been clobbered with notices [showing discount prices] detracting from any quality of the garment anyway.

The staff inside the shop also had to change:

> We could see where they should go. They had not got to break any new ground, as Burtons had done it. The one strength of Fosters was that they had traditionally been in casual clothes which is where all the market is at the moment, but as you go down you find that all these people who are selling it are very formal. They are doing casual advertisements but it was very formal.

Shop assistants were to wear casual clothes and they were told they should allow shoppers to browse rather than 'sell' to them. Only managers were to wear a suit. In the past all staff had worn suits but Saunders made a discovery here that affected his view not only of the merchandise, but also of the perception of shop staff of the Fosters business:

> We found that all the managers had to wear suits and they were all wearing Burton or Hepworth suits. When we asked why, they said our suits are rubbish. You wear them two days and they all screw up or fall apart. So how could they have confidence in selling suits?

In these early days Saunders requested, and was given, authority over shop design, layout, merchandise, selection, posters, staff and all aspects of trading in the test stores.

> When we tested the first shop we selected the merchandise. They laid all the stock out in the warehouse and we went round and said what we wanted. And we said we are not interested in the 45-year-old man; we kept out the stuff that looked terrible. We had three shops to test for a start-off and we had total god-like control which I insisted from the word go. We wouldn't change anything for six weeks.

This direct involvement was resented by the buyers in particular: as Norman Phillips explained:

> Saunders must be a good designer but I resented him getting involved in the merchandise – not his viewpoint. I resented the idea that because it was an outside view it was a guarantee of success.

The Peterborough shop was, however, an immediate success, with the sales performance well above expectations; and Saunders was retained to extend the 'new image' shops. The partnership between him and Haynes became a central force for change in the company over the next year. Davison appears to have remained somewhat removed from the early stages of the changes whilst giving support to the activities of Haynes and Saunders.

After the success of Peterborough, many managers increasingly came to believe that Saunders could effect the sort of changes they admitted they had not themselves been able to perceive:

> Self-flagellation had been going on around the building and had prevented people taking clear-sighted views of what they should do. The only person with a clear-sighted view of what should happen was Saunders.

If the retail side of the business was ready to change as the shop conversions went ahead, the changes were not so evident in the buying side. The situation worsened when Saunders became involved. His view was that, whilst in the past, the shops environment was inadequate, with his new image, it was now the merchandise that was unsuitable.

> The thing we are trying to exhibit, the thing we are trying to sell has got to be the best thing. That shop is a promise: when they go in there the merchandise has got to reflect that promise; it can't be another promise. You could send a buyer to a Burtons shop and he would come back and tell you that we had all the stuff they had got. He was convinced that they were equally as good. All I knew was that we were going to design shops for a particular slice of the market and their clothes would have to change to be in that market. In the end, we had a big meeting; it was the board of Foster Menswear and myself. And Barry Davison said 'what the hell are we going to do? And I said that if you like I will go out and show you what I think you ought to have. He spoke to Norman Phillips and said 'He has offered to help us. What do you think?' and Norman said 'OK', so Barry said 'Give him £25,000'. It was the Menswear Exhibition in London. I went down with Tony Gray and he walked round with an order pad. We wrote out orders there and then. The buyers did then actually get roused up; they had got the message by then.

There was resistance from the Merchandise Department. In Norman Phillips' opinion the views expressed were not well thought through, often wasteful and gave rise to confused merchandise planning.

> They came along with the preoccupation that spending money would solve everything. In 30 years with the company, you can become blinkered; but I just could not tolerate what I saw as waste. . . . Anything that was new was great. Richard would come and say 'we're having BRMB tee shirts – its new'. I just continued picking up the bits of other people. . . . These two would go to BGD and say 'it's new, its great'. It angered me that I wasn't involved and I knew I would be left to pick up the pieces.

This resentment that Haynes and Saunders appeared to be dominating the developments was made the worse when, at the opening of the redesigned Bull Street branch in Birmingham, Haynes publicly praised the various department for their help in the venture but forgot to include the buyers in his praises.

The other resistance, initially, was from the buyers themselves. Although it was the retailers who had been criticized at Stratford:

> . . . it swung to buying and the buyers took a lot of flak, as it was then said that the merchandise we were buying was staid, not imaginative, there was a lack of coordination and cohesion.

It was criticism the buyers resented:

> You're not going to give in and say I've got this completely wrong. That doesn't happen; it's not human nature. There was a period when there was fragmentation. No one wanted to be held as the prime responsibility for the decline. It took the form of a lot of tension. The lack of morale down this corridor was very bad. People thought that their judgement, their flair, their knowledge, of the trade, their ability to buy, was being questioned. They could point to eight or nine years of sustained growth, and most of the buyers at that time had been with the company certainly since the mid-1970s. So a buyer would say he'd done a good job for that time. We were great lads, what turned us into idiots? And the question was being asked 'Are you the right people?' To an extent we should have changed. We should have looked forward and said 'What we are doing now? Will it last for ever?'

The same problem, and causes, were given by Brian Wood:

> To change them (the buyers) was very difficult: they had so much success in the past. To change was a hell of a move: it was like turning a tanker.

Given that the merchandise managers had, perhaps more so than other managers in 1980, seen the competitive pressures for merchandise repositioning, the resistance to change from them was of particular interest. Richard Haynes observed:

> To change anything is a huge problem. If you have got a pair of trousers in the range and you are selling 20,000 a year and I say to you drop them, there's a fear that says 'Christ if I drop those what do I do? I know the styling, cloth, the supplier; if I go somewhere else I am going into uncharted territory.' We said to the the buyers 'You are going to spend 50% of your time buying for 490 shops and the other 50% of your time buying for 10

shops.' So they found that what we wanted to do was a bloody nuisance. It was taking them into uncharted territory.

Haynes himself was able to take a different stance with responsibility for the new image shops:

> I made a conscious decision when we decided to do something radical to shut myself off. I was just not concerned with what was happening in the grotty old shops. I targeted my thoughts entirely on the new concept. It had 100 per cent of my attention. Other people in the business did not have that and could not have that.

Certainly as far as the buyers were concerned, it was very difficult to change, both because of limited resources and also because, to them, the direction of change was still not clear.

> We watched morale slide. They [the buyers] started to question their own judgement. They start to question whether they can ever do anything right. There were also physical limitations: we didn't have many staff to handle a wide range of products. We should have recruited more staff and now we have done, from four buyers up to nine buyers. I would say that Norman [Phillips] failed to keep that morale up and possibly did not define clearly enough the direction in which we should be going, but that could have been because the board were unable to decide. The buyer does not work in a vacuum. I don't think he [Phillips] came down clearly enough on what our market was. They [the buyers] would ask me for advice and I would say 'That's the way I see the market', but in some cases I would be saying that unilaterally rather than knowing the policy of the board – but I suspect that for some time the board had no policy. I did take it up with Norman at the time that I thought morale was appalling – and bearing in mind that the Chairman is a man who wants success today, I felt that he was asking for something that we were not physically able to do, because of lack of staffing and clear definitions.

There was also genuine confusion amongst the buyers because the changes were being driven by a business conception promoted by Haynes and Saunders that was quite alien to their experience and, in their view, lacking in clarity. They had been brought up as buyers over years when there were clear and unambiguous expectations and procedures for buyers. They were now being expected to respond to what they saw as ill defined, unfounded proposals by people who knew little about the Fosters business.

Mike Adams was sympathetic as regards the problems and attitudes of the merchandise team and pointed out that Richard Haynes did not always appreciate the detailed merchandise planning required to change the mix:

They now point out the success of the Saunders shops, but they forget that the merchandise in those shops was organized during Norman's era – but Norman was stubborn. Richard does not see the problem through, there's a lot of I's not dotted and T's not crossed.

It is not difficult to see why the buyers were resistant to much of what Saunders and Haynes wanted. Not only were many of the demands difficult to implement because of lack of staff and lead times for merchandise, but they were being asked to reduce buying quantities to provide for more stylish fashion-orientated garments, buy branded merchandise and thus accept lower margins, look for 'good value' rather than low prices, and all this for a target market that was different and not clearly defined. It was not the Fosters approach to buying. Norman Phillips illustrated this:

> The best example I can give is Levi's. There's just no profit in it. Levi's were saying constantly 'We want more space'. Sure you need it represented in the range but there would never be a time, given their margins, when they would generate the profit.

Richard Haynes saw the problem differently:

> Gross margin as a percentage became an absolute tablet of stone. If you weren't making 164 per cent mark-up – it got as high as that – if you weren't making the margin, then you were breaking the tablet of stone. I had a hell of a battle with Norman Phillips; he seemed totally incapable of understanding what actually mattered was margin times volume, not margin on its own; that it was pointless making 160 per cent on something and selling two when you could make 140 per cent on something and sell them. Although they strenuously denied this, it was one of the reasons why it took so long to get branded merchandise into the shops.

Moreover, it was becoming clear in a very practical way that the power of the merchandise department was not what it was; more resources were being channelled into retailing and the objections by Phillips to the demands of Saunders and Haynes were being overruled by Davison.

According to his colleagues, Norman Phillips became more and more isolated politically and increasingly antagonistic to Saunders and Haynes. Haynes saw Phillips and the buyers as intransigent and myopic as they resisted change. Phillips saw Haynes as lacking an understanding of the detailed planning needed for merchandise change.

It appears, however, that other members of the Merchandise Department began to change their attitudes due to a combination of influences. Certainly they were facing pressure from Haynes and Saunders with apparent backing from Davison; by the end of 1982 it also became clear that the 'new image' shops were indeed generating more business. Tony Gray, by now New Projects Manager working with Haynes and Saunders on the implementation of refitting, said:

> It was the success of trade at Christmas last year [1982] which actually proved things were going to work. The best way of crushing doubt is to crush it with success and the thing was more successful than many cynics thought.

He also explained some of the internal difficulties in the Merchandise Department:

> We had a merchandise director who was extremely defensive in supporting what had been done instead of supporting change. He was genuinely looking for help but did not like the answers he was getting. To put it to extremes to make the point. We were providing our . . . the body cover business . . . a cheap type of garment which is bought by someone who needs to wear a garment, not because he cares about what he wears. I would be advocating that that was not appropriate to our target market. In the early days of the new project the buyers were seeing the market in a very different way from me: there was quite a lot of cynicism involved on the basis of saying we've seen this all before. We had some very stormy episodes. I gave you the impression that Norman would not back me and this is not accurate. He did but he was the most undiplomatic man you've ever come across; but on three occasions last autumn [1982] I could not get the kind of commitment that I felt we should be giving to the new shops and was forced, through an inability to put it right myself, to go to Norman Phillips. On three occasions he had the buyers together and made it very, very clear that their jobs were on the line. That if the thing did not work they would not be involved in the spring. They were saying 'no' because they did not think it would sell, they had not got the budget to buy it, you name it. The historical influence of Norman was creating that resistance.
>
> He [Norman] showed signs of tension. He was not very dependable: he was unpredictable. You couldn't predict how he would react and it was very damaging to confidence in the buying team. They were inhibited because of him. Rather than make the wrong decision they would prefer to make no decision. Norman would back me at crisis point but nothing else, not on a day-to-day basis. You can imagine what the atmosphere was like; it was absolutely appalling.

The stance taken by Phillips was not seen by his colleagues within his department as suitable in the circumstances either. Norman Phillips had been appointed to the main board of the company and as such had responsibility for merchandise policy throughout the company; but as one of the menswear buyers saw it:

> He was a buyer rather than a Merchandise Director – not making policies but being involved in range content. It would have been better if he had been director of purchasing rather than director of merchandise.

Despite the appointment of Norman Phillips to the Group Board, by the beginning of 1983 overcoming his resistance was seen as crucial to company recovery by Davison. Davison set about trying to recruit a new Merchandise Director for Foster Menswear. He was urged by Richard Haynes 'to pay whatever was necessary to get the best' and actively sought to recruit a senior buyer from Burtons. It was done, in Davison's view despite the unwillingness of Norman Phillips to cooperate, a view not shared by Phillips who explained the developments as follows:

> Barry and I went down to interview one of the Burtons guys; we spent about three hours with him in the London flat. Afterwards he [Davison] asked 'What's your viewpoint?' Well I think I said something like 'I think there's something there'. And his response was 'OK you think he's no good!. That developed into him not wanting me to be involved.

Barry Davison tried to attract this candidate and his attempts further annoyed Phillips:

> He [Davison] said 'Take him out to the Far East and get him involved in the next range'. He wasn't even working for us! What am I supposed to tell suppliers? 'Tell them he's a consultant'. I refused. What about my credibility and that of my agents?

The job was in fact offered to the Burtons buyer and a 'celebratory' welcome dinner was arranged for him. On the day the dinner was to take place, the new man turned the job down. Mike Adams believed that Barry Davison dealt with Norman Phillips 'very badly'. Richard Haynes also felt it was handled badly but believed Norman Phillips could easily have circumvented problems:

> Norman had the perfect out. He was on the main board and knew that Barry wanted to bring someone fresh into Foster Menswear. He could have remained on the main Board and said 'OK, bring someone in beneath me' and then have ridden on someone else's success; but Norman chose not to do that. He believed he had been discredited both within and outside his own department.

Such a position was not seen as tenable by Norman Phillips who saw the situation quite differently:

> When I got on to the main board, it was the biggest disillusionment of my life that there was only one voice. Colleagues were protecting their own patches, and I had expected that the non-executives would play a more important part.

He believed he had the responsibility to argue his case but was increasingly frustrated by what he saw as an unwillingness on the part of Davison to listen to anyone from within the business.

In May 1983 Norman Phillips resigned. It was a decision seen by many of the managers as inevitable though regrettable. Mike Adams saw it as a mutual loss of confidence between Davison and Phillips:

> Norman accepted the need for change. Barry had not got the confidence that he could bring about that change; therefore it became a lack of confidence, one between the other.

Norman Phillips saw it as a matter of personal peace of mind:

> I just decided there was a better quality of life elsewhere. The moment that trust, confidence and credibility was being tampered with, then I decided I did not need the aggravation.

Other Business Operations

Although the concentration of activity was on Menswear in this period, elsewhere in the Group there were other developments, although again with the underlying difficulty of turning the activity into profitable gain. Adams Childrenswear was by 1983 making losses of around £1 million and a revision of strategy similar to that for the Menswear side was imminent. Millets of Bristol, which was making £400,000 p.a. on takeover, made £40,000 in 1982, although the commitment to that market remained and was signalled by the acquisition of Millets of Sutton in 1982 for £2.8 million, adding 17 shops to the Group. Dormie remained a profitable operation, though with diminishing sales; the decision was taken in 1982 to revitalize the rather old-fashioned image of the shops and a test of four branches was begun under 'Esquires' as a trading name with an updated, more stylish range of merchandise.

Profit decline had been stemmed in 1982: on declining sales, trading profit had been held at £3.5 million and, with sales of properties, profit before taxation had risen to £5 million (see table 5.3).

TABLE 5.3   *A summary of the financial performance 1981–1983 (a) and a summary of key financial ratios (b)*

	1980/1	1981/2	1982/3
(a)			
Turnover: retail sales (£m)	94.2	91.2	82.5
Trading profit (£m)	7.8	3.7	3.5
Surplus on sale of properties (£m)	1.2	1.1	1.5
Less interest (£m)	—	—	—
Profit before taxation (£m)	9.0	4.8	5.0
(b)			
Growth in turnover (%)	+5	−3	−10
Growth in trading (%)	−26	−53	−5
Trading profit as percentage of sales	8	4	4
Profit before tax as percentage of capital employed	26	13	12

Source: Foster Brothers Annual Reports

In 1982 the group also acquired a 75 per cent interest in 'Anglo American Retail Inc.' which had a controlling interest in 'National Shirt' and the Biny Clothing company of America, giving them a USA subsidiary with a coast-to-coast coverage of 280 shops and a turnover of around $100 million. By the end of 1982 this acquisition too was experiencing difficulties with a downturn in expected sales in the last quarter of the year as the American economy slumped; this was despite a conversion of over 60 of the shops to a chain called 'His Place' catering for the 18–25 age group which by the beginning of 1983 was contributing 40 per cent of the chain's sales. By late 1983 Barry Davison had asked David Saunders to redesign the 'His Place' shops again and by May of 1984 the early trials of this new image were showing encouraging signs of turnover growth.

As far as other business ventures were concerned, by this time managers claimed they had learned many lessons from the way they had handled previous attempts at diversification and acquisition. Fosters had valued the principle of internal promotion and the acquisitions were normally staffed by Menswear managers both as a reward and also because there was the real belief that the way Fosters operated was worth transposing and could best be done by the transfer of people. By 1983 managers claimed that this was not so. Nor was it just people. Fosters valued high degrees of central control on merchandise selection and distribution, and evolved systems that had proved to be successful for

Menswear over the years. These too were transferred to the acquisitions. By 1983 this too was seen to be inappropriate by senior Board members.

> Millets of Sutton will make half a million this year but we haven't had time to interfere with that yet. We went into businesses that were making money and said 'We can do it a damn sight better'. With Millets of Bristol we put all their stock onto a computerized stock feed. Now the differences between Millets Bristol and Millets Sutton is that at Bristol they have computerized stock feed and at Sutton they do not. Computerized stock feed is a very good thing when you get over a certain size but at Millets of Sutton the managers are so fleet of foot. Our most successful shop in Foster Menswear is where the manager is able to buy the stock himself – our shop at Barnstable. The centralized control at Fosters is not appropriate to acquisitions when there are small numbers of shops. We would be much better to help where we can with the economies of scale – with the buying of jeans – but I don't care what anyone says, a shop run by an 'owner–driver' – a good owner-driver – will make more money than a shop run by a manager on behalf of a big organization. There comes a time when you switch a small organization over and you try and put the system in but unless it's over a certain size it won't do any better; in fact it will probably do a lot worse.

And again:

> We thought we knew enough about retailing to retail anything. It shows how foolish you can be. Where you've got a person running his own business he is totally motivated. The people in Discount for Beauty were totally motivated to produce their own profit. It went straight into their pockets. We take over and we've got a big group concept and there isn't the same pot of gold for the man at the end. Switching to current situations, a very live situation is Millets. Millets in Bristol is being run very much like Fosters – all computer systems – and it's run by ex-Fosters people so it's got a very similar logic to the way we run here. It doesn't make a lot of profit. We then have Millets at Sutton which is really run in the same way as Discount for Beauty was, by the people who are totally motivated in their own little enterprise for their own ends, and it shows. There is a difficulty within a group to have the corporate logic but allow the entrepreneurial drive to materialize.

Organization and Management Change

The period 1981 to 1983 was one of difficulty and change for Fosters that imposed a good deal of strain on the Fosters management team. It was a strain acknowledged by Barry Davison in the 1983 annual report:

When trading is difficult and success is hard to come by, it is always a problem for the people working in the business to maintain their enthusiasm and dedication. We are lucky to have an incredibly loyal and hard-working group of employees who have withstood the traumas of poor results and reduced staffing levels and have responded with even greater efforts.

By 1982 and 1983 what were seen as major changes in organization design and systems of planning and control by the management were in hand. There was an influx of new managers at senior and middle levels from 1982 onwards. This included new directors at Adams, additional middle management in the accounting and buying functions in Menswear and, most significantly, early in 1984, a new Merchandise Director, who had been with Burtons and brought with him what Fallon described as 'a whole football team from Burtons, Top Shop and Harry Fenton'.

In 1983 the company set up a Management Board consisting of the managing director of each subsidiary together with certain senior managers representing central functions such as personnel and finance. Figure 5.4 illustrates the changed structure. This was seen by senior management as a means of achieving two changes. First, there was the need for better planning and strategic control. John Fallon was given the additional responsibility of 'corporate planning' and described how he envisaged the system of planning would work through the Management Board:

Once a year we have a fairly extensive planning review whereby subsidiaries submit a standard accounting package for three years. Having done that we have for the major subsidiaries a day's review with myself, the Chairman, and their management team. In looking at their financial plan they outline their proposals in terms of their strategy. Before they get to that stage they have had independent reviews internally: so you would have a merchandise team giving the merchandise thrust and a retail team giving the retail thrust and so on. Having done all that it is all pulled together into a Group strategy. Having done that the Management Board get together to thrash out where we are and what we want to do.

The second purpose of the introduction of the Management Board was to achieve greater decentralization of strategic responsibility. A typical view of many of the middle and senior management in Fosters:

You could argue that, given a proper executive structure we could never have got into the mess we did get in. Middle management of our business knew many of the problems before the senior management. I believe our management structure is one which perpetuated what we have been doing rather than initiated. Perhaps the problem is we have not had a board strong

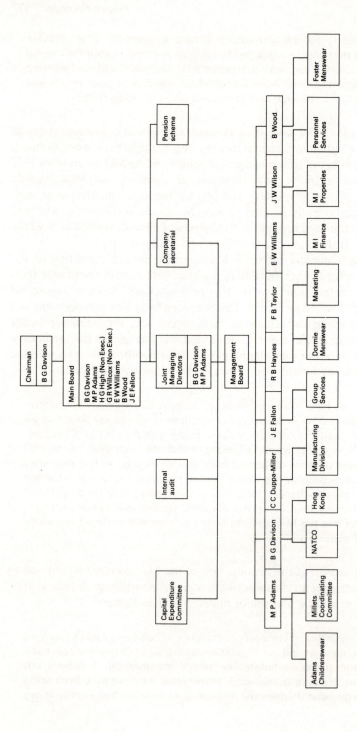

FIGURE 5.4 Foster Brothers Clothing plc; group structure in 1983

enough to stand up to the Chairman. Subsidiary boards do not have control, even at Foster Menswear, of their company. Investment is controlled by the main board. Now we've set up a Group Management Board between the main and subsidiary boards. That may be the answer.

According to some Fosters managers there was, by 1983, a real attempt by Davison to change the previous centralized decision-making mode of operation:

He is trying very hard to step back and let middle management take decisions, which was not the case in 1980; he was very much trying to make every decision.

It was not a view that Davison himself held about his own role. He believed that, in the past, he had seen much of the inertia but had failed to insist on sufficient movement because he had been persuaded that the way things were done was sensible.

I believe I saw a lot of the things that were going to take place. I tried to encourage people in the organization to do what was necessary but I am not a retailer in the sense of Conran or Halpern and was unable to totally influence it myself. I'm not a confident enough retailer in my own ability to say you will do it this way, when people who I have accepted as experts said it's not the way to do it.

His view of the Management Board and the planning role of the subsidiaries was that they should be required to go right back to basic questions of strategy and have this questioned by the Board.

The Board really says to the subsidiaries 'We want you to grow'; it's as broad as that. Then annually we go round and see what their plans are. This year we've tried to go right back to base and say 'What business are you in? Where are you intending to be? What's the future?' It's the Board that makes the plans.

Melvyn Taylor described how he saw a more de-centralized Foster Brothers working: he did not see a *laissez faire* attitude to decision-making:

Most companies that are successful are worked from very tight rules or very tight control, not on everything but certainly on the financial criteria which would include returns, costs and so on.

It was on the operational side that he envisaged decentralizing:

> If the businesses are different you've got to allow it in terms of marketing policy. Having said that the company has to identify who it is, where it is and where it is going, and that has to be agreed as a policy directive by the group. The subsidiaries then have to go off and do that.

It was a view very similar to that of John Fallon who claimed that:

> Genuine responsibility is being passed down with parameters to let them know just how far they can go.

His view on the mechanism of the Management Board was:

> It could be seen for many organizations as a retrograde step because it imposes a rigid structure. I do believe that somewhere you have to have some form of rigid structure that in itself can become flexible and malleable. Our problem was that we did not have that to start off with.

He was concerned that in the past there had been no mechanism by which any decisions of consequence were challenged. The main board was far removed from the operating companies which were run by power elites rarely required to justify actions other than to Davison. The decentralization to subsidiaries went hand in hand with an attempt to introduce a more participative style of management within the subsidiaries. John Fallon again:

> In order to make the whole of this process interactive, we had to involve the managers at the bottom and every level. There are several key things that have happened. We now call area sales managers, area managers. We are saying to those people 'Your prime function is not to sell but to manage your area in the broadest sense.' In doing that one of my introductions was to create a set-up called retail accountants. Their purpose in life is to act as advisors to area managers. They go out and review the performance of shops. We have undertaken financial training courses for our main board directors, our second tier of management and our third tier; we have not yet got down to our area managers. We get our accountant to go out on site and visit the area manager and talk through his problems. To follow on from that: as an example, until this year we did not have any opportunity for retail sales planning. If you think we have 500 shops in Fosters with two floors in a lot of them perhaps with 750 trading slots; and we have something like 16 departmental breakdowns in merchandise; that's a hell of a lot of departments. What used to happen was the sales director used to say 'This is what the sales budget will be for the next year' and the merchandise people

would add up the merchandise they sold last year and say 'This is what we will sell next year'. There was no involvement from anyone else. You would then breakdown the sales budget targets for each shop; that was the end of it. We had introduced a new sales planning mechanism whereby we can actually plan the sales of every shop or every department within that shop by week of the year. The way we did that was to get area managers here, and they sat down at the terminal with our accountant and . . . did a full retail branch plan for every shop. We built the plans from the bottom up. We also had the top down figure coming in. They met in the middle. The Area Managers now have plans which they have worked on themselves. There are people now in the business who are also able to challenge the Chairman's view and who the Chairman himself is prepared to listen to.

Business Performance

The first 'new image' shop was opened early in 1982 in Peterborough and with immediate success. This success was greeted with not only relief but an immediate decision to proceed with the conversion of other shops in which similar results occurred. Whilst sales and profits in the traditional Fosters branches still declined, the accelerating programme of shop refittings convinced the Fosters management that they could remedy the situation. By the end of 1982, 32 shops had been converted, accounting for 15 per cent of turnover. By mid-1983 a refitting plan including 300 shops for redesign over a three-year period was agreed with the likelihood that the other 200 shops would be sold, converted to 'clearance' shops or relocated. The target sales increase after the refit was set at 40 per cent and this target had been met on shops refitted up to mid-1983 although trade press sources reported returns as high as 150 per cent. Costs of refitting branches varied from £10,000 for a small one to £300,000 for the central Birmingham branch. By June 1984 the Group were able to report profits over £8.3 million (see table 5.4) as a result of a general upturn in demand and, in particular, a continuing growth in performance of the 'new image' shops of which there were 120 by early 1984.

The managers within Fosters were, generally, very pleased with their progress. The only notable reservations came from one of the chief architects of the changes, David Saunders:

They are beginning to get more greedy; the finance people are beginning to say 'We are making a lot of money; now let's make it more profitable'. They are coming and saying 'That shop there – we reckon out of 2000 square feet, we can do half a million pounds of business so you have got £120,000 to spend'. That's irrespective of whether the shop has got a side road with miles of windows. They have made a very rigid decision so it's coming back

TABLE 5.4   *A summary of the financial performance 1983/1984 (a) and a summary of key financial ratios (b)*

	£ thousand	Percentage change on 1982/3
(a)		
Sales revenue	101,703	+ 23
Trading profit	7333	+ 97
Interest and charges	(300)	
Sale of properties	1269	
Profit before tax	8302	+ 65
(b)		
	1983/4	1982/3
Trading profit as percentage of sales	7	4
Profit before tax as percentage of capital employed	22	12

Source: Foster Brothers Annual Reports

because they have all assimilated it and they think it's theirs and are beginning to tinker with the bits. . . . One of the de-motivating factors in retail is that they are moving the goal posts. They set him [the shop manager] a target and when he looks as if he is going to reach it, they move it. I thought we were working on a 40 per cent increase as a target; I now get the figures and find that some stores are 200 per cent up and people are going around saying we are below target. So I've started fighting the finance people. We will do our absolute best to make it work (within the finances) but they will find some that do not work; it's an absolute false economy.

Internally there were, however, concerns that the conversions were proving too expensive:

Budgets went over by literally thousands of pounds.

David Saunders, however, believed that there were dangers in 'old ways' reasserting themselves. He described how the property department tried to pare costs by, for example:

Knocking out spotlights. Every shop we go to they have closed down something. Its all the old disciplines coming back.

In May 1984 Barry Davison was, however, able to issue a press release on the previous year's performance that stated:

The substantial increase in both sales and profits reflects not only the buoyant conditions that have existed in retail trading during the year but mainly the increasing benefits which are now starting to accrue to the Group from the store modernisation programme which was commenced some two years ago.

Sales in all our retail companies show a satisfactory improvement against last year with an outstanding performance achieved by the major subsidiary, Foster Menswear, from its refurbished branches being the main reason for the doubling in trading profits. At present, some 125 branches are operating in the new image and the programme of conversion is being accelerated so that in excess of 250 modernised shops should be open by the end of the current year.

The other retail companies have achieved good progress. Adams Childrenswear has made substantial recovery and Dormie Menswear produced increase profits. The two Millets companies achieved worthwhile improvements in results and the amalgamation of the two companies is progressing.

In the USA a small profit was made and progress is continuing. A redesigned store format catering for the young fashion market has been launched and results are encouraging indicating that a substantial contribution to Group profitability in the years ahead is fully achievable.

CRISIS AND TAKEOVER

By the beginning of 1984 the management at Fosters were looking forward to a period of renewed profitable growth. In fact such profit growth never materialized; it was clear by the beginning of 1985 that the company was in serious financial difficulties, and by August 1985 the company had been taken over by Sears after a takeover battle between them and Ward White. The circumstances of this decline and the eventual takeover are re-told variously by the managers involved at the time, but the main reasons are generally agreed upon.

Fundamental to the declining fortunes were the activities in the USA. In 1981 Fosters had taken the 20 per cent interest in the American operation and by 1984 had gained a controlling interest. Barry Davison was known to be enthusiastic about the venture and, indeed, by the end of August 1984 the management of the operation were forecasting a one-million-dollar profit for the end of that year. In fact the results for 1984 were very different. As Barry Davison explained:

> In fact that year they lost $12 million. Sales targets were missed by 30 per cent. Sales were down 23 per cent on the previous year and the American market fell apart.

In company terms the result was a major cash drain on the UK parent.

There were several explanations for the downturn in the fortunes of the American business. His Place consisted of 246 shops in 35 states. In 1984 a refitting programme for the shops had been begun by David Saunders and his design team. Davison explained that:

> We had been achieving a 100 per cent increase in sales after the Saunders redesign, so we went ahead with the other branches which required more capital; and none of them made money.

In particular, sales in the Autumn period and during the Christmas period of 1984 were disastrous. Brian Wood attributes this problem to the new merchandise team for the company buying merchandise not suitable to the sort of stores the company had:

> They bought more fashionable, higher-priced merchandise which was New York style.

Melvyn Taylor believed, too, that:

> They price-structured the business from a New York perspective; it was unrealistic.

This combined with a major control and distribution problem; it had been decided to introduce a new distribution system based on computer control of stocks from central warehouses. The computer systems, when introduced, gave rise to major problems. At one period there was no means of knowing the stock requirements of shops or what stock was available for shops. Barry Davison agreed: 'We didn't know what was selling, or where to send goods to'. The result was a highly dispersed trading operation reliant on centralized deliveries without the assistance of computerized control and with no back-up staff to operate manually. Moreover, it was a crisis that coincided with the peak trading period in the USA. The result was a major drop in profits. Brian Wood:

> To keep the business going there was a necessity for mark-downs and at one point they were trading below cost.

Members of the Menswear Board insisted that the American operation was never discussed at their level, and the only executive director known to oppose the move was Mike Adams. They also believed that it was difficult to control Barry Davison in his commitment to expansion in the States. As

Brian Wood explained 'BGD wanted to take America. He honestly felt the company would make money out of it.'

The problems in America coincided with growing difficulties in the UK in 1984 and 1985. First, the American problems came at the same time as the growing capital costs of funding the shop refitting programme, as it was extended more widely throughout the Fosters chain. This itself cost something of the order of £20 million and required a major growth in bank borrowings. As Brian Wood explained 'this plus the losses in the USA would have meant Group end-year losses if they had been declared'.

However, the returns being made on the refits were not at the levels of 1983. Richard Haynes explained:

> Fosters had got a hotch-potch of sites – not a lot that they had taken on as prime sites. So the first 200 shops were the best. By the end of 1983 the best had been done. The big city-centre shops held up in performance, but the secondary refits didn't work to anything like the same extent.

Haynes attributed the problem to the legacy of the property policy of the company, in which sites had been acquired and retained even when they had become secondary locations: 'The property portfolio was an albatross.' The result was that they could not find a cost formula to refit the shops, when sales returns could not be relied upon, given the location of the stores.

Managers also attributed problems to the merchandise policy introduced by the new Merchandise Director. Essentially this involved a more fashionable range, but applied across all the Foster shops. Brian Wood commented:

> The merchandise package was changed. It was made much more fashionable, which did not suit smaller suburban branches. It neglected the rump of the business particularly in the smaller-town branches which were re-furbished later. It also brought margin down. It reduced own label by direct sourcing, did it through import houses, introduced more brands, and also stepped up concessions – sometimes by as much as 50 per cent. The overall margin then came down and we couldn't get sales up enough to counter that.

More broadly, some of the executives argued that one of the problems was that there were still too many links with the past; it was not just a matter of the inherited property portfolio but also the way in which the business operated. For example, Richard Haynes argued that:

> The principal personalities remained the same: they were still in charge; and they made sure they protected themselves with people who were loyal to them.

Most of the old guards who left were still replaced with people from within –
still the old school.

And in the view of Haynes:

Whenever the situation got tough, they would return to the 'foetal position'.
That meant big tickets, pile it high and sell it cheap and sales – and always
much longer than anyone else.

Other senior executives felt that, given the changes of 1983/4, there was
insufficient release of executive autonomy and discretion from the centre,
such that the requirements for greater contribution from middle management, in particular, was stultified. Brian Wood commented:

I can't think of anything that changed internally. Externally things changed
but not internally. . . . For example, when area managers came into the
building the attitude was the same: they felt they would be jumped on. If they
said 'we need brands' they would be told they didn't make any profits. They
saw no change in here.

To some of the senior executives there appeared to be little visible change
in the way the company was run. There remained, for example, a clear and
substantial gap between different executive levels:

The executive dining room remained the preserve of the main board and the
Menswear Board. If you wanted to invite anyone else you had to ask BGD.

The trading problems extended beyond the Menswear business. Despite
the difficulties previously experienced with acquisitions and new womenswear ventures, the Group board agreed in July 1984 to acquire Peter
Richards, a womenswear chain of 29 shops, some of which were 8000 or
10,000 square feet. It was a decision taken before the serious decline in the
fortunes in the USA. However, the failure of the operation to generate
profits, and its necessary absorption of investments, did nothing to help a
worsening situation. The decision to acquire was swift:

Peter Richards came to us on Tuesday and we took the decision on Friday.

According to Barry Davison:

It was something everyone wholeheartedly was in favour of doing; but it
didn't have time to work.

The basis for the decision appeared, however, to be fundamentally opportunistic and rooted in a belief in the financial strength of the Fosters Group. Brian Wood:

> BGD had always wanted a ladies business. Richards had no cash. It cost us nothing – but, then, they had no stock because they had no cash.

Indeed, not only did the business have no stock, or cash, but Fosters also agreed to take over a debt of around £2 million.

Brian Wood believed, however, that Barry Davison made a determined effort not to 'Fosterize' the Peter Richards business. He appointed a Merchandise Director from the Burtons' Dorothy Perkins operation and Richard Haynes as Managing Director. However, the venture never got off the ground. On taking over the business the management was faced with buying an Autumn range 'off the shelf'; not only was there insufficient time for this, but according to Richard Haynes:

> We went out and sold cheap and cheerful crap. We had learned nothing.

Also, by the time further funds were required later in 1984 and in 1985, the problems in the USA meant that availability of such funds had dried up.

By late 1984 the combined effect of the crisis in the States, the cash drain on the UK business, the lower returns from the refurbishment programme and the reduced margins of the new ranges, together with rapidly increasing bank borrowings, combined to place Fosters in a highly vulnerable position. The managers agreed that, had that year's financial results ever been declared, the company would have been a prime takeover target. However, in February 1985, before the USA problems had become known outside the company, the retail conglomerate Ward White declared an interest in the Fosters Group. Although the USA situation was not known, it did mean that the bid was the more difficult to defend. Sears, had, apparently, also been looking at the possibility of takeover, and in March, prompted by the Ward White offer, they too declared an interest.

Foster Brothers was taken over by Sears in July 1985 and the group became an operating unit within the holding company of Sears. By August 1985 Barry Davison had left as Chief Executive and was replaced by Mike Adams. Fosters became a division of Sears. The Divisional Board consisted of Geoffrey Maitland Smith, the Sears Chairman, two other Sears' Executive Directors, Mike Adams, Brian Wood as Managing Director of Foster Menswear, the Managing Director of Millets, John Fallon as Financial Director and Melvyn Taylor as Company Secretary. The American interests were sold off as was the Peter Richards chain.

A Strategic Postscript

In the Spring 1986 edition of Foster Group News there appeared this
interview with Mike Adams on the strategic future of the business.

- 'In recent years, your chains such as Fosters, Dormie and Esquires do not seem
  to have been targeted so precisely as, say, certain chains of your major rival, the
  Burton Group.

  M.A: I would not disagree with that, but as a management team we are
  currently rationalising and repositioning our shops to optimise our trading
  performance. Although we have plans for all our chains, the most significant
  changes will be seen in the Fosters chain, which currently has 511 shops. We
  have developed a new system for classifying branches which will enable us to
  match our shops with their local markets more efficiently than has ever been
  achieved before. To optimise our performance we need to become more
  relevant to the varying local needs of our potential customers.

- How soon will we see the effects of this development on the High Street?

  M.A: Some changes have been put into practice this season and the plan will
  be totally effected by February 1. In effect we are dividing the Fosters shops into
  six classifications. For large city centres we will be serving primarily the
  fashion-conscious 15–25 year old group with specialist young fashion ranges in a
  very up to date shopping environment; secondly, in large towns where there is
  high competition we will promote a modern fashion image, but with an appeal
  to a slightly wider age group; then, in the large country towns and suburbs,
  while there will be a younger fashion emphasis, we will have some conventional
  clothing and larger sizes. Here the shops will be modern but comfortable, so as
  not to alienate our older customers and their wives.

  Fourthly, for small country towns where there is very little competition, our
  research has shown that the demand is for mainstream fashion and conventional
  clothing, but over 50 per cent of the customers will be over 40 years old; moving
  on from this to small country towns and industrial suburbs, the demand is for
  conventional, but not old-fashioned, clothes. Basic clothing and work clothing
  will also be carried in these branches, where we expect 70 per cent of the
  customers to be over 40.

  Finally, in declining inner city areas we will have our clearance shops which
  already trade as Your Price.

- Won't it be confusing to have all this under the Fosters name?

  M.A: Although we have made no decision yet, we have considered
  introducing a new trading name for our specialist high fashion shops, which
  would help remove the 'old men's shop' image which some of our younger
  customers have of us. We may also use a different name for the chain aimed
  predominantly at the 40-plus conventional man.

- What numbers will be involved when the branches have been reclassified?

  M.A: We project that the young fashion chain will have 20 branches, the second chain will have 84 shops, and there will be 145 with a young fashion emphasis, but also some conventional merchandise. We are planning for 52 of the fourth category, and 37 of the fifth, with about 89 Your Price shops completing the strategy.

- Will you change merchandising strategy?

  M.A: Besides this being perceived more tightly to suit the local markets, a general tendency will be to feature more of our own brands, which currently account for 60 per cent of sales in Fosters. We now have a design team to provide us with what's right for us.'

By the end of 1986 the new Fosters senior management team, working within the Sears Group, were actively implementing the repositioning strategies outlined here.

Senior managers were confident that the difficulties of 1984 and 1985 were behind them and that the retail strategies for the Foster Group were both clearer and in tune with customer requirements. The Chairman of Sears, Geoffrey Maitland Smith, was able to announce, in Foster Group News, in the Summer of 1986

> . . . that in the forty two weeks to 31st January 1986, the Foster business made trading profits of £9.6 million. These results are quite satisfactory for the year of acquisition and integration. . . . I am pleased that the Foster Group executives and employees have responded well to the moves that have taken place and are finding a sense of determination and purpose in facing the challenges and opportunities that lie ahead.

At least one major group of stockbrokers agreed when they advised their clients in 1986:

> We see considerable scope for future expansion of the various business segments of Fosters. During the current year sales are likely to top £160m with trading profits of £15m.

Part III

Making Sense of the Strategic Management Process

The case study in the previous section aims to provide a fairly full, contextually rich account of strategic change in an organization. It cannot, of course, hope to detail all relevant aspects of what was a highly complex series of events and dramas. It is, however, an attempt to provide a rounded basis for a discussion of strategic management processes as they took place in Fosters, in the light of existing theory and research on processes of strategic change. The question that needs to be asked is to what extent such theory and research helps to explain and make sense of the developments in Fosters. In addition, to what extent does an examination of strategic change in Fosters, yield propositions that advance our understanding of such processes?

This last section of the book therefore sets out to explore the problems of the management of strategic change in a business. It utilizes the sorts of concepts and models discussed in chapter 2 as a means of examining the different patterns of strategic change observed in Fosters; how and why such change takes place at different rates and in different ways; why such change is problematic; and how problems of strategic change were, or were not, overcome. As explained in chapter 3, the analysis that follows is necessarily based on the wider data collected and not on the case study alone. However, there has been an attempt to avoid the introduction of new information as far as possible.

We begin in chapter 6 by considering the extent to which the analytic and planning modes of management of 'rationalistic' strategy models can be detected within the firm or can help explain strategic change processes; and, indeed, there is evidence that the behaviour of managers could be described in many cases in terms of such models. We then take an 'incrementalist' perspective and find that, indeed, patterns of strategic change that correspond to such a description do exist. Moreover we see that managers talk about processes of strategic management very much in terms of the 'logical incrementalism' that Quinn (1980) found in his research. However, the argument is advanced that essentially rational perspectives on the management processes at work in Fosters over the time of the case do not adequately account for what occurred. There is no denying that managers in organizations do act rationally; however, there is ample evidence that they also act politically, and that management cognition plays an important part in the interpretation of situations and guiding managerial action. The activity of managers is not capable of being reduced to any one perspective. Moreover if we are to consider the problems of managing strategy in organizations, and particularly the problems of managing strategic change, then we have to conceive of management not only in terms of the activities of individual managers but, essentially, as the activities of collectivities of managers, and their interaction among themselves and with other stakeholders in the organization. Managers, individually, have to manage within the events, dramas, routines and beliefs that are the day-to-day reality of an organization. As such we need to conceive of strategic management, not as something set apart, but as a management task within the cultural fabric of an organization.

The remainder of the book, then, takes a deliberately cultural and cognitive perspective on the management of strategy and strategic change. Chapter 7 develops this cultural theme and argues that we need to understand observed patterns of incremental strategic change as a process rooted in a 'cultural web', specific to an organization and acting, very conservatively in Fosters' case, to mould strategic response. It is argued that we can best understand the developments in Fosters by focusing, not so much on environmental impact on the business, as on the way in which the managers made sense of their strategic situation in terms of the 'realities' of their organizational world.

In chapter 8 the argument is developed that the management of strategic change can profitably be considered in terms of the ideas developed in chapter 7 together with the ideas about processes of managing strategic change developed by other writers. The sort of incremental change observed in Fosters up to the early 1980s and the attempts at more fundamental change from 1982–4, are employed for illustrative purposes in the discussion. This discussion is, then, an examination of the applicability of theoretical models of process to a particular context – that of Fosters' strategic development. Out of this discussion emerge further explanatory ideas and propositions about the processes observed, which develop the notion of the management of strategic change as an essentially cultural and cognitive process.

Finally, in chapter 9, these ideas are summarized and examined in terms of their relevance to the practice of management. Here the view is developed that by beginning from a conception of strategic management as a cultural and cognitive process, valuable and practical lessons can be learned. Moreover, in so doing, the value of analytical and planning modes of managing is more likely to be placed in a relevant and useful context.

6
Strategy and the Notion of the 'Rational Manager'

This chapter examines the processes of strategic management as discerned in Fosters from an essentially rational perspective: is there evidence of the analytical, planning modes of behaviour that might support 'rationalistic' accounts of management? Also, are there signs of the 'logical incrementalism' that, as some have argued, more accurately describes managers' approach to formulations and implementing strategy?

Overall, the view has to be that, whilst examples of analytical and planning behaviour can be observed, the characteristics of rationalistic models of decision-making do not typify managerial behaviour in Fosters for the period of the study and can only very partially account for the patterns of strategic development observed. Using the characteristics of such models discussed in chapter 2 this becomes clearer.

There is little evidence of *systematic and comprehensive environmental scanning*. Managers certainly had views about their business environment, but these tended to be personalized conceptions of what was taking place around them. There was no systematic mechanism to bring these perceptions together in terms of any organizational unity. For example, it was clear that, in the 1970s, store managers and area managers were increasingly aware of the growing influence of fashion changes on the core market of the company. This awareness gave rise to two sorts of activity. First there was growing political lobbying over a period of years; secondly, there was an infiltration of merchandise into shops on a piecemeal basis. This orientation towards action and implementation is also borne out, for example, at the most senior level in Davison's concern in the 1970s with the perceived threat of supermarkets in the home'n'wear activities. His perception of the threat is highly personalized; it was not supported by analytical study, and it resulted in action in the introduction of cheaper merchandise and an alliance with Tom Jacks in the 'pile it high' era. Environmental sensing may take place but it does so personally, with little evidence of systematic analysis, and with a leap from personalized problem awareness to action. It is a decision-making process much in line with the decision routines found in the research of Mintzberg (1976) and Lyles (1981) and reported in chapter 2 within the discussion of action-oriented incrementalism.

The evidence of any *infra-structure for long-range planning* is limited to that introduced in 1983 by the new Finance Director, John Fallon. This was certainly systematic; Fallon himself saw it as a system of planning that had to be fairly rigid to integrate different levels of management, different functional responsibilities and the overall new Management Board. However, the system he introduced could hardly be described as an archetypal corporate long-range planning system: it had no specialists associated with it; it was relatively short term in its horizons, concentrating mainly on the year ahead; and it was primarily a budgeting exercise with relatively less concern with formalized environmental analysis. Certainly, in part, it was seen as a management development exercise to involve levels of management, hitherto unconcerned with policy formation, in the consideration of operating plans for the company. Moreover, it has to be said that such systems were introduced *after* the attempted strategy re-formulation of 1982 and 1983. These planning systems did not contribute to the origins of strategic change at that time so much as arise from it, and attempt to plan implementation in an operational sense.

The extent to which there were any clear *objectives* or explicit *choice between strategic options* was minimal. Objectives were personalized and generally vague at least until the more formal planning systems were introduced by John Fallon. They were primarily concerned with 'continuing to grow' or 'increasing the number of shops'; there were no clearly stated financial objectives. Nor was there evidence that managers systematically evaluated strategic options against either an analysis of the position of the company or its objectives. We have to account for the strategy revisions introduced at Fosters in quite different ways.

Perhaps the overriding principle of rationalistic schools of thought is that the complexity of the organization's environment, and its position in it, can be understood, or reduced, through *analysis*. Yet the extent to which we find signs of systematic analysis at an organization level or an individual level is limited. Certainly managers gave the impression that they identified and gave consideration to important assumptions held within the business; but this activity took place largely at an individual level as managers considered the assumptions held by other managers, usually retrospectively: managers explained past strategy in terms of the assumptions of successive buying directors or chief executives for example. In this sense there was some individual retrospective analysis of what drove strategy. This is, however, not the sort of analysis that is supposed to underpin rationalistic decision processes. However, if the data are examined more closely it is possible to see that there were occasions when there were analytical processes at work that, at least on the face of it, appear to be pro-active rather than reactive.

The most obvious was the attempt to diversify away from the menswear market into other areas of retailing, most notably womenswear, in the mid 1970s. However, if this is examined more closely, it is difficult to support the contention that rational analysis drove the strategy. In the first place at the time of the Stone-Dri and Crowds initiatives, menswear and womenswear sales nationally were growing roughly in line with each other: moreover Fosters menswear sales were benefiting from their relative dominance in their market sector. Secondly, even if we take the view that it was an analysis of the advantages of the womenswear sector that attracted management, this says nothing at all about the bases upon which the strategy itself was formulated and implemented. Indeed there is a good deal of evidence, which will be examined later, that the strategy took form much more in terms of assumptions about how to compete in retailing based on the current menswear business than any analysed view about how to run a womenswear operation.

In the case of the development of Blue Movers in the late 1970s the company set up a study group to examine whether or not a jeans business would be viable. It was a committee on which chief executives of six of the smaller companies sat. It took six months to consider its views and recommended that the company should not go ahead because the resources it had available, particularly in terms of property sites, were not suitable. The findings were overruled on the basis of strong views held by the Group Chief Executive and a contra-piece of evidence in the form of the financial, rather than market, analysis of the performance of existing retailers of jeans. It was also clear that the decision was heavily influenced by the extent to which differing parties within the organization felt they might benefit in some way from a jeans operation – retail managers by additional opportunities for their management; buyers from the prospect of additional buying power for jeans; and despite the fact that he sat on the committee that recommended against the venture, Tony Gray, because he saw it as a possible route to a Board position. The evidence here is that the impact of analysis is low relative to the commercial benefits perceived by powerful individuals and the vested interests of such individuals.

There is also evidence that much of the analysis that did take place within the firm was financial. The example given above shows that the analysis of competitors' financial positions provided more powerful support for the view of the Chief Executive and vested interests of groups of managers than did the broader 'strategic' analysis of the committee. It became evident later in 1981, too, that the financial analysis carried out by the management services department under Melvyn Taylor was also a powerful stimulus to a discussion of how the company should turn itself around. However, such financial analysis did not so much perform the role in the decision process of diagnozing problems as of triggering action.

Perhaps the most striking example of the role and impact of analysis was that of the market research carried out in 1981. Richard Haynes, the new marketing director, as one of his first acts, had commissioned the market research survey of the position of Fosters in the market place. It was a comprehensive and thorough survey which showed how fundamentally the company was out of line with consumer expectations and attitutes. As a diagnostic statement it was full, powerful and prescriptive. Moreover it was the result of the intervention of a manager who appeared to believe in the importance of analysing market conditions as a basis for planned action. The immediate result of this analysis was that the report itself was 'rubbished' by senior managers and directors although, later, they were to claim that the report acted as a stimulus to a re-formulation of strategy. This initial rejection of the research can be accounted for in two ways: first many managers simply could not reconcile its findings with their perception of the company's success historically; and second the findings were fundamentally threatening to their position in the firm. For example, the report was critical of the merchandise range in the shops and, by implication, the expertise of the powerful Merchandise Department. The analysis may have been perceived by its initiator as diagnostic, but was received by its audience as a politically threatening statement.

It is possible to build up an argument for some degree of relatively *long-term orientation* in decision-making; however, such an intention has to be considered in the context of much shorter-term horizons within the processes of decision-making and action. For example, the account of how Fosters moved into Far-Eastern buying of merchandise shows that the managers were concerned about the possibility of other retailers making long-term gains by establishing channels of supply and gearing up their buying quantities. It could be argued that the management were here taking a long-term perspective in consciously seeking to dominate the supply end of the market given their powerful store representation in the 1960s and early 1970s. So too can it be argued that the attempts in the mid-1970s to re-orientate the merchandise range to more fashionable items, and the launch of Blue Movers, were attempts to make strategic changes with relatively long-term horizons. However, these moves need to be considered in terms of the way the policies were formulated and implemented: as has been shown, they were typically characterized by political activity and rather piecemeal, short-time-horizon action. For example, if the move to more fashionable goods might be said to have a long-term implications, it was nevertheless carried out by low-scale experimentation initially and a very gradual development of the retailing concept apparently by short-term operational constraints. It is one thing to recognize the presence of longer-time horizons in management's considerations or the longer-term implications of decisons; it is, however, quite another to suppose that a long-term perspective determines the policies adopted in the business month by month.

Overall, it is difficult to see evidence of a marked and explicit influence of rationalistic models of decision-making. None the less it might be that whilst the external evidence of such processes was absent, there might be more underlying, implicit evidence of such rationalism. A separate study was carried out of the language used to explain the management of strategy in Fosters by the Chief Executive in both 1980 and 1983 (Pitt and Johnson, 1987). In this study a content analysis (Holsti, 1969) of the transcripts of the discussions with the Chief Executive was undertaken, as a means of coding according to different theoretical models of decision-making. Though these models differed somewhat from those outlined in chapter 2 – specifically they were identified as 'analytic/planning' perspectives, 'incremental' perspectives, 'political' perspectives and 'cognitive/symbolic' perspectives – they none the less serve to show the extent to which different models of strategic management show themselves in the language used. Each of the perspectives was identified in terms of the sorts of rules of evidence described in chapter 2 and the transcripts systematically analysed and second coded against such rules of evidence. (Since the rules of evidence used were extensive, it is not possible to show them here (but see Pitt and Johnson, 1987). However, what follows are some examples of the sort of statements taken from the transcripts as coded according to the different perspectives.

Statements Coded as 'Analytical Planning'
• Strategy is the product of deliberate (intended), systematic, rational analytical behaviour involving search, evaluation (matching) and choice (decision) process, in the attempt to achieve optimal results.

'I felt that the low-overhead structure that they had would enable them to devastate our price structure and that they would take a substantial part of our turnover away'.

'Our decisions tend to be long term with an objective of growth for the group'.

'I think one of the reasons for our success is that we have tightly controlled our current-asset situation'.

'We anticipated the move to imported merchandise earlier than our major competitors'.

'If for instance you look at last month's statistics, menswear were up by 4 per cent, overall retail spending was 13 per cent up in cash terms . . .'

Statements Coded as 'Incremental'
● Strategy is the product of ongoing routines, procedures and action programmes, within an overall framework or pattern variously called a repertoire, recipe or paradigm.

'One of the differences between retailing and, let's say, engineering, is that you tend to take much shorter-time decisions'.

'We have no particularly entrenched ideas as to where we were'.

'There isn't any firm objectives for me in so far as I can say that it is where I want to be'.

'We are in a business of change; all of the time we have to have changes'.

'We arrived where we were without any concrete plan'.

Statements Coded as 'Political'
● Strategy is the product of organizational processes of influence, negotiation and bargaining involving the exercise of authority and power (and restraint thereof).

'There is a personal ambition element as far as I am concerned'.

'Gradually I started to try and get myself involved in what he was doing, which he didn't particularly like'.

'I am giving it full backing and making it appear that it is in total keeping with my ideas'.

'How I perceive that decision having been made? I said we are going to do it'.

'We did sell suits and then we dropped them because Tom didn't like the idea of selling suits'.

Statements Coded as 'Cognitive'
● Strategy is the product of ideas, constructs, perceptions, convictions and other outcomes of individual and share cognitive processes within the organization. Shared cognitions are typically referred to as 'world views' or 'theories of the world'.

'Self-satisfaction is what everybody is after'.

'I was absolutely convinced that we had to be in that area'.

'I've got to change my philosophy and it is a philosophy that has to be changed downstairs'.

'You develop over the years a theory which you believe is right'.

'We had an ingrained attitude in the business and I was part of that, saying that we were selling products and really that the environment wasn't a really important part of a trading philosophy'.

'There was a belief that the merchandise team was capable of virtually anything. There is a belief now that it isn't'.

Statements Coded as 'Symbolic'
● Strategy is the product of the prevailing signs and symbols inside the organization and surrounding it and of the meanings and ideology they represent.

'I believe that I generate inside and outside the business the identity of the company'.
'I do believe that it is possible to have a personality cult within a fairly large company'.
'Fosters have changed their face over the last ten years'.
'We are concentrating on big image'.

The analysis showed that no one model could explain how the Chief Executive talked about the processes of strategy formulation in the company; indeed all the different perspectives were represented in his accounts. This is evident in table 6.1. What also became clear, however, was that rationalistic perspectives scored relatively low in his accounts; and it must be remembered here that this is not based on his descriptions of any systematic analytical approach within the firm, but rather statements of a rationalistic nature no matter how isolated or unconnected. It also emerged that even in 1983, at a time when the company was actually introducing planning systems, there was still relatively little emphasis given by the Chief Executive to rationalistic modes of management. In fact the 'swing' is more markedly towards cognitive and symbolic perspectives of management – a theme that will be developed further in this part of the book. Similar analysis of the transcripts of other managers might, perhaps, show more of an orientation towards rationalistic processes; but we cannot escape the fact that, whether it be in the language they use, or in the processes observed in the company, rationalistic modes of strategic management were not markedly dominant in Fosters in the period studied.

How do we interpret such findings? The point might be made that it is precisely because Fosters did not have an orientation towards some sort of planning approach to strategy formulation that they eventually suffered the problems they did; and that the Fosters example is too context-bound and that other companies have more of an emphasis on a planned approach to the management of strategy. A number of points arise here. First of all,

TABLE 6.1 *Frequencies of observed perspectives on managing strategy*

Perspectives	Percentage of observations	
	1980	1983
Analytic/planning	18	21
Incremental	29	25
Political	30	9
Cognitive/symbolic	23	45

whilst we are not here directly concerned with the performance of the business, it should be pointed out that there exists in the research little correlation between the presence of planning systems in companies and the performance of those companies. At best the evidence of a relationship is equivocal (Armstrong, 1982; Schrader et al, 1984) and there is a good deal of evidence that it is non-existent (Grinyer and Norburn, 1975; Kudla, 1980; Leontiades and Tezel, 1980). Moreover, formalized planning systems are not common in retail companies (Feinberg et al, 1983; Gilligan and Sutton, 1987); and whilst such systems may be more commonly found in large manufacturing-based companies (Al-Bazzaz and Grinyer, 1981), the extent to which they are used by managers may be limited (Hall, 1973) and their role, as we saw in Chapter 2, analytical and programatic (Mintzberg, 1981; Bahrami, 1981) rather than one of contributing directly to strategy formulation.

In short, while there is no attempt to suggest that the Fosters situation is entirely typical, it is certainly not unique. We are here concerned with the process of strategy formulation and it does appear that planning systems do not provide a sufficient explanation of strategic decision-making in companies. Whilst planning systems and rationalistic modes of management might be seen as a component of strategic decision-making, it is necessary to look much more widely than this to understand how and why strategic changes take place in organizations. By exploring further the processes that work in this company, the remainder of this part of the book seeks to illustrate processes that, it is argued, are also at work in other organizational settings.

PATTERNS OF STRATEGY

If rationalistic models of strategy formulation are insufficient to explain the management of strategy in Fosters, how then can we explain it? One way is to examine the development of the strategies of firms in terms of output; that is strategy as it can be observed. This can be done by 'mapping' the strategies in much the same way as Mintzberg (1978) did in his historical studies of Volkswagenwerk, Saturday Night Magazine and the US government's strategy in Vietnam from 1960 to 1968. This mapping exercise was undertaken for Fosters with two purposes in mind: first to examine what patterns of strategy could be seen to exist historically; and second to assess what could be learned, if anything, about the process of strategy formulation through an examination of such readily observable manifestations of strategy. Figure 6.1 is a visualization of the patterns of strategic change in Fosters over the period up to 1983, coded so that discernible strategic moves can be identified.

Strategy and Environmental Change

This simple mapping of strategies is in itself illuminating, in that it provides some bases for inferring lessons about the formation of strategy, building on previous research and theory. The notion of strategy as a response to environmental change is supported in so far as, over the 13-year period, company strategy did apparently change to deal with environmental changes. For example, the era of branch acquisition, (2), (3), can be seen as a response to the development in the 1960s of shopping precincts in the UK. The introduction of more fashionable merchandise for a rather younger age group, (6), can be associated with a growing customer demand for more fashionable menswear. The discounting and cost-cutting, (7), can be seen as a response to the negative pressures of recession on sales volume; the efforts throughout the 1970s diversify out of a sole reliance on menswear and, in particular, into womenswear (5a), can be interpreted as a response to a real decline in expenditure on men's clothes and the relative bouyancy of womenswear retailing.

Thus the notion of strategy as a response to environmental change, promoted by writers on the subject from Andrews (in Learned et al., 1965) onwards can be supported. Indeed it is possible to take the notion further from this evidence. More recent work has shown how companies, more or less successfully, achieve competitive positioning in terms of key environmental forces (Porter, 1980). Taking Porter's five main environmental forces, (a) a threat of entry into the industry, the power of (b) suppliers and (c) buyers, (d) the threat of substitutes and (e) the extent of competition within the industry, it is certainly possible to construct an explanation of strategic change in such terms. Porter argues that it is the task of strategists to assess the relative power of these forces and the way in which competition copes with them, and design strategy so as to position the firm to its best advantages. The strategy of Fosters can be conceived in such terms as these (see figure 6.2). The company's success in the 1970s might be explained in terms of their ability to dominate what was a separate retail sector of 'outfitting', by their number of branches and the early realization of the economies of imported merchandise from overseas suppliers. In such a way their dominance of the supplier–competitor–buyer chain was very real; they were not dependent on suppliers since they could shift between any number of capable sources; there were no competitors who had a comparable branch representation or volume of

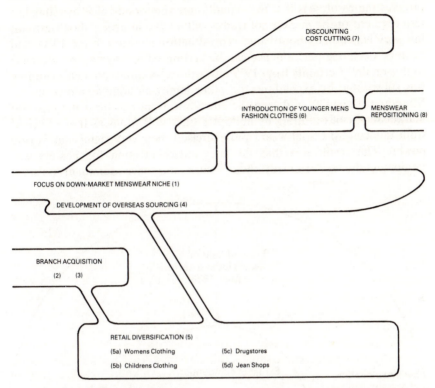

| 1960's | 1970 | 1971 | 1972 | 1973 | 1974 | 1975 | 1976 | 1977 | 1978 | 1979 | 1980 | 1981 | 1982 | 1983 |

DISCOUNTING
COST CUTTING (7)

INTRODUCTION OF YOUNGER MENS
FASHION CLOTHES (6)

MENSWEAR
REPOSITIONING (8)

FOCUS ON DOWN-MARKET MENSWEAR NICHE (1)

DEVELOPMENT OF OVERSEAS SOURCING (4)

BRANCH ACQUISITION

(2)   (3)

RETAIL DIVERSIFICATION (5)

(5a) Womens Clothing   (5c) Drugstores

(5b) Childrens Clothing   (5d) Jean Shops

1. A traditional and continuing focus on low priced, high margin merchandise to the lower end (the working man) of the market.

2. A policy of growth through branch acquisition from the mid 1960's culminating in 1970 with the acquisition of Bradleys.

3. In the early 1970's branch acquisition continued though not through acquisition of businesses.

4. The development of large scale direct importing in the early 1970's, forming a base of merchandise strategy throughout the 1970's.

5. Efforts at diversification pursued throughout the 1970's;

(a) into specialist womenswear retailing
(b) into childrens clothing retailing (Adams)
(c) into discount drug stores (Discount for Beauty)
(d) into specialist jean shops (Blue Movers)

6. From 1985 onwards the introduction of younger mens fashion merchandise into the main line mens wear shops (Fashionpoint).

7. Faced with a declining performance in the early 1980's a cut back on costs and emphasis on discounting.

8. From 1982 onwards the repositioning of the shops as a fashion retailer.

FIGURE 6.1   Observable patterns of strategy: Fosters 1970–1983

offtake; the result was that they could offer very good-value merchandise to a segment of the market not traditionally too concerned about fashion, but very concerned about value. The situation changed in the 1970s and Fosters' declining performance can be accounted for, again, by reference to this model. Certainly from 1979 onwards expenditure on men's clothing was substituted by expenditure on other family clothing as recession bit. Moreover, the 1970s had seen the entry into what had been the separate market sector of outfitting by multiples such as Burtons as they switched from tailoring to casual wear, and exercised their very significant buying power. The result was that the competitive position for Fosters was fundamentally undermined; their secure and once dominant position

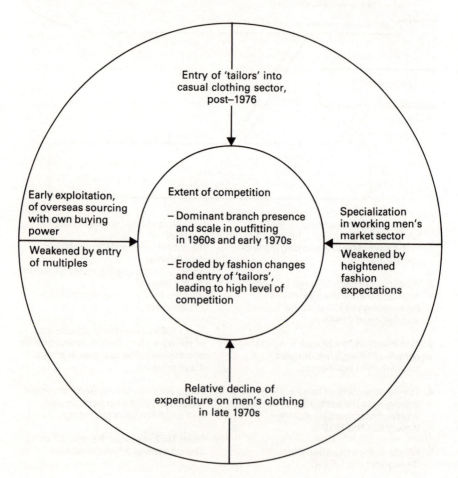

FIGURE 6.2   Fosters' strategic position in terms of a model of competitive strategy

changed to one of intense competition against major rivals. In short, Fosters problems can be accounted for by their inability to prevent entry into their market and, once the entry had occurred, the difficulties of competing with new and much more threatening competition.

The significance of environmental impacts and influences on strategy should not be minimized. Undoubtedly the action taken by the company to cope with a changing environment affected its performance. Moreover, there is ample evidence that managers saw and attempted to respond to such changes. We must accept that the business environment influenced and constrained strategy. Indeed the sort of mapping carried out above is a useful exercise in describing the strategies followed, and examining and explaining *post hoc* how a company's strategy coped with the external forces it faced. It can also yield explanations that can help account for the performance of the company. It is, however, quite another thing then to argue that it was these environmental and competitive forces that directly shaped the strategies followed by the company. This would imply that the environment is deterministic of strategy: it is not. It is more realistic to see environmental forces as both constraining and enabling the formulation of strategies by managers: they provide managers with the strategic arena that they must understand, that they seek to transform and in which they act (Bhaskar, 1979).

We must also be careful to distinguish between strategies as espoused and strategies as formulated and implemented. For example there is evidence to support the view that at least some of the managers were aware of threats to the core menswear business of Fosters and took the view that the company should diversify as a result, but this says nothing at all about how that espoused strategy took shape or how it was implemented. We should be wary of notions of strategic management that suggest a sort of linear, deterministic model in which environmental change, through analysis by managers, yields espoused strategies which in turn are logically configured within resource capabilities to meet environmental forces.

In Fosters this did not appear to be the case. Such changes as did take place were not sufficient to cope with the forces at work in the market. Moreover, if we widen this from an examination of Fosters, we see that in the rest of the clothing industry similar phenomena occurred. Both Burtons and Hepworths, major multiple tailors for decades, were faced with similar sorts of fashion changes in the 1960s and 1970s. The management of Burtons in the early 1970s made major efforts to switch from an over-reliance on made-to-measure suits, first to ready-to-wear and then to more casual wear (Channon, 1972; Johnson, 1986). The forces for change were evidently seen by the management, even if the extent and speed of the changes were perhaps not fully understood, but the strategies that were formulated were insufficient to prevent a major decline in the fortune of the company. For Hepworths, despite the changes that were taking place in the market, the company clung to a tailoring base for most of the 1970s. Nor is it sufficient to suggest that these difficulties are limited to clothing retailers. To take examples that are quite different, Pettigrew (1985b) also shows in his study of ICI how strategies being followed by companies tend to continue despite contra-forces at work in their environments; and research work, current at the time of writing, by the Centre for Corporate Strategy and Change at the University of Warwick (Whipp et al., 1986) also shows similar patterns in the automobile industry and merchant banking. Moreover this 'momentum' of strategy has also been demonstrated more generally by Mintzberg (1978) and Miller and Friesen (1980) in other industry contexts.

There is of course again the argument that what we are witnessing is not the failure of rationalistic models of strategic management here, but the failure of managers to be effective rational managers. If managers were more analytical, carefully evaluated options and planned resource allocation more carefully in line with needs determined by matching competitive forces and resource capability, then all would be well. There is no claim here – and none would be made by the managers in Fosters – that many of the strategic decisions might not have benefited from more penetrative market analysis or have been planned more effectively. However, this fails to explain why the prevalence of an analytical approach was relatively low; and why, when analysis did occur, it seemingly lacked influence. The fact is that we need to place the role of analysis and planning within the wider arena of management and organizational life to understand what it can and cannot contribute.

Strategy cannot be explained in terms of the process of its creation simply as a rational response to environmental change. Traditional approaches to the study of strategy do, of course, offer explanation as to why strategy is not simply a product of environmental change. As early as 1938, Barnard (1938) argued that it was necessary to reconcile the sub-systems or 'economies' of the firm with the environment. He pointed out that these 'economies' – which correspond to physical and people resources and activities – are different between firms, so one company's response to a given environment will not be the same as another's. It is a notion similar to that of Learned et al. (1965) who identified four components of strategy in an approach that typifies what has become known as a 'business policy' approach to strategy. Their components were: '1) market opportunity, 2) corporate competences and resources, 3) personal values and aspirations and 4) acknowledged obligations to segments of society other than stockholders' (p. 21). They stressed that strategy-making is complex because of the need to, and difficulty in, reconciling these different components. This approach thus recognizes that strategy formulation is a problem of *management and management choice*. If we are to understand why organizations' strategies are the way they are, we must understand it from a management perspective; and this means we must understand the management process that accounts for strategy formulation and strategic change.

An Incremental Pattern of Strategic Change

A further observation that can be made from the mapping of the development of strategy in Fosters as shown in figure 6.1 supports the idea of an incremental development of strategy. There are, it is true, some clear breaks in strategy but, in the main, strategies merge into each other, or grow out of another strategy. For example, before Fosters attempted to reposition their menswear business in the early 1980s, (8), it had already embarked on a change in merchandise policy some years earlier, (6). This attempted change, begun in the mid-1970s, was itself very gradual, and built on a long tradition of selling clothing items such as shirts, sweaters, jackets and trousers as 'separates'. The idea, then, that an incremental approach to strategy formulation is, in effect, the way in which an organization learns strategically can be inferred from the patterns that emerge.

What becomes clear is that the strategy of Fosters needs to be seen as substantially explained by its own history. The impact of the strategy of one period can be traced through to the strategy of another. The company developed throughout its history as a men's outfitter – a buyer and seller of men's clothing – with an emphasis on working clothes and boyswear, and little commitment to manufacturing (1). Its strategic emphasis on the centrality of merchandise bought for the working man, and on boyswear, was still strong throughout the 1970s and, indeed, the 1980s. The strategic changes of that time appeared to build on that history, rather than to change it. The branch acquisition phase of development in the 1960s (2) also had its legacy. By the 1980s the company had many branches not suited to current forms of trading, or poorly sited, yet it was unwilling to dispose of them. Indeed it actively sought to develop businesses such as Blue Movers (5d) in order to retail those branches. The development of overseas importing (4), so beneficial in margin terms in the 1970s, was a central plank of its strategy that persisted, and, to some extent, moulded the development of later strategies. 'Fashionpoint' (6) could be seen as an attempt to develop a more fashionable business with the constraints of the buying strategy already in existence.

The picture emerges of prior strategy moulding or constraining strategic development: it would be quite wrong to conceive of strategies being developed from a zero base, given the identification implicitly or explicitly of environmental forces. Rather, we need to see any identification of such forces as informing the managers of the requirement to amend or develop existing strategies.

A Logic to Incrementalism

If the exercise of 'mapping' shows patterns of incrementalism from which inferences of gradualism and experimentation can be made, so much more is the idea, and espoused logic, of incrementalism evident in how the managers in Fosters explained the company's strategic development. Certainly in 1980 it was the view of managers that the company adopted quite deliberately an adaptive mode of strategic development. It is worth repeating the account by Barry Davison in 1980 of Fosters' development. Here, however, some of the more detailed content is omitted to highlight his views on process:

> Why is the company successful and other menswear businesses are not successful? Luck, doing a lot of little things at the right time. . . . We, as a multiple company, grew rapidly in the number of branches at a time when it was not too difficult to do it. The development of shopping centres in the UK was going on rapidly and we gained a lot of representation when there was a polarization of change in shopping habits from developed centres. We took advantage of that situation when a number of others did not. We anticipated the move to imported merchandise earlier than our major competitors. We have got a very tight control on cost, tighter than a lot of our competitors. We were in the casual menswear business before we realized we were; that happened without a conscious decision being made. We were jacket-and-trouser sellers whereas they (Burtons) were suit sellers. We were a workwear specialist and it was a natural progression to move into jeans. We got the jeans trade without consciously going out to get it; so from that point of view the growth from until the big surge forward really came without any concrete plan. There was the plan to get more and more branches – there was that plan. We created not a big leap in turnover, but leap in turnover sufficient to dramatically increase our profits. In retailing you do not need a big leap in turnover in order to push up your profits. That increase in turnover has come without a corresponding increase in overheads. This is the thing about retailing; you have a very large fixed overhead. You only have to put your turnover up by 10 per cent and you have an enormous profit increase.

Later he was more specific about what he saw as the perceived advantages of this process of development:

> We have no particularly entrenched ideas as to where we were. We had no ideas as to what market we were in, other than that we wanted cheap clothes. So there was an infinite amount of flexibility. One thing we decided was that we wanted to keep this wide appeal – it might not bring us an enormous leap forwards, but as long as we can keep adjusting our merchandise mix and image satisfactorily we can keep a fair share of the market. I don't think it will give us any dramatic change.

Davison believed there were good business reasons for this approach to strategy development. In talking about the relationship with and influence of the City, he said:

> I can't really make a decision which says, like a private individual could do, this would be good for us in five years' time, but would be bad for us for the next five years. I can't do that because if I do that we would be down-graded in the stock market and our shareholders will not be happy with that. And that would give someone the ability to come and snap up what we have done. It is a primary reason for policy-making now in that we can only take small things that have not got an immediate return and when we go for something large it has to have a satisfactory return immediately. Experimenting with something new that you absolutely believe is right to do – let's say there was a project that we coyut £15 or £20 million into, because if I looked upon it as my own money I believe that long term that would be the right thing to do, but it was going to knock us about desperately in the short term – that would now be a prime restraint. I would just totally disregard the possibility of doing that because of the risk to which it would put the organization. It is not the risk that it would put to our financial state, but the risk in the open market.

He also argued that the nature of retailing is such that small, incremental steps make a lot of sense given that even fixed assets in retailing are, relatively speaking, not that fixed. He expected, and believed he was expected, to provide short-term return on investment that was, in the main disposable as property:

> One of the differences between retailing and, say, engineering is that you tend to take much shorter-term decisions. I am going after immediate return; I am not in the position of Michael Edwards who says 'Do we lay down £150 million pounds to try and make the Metro: because that might make us profit in five years' time?' We do not have that sort of situation.

It was a view of management process that was espoused by other managers too:

> The real strength of the company is to be able to follow these peripheral excursions into whatever, because most of them are lossmakers. . . . One has got to keep thrusting in these directions: they are little tentacles going out, testing the water.

Also:

> We haven't stood still in the past and I can't see with our present set-up that we shall stand still in the future; but what I really mean is the path of evolution rather than revolution. Some companies get a successful formula and stick to that rigidly because that is what they know – for example Burtons who did not really adapt to the change in climate from bespoke to casual, so they had to take what was a revolution. We hopefully have changed gradually and that's what I think we should do. We are always looking for fresh openings without going off at a tangent.

Other examples, many of which are included in the case itself, serve to show that in 1980 the nature of the management system described was incremental in the sense that Quinn (1980) means it; and that the logic of this, according to the managers, included the following:

- Small movements in strategy allow deliberate experimentation and sensing of the environment through action; if such small movements prove successful, then further development of strategy can take place.
- Shareholders expect short-term returns; therefore, it is not sensible to commit large sums of money or other resources to major shifts in strategy.
- It is better to make continual adjustments to strategy so as to keep in line with market changes; if this is not done, then the company's strategy will become atrophied and over time will lead to the need for radical repositioning. (It is ironic that this reason was given quite explicitly in 1980 and it was felt then that a good example of atrophy and attempted radical repositioning was Burtons, whereas Fosters had been more able to change in line with the market.)
- Opportunistic management are able to search for ways in which they can take advantage of the matching of an historic and developing strategy with a developing market.
- The nature of retailing is particularly suited to incremental adjustment, since there are few really fixed costs and assets; for example, property is

saleable. It is, therefore, much less of a commitment and risk to try out a new strategy, because it can be done by opening a few new shops, or adjusting merchandise in shops; if this does not work, then the shops can be disposed of, or the merchandise sold off with relatively little loss.

- In a business in which there is a high regard for people, it is important not to 'rock the boat' too much; people will go along with change much more readily if it is gradual and they can become used to it.

These are the sort of reasons given by the managers at Fosters for what amounted to an espoused theory of incremental strategic management; they are reasons which do, indeed, bear a striking resemblance to those given by managers to Quinn in the research he conducted in the late 1970s and that resulted in his advocacy of 'logical incrementalism' as a system of strategic management.

In so far as there are observable patterns of incremental development both to the managers and the outsider, the phenomenon of incrementalism can be said to have been confirmed. Moreover, if the espousal of the logic of incrementalism is examined in the context of the company's performance to 1980, it would be tempting to concur with the view that such a process is, indeed, beneficial. Fosters had just enjoyed a decade of virtually continuous profit growth and a four-year period in which it had achieved record profits, whilst more large competitors could only generate book profits through the sale of properties. There are, however, two dangers in this interpretation. The first is a danger of dubious causality: it is one thing to recognize the phenomenon of incrementalism, even to note the espousal of 'logical incrementalism'; it is quite another to suppose that a good record of profit performance can be explained by it. Indeed the events in Fosters between 1980 and 1983 were to show that the processes of management in the firm were not adequate to prevent a dramatic decline in company fortunes.

The second danger is that of assuming that the logic of the processes described by the managers is necessarily a reasonable description of the processes that actually account for strategy formulation. This research was concerned to study strategic change as a longitudinal, contextual process, rather than as the espoused theory of the managers. It will be shown that a somewhat different picture of the process of strategic management emerges if patterns of development of strategy in the business are examined in terms of the historically reconstructed events, dramas and routines of organization life and the belief systems of managers. The evidence of the Fosters case confirms that incremental patterns of strategic change are typical, but we need to look beyond rationalistic models of management to explain why this is so. This is one of the tasks of the chapters that follow.

7
Strategy and Organizational Culture

The review of strategy-making in Fosters from a 'rational manager' perspective has proved to be inadequate as an explanation of the change processes observed. The rationalistic explanations we have examined and the associated analytical, planning models, remove strategic management from day-to-day management activities and suggest that strategic decisions are set apart, perhaps even institutionalized, in systems of strategic decision-making. We saw, however, that explanations of incrementalism have their roots rather more in the organizational processes, often routinised, through which managers operate. In this sense, incrementalism is seen to be a sort of bridging process between environmental changes and organizational processes. In this chapter we examine in more detail an explanation of the process of strategic management which is rooted in the day-to-day 'realities' of the lives of managers in an organization.

There is no denial here that planning goes on in organizations or that senior management, or other levels of management, consider the nature of their business environment and how to adapt business strategies. There is no denial that these processes occur; what is questionable is the extent to which they actually account for the formulation of strategy and the processes of strategic change.

However, if the perspectives on strategy discussed so far are inadequate explanations, this still leaves questions as to why the strategies followed were adopted; why they persisted and what the mechanisms of strategic change were? Central to the explanation that will be provided here is the view that strategy formulation is characterized by the way in which individuals in an organizational context make sense of, and respond to, a changing environment – that strategy formulation, and the management of strategic change needs to be seen as a social, cultural, political and cognitive activity.

A problem in the literature on decision-making and change is that at the level of psychological explanation, explanatory models are in almost every case individually based and devoid of social specificity. The social context of decisions is seen as 'background noise' rather than an essential part of the problem. It is clear enough why this should be the case: psychologists and decision theorists have found it difficult enough to explain how individuals go about taking decisions; it is the more difficult when the individual is interacting in a social setting, in which other individuals are also tackling the same problem or one that is related – moreover where groups or individuals are competing with others for organizational resources. Figure 7.1 summarizes the arena in which we need to consider strategy formulation: it suggests that any explanation must take into account at least three aspects of the process: (a) how individuals make sense of environmental stimuli, (b) how, if at all, the collectivities of individuals we call organizations make sense of the same stimuli and (c) how the interactions of organizational life affect decision-making.

As far as this third aspect of organizational life is concerned, explanation must take account of at least (a) how individuals make sense, not just of their external environment, but of their organizational context; (b) how the nature of the organization influences the behaviour of individuals and

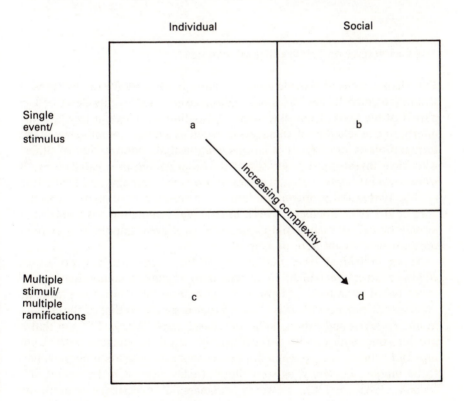

FIGURE 7.1 Levels of complexity in decision-making

groups; and (c) how individuals and groups seek to manipulate others to achieve their ends. Explanatory models must therefore embrace cognitive, cultural and political dimensions of decision-making and change at both an individual and organizational level.

It is precisely because of this level of complexity that rationalistic models of strategy formulation have been so attractive. They have the merit of simplicity: they recognize the need to understand a changing environment and provide an analytical framework by which to do it. The complexities of the organizational context in which it might be done are regarded as a sort of 'black box' which can be conceived of in essentially structural terms. The danger of such an approach is that the problems of strategy formulation are reduced to such an extent that they fail to provide relevant guidance to the manager who must live and operate within an organizational context. In such a context relevant 'lessons' about the management of strategy must build on, integrate and be expressed in terms that address the realities of organizational life.

THE CENTRALITY OF INTERPRETATIVE SCHEMES

This chapter aims to provide an explanatory framework for the patterns of strategy formed by the decisions, non-decisions and events described in part II of the book. Central to such explanation is the extent to which the interpretative schemes of managers are seen as a dominant influence in the formulation of strategy. It is an observation that confirms that of others who have investigated processes of decision-making in organizations. It was shown in chapter 2 that in stages of problem awareness and incubation (Lyles, 1981), and problem resolution and solution development (Mintzberg et al., 1976; Soelberg, 1967), in strategy formulation has what might loosely be called 'managerial experience' is of great importance. A brief recapitulation might here be helpful.

At an individual level the notion of the 'script' as 'a hypothetical cognitive structure which, then activated, organizes comprehension of event based situations' (Abelson, 1981) helps explain what is meant by 'managerial experience'. It is a notion that is similar to that of the 'theory in use' (Argyris and Schön, 1978) or 'causal map' (Weick, 1977) in that it provides the manager with 'a repertoire of examples, images, understandings and actions . . . [so when he] makes sense of a situation he perceives to be unique, he *sees* it as something already present in his repertoire' (Schön, 1983, p. 138). However, 'managerial experience' cannot be accounted for solely as a function of individual cognition. Others have observed sense making systems at industry and organizational levels. Spender (1980), Grinyer and Spender (1979a) and Huff (1982) show that industry-level 'recipes' or 'frames' play a role in defining situations and providing guidelines for response. And at an organizational level there are discernible configurations of beliefs reported, variously termed 'myths' (Hedberg and Jönsson, 1977), ideologies (Beyer, 1981), interpretative schemes (Bartunek 1984), paradigms (Sheldon, 1980, Pfeffer, 1981b), that serve the same function. Those who take a cognitive perspective on strategic management would thus agrue that the 'reality' of the complex world the manager faces is configured in terms of structures of meaning lodged within the individual, the organization and at an industry level. What is less clear is just *how* such structures take effect in strategy formulation. Daft and Weick (1984, p. 293) assert that 'the process of interpretation is so familiar that it is taken for granted, which may be why little research on this topic has been reported'.

In what follows, these interpretative schemes are explained specifically in the Fosters context and there is developed an explanation of how such interpretative schemes take effect in action. This is done by identifying and explaining the nature of interpretative schemes that helped to configure strategy in Fosters, seeking to understand how such schemes were preserved, how they took effect in action, and how strategic change occurred given such interpretative schemes.

THE NATURE OF INTERPRETATIVE SCHEMES

Interpretative schemes in the context of organizations are systems of beliefs that, for those in the organization, make sense of that organization. As such we are concerned with 'ideology', in so far as we can conceive of ideologies as 'relatively coherent sets of beliefs that bind some people together and that explain their world in terms of cause and effect relations' (Beyer, 1981, p. 166): and we are concerned with 'ideational culture' in Schein's sense of 'assumptions and beliefs [as] learned responses to a group's problems of survival' (Schein, 1985, p. 6). Like Schein, Mannheim (1936) has argued that it is necessary to conceive of different levels of beliefs: there are those that are concerned with 'world views', more 'total' or general in their nature, and associated with groups of societies; and those that are 'particular' in so far as they are related to a more specific context. Such distinctions raise questions about the role and nature of ideology in organizations. In particular, in the context of this study, to what extent are individual belief systems related to organizational ideologies? Are we, for example, to assume that they are somehow subjugated to more total organizational ideologies? If not, then what mechanisms are at work to provide a degree of cohesion or consensus for organizational action? Also, what is the role of ideology in an interpretative sense: what sorts of beliefs 'bind some people together and . . . explain their world in terms of cause and effect relations' as Beyer has it, and how does this occur?

An analysis of the individual belief systems of the managers at Fosters was undertaken. This analysis was not so much concerned with their views about particular situations or problems, as with the views they expressed about their underlying and personal expectations for and about the business, their role in it and its role vis-à-vis themselves and others in the organization. The aim was to establish the extent of unity of individual ideologies at a fairly fundamental level – in short, whether or not the managers saw the relationship between themselves and the business in the same sorts of ways. The analysis was conducted on the basis of the interviews carried out in 1980 – that is, after the years of growth – and took the form of a thematic content analysis of the transcripts, yielding a binary data base which facilitated a cluster analysis of the individual managers. What emerged were two quite different clusters of ideologies, which could be further subdivided into five. These were in summary as detailed in the following.

Cluster A

This group of managers was characterized by a rather personal orientation towards the business: they saw the business as a vehicle for personal fulfilment, challenge or ambition.

Cluster A1 comprised managers who wished to be associated with a publicly successful, growing company in which such growth was seen in terms of profits and increased retail presence in new locations. These managers were mainly members of the Board and buyers.

Cluster A2 was a group of managers who saw business in terms of a challenge, gaining satisfaction personally from association with that challenge, and believed that others did so too. Amongst these managers there was a good deal of discussion about the way in which employees gained from and expected a challenging environment.

Cluster A3 was a group of managers who again emphasized the challenging nature of the organization but also emphasized their desire for personal promotion or 'a bigger job'. These managers were, by background, senior managers who had risen from shop management. They saw the growth of the business in terms of numbers of retail outlets.

Cluster B

Managers within this cluster held beliefs that were rather more orientated towards the external world and the role of the business in the external world. They were, typically, more junior management than those in cluster A.

B1 was a group of managers who saw a need to maintain continual growth to keep the City happy, avoid takeover and keep ahead of competition. There was a marked lack of discussion of personal expectations and a generally conservative view about the development of the business in so far as they regarded historical strategy as important to maintain and build upon. Managers here tended to be head-office service managers rather than field operators.

B2 were managers who also discussed their views of the business in fairly operational ways, particularly in terms of the need to keep ahead of competition. There was here a recognition of personal benefits of a growing business. This cluster of managers was also typified by a view about dangers of 'standing still', which they saw as inevitably meaning a declining business in retail terms; but, again, change was seen as, necessarily, building on historical strategy.

With so few managers it would be foolish to draw too many conclusions from such an analysis. However, what the exercise illustrates is that managers within Fosters saw the business, and their role in the business, rather differently. It would be wrong to assume that, despite the fact that there was a very high proportion of long-serving managers in Fosters, they all had the same expectations about the business. In other words there is reason to believe that individual ideologies are potentially quite divergent, and this within an organization that might be typified as clannish (Ouchi, 1980). Yet it is equally clear in reading the transcripts that there was a high degree of agreement on the overall strategic position of the business. There are a number of ways in which the divergence at one level and congruency at another might be explained.

The process might be accounted for by essentially political models. The process of bargaining might reconcile divergent ideologies, and accommodate them through compromise or the 'quasi-resolution' of potential conflict (Cyert and March, 1963; Pettigrew, 1973) within what amounts to the 'negotiated order' (Strauss et al., 1963) of an organization. Such a model implies that the organization is in a state of relative ideological turmoil, the resolution of which is a coping process through negotiation within 'rules' which build up over time and are specific to the organization. An implication is that 'change is inevitable and continuous (though often slow)' (Fine, 1984). A second model would suggest that potential divergencies are dealt with by achieving 'compliance' (Etzioni, 1961) through a coercive, remunerative or normative exercise of power. Such a model would argue that the disincentives of not harmonizing, or apparently harmonizing, around some common set of beliefs outweighs any natural inclination towards divergence.

There are indeed examples in the Fosters case of political activity. Certainly the Chief Executive and other senior executives – notably the Merchandise Director – exercised considerable power. Indeed many of the managers explicitly commented on the extent to which the Chief Executive exercised high degrees of centralized authority.

There is also the implication in many of the decision routines that different groupings were indulging in what might be regarded as a process of bargaining and negotiation in which their various interests and inclinations were traded off against each other. For example, the incremental resolution regarding 'Fashionpoint' could be seen very much in these terms. However, such approaches fail to account for two persistent phenomena. The idea that managers saw the firm's strategic position in quite different terms, such that political bargaining processes were somehow necessary to sort out such divergences, misrepresents the case. Generally managers saw the strategic position of the firm in quite similar ways. We are left with having to account for why such unity of beliefs about the organization's position should exist and persist. Second, even if we accept that the political dominance of certain individuals helps explain why strategies were followed, a purely political perspective does not explain why they advocated the strategies they did. We will return to political influences on strategy but it is necessary to explain further interpretative process before we do so.

Another view about the relative unity of ideology at a strategic level within an organization is that beliefs that managers have are 'regularized' within the organization. Such processes of regularization have been shown to include initiation rites, designed to show new managers that they 'have things to learn' (Schein, 1974), through 'intimidation rituals' (O'Day, 1974), of isolation and defamation, to the control of recruitment and training (Pettigrew, 1973; Schein, 1974) in the attempt to ensure that new arrivals 'fit in'. A more benign view of such regularization is implicit within the notion of Kelman (1958) of 'identification and 'internalization' as bases for compliance. Here it is argued that managers take an organization perspective not because they are forced to, but because they accept such a perspective. Kotter's (Kotter, 1973; Kotter and Lawrence, 1974) argument that individuals enter into a sort of 'contract' with an organization, the basis of which is the matching of their personal 'agenda' with that of the organization, to some extent squares these two views. In other words whether through regularization or through a voluntary matching of the agendas of individuals and organizations, there emerges some ideological congruence.

Again, in Fosters we see such processes at work. The history of the company was one of recruitment at an early age into the company and promotion from within: even relatively senior managers joining from other retailers were required to start on the 'shop floor' and learn the Fosters way of doing things. Managers or consultants who were regarded as 'deviants' were liable to find themselves subject to regulatory behaviour; for example when Richard Haynes moved into the company as a director he nonetheless found himself without any clear job definition, what he perceived as relatively non-compliant fellow directors and an implicit message that he was expected to conform and that 'the mafia' might 'get him' if he did not. One result was indeed a system of homogeneous beliefs about the nature of the organization within its business environment.

This does not, however, explain what the nature of the beliefs was and how they affected the formulation of strategy. The argument that will be put forward here is that an understanding of just what constitutes the core beliefs about the strategic position of the business is central to understanding why strategy is formulated in the way it is, and indeed many of the mechanisms associated with the process of formulation. We now move on, therefore, to an investigation of how an interpretative perspective on strategic management helps explain the process at work in Fosters. In so doing we develop a model of interpretative systems at a strategic level that incorporates and explains incremental and 'organizational action' notions of strategic development.

THE NOTION OF THE PARADIGM IN AN ORGANIZATIONAL SETTING

Returning for a moment to the notion of total and particular ideologies, we might expect, following Mannheim, that it is total ideologies that bind managers within some degree of organizational unity. Such beliefs would presumably be concerned with the role of the organization in society, the bases or boundaries of competition, the ethos of the organization and so on. They would be general, overarching ideals about the way the organization is, or should be, which most managers could embrace. The suggestion here, however, is that such total ideology is difficult to locate within Fosters and not especially evident in the processes of strategy formulation. This is not to say, however, that there is an absence of unifying ideology. On the contrary, the proposition that will be elaborated here is that a set of beliefs held relatively commonly throughout the organization, taken for granted, but discernible in the stories and explanations of the managers, played a central role in strategy formulation. However these beliefs, in Fosters, were of a very particular nature. It will be argued that this set of beliefs, specific to the organization, configures organizationally relevant meaning in such a way as to inform and help formulate strategy. This is not a new idea: the notion of organization-specific belief sets as sense-making mechanisms is encapsulated in the concept of 'ideational culture' and described and discussed, using a variety of terms, by many different writers (see pages 41–42, 216). The term used here to describe such a belief set, borrowed from Brown (1978), Sheldon (1980) and Pfeffer (1981b) in the organizational literature, is 'paradigm'*, that is:

> Those sets of assumptions, usually implicit, about what sort of things make up the world, how they act, how they hang together, and how they may be known . . . organisational paradigms provide roles to be enacted in particular ways, in particular settings, and in particular relation to other roles. (Brown, 1978, p. 373)

This set of beliefs and assumptions labelled 'the paradigm' is linked to action in so far as it

> . . . provide[s] organisational participants with a sense of belonging and identity as well as demarcating the organisation from its environment and assisting in the control and commitment of those within the organisation. (Pfeffer, 1981b, p. 13)

If the general concept and specific terminology are established in the management literature, what is less clear is just what role the paradigm plays in the formulation of strategy. It is this issue that will now be explored using the Fosters case as a context for analysis and discussion. However, first it is necessary to identify the core beliefs that made up the paradigm in Fosters.

It has been shown that there was relatively little discussion by managers in 1980 of matters external to the firm, for example about competition or the nature of the market. However, such evidence of an external focus as does exist indicates that there was some measure of disagreement about

---

*(I have elsewhere (Johnson, 1984; 1985) used the term 'strategic formula' to signify the same phenomenon. I am persuaded, however, that there is no value in the proliferation of terms for describing similar phenomena.)

the market place. We saw how in the 1970s Fosters' management saw the changing fashion trends in different ways. Retail managers and some younger managers viewed the changes as potentially threatening but also as opportunities that needed to be built upon. More established and older managers, and the Merchandise Director in particular, saw the changes as relatively peripheral to Fosters. In 1980 there were also some disagreements about the nature of the market place and Fosters' place within it. Brian Wood saw a need to move towards what he termed the 'Hepworths end of the market'. Mike Adams clearly disagreed about the opportunities that existed within the retail markets for jeans. Melvyn Taylor felt that there was a risk that the Fosters image in the market place might become confused. Some saw the major multiples as having entered Fosters traditional market; others were relatively dismissive still of the threat of competition. The point is that the way in which managers in Fosters saw their competitive environment varied; there was not a common view of the external situation in which Fosters was competing; moreover the evidence was that such differences of opinion had existed through the 1970s.

However, if the views of managers about their competitive environment differed, there were quite homogeneous views about other aspects of the market and, especially, matters internal to the firm concerned with 'the way we do things around here' (Deal and Kennedy, 1982). There were, in effect, sets of beliefs that were persistent and held relatively commonly about the ways to compete in the market and the legitimacy of the routines (Nelson and Winter, 1982) of the organization in coping with the business situation. These were beliefs that had built up over time and been reinforced through the activity of managing.

Taking 1980 as a focal point we can identify a number of discernible constructs, illustrated in table 7.1, that were just such shared assumptions held in common by virtually all the managers, and are detectable in the transcripts of the discussions held with the managers at that time. There was a strong emphasis on the role and importance of merchandise and buying, specifically the strong belief that the company's success hinged around the ability and experience of the buyers to locate and negotiate the provision of ranges of merchandise, suitable for the Fosters working-men's market, so as to provide low cost, high margins and yet good value in the market place. Fosters was, essentially, a merchandise-driven company. As Brian Wood was, later, to put it, they had the view that 'if you've got the merchandise right, you can sell it out of fish barrels'. The shops had been long regarded as the vessels through which the merchandise was driven; by 1980 many were in second-rate positions and in poor states of repair. This orientation around the primacy of merchandise was not an issue on which managers had differing views. They might differ as to the nature of the market place; they did not, however, differ when it came to the central means by which Fosters would succeed in the market; it was by getting the merchandise right, and that meant buying in bulk mainly from overseas suppliers, and maintaining a high-margin policy for merchandise suited to the working man.

TABLE 7.1   *Constructs of the paradigm in Fosters in 1980*

* Low-cost, good-value, high-margin merchandise * Skills and experience of buyers in negotiation and range planning	A merchandise focus
* Fast, growth-orientated, entrepreneurial decision-making by top management * Caring top management * Loyal, experienced, committed staff * Centralised, tight control of stock and distribution	Supported by a mode of management
* Dominant in secure working-man's market segment	Yielding a clear market position

The central focus on merchandise was supported by other constructs within the paradigm, largely about the way in which the company was managed. It was generally accepted that the company was centralized primarily upon the Chief Executive for virtually all significant decisions. All the managers had stories to tell about the centrality of Barry Davison or Mr High; they were seen as entrepreneurial, fast-moving decision-makers, always ready to intervene and assert their point of view and with an ability to take decisions fast. The stories often had the flavour of mixed irritation and amusement at the extent to which the Chief Executive might interfere, but with the virtually universal acceptance that, as a mechanism for 'getting things done', it worked. Moreover senior management, and the Chief Executive in particular, were seen to be part of a caring organization for those loyal to the company. Fosters was not the sort of place where people were hired and fired; the company provided secure employment and an environment in which staff could find their appropriate level of expertise. It was in many respects rather like a family company; and if managers talked about the inevitability of this changing, they did so reluctantly and still with the view that its benefits could and should be preserved. This caring style of management from the top was balanced, and benefited from, the loyalty and experience of committed staff, many of whom had been with the company for very many years. This too was seen as a great benefit; it meant that, if changes needed to be made, whether they be a shop refitting or the staffing of some new enterprise, such changes could be made swiftly and with commitment by a team of managers who knew how the business worked.

A more mechanistic construct within the paradigm was the perceived benefit of the centralization and tight control of current assets in the form of stock through the centralized buying process and the supporting distribution system. Managers prided themselves on working for a company that was good at controlling its costs; the high margins that were to be made on merchandise, combined with the low costs resulting from the means of control, were seen to have provided many years of profitable growth that provided the security of employment valued in the company.

Underlying these constructs was a particular view of Fosters' place in the market. All managers agreed that Fosters was in 'the C2D market for men's clothing'. Fosters sold clothes for the working man and benefited because this market sector was secure and Fosters dominant within it. Moreover their experience in managing the merchandise and distribution systems so as to provide very healthy profits and yet highly competitive prices in the market place meant that smaller retailers could not hope to compete as effectively.

Before we move on, it is important to make a number of points clear about the claims being made for this notion of the paradigm. First, it should be emphasized that these constructs were not necessarily made explicit by the managers. They were identified from the themes and explanations embedded in the stories and accounts of events told by the managers. What distinguishes these constructs, in particular, is the extent to which they recurred over and over again in various forms in the transcripts of the discussions with managers and were the common property of managers at different levels in the firm and with different responsibilities. It is not suggested that such homogeneity of beliefs is always the case in all organizations: indeed it will be shown how such homogeneity broke down in Fosters in the 1980s. However, other empirical studies (e.g. by Grinyer and Spender, 1979a; Davis, 1984; Janis, 1972; Miles and Snow, 1978; Smircich, 1983a) theory development (e.g. by Abravanel, 1983; Kiesler and Sproull, 1982; Wilkins and Ouchi, 1983; Weick, 1977) and practical experience suggest that there are many organizations in which just such homogeneity around a core set of beliefs occurs. This is not to say of course that they are the same sort of beliefs as those identified in Fosters; but it is likely that their existence may have similar effects.

Second, the distinction between 'strategy' and the 'paradigm' needs to be clarified. Following Mintzberg (1978) it is useful to distinguish between 'intended' and 'realized' strategy. Realized strategy is taken to mean the observable output of an organization's activity in terms of its competitive positioning over time. Realized strategy can be seen in what the organization does in the market place. This may or may not arise directly from 'intended' strategy. By intended strategy is meant the strategy that managers espouse perhaps in some sort of formal plan or public statement. The paradigm, on the other hand, is a more generalized set of beliefs about the firm and the way it is or should be. The argument that will be developed here is that both intended and realized strategy are likely to be configured within the parameters of this paradigm but this does not mean that they are the same phenomena. For example, the move to more fashionable merchandise in Fosters, and managers' espousal of Fosters becoming a fashion retailer, could not be said to be part of the paradigm. There were in fact quite considerable differences in views about what it meant to be a fashion retailer. However, the way in which realized strategy actually took shape will be shown to have its roots in the paradigm. There may also be intended strategies that have nothing apparently to do with the paradigm. The espousal in 1980 by most of the Board of Fosters of the need for diversification was not easily traceable to the paradigm; but again whilst there were disagreements about the wisdom and nature of diversification, the ways in which diversification strategies were followed were very much in line with the paradigm – the realized strategy was developed within its bounds.

Nor is it suggested that the paradigm is fixed. Certainly if the history of Fosters is examined there is evidence to suggest that the paradigm current in 1980 had evolved somewhat over the 6om one that, in the 1960s, had much less of an emphasis on merchandise and a much greater emphasis on branch acquisition. The paradigm changed with time and in action. It will be shown that its constructs are, in effect, what managers perceive as the lessons of operating – what might be regarded as collective managerial experience. However, whilst the paradigm is not fixed, it is not typically susceptible to rapid change, and again it will be shown later why this is so. What is clear is that constructs of the paradigm are likely to have a persistent influence. For example the residue of the 1960s' combination of opportunistic property acquisition and low-cost operations were still evident in the firm in the 1980s. Mike Adams gave as an example in 1980 the acquisition in that year of a large branch in Cardiff:

A £2 million investment and [Menswear] is paying a rent to the Property Division of £80,000. No way can you say in commercial terms that this is a return. If you take it as a property investment and say that property is inflating at 10 per cent or 15 per cent, or whatever, you can justify it though.

The dominant influence of the paradigm is more than a phenomenon observed by the researcher. The dominance was realized by the managers, certainly by 1983. For example, one senior manager cited the dominant influence of the merchandise focus in the 1970s:

> We did have the belief in this company in the 1970s that the critical factor in successful menswear retailing was not the [shop] environment but was the product.

He went on to illustrate how those who were arguing for improved shop presentation found little sympathy within the company, and particularly from those at the top of the company, who were convinced of the supporting constructs of a merchandise-driven operation with a low-cost base.

Much the same sort of comment was made by a director as to why shops, which were being re-designed in the late 1970s by the Fitch design company, failed:

> There wasn't a commitment to change the branch environment at that stage. We were going through Fitch and other designers to try and get new designs for shops without any real success because they were coming up with designs that had to take into account our merchandise.

In 1983 Barry Davison also related the same lesson about neglect of the shop environment to the total decline of the business:

> Fosters made improvements in their shops over the past 10 years but only in line with their sector of the market; we did not really do anything new to bring people into the shops. Now Burtons took a very different stance. They said there is a very big market available to make shops extremely attractive.

The extent to which they relied on current methods of buying and the belief that traditional merchandise provision was adequate was later seen to have been harmful. For example, they saw they had deluded themselves with Fashionpoint because, as a marginal adjustment, it disguised the need for more fundamental change:

> There were two themes running along at the same time. One was 'Let's have a Fashionpoint area of the shop and just try with a bit of tinsel or paper to create an image'; but the rest of the shop was still the working-men's outfitters. So there wasn't a clear dedication to follow through the fashion logic as there is now.

The dominance of the merchandise mix as a defining influence in perceived market position and as an assumed central factor in generating demand was not the only reason for the neglect of the shop environment. By 1983 managers themselves saw that another element in their paradigm that worked against shop re-design was the perceived importance of cost control and minimization. Barry Davison:

> What was happening was that we were doing very cheap jobs and getting enormous increases by making very nominal changes. We laughed at all this money Burtons were spending because spending £2000 on a shop brought us an increase in trade.

So whilst success, measured in financial terms, continued, it re-inforced the paradigm. The likelihood of a challenge to the dominance of the merchandise focus was thus even less:

> It was not necessary to make changes to fashion because we were doing very well as we were, mainly on price first. We are able to sell everything we buy. . . . If you don't need it you're not going to say – fine as it is but where are we in ten years' time? We didn't ask ourselves those questions in the 1970s because every year was a record.

THE PARADIGM AS A CULTURAL PHENOMENON

It has already been argued that the paradigm is durable. The reasons for its durability also begin to explain why it is important in the decision-making of the organization.

First, as has been said, a characteristic of the paradigm is that its constructs are held more or less in common throughout the organization. Moreover, they are not seen as problematic; that is, we should not think of them as an explicit set of issues for potential debate: they are, rather, powerful but tacit assumptions about the business. This is illustrated by the problem that I found when wishing to pursue questions about assumptions and beliefs that went to make up the paradigm; such questions were either treated as a symptom of the questioner not knowing about retailing, or they elicited confused and mildly irritated re-assertions of what was seen to be 'obvious'. The paradigm as an aspect of 'ideational culture' is a 'set of important assumptions [often unstated] that members of a community share in common' (Sathe, 1985, p. 10). Fosters was, then, a 'clannish' organization, a 'thick culture' in the extent to which beliefs and assumptions were shared and held in common.

The set of assumptions that comprise the constructs of the paradigm also provide a system of meaning that makes sense of a complex environment in terms of 'what works' and is therefore relevant to managerial experience. Indeed the internal consistency or 'logic' of the paradigm is self-preserving and self-legitimizing. The belief in the efficacy of bulk buying was consistent with the accepted wisdom of centralized control over stocks and distribution; the belief that the company could be 'fast on its feet' because of the entrepreneurial approach of top management and the loyal workforce helped managers to account for how an apparently rigid and closed system could be regarded as capable of flexibility. It is not an easy matter to challenge or repudiate one construct of an internally supportive and consistent whole. Moreover as a self-supporting package of beliefs, it was readily applicable to situations both to explain problems and provide solutions – as will be shown later.

We can go further however. As was discussed in chapter 2, there are views on culture that would suggest that it is possible and sensible to differentiate between ideational culture and an adaptationist's view of culture as represented by systems of behaviour that can be passed on within society (Keesing, 1974). The ideational view concentrates on ideas and the adaptationist view on behaviour or action. As has been consistently argued here, one of the important points about the significance of the paradigm is the extent to which it bridges beliefs and assumptions and action. Indeed the proposition here is that the paradigm is preserved and legitimized within a 'cultural web' of action – myths, rituals, symbols, control systems and structures – which support and provide relevance to core beliefs (see figure 7.2)

A few examples help make the point. It is clear that many of the constructs of the paradigm were embedded in the formal systems of the organization. The assumptions about the approach to buying and merchandising and the emphasis on centralized control of current costs and assets were not only linked themselves, but institutionalized, indeed capitalized, in the stock control and distribution systems, with computerized control systems, a specialist distribution department and a management information system built around it. This is the inertia of technical organizational commitment and is not lightly ignored or overturned. These routines and structures are elsewhere seen as 'instrumental' (Daft, 1983) or 'operational' (Abravanel, 1983) symbols of organizations which, as the more formal aspects of control, have major symbolic significance in so far as 'the idea of culture rests on the promise that the full meaning of things is not given *a priori* in the things themselves. Instead meaning results from

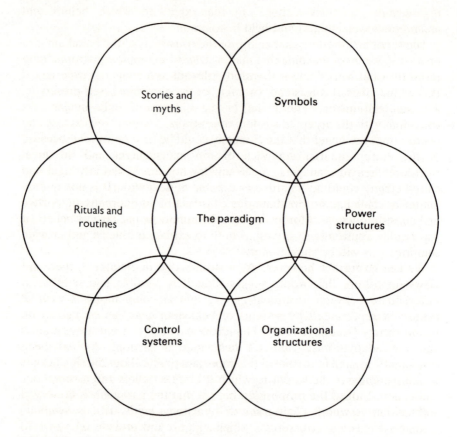

FIGURE 7.2   The cultural web of an organization

interpretation, (Louis, 1983). It is not the control systems *per se* that are significant but the fact that they are 'symbols' – they 'express much more than their intrinsic content' (Morgan et al., 1983). The manager responsible for distribution systems, for example, would conceive of his or her job not merely as the utilization of a computer system or the interpretation of data on stock movements but as a contributor to, indeed a manager of, the strategy of the business through day-to-day activities. Moreover, because such systems are about the day-to-day activity of managing, they represent the reality of what strategic management is about for the managers. The reality of managing the strategy of the business becomes the management of those systems through which the business achieves its success.

The significance of many of these operational aspects of managing the business was highlighted and arguably preserved in the 'softer rituals, myths and symbols' of the organization (Wilkins, 1983; Daft, 1983; Dandridge et al., 1980). For example the dominance of buying and merchandise could be seen in the shop window displays of the 1970s, crowded with every item of merchandise the shops stocked, with an emphasis given to what the buyers had procured; window displays that, themselves, were typically finally approved by the Merchandise Director before they were put into effect. The assumption of the dominant importance of merchandise and buying was also symbolized in the greater freedom and discretion enjoyed by buyers (e.g. on buying trips) in an otherwise tightly controlled business.

There were other aspects of the organizational life less capable of formal rationalization that were nonetheless encapsulated and preserved symbolically. On the 'caring' nature of management there were stories that emphasized the concern of management for staff, for example an emphasis on the difference between retailing and manufacturing because retailing was run on 'trust' and 'love'. In 1980, managers emphasized views about the way in which they were always given the opportunity for career progression: promotion was always from within, and if someone was promoted beyond his competence then he would still be 'looked after'. He might be moved sideways or, if he lost status, would retain the salary. Fosters was not a company that sacked people. The managers also recounted how the Board members took a personal interest in the well being of individuals and their feelings: Mr High gave personal advice to people about courses or career opportunity; Mr Davison sent people Christmas hampers and bottles of brandy, and took them to Athens.

The caring attitude was supported by the emphasis on the importance of staff loyalty and the know-how built up over years of experience in retailing or buying. For example, managers were proud to tell how staff would work extra hours, perhaps 'till three in the morning' or over the weekend in their store or someone else's to help with a refit.

There were rituals of 'Fosterisation' that ensured that everyone knew the Fosters way of retailing. Particularly in the 1960s, this did not only include the training programmes, but included bringing in some quite experienced retailers who were at area manager level in Hepworths, for example, and starting them at branch manager or assistant branch manager in Fosters. Everyone could expect to 'start at the bottom'.

The nature of top management in the firm, its entrepreneurial flair, the speed of decision-making and the centrality of the Chairman were enshrined in stories – such as stories of the speed of decision-making on new shop properties or the annulment of redundancy notices and the conversion of the Jessops factory to the making of blazers. The Chairman was involved in everything, he 'had his finger on the pulse' or 'in every pie' and if that meant that he would interfere in your area, perhaps even be rude to you, well that was just part of the way the business was run. The power of the Chief Executive was also symbolically enshrined in the practices of referring to him as 'Sir'. Moreover the story was told by some that at board lunches the directors left after the meal in order of seniority.

There are other examples, but these serve to make the point that such stories and rituals not only exist but perform an important role. That role is to legitimize and maintain informal systems (Dandridge et al., 1980; Wilkins, 1983) which cannot be routinized. They are particularly prevalent in the thick cultures typified by Fosters, with long-serving, stable staff and where loyalty and long service are highly valued (Wilkins, 1983; Wilkins and Ouchi, 1983) and where there is a congruence of general organizational goals but ambiguity in performance criteria (Ouchi, 1980).

Two points of importance need emphasizing as far as the role of these symbolic aspects of organizational life are concerned. First, as illustrated diagrammatically in figure 7.2 and discussed above, these myths and rituals ground the aspects of ideational culture termed here the 'paradigm', in the behaviour and systems (formal and informal) of organizational life. The way in which that paradigm influences strategy will be explored in more detail in what follows. It is enough here to point out that, as an aspect of ideational culture, it is not preserving of itself: it is threatened by changing external influences and potentially divergent individual beliefs and values. What helps to preserve ideational culture are the wider cultural systems – the myths and rituals we have discussed – to which it is linked and that legitimize it. Secondly, Abravanel (1983) demonstrates that within a dominant ideology there are likely to be conflicts between what he terms the 'fundamental' and the 'operational'; that is, between what the organization sees itself as, or wishes to be, and what it has to do to operate. For example, in Fosters the high value placed upon a caring view of employees and the need to retain and cherish 'team spirit', particularly on the retail side, came increasingly into conflict with the developing of more and more stringent central control, the tightening up on current expenditure and the spending of little on shop refurbishment, in line with the emphasis within the paradigm on centralized and tight control of costs. Both sets of values have been identified as constructs with the paradigm, and illustrate the difference between the fundamental and the operational, and how they might be in conflict. Abravanel argues that this conflict has to be 'mediated' and that this is an important role of 'myth'. Whilst the systems of the organization may represent and account for the operational, many of the stories and rituals described above represent the 'higher-order' perceptions of what the organization is about. In this way such stories and rituals preserve the ideological homogeneity that has been referred to, in the face of such potential contradiction. In these ways the paradigm is likely to be enduring even faced with 'logical' contradictions or threats.

THE PARADIGM AND POLITICAL PROCESSES

When Barry Davison described Fosters as it was in the 1960s and early 1970s he did so as follows:

> Retail companies are very much property companies. In those days they were very much a branch acquisition business more than a retailer. I think I'm the third Managing Director in line that has been a Chartered Accountant. I think it was logical for property people to be very senior because the individual company big decision is acquiring a branch. You are doing it very regularly, much more so than in a manufacturing operation. When you are in a growth pattern, like we were in, it was a very regular procedure. At one stage we opened 50 shops a year. We were always very entrepreneurial about our property decisions; we made quick decisions which gave us a big advantage over companies that take a long time to make decisions. Very much at that time of business the sales people were at a very low profile; and although there was a Buying Director, he was the most junior person in the management team.

And when Mike Adams described the power bases in the company as they developed in the 1970s he did so as follows:

> The emphasis was very much on the buying side of the company dominating the selling side of the company. Tom was a very strong personality. He felt he had to dominate the selling side although he was merchandise director because the volume he was purchasing in the Far East had to be sold and therefore he had to have a strong influence on retail. There was a period of several years when the retail side was very much the poor relation. It was a very successful period in financial terms. They had sales promotions; and if you went downstairs to the display room it would be Tom Jacks who would be saying what went where and why (in the windows). It wouldn't be the retailers saying 'This is how we're going to do it'.

There had been changes in the power bases of the business. First, it was those associated with property decisions when the company, under Geoffrey High, saw branch expansion as the bases of its development. By the mid-1970s it was the buyers who exercised power as the buying formula of the business became established. The source of such power can be conceived of in several ways: the buyers, and the Merchandise Director in particular, in the 1970s were the providers of resources upon which others were dependent (Emerson, 1962; Pfeffer and Salancik, 1978). The Merchandise Director had the confidence of and access to the Chairman (Pettigrew, 1972, 1973, 1975). The buyers were the technical 'gatekeepers' in terms of the key aspect of merchandise policy (Pettigrew, 1972, 1973, 1975). Perhaps most illuminating, however, in terms of the argument being developed here, they were, in effect, in control of operations that reduced uncertainty for the company. It is an observation made by many researchers that 'power accrued to the those sub-units which could best deal with organisational uncertainty' (Pfeffer and Salancik, 1974, p. 137; Hickson et al., 1971; Crozier, 1964; Thompson, 1967; Salancik et al., 1978). The buying policies being followed by the mid-1970s arguably bestowed power on the Merchandise Director for much the same reason as power was bestowed on the property specialists of the 1960s. Both the branch acquisition strategy and later the merchandise strategy were perceived to have the effect of insulating the company from market threats: in the case of branch acquisition, because it established Fosters as the dominant force in, at that time, the distinct and fragmented market sector of outfitting; and in the case of the merchandise strategy of the 1970s, because the price and margin advantages reduced the likelihood of competitive incursions and buffered them against downturns in demand. Changes in fashion were less important to Fosters than to some other companies because they had elected to concentrate on 'commodity' merchandise. Buying sources were also kept to a minimum and provided with opportunities for large production runs so that they were keen to obtain Fosters' business. At the hub of this was the merchandise department. Growing in significance through the 1960s, as the company switched to centralized distribution of merchandise and reduced the shops' freedom to select merchandise, the merchandise strategy became the mechanism through which company profits were to be guaranteed.

The links between the paradigm and power bases in the organization are likely to be close. The paradigm is, in effect, the set of assumptions about the basis upon which the business can compete in an uncertain world. In as much as power has been shown to devolve upon those associated with uncertainty reduction, we might expect the most powerful individuals and groups to be those most identified with the elements of the strategic formula. Moreover, in relation to the earlier discussion about the cultural mechanisms that preserve the constructs of the paradigm, it is also possible to see how the established power structures in the organization are also likely to act as a mechanism for their preservation.

This association of the beliefs culturally bonded into a paradigm and power in the organization means that changing the paradigm is made the more difficult. Strategic change processes traditionally advocated in the literature are linked to rational analytic planning models or the introduction of new ideas through the mechanism of new management. Both of these mechansims were evident in this study and both illustrate why change is problematic.

The notion that it is through analysis of the business environment and of the competitive position of the firm that managers yield insights into strengths and weaknesses that help identify the need for and opportunities for change overlooks the political implications of such analysis. Such analysis was undertaken in Fosters – for example the market research report of 1980. In the period following the analysis, the evidence thrown up was either denied by management, discredited, or led to minimal changes at an operational level. The reason for this was not that the analysis lacked clarity or cogency – quite the reverse. The 1980 market research report pinpointed the problems facing the business and illustrated them with verbatim customer quotations most graphically. The reason the report was initially discredited by senior managers was because it pointedly questioned tenets of belief fundamental to the strategies being followed by the organizations; in other words, that it raised explicit challenges to the paradigm and, as such, constituted not merely an intellectual questioning of strategy but a political threat to those whose power was most associated with it. Moreover, when the relevance of the report was, more than a year later, admitted into the debate on the future of business, clear and unambiguous as its analysis was, and freer as the debate had become by that time, the policy options considered were still along lines compatible with the dominant paradigm. Clarity of analysis does not, in itself, appear to be a sufficient basis for breaking the powerful momentum of the fundamental assumptions here called the paradigm.

Moreover, as we have seen, when new management were introduced and voiced any dissent, such managers were re-educated into more acceptable ways of conceiving of problems most often by immersion in the day-to-day problems of doing things with their associated coping routines, or by being intimidated into accepting the ways of the organization.

8
Processes of Strategy Formulation and Strategic Change: An Interpretative View

The previous chapters in this part of the book have argued that to conceive of strategy in organizations as the outcome of analytical procedures or 'logically' incremental processes is to impose a dubiously rationalistic perspective on organizational behaviour. Rather, it has been suggested that an essentially interpretative cultural and political approach has more explanatory power. We need to understand that organizational environments take on meaning, not independent of organizational context, but within it; specifically that organizations are likely to have more or less homogeneous ideologies, the constraints of which provide meaning and legitimize organizational action. It has been proposed here that there are likely to exist a core set of such beliefs that are taken for granted, endure over time and account for the way the business competes. This has been termed the 'paradigm'. Moreover, these beliefs are to do with organizational characteristics and systems and are embedded in the cultural and political web of organizational life. They are not remote from the day-to-day lives of managers but part of them.

The purpose of this chapter is to re-examine processes of strategy formulation and strategic change, using the Fosters example, given our understanding of the dominance of the set of beliefs and assumptions termed here the paradigm, within this cultural framework.

Understanding Incremental Change

Fosters provides a convenient chronological structure with which to explain how strategies come about and how they typically change. The period up to about 1981 represents one in which we can examine essentially incremental change in which the managers claim they saw themselves attempting to grow a core business and experiment around it. The period 1981–4, in contrast, sees the managers wrestling with more fundamental strategic change following severe performance decline. This chronological device will be used to examine the processes at work in the formulation and re-formulation of strategy.

Taking the case of the strategic development of Fosters in the 1970s, we see an organization that displayed the capacity and willingness to adapt, albeit much as Ouchi (1980) would have it, within their basic assumptions. This is not a company that was strategically stagnant, but one that was continually adapting its product range, building its market presence and experimenting with new ventures. Its managers quite understandably saw it as a successful, adaptive, energetic business in 1980. Yet despite the activity and success of the 1970s, outside observers and the managers themselves were by 1983 able to see that the business had become out of touch with a changing market and had continued to follow inappropriate strategies. There are characteristics of strategic change here that demand more detailed explanation. We have a company that was changing incrementally – if we are to pay heed to the managers accounts in 1980, logically incrementally – yet apparently failing to keep in touch with market realities. We see managers who realized, over time, that the market, and their customers' expectations, were changing, but failed to adjust their retail offering to meet those expectations.

We know that managers were aware of the changing strategies of other retailers: yet they failed to see their full relevance to Fosters.

It was not that changes in the business environment were not seen, nor was it that changes in strategy did not take place: it is evident from the case study that managers were aware of changes taking place in the market and were, in their own terms, implementing policies to deal with those changes. It was rather that the processes of strategy formulation and change were, with hindsight, inadequate and sometimes inappropriate given the environment the business faced a situation not uncommon in the strategic development of other organizations.

An Interpretation of Strategy Formulation in Fosters

It is useful to build on the idea of 'relevant environmental change' as propounded by Rhenman (1973) to explain what we observe in Fosters. We have already seen that in more traditional economic theory environmental change is seen as an independent, external force impacting on the organization. Strategy in this respect is conceived of as a sort of 'stimulus–response' mechanism. We have also seen that those who have written on strategic management have long recognized that, at a minimum, management is a sort of intervening variable; strategic decisions are here seen as a trade-off between environmental forces, organizational resources, management capabilities and the beliefs, values and aims of stakeholders – including the managers themselves. Those who have examined cognitive decision processes adopt a much more managerial orientation. To them the environment's impact on strategic decisions cannot be divorced from managerial cognition: the environment only has significance in terms of decision-making in terms of the way in which it is perceived, interpreted and enacted by the managers.

The argument here is in sympathy with this cognitive perspective. The business environment is seen as a complex, atomistic mix of potentially divergent and ambiguous signals. It is not possible for managers to make sense of such a situation through continual objective analysis – so much has been shown well enough through the work of managerial and social psychologists. Rather, managers must employ some cognitive devices by which to make sense of the complexity and diversity they face. There is nothing new in this as a proposition (see Weick, 1979 a & b; Argyris and Schön, 1974; 1978; Schön, 1983; Hedberg and Jönsson, 1977; Kiesler and Sproull, 1982; Shrivastava and Mitroff, 1983). However, understanding more fully the reasons for the developments in Fosters may help illuminate, within an organizational context, the nature of those devices that provide for the re-ordering of environmental stimuli.

The proposition arising from an analysis of the events in Fosters is that environmental signals will be re-ordered in terms of the paradigm. We can discern a pattern in this that allows a clearer understanding of what is meant by 'relevant environmental change'. The overall proposition is that relevant environmental change will be defined in terms of consonance or dissonance with the paradigm, and it is on these bases that strategic action will be taken. We make this specific below.

(1) Some environmental signals will simply not be perceived as relevant in terms of the paradigm and will be ignored. For example, it would be a mistake to think of the competitive activity of the late 1970s and 1980 as clearly relevant environmental change. The development of Burtons was interesting to observe, deserving of comment, but of no direct consequence and requiring no specific action. After all, Fosters was seen by its management to be in a distinct market sector. Moreover Burtons' huge expenditure at that time on shop refurbishment was viewed with mild amusement by some and seemed to confirm that they were in some other market sector. The other traditional tailors were seemingly remaining within their traditional sector and, although performing badly, were

apparently not in a position to challenge Fosters. To Fosters' management the company remained the largest outfitter in a separate market sector and, in any case, was out-performing all competition.

(2) Other signals might be seen as 'consonant' with the paradigm, in so far as they were capable of interpretation and action within the bounds of that paradigm. For example, regrettable as it might be, the apparent decline in consumer expenditure within the target market in 1980 was seen as a matter that could be handled by a more aggressive sales effort from loyal staff, price competition and even tighter cost control. The paradigm here provided a ready-made menu of responses to a set of circumstances.

(3) There might also be signals from the environment seen as 'dissonant' with the paradigm; that is they might be actual or potential perceived threats to its basis or not capable of being dealt with strictly within its bounds. For example, it appears that the management in Fosters found the changes in buying behaviour of the 'working-class lad' through the 1970s as potentially threatening. It became clear that there was a growing expectation of more fashionable merchandise within the C2D market, and youngsters in particular were increasingly shopping elsewhere for clothes. This was clearly relevant to the merchandise formula of the company, but, as we saw in the mid-1970s, not capable of being handled by the 'pile it high and sell it cheap' approach of that time. It would of course, theoretically, be possible to see the same signals in quite different ways; analytically it might be argued that their notion of a defensible market sector was groundless; or that changing fashion expectations were not simply to do with merchandise but also to do with retail shop ambience. This however, is to take an analytical perspective rather than a cognitive perspective. Market signals were not analysed in this sense but perceived in terms of the organizationally and operationally relevant ideology – what we have called the paradigm.

Given perceived dissonance there appears to be a pattern of response. Dissonance with the paradigm is potentially threatening to its integrity. The responses, given such a threat, seem to follow a pattern.

(1) Dissonance will be mediated symbolically; that is the symbolic mechanisms within which the paradigm is embedded will perform the dual role of maintaining the legitimacy of the paradigm in the face of the apparent threat.
(2) Since such a threat may take the form of a political challenge to those most associated with core constructs of the paradigm, such threats may well take on a political complexion and be strongly resisted.

(3) The problem will be resolved by managers seeking for consonance within the paradigm. That is, managers will seek to resolve the extent to which elements of the environment and the paradigm are in a state of dissonance. It is here that the most significant acts of strategic adaptation take place. The evidence throughout the period under study at Fosters is that such consonance is achieved by:

(a) interpreting the dissonance in terms of the paradigm;

(b) where necessary marginally adjusting the paradigm, but from within its own bounds, and whilst maintaining its essential form;

(c) taking action in line with the (adjusted) paradigm.

Moreover such processes take place within the social and political arena of organizational decision-making characterized by qualitative data search, solicitation of opinion, lobbying, iterative problem resolution and the application of the familiar, which characterizes strategic decision-making, and is illustrated in figure 8.1. In order to illustrate this pattern of strategy

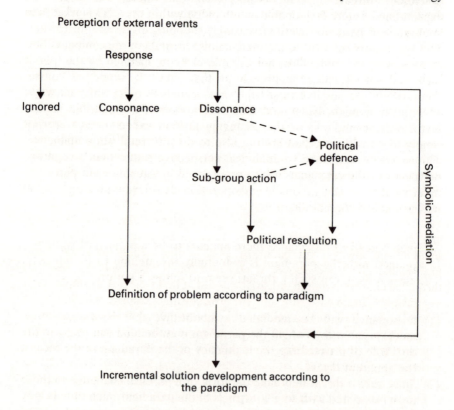

FIGURE 8.1   A pattern of problem resolution and strategy formulation

formulation, a brief review of some examples from the events in Fosters over the period might help. These examples are drawn from the case study in part II of the book and re-interpreted in terms of both the 'lessons' advanced by the managers themselves with the benefit of hindsight, and the explanatory models that were discussed in chapter 7.

'Fashionpoint' – A Process of Lobbying and Incremental Adjustment

It is clear enough that managers in the business were well aware of fashion changes early in the 1970s. The picture emerges of more junior management, mainly from the relatively low-power base of the retail side of the company, sensing the need for change and in some cases trying to put into effect such changes, if only locally, by the infiltration of merchandise. Moreover they were lobbying for merchandise changes, apparently over a period of years, but their appeals for change were ignored or blocked by senior, more powerful managers. Arguably it was these managers, and in particular senior merchandise executives, who were most wedded to, and arguably derived power from, the established and hitherto successful strategy rooted in the dominant paradigm. Those resisting change could draw on a whole raft of justifications for such resistance: lead times on high-volume purchasing were long; more fashionable items might jeopardize volume purchases and hence margins; it would be more difficult to control a widening merchandise range; in any case, profit growth was continuing and there was no other serious competitor in their market sector. In short, they could draw upon well established bases of the strategic success of the business to defend the legitimacy of the approach to business upon which their power had been built.

However, it has to be noted that those from within the business advocating change were also conceiving of problems and solutions within much the same paradigm constraints. To them the customer was much the same as he always had been; he just wanted access to some more fashionable goods. Moreover it was a problem that could be resolved through a change in merchandise: it was not at that time, for example, seen as a problem to do with shop design, or requiring a change in definition of target market. There is no evidence to suggest that anyone was conceiving of problems or solutions in ways fundamentally different from that configured by the paradigm. And there is certainly no evidence of any systematic gathering of data or analysis of market data by which to challenge an essentially internalized view of how to deal with the problem.

The picture emerges of two 'lobbies', one more powerful than the other, but both operating within much the same cognitive bounds. Shop management did not see themselves advocating fundamentally different strategies; however, more senior management, particularly on the merchandise side of the business, did see the advocated changes as potentially substantial shifts in strategy. The divisions between the two groups appear to have lasted a number of years; yet the essential homogeneity of the management team was maintained. One of the mechanisms for its maintenance was undoubtedly the continued profitable growth of the business. Arguably another was the mediating role of the myths and rituals of the organization. The ritually elevated power base of merchandising, embedded in stories about the dominance of Mr Jacks in decision-making on operational issues, legitimized the relatively lower influence of the retail managers. Any potential schism was, however, overcome by the apparently benign and patriarchal role of Mr High: he embodied the caring nature of the firm and managers could be ensured of a career of progression within a system known to look after its own.

The resolution of the problem was through the mechanism of what managers saw as logically incremental action. Fashionpoint can be seen as a change in strategy that was defined in terms of the paradigm and implemented gradually so as not to interfere with what was 'known to work'. Although the aim was to 'become more fashionable', this was done in such a way that bulk buying from overseas, could be retained, so each new range had to be tested to ensure volume sales. Fashion was defined as imitating what other retailers demonstrated they could sell in volume: buyers explained that 'we would take a garment to the Far East and ask them to make it for us; perhaps changing it a bit to meet the needs of our customers'. There was to be no loss of control on stocks: distribution was retained at the centre and shops had to 'qualify' for Fashionpoint on the evidence of past sales of the limited range of fashion merchandise available. The shops themselves were hardly changed; Fashionpoint was introduced in most shops as a display area only, kept separate from the traditional outfitting merchandise and perhaps highlighted in a section of the window. Moreover such changes were moderately successful and the effect of this success was to offer evidence that the changes that were taking place were sufficient and sensible.

Blue Movers

Whilst on the face of it, the setting up of Blue Movers appears to be a move away from the traditional retailing approach by Foster, the way in which the operation was set up was very much within the generalized processes of strategy development we have already discussed and, specifically, much influenced by the dominant paradigm.

Fosters had built up its sales of jeans almost by default and, originally, out of its workwear merchandise base. Throughout the 1970s it had become one of the largest volume retailers of jeans. However the 1970s had also seen the growth of speciality jean shops and these were eroding Fosters' share of that product market. Initially this was seen as a problem for which the current paradigm provided potential solutions – here was an example of 'consonance'.

In particular such developments coincided with the fact that there were shops within the menswear company that were performing badly. There were two possibilities; one was to close them down and the other to develop them to return to profits. The closure of such shops would have been contrary to the central tenet that the company had a responsibility for the well being and appointment of staff and that motivation on the retail side of the business was maintained in this way. It would also have meant the disposal of properties at a depressed price within a business that saw itself good at making it properties work profitably. After all, the fortunes of the business had been built on the acquisition and therefore growth of branches. The closure of the shops would have been seen as a negative move; the development of the shops was a positive move.

The early development of the test shops was characterized by the application of the experience of those within the menswear operation. The work was carried out by the Regional Sales Manager in terms of choice of shops, the commissioning of their design, their layout and window design; it was based on what existing retail management saw as 'fashionable'. There was no attempt to recruit new sales staff; rather, existing menswear retail staff were provided with the opportunity of developing a new business within the control of existing retail area management. Buying was done by a young trainee buyer who was given the job. In short, in its early stages the experiment took the form of application of what management saw as the requirements for a jeans business based on their understanding of their existing business.

If these early developments were an example of consonance with the paradigm and the application of the familiar in line with that, later developments were rather an example of the way in which a strategic experiment emerged given increasing 'dissonance'. By 1979 it was becoming clearer that Fosters had to respond to the growing fashion consciousness of customers. They had attempted as much with Fashionpoint and were rolling out that initiative into more shops; but was that enough? Did the experiments with the jean shops provide another opportunity for development? Barry Davison was convinced it did; others less so. There were different interpretations of external opportunities and the extent to which Fosters could take advantage of them. In this sense a state of increasing dissonance emerged.

The decision to proceed with the Blue Movers chain was characterized at least as much by political convenience as by considerations of market and competitive needs. It is clear that such opposition as did exist at an early stage to the notion of developing a specialist jean operation had relatively little impact. First, consider the recommendations of the retail committee, set up to examine the feasibility of such an operation. Their conclusions were negative to such a development, and were made by managers not directly associated with the dominant paradigm in the menswear business; in this sense they were outside the arena of influence on this decision; their view was based on an evaluation of the suitability of sites in terms of perceived market need. The same applies to the opposition from Mike Adams: he saw his role as making his views known to Barry Davison rather than becoming involved in debate at any operational level. In this sense he was taking a rational, analytical perspective on the issue, his argument built on a diagnosis of market conditions and the reconciliation of Fosters' capabilities with market need. A major problem arising from both their cases was that it raised the spectre of shop closures without providing an answer to declining sales. The alternative of developing a specialist jean operation not only utilized the shops and sought extra sales but maintained, indeed enhanced, the belief that the company sought to provide opportunities for its staff.

If such misgivings raised doubts about the viability of a jeans chain, the resolution of the situation took an essentially political form, much as Fuller and Myers state:

> Conflict over policy determination can best be observed by charting the alignments of different interest groups who have various stakes in the solution of the difficulty. These groups represent certain institutional values, many of which appear incompatible with each other, all of which must be reconciled or compromised before the community can go ahead on a collective policy of reform.(1977, pp. 115–6)

Faced with continued declining performance in a number of shops, those whose status or reputation could be harmed by closure appeared to be seeking a solution that would reduce the threat, or enhance their standing. The possibility of using these branches for some other venture was attractive because it did precisely that. The accountants saw the possibility of increased productivity through badly performing branches. It also meant that the necessity to close branches and make staff redundant could be avoided; indeed the retail management could use it as a means of demonstrating still further their determination to look after the well being of staff and provide them with new opportunities. The buyers, concerned that moves to introduce branded merchandise would reduce margins, were initially wary of a specialist operation that might highlight branded goods: but this fear was reconciled by turning it on its head; the introduction of a limited quantity of branded merchandise would show just how comparatively good Foster' own-brand merchandise was. If there were reservations amongst operating managers about the wisdom of the move and their ability to make a success of it – and there were such reservations – then they were submerged within the general acceptance of rightness of developing shops and providing new opportunities for staff; and, in any case, it was known the Chairman was in favour of the idea.

The implementation of the decision through the development of the Blue Movers operation illustrates two further points. First, despite the apparently different image that was intended, much of what was done could be seen to grow directly out of current ways of operating. The additional branches that were added were from the existing stock of branches, rather than from branch acquisition, even if they were somewhat secondary sites. The operation was eventually placed officially within the menswear business. Staffing policy remained firmly one of redeployment from the menswear business and the buying influence remained within menswear. Tony Gray, appointed General Manager, had had years of experience within the company, again within menswear. Despite the fact that the business was originally conceived as targetted at both men and women, there was virtually no expertise brought in on the buying or selling of women's clothes.

The second point that Blue Movers illustrates is the extent to which those responsible for its operation rapidly found themselves unable to commit themselves to it as it moved away from their conception of a 'fashionable' menswear shop. The outside commissioning of shop design and the insistence by Tony Gray on creating a different image in the shop in terms of ambience, staffing and merchandise, led to the menswear retail team feeling uncomfortable with the venture. With hindsight Blue Movers may have been 'too little, too late' but, at the time, and as it developed, it was seen as a move into a higher-fashion operation and foreign to many of those who had been directly involved in developing its test operation. It provides an example of how constrained the degree of variance from the current paradigm can be.

Acquisitions and Diversification Policy

Throughout the period of this study Fosters attempted on several occasions to launch womenswear chains; they also diversified through acquisition into Millets, Discount for Beauty and Staff Facilities. It was the avowed intent of the main board, at least, to move away from a reliance on menswear; and on the face of it this would appear to indicate an intended break from traditional ways of operating. Yet if we look at the policies adopted on acquisition, yet again we find the interpretation of opportunity in terms of the paradigm and the application of the current modes of operation.

There appeared to be little dissent about many of the acquisitions before the event. There were perhaps two reasons for this. The first was that acquisitions policy was the responsibility of the main board, and therefore involved few executives involved in the core menswear business. The second was that there was no reason, at least in the 1970s, for managers in the operating companies to see themselves threatened by such activity. Indeed, the perceived opportunity, as conveyed to managers, was to seek for growth by applying the Fosters expertise and experience to new companies in new markets and, moreover, provide greater buying power in so doing. In short such new opportunities were consonant with the current paradigm. In such circumstances we would expect the application of the familiar Fosters mode of operations.

Going back as far as Stone-Dri, Barry Davison asserted that the main attraction at the time was the property portfolio of the business. That, combined with the opportunity to increase buying power in the Far East, and increase margins as a result, was sufficient to ensure the support of the powerful merchandise department. If Davison's version is to be accepted (and it is supported by colleagues), then it does seem to be the case that the Stone-Dri acquisition can be considered as an expression of the dominant paradigm at the time. The board was committed to growth through branch acquisition – the merchandise team in particular to the benefits of overseas buying; and most of the management saw this and the possible transferability of the Fosters systems as major reasons for the acquisition. There is of course nothing here that runs counter to the wisdom of management literature. Synergistic benefits of acquisition have long been argued. What is clear here, however, is the extent to which there was little or no discussion 'strategically . . . about what merchandise profiles we were in'. In other words there was little discussion about the market logic of the Stone-Dri acquisition: it was driven by perceived reasons for the success of the past.

The demise of Stone-Dri saw the experiment with Crowds which used some of the Stone-Dri shops. In this case, too, the pattern of organizing the operations was essentially similar. Fosters put in their control systems and transferred managers from the menswear operation to run the acquisition. An area sales manager was put in as the General Manager and buyers, sales and display personnel moved across with the brief to introduce Fosters' procedures into the new ventures. This too failed. The reasons for failure of the womenswear ventures stated by Mr High in the annual reports were essentially that the type of trade was not one that Fosters had sufficient experience in. Another way of saying this would be that Fosters imposed their own modes of operation on businesses that required different modes of operation.

Yet the policy continued. In the late 1970s the company turned away from its search for womenswear chains and acquired, first, Discount for Beauty, then Staff Facilities and then Millets. Certainly in the first two cases management adopted almost exactly the same approach; Fosters' control systems were introduced and Fosters' management transferred to run the operations. The first two of these operations failed and were disposed of. Arguably some of the same sorts of problems occurred in the U.S.A. in the 1980s – the acquisition was followed by an attempt to centralize distribution and merchandise control despite the fact that there were over 200 branches spread throughout the United States.

By 1983 the managers themselves could see why the attempted diversification had been so problematic. To repeat the lessons drawn by the managers:

We thought we knew enough about retailing to retail anything.

The centralized control at Fosters is not appropriate to acquisitions when there are small numbers of shops . . . there comes a time when you switch a small organization over and you try to put the system in but unless it's over a certain size it won't do any better; in fact it will probably do a lot worse.

Managers were able to see, with hindsight, why the acquisitions took place; it was because senior executives saw opportunities in terms of the Fosters paradigm and went ahead and applied the logic of these 'taken-for-granted' ways of operating to the companies they acquired. As one senior manager commented, looking back on the Stone-Dri acquisition, it was seen as compatible at the time in terms of perceived logic with the Fosters operation:

Stone-Dri was the body cover market, basically cheap awful crap. You could see the logic in the acquisition.

The Response to Declining Performance: 1980/1981

By the middle of 1980 it was clear to managers that the growth of recent years would not be maintained. By the middle of 1981 it was clearer that the group was in a state of serious performance decline. The period provides some good examples of a management team, faced with a problem it found difficult to understand, making sense of it through, and exerting greater efforts within, its paradigm, whilst seeking to preserve the legitimacy of that paradigm from the threats of growing contra evidence and argument.

In the first place, the external events of that time were interpreted initially as remote from the strategy of the firms. Performance decline was to do with an economic downturn which was regarded as temporary. Indeed, Barry Davison, in comments to the financial press stated as much: 'As soon as the public returns to normal spending levels, upward growth in profits will resume'. The downturn was not seen as anything to do with what Fosters were doing; rather, it was to do with what the customers were doing. The expectation was that the customers would come back to see the benefits of what Fosters were offering. The market sector was seen as essentially reliable and Fosters' approach to it appropriate.

In the meantime the paradigm offered a menu of response to the problems the business faced. This included the tightening of controls and the cutting of controllable costs – for example, branch refurbishment costs. It also meant that managers sought to do better what they had always done; to stack the merchandise higher, pack the windows more fully, make sure the staff were selling more aggressively and, as one manager said, 'chase around the branches asking the managers if they were doing everything right'. In addition there was the ability to manipulate price through the reduction of the normally healthy margin and seek even better prices from suppliers.

By 1981 when such measures were still showing an insufficient ability to turn declining performance around, management opted to deal with what it knew how to control best, the costs. This was the year in which Metra Proudfoot introduced their package of cuts to slim down the retail operations. For a company wedded to the belief that it was an efficent cost-controller, the move was both a natural one and yet led to a significant contradiction of ideologies. It was not easy for some managers to reconcile the ideal of more efficient cost control and redundancies with the notion that they had always been efficient anyway, and also the ideal of a caring management loyal to its staff.

Conflict and contradiction arose elsewhere too. If the initial response to downturn was to apply more vigorously those familiar aspects of management practice embodied in the paradigm, by 1981 there was also growing dissonance. Whilst most of the managers may have accepted that the market would return to Fosters, the new Marketing Director was equally convinced, through the research he had commissioned, of the dubious reliability of traditional Fosters market. The market research report questioned not only the validity of Fosters' management conception of the clothing market, but attacked their way of operating within it. The response to such questioning was much as Pfeffer (1981a, p. 325) has separately indicated: 'attacks on the dominant beliefs or paradigm of the organisation are likely to be met with counter argument and efforts to reinforce the paradigm'. Also, as has already been argued, the report had the effect of being a major political threat to established senior management. We have already seen that it elicited heavy initial resistance from these managers. The resistance was concerned with more than the report itself; it was also addressed at Haynes who was regarded as an outsider with little understanding of the way Fosters did things.

The responses illustrate well the role of symbolism in mediation. There was raised the 'myth of retailing experience'. Haynes was deemed not to have this retailing experience; and reasons for condemning the research were found, for example, in the obvious lack of retailing experience of those who presented it. For months the findings and conclusions that the research arrived at were disregarded.

It was, however, a time of increasing conflict and contradiction. Managers thoughout the operation found themselves facing evidence that conflicted with their taken-for-granted assumptions about sensible ways to operate at the same time as they were having to take decisions to make staff redundant. The argument of Abravanel (1983) about the mediatory role of myth in such circumstances is borne out. Such contradictions could not be explained logically; yet managers would tell stories about the flexibility of the company in crisis, the speed at which decisions could be taken, and the historical ability of successive chief executives to manage the business into growth through entrepreneurial decision-making.

The attempt to resolve the situation politically also took place at a senior level. Attempts were made to pull together solutions that would be acceptable to those who had been within the business and had 'owned' the paradigm. Certainly the reversion to mass merchandising, reduced pricing and exultations to 'sell more', whilst giving head to the accountants to cut and control the costs more aggressively, brought together senior manage-ment for a time. The politics of resolution took the form of attempts to re-assert the core aspects of the paradigm. In this case, however, it failed for two reasons; in the first place the expected performance improvement did not occur, and in the second place, the chairman set in motion a chain of events that led to substantial strategy re-formulation outside the bounds of the paradigm. It is this chain of events we will examine more closely in the next chapter.

RE-CONCEIVING INCREMENTALISM – AND THE NOTION OF STRATEGIC DRIFT

The period up to 1981 has been used as a basis for analysis and the generation of explanatory propositions. There is, however, a further issue that needs to be dealt with that is particularly relevant to the same period. It should be remembered that it was in the discussions with managers in 1980 that they quite explicitly talked about the way in which they managed strategic change in terms very similar to what Quinn (1980) would identify as 'logic incrementalism'. They saw the business sensibly being managed adaptively, building on a strong core but with 'side-bet' experimentations, and they saw themselves as sensing agents of an essentially flexible decision-making system. The question here, however, is whether this idea of 'logical incrementalism', as exposued, bears more empirical and objective scrutiny. The discussion that follows seeks to relate the contextual data from the research study to some of the theoretical perspectives on the management of strategy discussed earlier in part I.

Whilst organizations as collectives of individuals may generate individ- ually divergent views about the position of the business environment – views that are not typically well defined, but are 'feelings' that 'something is amiss' – the process of defining a problem or its solution in an organization sense must be seen as a social process. As such it can be seen in terms of the culturally preserved collective experience of managers that has been termed here the paradigm. Environmental change is likely to be detected by managers – in Fosters the fashion changes of the 1960s and 1970s were seen by managers. It may be that individuals or sub-groups will hold that there is need for some organizational action because of these changes. However, this study confirms that there is unlikely to be any significant ntegy unless there is some performance decline as with Fosters in 1981 and 1982 (Mintzberg et al., 1976; Smart and Vertinsky, 1977; Grinyer and Spender, 1979a & b). Indeed individuals who argue for change without such 'evidence' of impact are likely to achieve little success. Without such evidence, arguments for such change are essentially intellectual: they are based on the premise that rational argument can and will change the beliefs and assumptions held in the organization, and hence the strategy of that organization: that such argument will change the paradigm. However, the paradigm must be understood as not just a set of beliefs and assumptions: as we have seen it is grounded in the routines, rituals and formal control procedures of the organization; moreover, it is in effect the accepted way of 'reducing uncertainty' or ambiguity and is, in consequence, likely to be associated with the power elites in the organization (Hickson et al., 1971; Hambrick, 1981). In the case of

Fosters, it has been seen that successive attempts to amend strategy through argument foundered on their potential disruption of 'the way we do things' and were perceived as politically threatening. Moreover such changes as were made in the 1970s were configured in terms of the paradigm. Problems were defined and solutions configured in such a way as to preserve the integrity of the paradigm, and stimuli for change or aspects of change lying outside it were likely to be discounted.

'Logical incrementalism' assumes a tension between identified environmental stimuli and 'the way we do things around here'. Indeed Quinn claims that such an approach explicitly recognizes the need for managing such ambiguity: in terms of the arguments in this book, the process allows for the admission of threats to the paradigm. The argument here its that the paradigm effectively defines environmental 'reality' and responses to environmental change, and its cultural and political context means that it is likely to stifle such tensions and such threats. The logical notion is that strategic change – through the environmental sensing by managers within sub-systems and, the interplay between sub-systems and continual testing out of new strategies – results in a learning and re-adjustment process in organizations, which is shown in representative form in figure 8.2. The argument here is different: it is that managers may well see themselves as managing logically incrementally but that such consciously managed incremental change does not necessarily succeed in keeping apace with environmental change. Indeed there is a high risk that it will not. The situation in Fosters as it evolved through the 1970s was not as shown in figure 8.2 but rather as shown in figure 8.3. Gradually the incrementally adjusted strategic changes and the environmental, particularly market, changes moved apart.

The reasons for this assertion have already been discussed and may be summarized as follows.

(1) Sensing of external stimuli is muted because the stimuli are not meaningful in themselves; they take on a relevance, and responses are operationalized, in terms of the paradigm.

(2) Managers believe they are adapting to a changing environment when in fact they are adapting to signals that coincide with the paradigm.

(3) There is likely to be resistance to 'deviant' interpretations of the environment if they threaten the paradigm. This results in political pressure for conformity or only marginal adjustments to strategy.

(4) Strategic drift is not easily discerned by managers. However, in the event of its detection remedial action is likely to take the form of solutions constructed within the bounds of the paradigm, thus escalating commitment (Staw, 1981; Fox and Staw, 1979) to the information supporting the existing strategy.

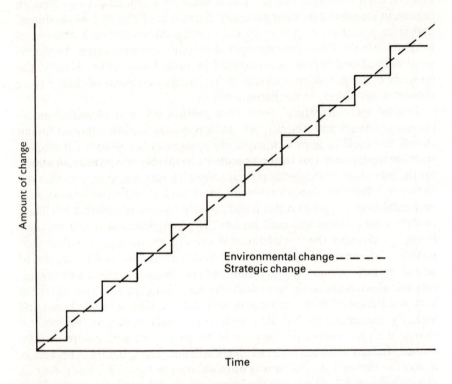

FIGURE 8.2   A notional pattern of incremental change.
The environment changes gradually and organization strategy develops incrementally in line with it

(5) Moreover these adjustments may well be enough to demonstrate the efficacy of the action to the satisfaction of stakeholders since, given the application of the familiar, there is a good chance that there will be some signs of performance improvement at least in the short term.

The proposition here is that strategic drift is likely to occur imperceptibly, and for at least two reasons. The first is that the notion of an 'optimal' or logical strategy – one that keeps in line with the changing environment – assumes that the environment can be known objectively; it has already been argued here that this is not so. It environments are enacted, it is not likely that deviance from what is 'logically' appropriate can be perceived by managers. The second reason is that, because marginal changes are taking place frequently, and are likely to be associated with some performance improvements, the view that change is in line with what is required to keep

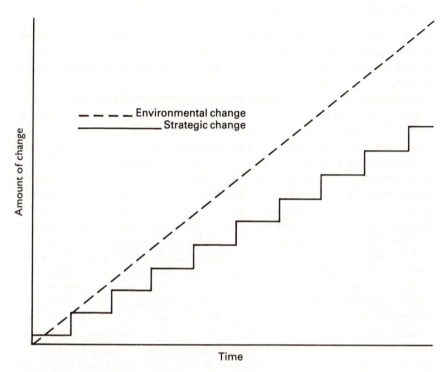

FIGURE 8.3   Incremental change and 'strategic drift'
The environment changes gradually but organization strategy fails to develop in line with it

'in touch' with environmental change will be supported. The implication is that managers are unlikely to be aware of strategic drift until it is so marked as to give rise to levels of performance decline for which marginal adjustments provide no significant performance improvement – indeed until a state of crisis is perceived within or outside the organization.

This notion of strategic drift, whilst accounted for differently, is similar to phenomena observed by other researchers. Mintzberg (1978) shows how organizations go through periods of strategy adjustment characterized by continuity, flux or incremental change but infrequently require more global changes. Greiner (1972) charts periods of evolution and revolution in corporate development and Chandler (1962) also noted the resilience of current strategies and structures, as more recently did Grinyer and Spender (1979a & b); indeed, Miller and Friesen (1980) show how 'strategic momentum' persists and leads to the need for periodic more 'revolutionary' re-alignment.

FUNDAMENTAL STRATEGIC CHANGE

Whilst strategic change is typically adaptive and incremental, as it certainly was throughout most of the years studied here, it is also the case that, periodically, organizations experience more radical, more fundamental, strategic change. The argument has been advanced that such re-alignment is likely to occur at a point when strategic drift has become so marked that a significant grouping of managers recognize that performance decline cannot be overcome by typical adaptive change. Rather, what occurs is a break with the constraints of the paradigm, and a more fundamental re-alignment of strategy as a result. Such changes began to occur in Fosters from 1982 to 1984. There evolved a different conception of the market place, with managers accepting that they no longer had a secure market sector in what they conceived of as the C2D market, and that they had to face major competition that had largely taken over their historical market position. They recognized a need for change in marketing strategy and, as significantly, that merchandising must serve that marketing strategy rather than lead it: merchandising had to be part of a strategy in which shop ambience and design and the approach of staff to their jobs had as significant a role in the retail mix. There were changes in approach that, for Fosters, were fundamentally different from what had dominated their thinking for over 15 years. As events were to show, the changes that were to be made were not, in fact, to turn around the company's fortunes as quickly as was hoped. They were nonetheless very significant changes for the managers to make and represented major and rapid strategic change. This research provides an opportunity to examine more closely some of the processes at work during that time that helped effect such changes.

The triggers for change can be traced to the decline in performance that managers became aware of in 1980 and were reflected in the 1981 accounts. What follows seeks to understand the management processes by examining the dramas of that time. Although this is not done strictly chronologically, the analysis follows the early triggering and the responses to declining performance: the impetus for change that the Stratford meeting can be seen to represent; the role of the Strategic Planning Committee and the activities surrounding that; the briefing and intervention of David Saunders, and the difficulties between the merchandisers and the activities of Haynes and Saunders. The role of the Chief Executive in the process is considered, as are the changes in structure and control procedures, and the political activity of the time. Throughout, however, the underlying question is what mechanisms for change can we discern at work and how do these square with our wider understanding of strategic change processes.

In broad terms, the analysis leads to the conclusion that the processes as observed bear similarity to those noted by other researchers. Following the early triggering of the need for change, there was, for example, early resistance to attacks on the dominant paradigm from those who saw themselves threatened by such change (Harvey and Mills, 1970; Pfeffer, 1981a & b; Schein, 1973) has argued that to overcome such resistance it is necessary to go through processes that closely resemble the events in Fosters at the time. Individuals must question their beliefs and values and by exposing them to critical examination and testing them out in action. There will be dissatisfaction and tension with the *status quo*, a precursor to the sort of 'unfreezing' of past beliefs and assumptions noted by Lewin (1952) and others that is necessary before change can take place. Within the context of such tension, there needs to be some sort of 'psychological safety net' in the form of new beliefs and values with which managers can identify. Such general patterns as these are discernible. What can be seen more specifically are the sorts of mechanisms for change that helped to break down the dominant paradigm of so many years, and contributed to the acceptance of new strategies.

An interpretative perspective on strategic change is, again, useful in understanding the processes at work. The management of strategic change is the management of individual and collective cognition; and management processes can usefully be seen in this light. As such the role of symbolic aspects of change also emerges as particularly important.

The 'Unfreezing' Process

Given the forces we have observed for adaptive, incremental change, it is to be expected that, faced with decline, management would seek greater productivity through both tighter controls and a concentration of activity within the bounds of the paradigm. In the case of Fosters it included their staff-reduction exercise, the 1981 sales, and 'Year of the Salesman', the re-emphasis of the priority of sales margins, tighter central control of costs and current assets and the exhortation of a loyal sales force for greater effort, whilst seeking for lower and lower costs.

At the same time as this re-assertion of the familiar was under way, there were, however, significant moves within and outside the organization that provided a context for change. It is worth noting that it was not declining performance alone that triggered concern about the stategic position of the firm. For senior directors, and Barry Davison in particular, there was growing outside pressure that played a part. For example, John Fallon recounted how questions began to be asked in the City as to why Fosters were clinging to some of their acquisitions and why they were beginning to lag behind Burtons. This heightened what was for Davison a personal affront that Burtons were doing as well as they were, and that their Chief Executive, Ralph Halpern, was becoming so well regarded in the City. The impetus for change was, then, not solely from within the organization.

There were, however, some divergent views about the causes of decline and what should be done about it from within the company – for example, the different views on merchandise and target market of Brian Wood, and the growing disquiet amongst some managers about the cost of diversification. These divergent views were not welded into, or directed towards, the creation of any coherent alternative strategy; in this sense they were not a movement for change but rather individual and diverse expressions of discontent. Nor were they in a form that fundamentally or explicitly challenged the tenets of the paradigm. If anything they took the form of resentment that some of its more fundamental aspects were being compromised; for example, the image of the caring company was not seen to be consistent with wholesale redundancies, whilst the Chairman sought diversifications in the USA taking the company further away from its traditional base. Some retail shop managers also began to resent the apparent lack of concern of senior management for the shops and staff. The importance of the discontent was not that it was directed toward specific strategic change, but that it was there at all. It was a momentum that was not specific but, as also noted by Dalton (1970), is a likely prerequisite for change. It represented the first signs of what is a necessary process of 'unfreezing' (Lewin, 1952), or breaking down, of the homogeneity of assumptions and beliefs that, it has already been observed, characterizes low levels of change in strategy. This 'destructive' process, also observed by Biggart (1977), is likely to take the form of mounting tension, a lowering of self-esteem and the interruption of traditional social ties and alliances.

The social pressures for conformity to norms of organizational behaviour also broadly correspond to those observed by others; they included the resistance of powerful elites to change (Pfeffer, 1981a) and their assertion of power over potentially divergent subordinates (Friedlander, 1983; Pettigrew 1973; 1985a & b); the conformist influence of myths and symbols (Dandridge et al., 1980; Abravanel, 1983); and the likelihood that divergent group members will be 'ridiculed, treated severely and finally ousted from the group' (Lewin, 1952, p. 226), a phenomenon also observed by O'Day (1974). It has been shown that all these pressures for confirmity lead to a typically incremental/adaptive mode of strategy development. To make fundamental change it is necessry to break the mechanisms for conformity so as to release latent divergent views and perceptions and to provide the mechanisms for challenging power bases to emerge. The process involves the necessity to devalue or discredit elements of the paradigm that form the basis for such confirmity. In so doing there is likely to be the 'emotional stir up' Lewin (1952) or 'pain' as noted by Schein (1973) as individuals find themselves questioning their assumptions and facing a fall in self-confidence.

Mechanisms for Strategy Re-formulation

Such processes of unfreezing may be necessary as a precursor to change but they cannot effect change in themselves. They continued in Fosters for some time but, concurrently, there were other mechanisms of change that began, more specifically, to break down the tacit assumptions and cultural blocks that defined and protected the existing paradigm. Such mechanisms were several, as listed below.

The Outsider   A number of writers on management have observed that major strategic change is often accompanied by the intervention of an outsider, often in the form of a new chief executive (Mintzberg, 1978, Grinyer and Spender 1979a & b; Huff, 1983; Slatter, 1984; Schein, 1985; Tushman and Romanelli, 1986). Whilst at Fosters there was no replacement of the Chief Executive until 1985 (and then from within the company), there did take place the intervention of outsiders from 1980 onwards. For our purposes an 'outsider' is not defined so much as someone who is physically from outside the company (though this is quite likely to be the case), but rather as someone with little or no commitment to the paradigm. (Schein calls such individuals hybrids.) What that individual is likely to bring is a questioning attitude as with Haynes and Fallon, or disregard for the paradigm as with Saunders. They are not likely to start from or be as restricted in their approach as are the existing managers, and in consequence are more able to perceive the limitations inherent within it, use mechanisms for change and promote more radical conceptions of change. For example Haynes's initial step was to commission research to establish the customers' view of the shops; and he saw himself, not as a retailer, but as someone who viewed the shops through the eyes of the customer. The effect of the market research report, critical as it was of the operation, was not to galvanize action as such but to create a more questioning and less secure view of the situation.

The Exposure of the Paradigm   A second unfreezing mechanism was the public exposure of the paradigm itself; again this is observed by Schein (1985). In a situation where there was growing disunity and questioning about the causes of decline, then the requirement of managers to be explicit as to what they saw as the reasons for past success and present decline, in terms of competitive position and the operation of the business, amounted to an encouragement of an individual divergence of views. That is precisely what happened at Stratford. Each department, but particularly those of sales and buying, defended their own territory. The effect was to force a critique by each party of the other and of what each saw the company as doing well or badly. This making explicit doubt and criticism in public, had the effect of breaking down the hitherto unquestioning adherence to the operational constructs of the paradigm. It was a process that was to aid the ability to change. The managers later dimissed the meeting as negative and achieving nothing. Its value, however, was not to be measured in the extent to which it created anything, but in the fact that it increased the pace at which homogeneity around the paradigm was broken down. Moreover, it made explicit, at a formal, organizational level, the recognition that something was very wrong and that action was needed. It was a sort of institutional symbol of the necessity for change. Certainly in the 1983 interviews, whilst managers were dimissive of the outcomes of the Stratford meeting, they all talked about the meeting's activity and drama. The importance of such a symbolic influences in change will be discussed further later.

Power Re-configuration   The steps taken to re-configure power in the organization were apparently intentional. They began with steps to disrupt what Barry Davison saw as the conservative influence of powerful groups and individuals. The configuration of the membership of the strategic Planning Committee had such effects. The decision of Davison to leave Brian Wood and Norman Phillips off the Committee was seen by them and others as a snub and an undermining of their authority; and Davison's support of Haynes's right to pull managers out of departmental functions to take part in Committee activities underlined this. In addition, it demonstrated his overt support for an outsider not linked to the past. Moreover, by associating Committee members with top-level decisions about briefing designers and refitting shops on behalf of the Chairman, Haynes (or Davison, through Haynes) effectively raised the status and self-esteem of junior and middle managers within the buying and sales departments and provided these groups fresh social links outside the influence of more traditional and powerful elites, a process also identified by Dalton (1970) and Tushman and Romanelli (1986). A role of the Strategic Planning Committee was, then, political in the sense that it isolated and diminished existing power elites and increased the power of those that were more likely to support change.

Activating and Legitimizing Dissent   It is interesting to compare the title 'Stategic Planning Committee' with the nature of the discussions in that committee. There was, on the face of it, little 'strategic' debate – little discussion about the nature of the changing competitive environment, or of broad strategic options and the criteria upon which they should be evaluated. On the contrary, virtually all discussion, criticisms and actions were operational in nature. Initially this took the form of discussions and suggested improvements about window displays, staffing levels and in-store layout, but as the re-merchandising of the Chester and Cardiff shops got under way, the discussion became more specifically addressed to some of the more pivotal aspects of the company's operations such as merchandise selection, the need for branded merchandise and more fashionable clothes. The effect was to activate dissent about sensitive areas that, hitherto, had been little questioned by middle and junior management. In producing this effect the Committee provided a forum through which the momentum, mainly from the shop operation managers, for change and action, was stimulated. Through this mechanism the tension already noted as a requirement for change was heightened and a 'felt need for change' (Dalton, 1979, p. 234) promoted.

It has been suggested previously that the power blocks in the company were those that derived power from their association with the dominant paradigm. Dissent about company operations would therefore normally be expected to be successfully resisted. In 1981, the most obvious critics were from relatively weak power bases; they were 'outsiders' such as Haynes, and some middle and junior retail managers who were concerned with what they saw as the run-down of the retail operation in the name of cost control. The Strategic Planning Committee helped legitimize the dissent of members of these lower power groups. It also acted to internalize, and therefore further legitimize within the business, a push for change by 'outsiders' (Kanter, 1984).

Challenging the Paradigm   In a sense all the instances of the activity cited challenged aspects of the paradigm. Managers, already with some recognition that current ways of doing things were inadequate, were persistently faced with practical questions of how things could be done differently or better. There were, then, repeated challenges to taken-for-granted assumptions. There were, however, more specific challenges too. First there was activity that demonstrated practically, if unintentionally, the inadequacy of the paradigm. The mechanism of the Strategic Planning Committee was the ultimate opportunity for individuals wedded to a particular view of the way the company should function to test out their views in action. The re-merchandising of Chester and Cardiff was, though nominally the responsibility of Haynes, in many respects an exercise in the application of the paradigm of the late 1970s. The refits were essentailly to do with changes in merchandise, presentation and price. There were no organizational or particularly restrictive financial constraints placed upon the exercise that could be used to excuse the fact that the application of the formula was insufficient to achieve the improvements required. It was a practical and comprehendable demonstration of the inadequacy of the prevailing beliefs about how to run the business.

There were other less direct but nonetheless powerful challenges to the paradigm. These took symbolic forms, a phenomenon, again, noted by Schein (1985) and others elsewhere. The crowded window displays, traditional in mens outfitting shops, were done away with and replaced by less cluttered displays designed to be more aesthetically appealing. The view of the company as reliant on the entrepreneurial skills of top management was challenged through the vehicle of the Strategic Planning Committee which included none of them. The reverence for the position of the Chairman was challenged by Saunders when he first arrived in Fosters and insisted on calling him 'Barry'.

> How do you say 'you are wrong Mr Chairman' when you call him 'sir'? The very first thing I did was to call him by his first name. I have to be an equal and he's got to listen to me.

Perhaps the most striking example of symbolic intervention for change, however, was that of the clothing worn in the retail shops. At the time when the new image shops and new ranges were being introduced, it was found that most of the shop staff were wearing suits and clothes bought from Burtons. Despite the changes in shop design and type of clothing displayed, they did not identify with the merchandise they were selling. Richard Haynes and David Saunders persuaded Barry Davison and Brian Wood to insist that all staff in the new image shops should wear clothes bought from their shops. It was an immensely powerful move in a number of respects. First it forced those serving in the shops to take responsibility and possession symbolically of the merchandise they were selling; they could no longer think of the ranges as 'yobos' uniforms'. Second, it exerted pressure on the buyers from the retailers; the retailers were no longer prepared to receive uncritically the merchandise they were sent. Also, third, and perhaps most important, it encapsulated and communicated the new strategy to be followed in a way that was eminently meaningful to those who worked in the shops and also to the buyers: the strategy was not just a set of ideas; it became meaningful in an everyday way throughout the organization.

Powerful Advocacy – the Role of the Chairman   None of these mechanisms could have been effective, indeed they could not have occurred, without the support and encouragement of Barry Davison. The impetus for change needs a powerful advocate: that is the role that Davison undertook, and in this respect his role underwent something of a change in the period 1981–3. He had always had the reputation of being autocratic – some managers would have said bullying – and of intervening in trading decisions to the point of detail. Yet in the early 1980s as the company proceeded through first the Strategic Planning Committee and then the initial exercise with Saunders he took what some managers described as a 'more of a back seat'. Whilst it does appear that his involvement was less detailed in nature, it also appears to have been significant in the change process. His admission that he did not know the answers to the problems was, in effect, a public statement that the old ways were insufficient. It was Davison who called the Stratford meeting, demanded a public review of performance and decision premises and, in effect, heightened the tension. Whilst he did not involve himself in the deliberations of the Strategic Planning Committee in detail, in choosing its members, and in openly backing its activities, he substantially asserted the re-configuration of power. His role in the menswear operations apparently ceased to be that of busying himself so much with the detail of trading, and switched to the dual roles of reorganization and the bestower of political backing. Managers at the time, and with hindsight, were critical of the management style of the Chairman, of what was seen by some as potential manoeuvring to remove Norman Phillips, of the pursuit of US diversification; and Davison himself was later self-critical of his failure to follow through strategic change to the point of recognizing the impracticalities of retaining one high-street identity for all the menswear shops. However, what must be acknowledged is the role he played in the promotion of the processes of change in the early 1980s. He did not know the answers and publically admitted as much, but knew that they did not lie within the business; his role on this became that of introducing a context for change and backing those who he believed might achieve it.

These then are some of the mechanisms that can be observed in Fosters as contributing to the breakdown of the paradigm that has preserved the *status quo*, and resulted in adaptive strategic change. The proposition is that more fundamental strategic change requires a change in that paradigm and that that change results from confronting the paradigm itself. This is a different conception of the impetus for strategic change from the rational models that still predominate in the literature; the inference in such literature is that an analysis of the strategic position of the business, if argued and presented logically, will result in the realization of the need for change followed by the planning of such change. The assertion here is quite different; argued analysis of competitive position may well give rise to initial resentment and resistance followed by the tailoring of conclusions into a form that is reconcilable with the prevailing paradigm. For strategic change of a fundamental nature to occur, the influence of the paradigm and the power elites associated with it need to be reduced.

A good example that illustrates the point being made here is that of the position of the buying executives in the early 1980s in Fosters. They argued in 1980 for changes that were, if anything, more radical than those proposed by other managers; yet after 1981, as the changes brought about by the intervention of Haynes and Saunders progressed, it was they that were considered to be most resistant to change. There were certainly political dimensions to such resistance; but it also stemmed from their perception of what needed to change and what did not. In 1980 they talked about a need to change merchandise in response to the environmental change they perceived; but this was a need expressed very much in terms of the current paradigm. There was no fundamental questioning of the way in which merchandise should be bought, of the necessity for bulk buying or of pre-set standard margins; and no thought that re-adjustment might entail any fundamental change in the target market. Argued need for more fundamental strategic change at Stratford, based on the data from the market research, had little effect on the merchandise department managers. They did not see the report as an attack on merchandise policies or requiring a change to those policies; it was a criticism of the operation of the shops. Indeed, there is little evidence that any of the managers who had been with Fosters for any duration were persuaded that fundamental change was necessary as a result of what was a sweeping and comprehensive analytical questioning of the competitive position of the business by the research. Fundamental change did not result from an analysis of the competitive position; it resulted from the political and symbolic confrontation of the paradigm that gave impetus to its breakdown – what has here been described as the 'unfreezing' process.

The Re-formulation of Strategy

The mechanisms so far described relate to the establishment of conditions necessary for fundamental strategic change. There may be conditions essential in that process of strategic change but do not, in themselves, define the nature of that change. There is also a need for the re-formulation of strategy during or after the processes that have already been described. Fundamental strategic change implies fundamental change in the paradigm. We have seen in Fosters that, typically, strategies are configured *within* the bounds of the paradigm. (It is an observation made elsewhere by Grinyer and Spender (1979a) although they use different terminology.) Here we are concerned with strategies that are formulated outside that paradigm.

On this issue, it can be argued that the insights from the study of the experiences of the Fosters management are more limited. After all, it could be argued – and some managers within Fosters did – that, despite all the changes of 1982–4, the company never really made the sort of fundamental strategic changes required to compete effectively. The statement in the Spring 1986 edition of Fosters News (and reported at the end of Chapter 5) that the company's shops were not targetted precisely at relevant market segments was a recognition of a failure to move away from a national, single-identity retailer with all the connotations of bulk buying, distribution and lack of market sensitivity implied by that. However, undeniably, the management in Fosters did embrace strategic change, within a period of two to three years, of a magnitude far greater than hitherto. In understanding how this came about, and also in asking why it was not even greater in magnitude, we can gain Vseful insights into the process and problems of strategy re-formulation.

The first point that needs re-stating is that a primary requirement for the achievement of fundamental strategic change in Fosters appeared to be the setting in motion of those processes, already described, necessary to reduce commitment to and acceptance of established beliefs anu routines, with all the upheaval and tension that they are likely to cause. This does raise the question of the relationship between the *processes* of change and the *content* of those changes: the implication is that the sorts of processes of unfreezing already discussed may need to precede the formulation of content of new strategies in any precise terms. It is an issue that will be discussed more fully in the final chapter.

Given this general point about the conditions for strategy change we can move on to a consideration of more specific mechanisms of formulation and adaptation that are discernible. New strategies tend to be associated with the arrival or intervention of what has here been called 'outsiders'. Grinyer and Spender (1979a) concluded that the arrival of new chief executives was an important mechanism for promoting fundamental changes in strategy. Pettigrew (1985b) was less specific but painted the picture of groups of executives, perhaps physically within the organization, but with a distinct ideology, often zealously trying to effect change. Both suggest a pattern that is in line with that observed at Fosters. Fundamental strategic change in Fosters arose because of the intervention of individuals who were not subject to the same conditioning environment that helped evolve and protected the dominant paradigm.

The proposition by these writers is that the content of paradigm-breaking strategies tends to come from outside the organization. It is not suggested that outsiders necessarily 'invent' new solutions; rather, it is accepted, as argued by Grinyer and Spender (1979a), that the outsider's role may be to import or borrow from his or her previous experience. The outsider's influence is valuable because he or she follows a different path in the formulation of strategy precisely because of previous experience. It is still possible to argue that the process is essentially adaptive; that is, the outsider is bringing to bear his or her experience on a situation and the strategy is being adapted as a result of the interaction between this and the current situation of the business; but the conditions that prevail within the business facilitate more fundamental change in two respcts. First, if the sort of unfreezing process already described has taken place, then the extent to which the current paradigm in the business will act to mediate the influence of the outsider's new approach will be more limited. Second, that unfreezing process may facilitate a situation in which the outsider (or outsiders) may more readily obtain differing views of the business situation at a strategic level; the managers are more likely to be more critical of the strategic position of the firm.

In the case of Fosters there were at least four clear outsider interventions in a period of five years. The first was the recruitment of Richard Haynes, the second that of John Fallon, the third the appointment of David Saunders and the fourth the arrival of the new Merchandising Director. They each played different roles but each illustrates points made here. Haynes approached the job, not as a 'Fosterized' retailer but as a marketing man and a consumer. It is evident that he had no directly appropriate strategic remedies but set about a programme of market research and market redefinition that, together with his broader political activities, helped to give rise to the climate for change. John Fallon admits that he played the important role of bringing outside values and information into a business working within essentially internally bounded assumptions – so, for example, he reported on the financial expectations of the Burtons refits. It was clearer that Saunders brought with him an approach to solving Fosters' strategic problems built on his past experience, but adapted to the particular competitive environment faced by the company. It is arguable that the value of the outsider lies especially in this approach; whereas typical adaptive change stems from the interpretation of the business environment in terms of the organization's paradigm, the outsider provides a quite different impact. He or she may draw upon past experience and beliefs that stem from that; but these are likely to be foreign to the new organizational context, and in any case, have to be interpreted in terms of what, to that outsider, are quite new circumstances. The result is a necessarily fresh perception of the business environment he or she enters. Saunders arrived with a repertoire of skills and experience and took advantage of a more fluid internal perception of business problems, in order to modify and apply that experience. These three 'interventions' not only illustrate the role of outsider perspectives, but their influence in the business also suggests one other condition that governed the efficacy of their interventions. The successes they could claim in achieving change also depended on their ability to carry with them an internal alliance of managers willing to build on a critical appreciation of the company's past. Haynes, for example, was effectively blocked until he had the support of members of the Strategic Planning Committee. Saunders immediately sought to establish creditability with the retailers. Indeed, arguably, the problems encountered by the fourth outsider – the new Merchandise Director appointed in 1983 – to refine further the change momentum into a coherent merchandise strategy appropriate to the company, illustrate some of the problems of an outsider drawing upon past experience. If the reservations of Fosters' management are to be accepted, the problems here were that the application of that experience paid too little heed, first to the business situation in which the company found itself – what Kanter (1984) would regard as a lack of appreciation of company 'pre-history' – and, second, drew too little upon the internal critical momentum that had built up.

This interrelationship between the constructive intervention of an outsider and the facilitating alliance from within helps explain the importance of outside intervention. Pettigrew writes:

> The most general dilemma for an innovating group is how to change the world whilst living with it; how to be exclusive or different enough to retain a vision or process to facilitate change but not so different that the group creates a moral panic, acquires the stereotype of folk devils and is controlled by overt attempts to limit contacts, tasks and resources or more subtly is ignored and allowed to slowly disappear. (1985b, p. 513)

In Fosters such fundamental strategic change as did occur was dependent on at least four conditions: (a) a conducive climate for change; (b) the introduction of an outsider perspective; (c) the building of an alliance with allies from within who have arrived at a position critical of the dominant paradigm; and (d) through this alliance an appreciation of 'pre-history', important in developing outsider perspectives into new relevant strategies.

If we are to look for why the introduction of fundamental strategic change in the business foundered around 1984 then, arguably, it is from considering this fourth point that we find some answers. Managers within Fosters came to accept the need for change; they were prepared to welcome outsiders' ideas and embrace them; but the extent to which they were able to refine those ideas, through a rigorous critique of their own pre-history, into specific strategies suited to a menswear retail business in the competitive situation of the early 1980s, was more limited, and did not effectively get underway until 1985

The Adoption of Fundamental Strategic Change

A new vision of strategy is, in itself, an insufficient means by which to manage its introduction. Just as there were identifiable mechanisms in Fosters that helped account for the unfreezing process, so there were mechanisms that could be observed that helped account for the adoption of re-constructed strategy. After the intervention of Saunders, and during the re-launch of the 'new image' shops, the sort of pattern described by Kanter (1984) in which conflicts turned to an emerging consensus, as the new ideas were adopted and internalized, could be explained in several ways.

The conditions were such that many managers were anxiously seeking what Schein (1973) refers to as a 'safety net'. The unfreezing process had been disruptive and painful for many. In such circumstances there is likely to be a felt need for some new ideas, which could be seen as a potential way forward. This needed to be linked to some means of generating confidence in the action that is to be taken. This appears to have occurred, for example, through the nature of the intervention by Saunders in at least two ways. First, as a change agent he was credible. He had a track record in retailing – he could 'talk' retailing. Second, he had the advantage of being able to demonstrate the success of his recommendations very quickly through the design of the first shop in Peterborough, a success that further increased his esteem amongst managers and their confidence in the new strategy.

There is a point of some significance here. The demonstration of the inadequacy of the old approach was not enough in itself to create acceptance of new ways of thinking; nor did confidence in the new strategy appear to be based primarily on argued views about the logic of the strategy. Whilst generally impressed with Saunders, many managers needed the evidence of successful action before accepting that the new approach would work. The power and importance of 'showing through deeds' rather than words that change is meant and is irreversible is noted too by Sathe (1985).

It has been shown that the resistance to change in strategy is at the level of the paradigm, and that this resistance is linked to the preservation of power structures associated with that paradigm. The unfreezing processes may have the effect of 'levelling' such power bases. However, to manage the introduction of change it is necessary to carry management, or a coalition of managers, with the strategy; these managers not only have to be convinced of the changes but have to change the way they conduct their jobs, persuade others of the wisdom of the changes and get them to change the way they behave too. The changes have to take place, not only through managerial acquiescence, but through managerial action.

In the case of the changes at Fosters in 1982/3, the internalization of change was not achieved initially for the buyers but was more so on the shop operations side of the business. The acceptance of such shifts in behaviour appeared to be linked to the extent to which such change enhanced or diminished status. In implementing the changes in strategy at Fosters there was heavy investment in refurbishing shops – a step that had never been taken before to a comparable extent. This was accompanied by overt dissatisfaction with the merchandising side of the business felt by those most identified with promoting the changes: as the shop refitting programme progressed, the view grew that the quality of merchandise was 'letting down the shops'. As the recognition grew of the performance improvement in the 'new image' shops, the extent to which merchandising was accepted as the central reason for company success was reduced, and the importance of shop operations enhanced, together with the self-esteem of those managing the shops. It is a phenomenon also noted by Dalton who observes that the ability to change behaviour does not depend so much on the achievement of self-esteem by individuals as the fact of movement from relatively low esteem to relatively higher esteem. He states: 'The abandonment of previous patterns of behaviour and thought is easier when the individual is moving towards an increased sense of his own worth. . . . The increased sense of one's own potential is evident through this continuum, not merely at the end (Dalton, 1970, p. 247).' One further way in which the acceptance of a re-constructed strategy was achieved was to find mechanisms at an early stage of involving and identifying managers with it. One of the main vehicles for this at Fosters was again the Strategic Planning Committee, the members of which could identify themselves with the selection of Saunders as a consultant, the architects of his brief and the collaborators in his work.

They also effectively evangelized about the changes that were being promoted. Saunders actively encouraged their initial participation and involvement, taking pains to discuss his ideas with retail management, for example. Whilst this was, no doubt, a genuine attempt to understand the problem from their point of view, it also had the effect of continuing to involve a wide range of managers in the decisions on changes that were taking place.

There was, again, a good deal of symbolic activity which had the effect of emphasizing the overturning of the old ways and the legitimizing and consideration of new approaches. These took several forms. As Pfeffer (1981b) and Tushman and Romanelli (1986) have noted, organizational and personnel changes may perform such a symbolic role. In Fosters there was, at first, the search and, later, appointment of a new Merchandise Director for Menswear accompanied by the departure of Norman Phillips. On the shop operations side of the business the two senior regional managers became ill and were not replaced; instead authority was passed to the level of management below them. At the same time the decision to set up the Management Board was taken, with more responsibility for decision-making and planning devolved to the businesses and away from the main board. These organizational changes were supported by others in the control systems in the company. The financial systems were beginning to be developed, not only for centralized control, but for more localized planning and budgeting and the provision of management information to lower levels of management. The boards of companies were required to present their views on strategy to be discussed at the Management Board. Reward systems were becoming geared to the profitable performance of the business and managers were expected to attend to matters of profit at levels where hitherto they had not had such information. Such changes in the systems and structure of the organization had the effect of, symbolically signalling a 'new order'; of consolidating the changes that had taken place.

There were also less formal but nonetheless powerful symbols of change, for example through the stories and rituals of the business. The power of stories has been noted elsewhere in organization change situations (Martin, 1982; Boje et al., 1982) and arguably lies in their relatedness to concrete rather than abstract information. The most common story that pervaded the company in 1983 was some variation on the theme of how a converted shop, whether in the city centre or market town, had had outstanding sales increases after its refit. Another common story was how the shop managers, 'even the older ones', had adapted to the new ways of retailing; for it was in the shop that the rituals signifying change were most pronounced. There was to be no intrusion on the customer's right to browse; staff were to wear clothes that could be bought in the shop and only the manager was to wear a suit; staff were to wear name badges with their first names on them. The emphasis was on informality. By 1983, the buyers, too, had identified themselves with the new retail approach. A powerful symbol of the irreversibility of the changes was, then, the conversion of individuals and groups who were previously associated with the old formula. They provided a focus for the personal corroboration of change.

The most powerful symbol of all, however, was the layout and design of the new shops. Their difference from the previous shops was pronounced, with mirrors, chrome rails, angular surrounding walls, windows with an absence of merchandise, a pervading, and Fosters-specific, green house colour and a new logo. The new shops were so entirely different and perceived to be so 'glossy' that they underlined the removal of the new strategy from the past.

It is, of course, also arguable that there remained powerful symbolic links with the past which prevented more substantial moves away from its influence on the business. With the exception of Norman Phillips, the most senior directors remained in their posts. The most powerful of these was Barry Davison and certainly many managers regarded the continuing of a relatively autocratic style of management as incompatible with the changes that were being introduced in the company.

It was argued by some of the managers after the event that the strategic changes of 1982–3 were not fully accepted by some, never fully implemented, and not entirely successful. This, then, raises the question of compliance. It has already been seen that there are different bases for compliance with change in organizations. The ideas discussed previously are based around those of Kelman (1958) and Etzioni (1961), yielding a typology of compliance as summarized in table 8.1. Essentially these different bases vary from the use of explicit power, as in the case of coercion, through political and symbolic bases of persuasion and manipulation – and the more implicit use of power – through to the cognitive internalization of change. All of these bases for compliance are observable within the change processes in Fosters in the 1980s. They are illustrated in table 8.1. A number of points emerge.

Whilst all the bases for compliance are observable, it is the more symbolic and political activity that appears to have been more effective

TABLE 8.1 *Illustrations of bases of compliance*

Coercion	Remuneration	Persuasion/ manipulation	Identification	Internalization
Buyers threatened with loss of employment for failure to comply with, or lack of commitment to changes	Reward systems linked to achievement of profit targets	Allocation of funds to retail for refitting of new image shops Shop staff required to wear Fosters clothing Group reorganization and systems changes	'Conversions' of senior retail and senior management Involvement of managers in 'partial implementation' of changes	Early appeal and adoption of ideas by shop management

Explicit power ←—————————————————————————→ Implicit power

than the more coercive activity. The speed of acceptance and implementation of change was greater the more the bases of compliance were rooted
in identification and internalization, and the slowest where coercion was
required. This is perhaps to be expected. What is more significant is the
extent to which political and symbolic acts of persuasion and manipulation
were frequent and also appeared to achieve more rapid compliance than
more explicit coercive power, bearing out arguments made previously by
Pfeffer: 'The argument can be made that it is the symbolic identification
with organization or decisions, as much as real choice and participation,
that produces commitment and action on behalf of the organization and its
decision' (Pfeffer, 1981, p. 207a). It appears that this 'middle ground' of
managing was particularly effective in achieving a climate for change and
moving managers towards the identification with that change.

It is a point that, again, illustrates the value of an essentially
interpretative view of managing strategy. Traditional rationalistic models
might suggest that, following strategic analysis and the rational determination of strategy, it is either the intellectual internalization of the need for
change or reward and punishment systems that are likely to form the basis
of strategy implementation. The argument here, rather, is that the
symbolic and political activity of everyday life may be a more powerful
basis for achieving change. Some of the most effective means of change
were the most mundane and in this respect the most relevant to the
managers throughout the organization. As a lesson it is well illustrated by
the way in which an identification of shop managers with the 'new image'
merchandise was achieved. The explanation of the new strategy had been
made to shop staff and the need for change was accepted logically; yet the
staff still did not identify with such change. They still saw the merchandise
and thought of the customer in terms of the past. Managers in Fosters bear
out that one of the most significant changes was the requirement for staff to
wear Fosters clothing themselves. From that point onwards they identified
with the new strategy, began to argue for its more rapid implementation
and sought to influence its progress. The intellectual argument for change
may have achieved an intellectual response, but this is not to say that it
achieved a movement towards identification and internalization: and
incentives and coercive threats could not change the traditional ways of
behaving. A simple act that linked the strategy with the everyday life of
those who were required to implement it was more powerful.

There appeared to be three broad states of potential compliance. The
first was that of those who complied because they were committed to the
solutions being proposed; the second was that of those who resisted
because they were under political threat, directly associated with the
discrediting of the paradigm. It was, however, those in the third state,

characterized by uncertainty and doubt, that were particularly affected by the sort of political and symbolic activity observed here. And it is, arguably, those within this third state for which the achievement of compliance with change most affected the achievement of strategic change. It was also in this third state that symbolic and political bases for change were the most powerful. In this third state, characterized by uncertainty and doubt, some form of 'psychological safety net', was also particularly important in the management of change. The political and symbolic activity may have been effective in creating a momentum for change, but the eventual internalization of that change required sufficient confidence by managers to cast aside the old ways of doing things and accept the new. To some extent this was achieved by the observation of the acceptance of change of their peers and of more senior management; but, also to a considerable extent the prevailing state of uncertainty and ambiguity for their managers were 'made sense of' in symbolic terms. As Boje et al. (1982) point out:

> This milieu of uncertainty is the foundation upon which organizational cultures arise to provide a framework within which shared meanings are developed. Organizational culture, as used here, includes the language, symbols, metaphors,and myths that arise from the organization's situation and the interactions of its participants. There particular components of culture facilitate the feelings of rational action in the midst of otherwise overpowering uncertainty and political manoeuvring. (Boje et al., 1982, p. 18)

In the end however, the most powerful safety net was the evidence of improved performance. The managers at Fosters noted the extent to which the speed of change increased markedly as the evidence of improved profits from the 'new image' shops in the early days of conversion grew. It was also evident that, as the roll out of the 'new image' shops progressed to the more secondary sites and evidence of increased profits diminished, so too did the commitment to the new strategy.

AN INTERPRETATIVE VIEW OF THE REASONS FOR DECLINE

The decline in the fortunes of Fosters in 1984 and 1985, and the eventual takeover of the business, clearly owed much to events not directly associated with the introduction of the new strategy in menswear. Managers in Fosters insisted that the primary reason for the problems was the American venture, which was such a drastic cash drain upon the business. Moreover, this cash drain also coincided with a slowing down in the profit turnaround of the business at home at the very time when a major investment was required in shop refitting. Again, this can be viewed as a straightforward matter of logistics. Any company that is investing in change is likely to go through a period of reduced profits and the coincidental problems in the USA became a burden that rendered the company defenceless against a takeover bid. However, this state of affairs also illustrates some of the points already discussed concerning the management of strategic change.

In the first place the declining performance of the business in 1984 and 1985 had the effect of diminishing the very 'safety net' so important in consolidating the internalization of strategic change. The evidence of the effectiveness of the new ways of looking at or doing things was substantially removed during this period. At the very time when it was most important that managers should be constructively helping to implement or question the bases of change, there re-emerged doubts for some about its efficacy. And, as has been noted, there remained substantial symbolic links with the past, not least in the form of powerful individuals in the business. However, some of those individuals who symbolized the process of change itself departed or became less visible – Richard Haynes departed from an active involvement in the menswear business; the new Merchandise Director left the company; and David Saunders, though remaining involved in the company, became less actively involved.

Indeed, it can be argued that some of the problems of 1984 and 1985 were traceable back to the dominance of the paradigm of the past. Certainly there was still the hangover effect of the property acquisition era of the late 1960s and early 1970s. Throughout the 1970s Fosters had still not been able to break with their commitment to the maintenance of their property portfolio and the maintenance of jobs. Disposal of properties and the consequent loss of jobs was anathema to Fosters' senior management. In 1983 and 1984 as they sought to refurbish such shops they reaped the consequences. The costs of refurbishment of small secondary sites in locations that could not provide them with an adequate return resulted in a major cash drain at the very time when they could not affort it. Also in the new ventures of that era we still see some of the features of the application of the old strategic formula. Distribution of stock in the USA was to be centrally organized and computerized, and stock ranges centrally bought and planned, despite the fact that the 246 stores were spread over 35 states. Also, arguably, the Peter Richards acquisition was essentially financially driven rather than market-driven. There appeared to be relatively little assessment prior to the takeover of just what the strategy would be; rather, the assumption was, again, that Fosters needed and could make work a womenswear chain.

Perhaps most significantly, however, the new strategic 'images' introduced were not refined and defined sufficiently both internally in the company and externally in the market. In terms of the market place, even during the period of change, it was not entirely clear just what the intended market positioning strategy for Fosters was. Tracing this back to 1981 and 1982, it could be seen that the marketing brief intitially issued by Haynes was not in fact pursued. It was amended by David Saunders and the 'new image' shops substantially built upon that view of the market place. Managers themselves later questioned just exactly what the positioning of the Fosters shops was intended to be; was it possible to try to sell a range of clothing in essentially similar shops to such a wide age range and through stores located both in major city centres and in small suburban towns? Arguably the profit improvements of 1983 were a function, first, of the fact that it was the best-positioned stores that were being converted mainly in city centres, second, that it was in these stores that the sort of change was most appropriate, and, third, that the symbolic power of change in itself stimulated, both internally and externally, a greater enthusiasm for Fosters. As the conversion programme continued, however, the questions as to the relevance of the positioning of Fosters more widely in the market was increasingly evident.

Internally, the problem was similar. The strategy was initially reliant on outsiders with relatively low-power bases. The power within the firm remained, at the time, essentially in the hands of those who had been with that firm for many years. They were committed enough to the changes that did take place but apparently unable to refine those changes to the specific needs of the company. Later, the introduction of senior management from outside the firm led to even more rapid changes in merchandise ranges and moves away from the buying formula previously so dominant in the firm. Yet such changes were still not built on any clear 'image' of what the strategy signified for those managing the day-to-day affairs of the business. They knew that the old ways of doing things had to change; they recognized that strategic change was under way and necessary, and they appreciated that the 'new image' shops had produced improved results. However, from this initial euphoria of change emerged the questions as to what specifically the strategy of the company was. It was not until 1985 and 1986, after the further profit declines of 1984/5 and the takeover, which is largely outside the scope of this study, that managers began to plan such refinements.

It was in the Spring of 1986 edition of the Foster Group News that Mike Adams, then the Chief Executive of the taken-over Foster Brothers, was to confirm openly the relatively weak competitive positioning of the Fosters chain and the activity then underway to develop and refine the strategy that had been introduced four years earlier.

The argument has been made previously that major strategic change requires both an alliance between outsiders and internal managers and also the ability of those insiders to refine and develop outsider innovations on the basis of a critical re-interpretation of 'pre-history'. What we observe in Fosters is that the first condition was substantially met but the second was not, at least in the period under study. A momentum for change may be a necessary precursor to strategy re-formulation, and the commitment of managers to that change process vital. However, the problem is that in the absence of any real clarity of what the strategy is, managers will fluctuate between a dependence on outsider interventions, which might continue a momentum for change but in divergent directions, and a search for security in the past. The idea that a clarity of strategy will somehow naturally emerge out of the change process itself is, on this evidence, misplaced. This raises the question again as to the relationship between *processes* for strategic change and the *formulation* of strategy, an issue to be discussed more fully in the final chapter.

9
Wider Implications

This chapter brings together the evidence, propositions and arguments in the rest of the book and examines the implications for practitioners. The chapter commences with a recapitulation of the key propositions developed in the book. There follows a discussion on the extent to which it is sensible to generalize about these beyond the bounds of this study; and the remainder of the chapter concerns itself with translating the findings of the study into practical implications for those concerned with the management of strategic change in organizations.

The theme of this book has been that the characteristics of the management of strategy that make it distinctly different and important in the practice of management are essentially to do with the magnitude of complexity of strategic issues, to the extent to which they are concerned with uncertainty and change within the political environment of organizational systems. In such circumstances the tenets of 'scientific management', whilst providing neat conceptual models, may be of much less assistance in managing strategic change. The argument developed here is that practitioners may beneficially approach the management of strategic change by conceiving of the problems, and of remedial action, in cultural and cognitive terms, and that this yields practical management guidelines. This is not to suggest that there is no room for, or no relevance to, notions of 'scientific management', but that the analytical and evaluative techniques associated with such an approach need to be seen as an integral part of a wider process. So much will be argued in this chapter.

A SUMMARY OF KEY PROPOSITIONS

The sort of framework described in chapter 2 under the general heading of 'rationalistic' models has traditionally dominated both writers' and practitioners' approaches to the complexity we call strategic management. There are, however, other well established ideas deriving from the study of management in organizations concerning how managers cope with complexity in the task of management. These other models, many of which are also outlined in chapter 2 of this book, appear to describe for Fosters, and for studies by other researchers, rather better how strategies are actually formulated and implemented in organizations.

There are discernible patterns of strategic development in organizations. Typically, for example, organizations go through long periods when strategies appear to be developed incrementally – that is strategic decisions build one upon another, in small steps, following a path in which history appears to play an important role in shaping future strategy. Again, typically, there occur in organizations, infrequently, more fundamental shifts in strategy as more major re-adjustment of the strategic direction of the firm takes place. Some writers, notably Quinn (1980) and Lindblom (1959), have argued that such incremental development in organizations is not only inevitable, but also logical. Managers consciously pursue an incremental approach to the management of complexity: they are aware that it is not possible to 'know' about all the influences that could conceivably affect the future of the organization. Moreover, they are aware that the organization is a political entity in which trade-offs between different groups are inevitable; it is therefore not possible to arrive at an optimal goal or an optimal strategy; strategies must be comprises that allow the organization to go forward. To cope with this uncertainty and this political compromise, strategies must be developed in stages, carrying the members of the organization with them, and trying out new ideas and experiments to see which are likely to be effective and to induce commitment with the organization through continual but low-scale change. This is what has become known as 'logical incrementalism'; certainly it was evident in this study that the managers, though not using such words, espoused such an approach. They saw themselves as logical incrementalists, and believed that this was a sensible way to manage.

There is no denial here that an incremental pattern of strategy is discernible in many organizations; Fosters was certainly one of them. However, there are other explanations as to how such patterns of strategic development come about. Indeed the whole idea of 'logical incrementalism' can be seen as a rationalistic interpretation of processes that can be accounted for in quite different ways. Pettigrew suggests as much about Quinn's work:

> Quinn's style of presenting his ideas, moving easily from description to prescription, makes his book extremely attractive as a teaching medium, but the clarity of his belief in the prescriptive value of logical incrementalism means it is not always easy to disentangle what he has discovered empirically from what he would like to see. (Pettigrew, 1983, p. 14)

We need to be careful about building too much upon what managers espouse: because they espouse the idea of logical incrementalism does not necessarily mean they behave in such ways. Still less does it mean that we should build normative models of management upon such espousal. Our explanations of management, and such lessons as can be drawn, must, rather, build on the empirical investigation of practice in the political, cultural and cognitive arena we call the organization. If the management process is viewed in such a way, what emerges is that the complexity that managers face cannot be objectively analysed continually within the managerial task. So much has been well enough established by other researchers. The analysis of the data in this study has yielded findings, however, that build on other developing concepts and add further explanations concerning the complexity of strategic management.

Managers hold to a set of core beliefs and assumptions, specific and relevant to the organization in which they work. Whilst individual managers may hold quite varying sets of beliefs about many different aspects of that organizational world, there is likely to exist at some level a core set of beliefs and assumptions held relatively commonly by the managers. This has variously been called ideational culture, myths, interpretative schemes, or the term used here, paradigms. In Fosters this set of beliefs, which evolved over time, embraced assumptions about the nature of the organizational environment, the managerial style in the organization and the nature of its leaders, and the operational routines important to ensure the success of the organization.

This paradigm is essentially cultural; that is, it is held relatively commonly and taken for granted. It may be more easily perceived by those outside the organization than those inside the organization to whom its constructs may be self-evident and 'obvious'. It is this paradigm that, in many organizations, creates a relatively homogeneous approach to the interpretation of the complexity that the organization faces. The various and often confusing signals that the organization faces are made sense of, are filtered, in terms of this paradigm. Moreover, since it evolves over time and is reinforced through the history and success of the organization, it also provides a repertoire of actions and responses to the interpretations of signals that are experienced by managers and seen by them as demonstrably relevant. It is at one and the same time a device for interpretation and a formula for action. The strategies organizations follow therefore grow out this paradigm.

Managers may therefore actually or conceivably recognize changes going on around them within or without the organization, but this does not necessarily mean that they see such changes as directly relevant to their organization. It is quite likely, for example, that the objective observer from outside the organization could perceive competitive actions as impinging on or threatening the organization, when managers internally, whilst knowing about such activity, do not see it as relevant to their organization. Relevance is determined, not by the competitive activity, but by the constructs of the paradigm; if such stimuli can be explained within that paradigm then that becomes 'the reality' for organizational action.

The paradigm is hedged about and protected by a web of cultural artefacts – symbols, myths and rituals that legitimize its constructs; organizational routines and systems that programme the way organizational members respond to given situations, delineate 'the way we do things around here', and may even be capitalized in hardware such as computer systems. Moreover, it is likely that those with the greatest power in organizations derive that power from, amongst other things, their association with the constructs of that paradigm; their association with its complexity – and uncertainty-reducing mechanisms enhances their status and links them to the perceived success of the organization. It would therefore be a mistake to conceive of the paradigm as merely a set of beliefs removed from organizational action. It lies within a cultural web which bonds it to the action of organizational life.

It is therefore very difficult to challenge or change aspects of the paradigm unless such changes are evolutionary. Challenges to the legitimacy of constructs within that paradigm are likely to be perceived as cultural or political threats to the organization. Such challenges are not only likely to be disturbing because they attack those beliefs that are central to managerial life, they are also likely to be interpreted as threatening by the political elites in the organization. Challenges to the paradigm need therefore to be seen as political and cultural actions rather than a matter of intellectual debate. This is an important distinction, not often understood by those who take an essentially analytical perspective on management. Those who believe that an objective, analytical assessment of, for example, a changing environment can yield knowledge that managers can, or should, interpret intellectually and objectively and assimilate in such a way as to change strategy, neglect the understanding that such analysis may well achieve a political rather than intellectual response.

When changes occur in the organization's environment that appear to conflict with or require action outside the paradigm, there is unlikely to be a wholesale change of the constructs of the paradigm. Rather, conflict resolution is likely to be political with symbolic mediation. If the paradigm does not provide a ready-made solution, organizational action will be dependent on solutions advanced by those who can exercise the greatest degree of power or that can bond together a political alliance that can dominate others. If this means that constructs within that paradigm conflict with one another – in Fosters for example in 1981 the need for greater cost control conflicted with the traditional paternalistic management – then the myths and stories, rooted in history – in Fosters case about the caring nature of the management – have the role of legitimizing action and preserving the fundamental integrity of the paradigm.

If one views the process of strategic management in such ways, then it is clear that incremental patterns of strategic development in organizations are very likely to result. However, it also becomes clear that, since the organization is likely to be responding over time to a business environment that is essentially internally constructed rather than objectively understood, it is likely that, over time, the phenomenon of 'strategic drift' will occur. That is gradually, probably imperceptibly, the strategy of the organization will become less and less relevant to the environment in which the organization exists. This may be a process that takes very many years and it is likely that it will not be discerned by the managers until the drift becomes so marked that major performance decline results. It is then that more fundamental changes in strategy are likely to occur.

Managerial processes that account for more fundamental changes in strategy can also be understood within the same essentially interpretative models of management. There is a need to 'unfreeze' the paradigm. This is likely to occur through mechanisms that concern themselves with the very devices that normally preserve that paradigm. So, for example, the break up of political alliances and the challenging or changing of rituals and routines within the organization play a role in surfacing and making explicit the constructs within the paradigm and, in turn, challenging them. In particular there is evidence that 'outsiders' – that is, individuals with little loyalty to that paradigm, usually because they come from outside the organization – may play a vital role in surfacing and challenging what is taken for granted in the organization.

As the paradigm becomes more fluid, so it becomes possible to provide new perspectives and new ideas. These too may well be introduced by outsiders who will draw on their own experience and beliefs, introducing them to a new context in a less rigid situation. The extent to which such new perspectives can be developed into a fundamentally different strategy is likely to depend on the extent to which managers from within the organization are able to feel confident enough about the need for change to become constructively critical of their own history and its dominant paradigm. In this way the extent to which new perspectives introduced into the organization take root and are developed effectively is likely to depend on the extent to which there is an examination and understanding of the 'pre-history' of that organization.

The likelihood of members of the organization complying with the changes being introduced and the challenges made to the paradigm will depend, not so much on the intellectual case made for change or on the overt reward and punishment systems, so much as on symbolic aspects of change which, again, legitimize the change process itself. It is also likely to depend on the extent to which deeds of change rather than words are communicated clearly, and the extent to which performance improvement visibly demonstrates the efficacy of such change.

It is likely that the change process that occurs will be, relatively speaking, ill defined and general. Members of the organization will know that change is occurring but may not be that clear about where it is leading or what it signifies. However, it may be that this process of change is a necessary precursor to the introduction of specific strategies. The change process itself is, however, unlikely to define those strategies, so there is a need for this rather general process of change to be converted and refined into more specifically understood action and direction. This refinement of strategy may well require the sorts of analytical, planning approaches more usually identified with rationalistic, scientific approaches to management. To come full circle, the problem may be that proponents of such rationalistic approaches neglect to understand, or fail to emphasize sufficiently, that they cannot be effective unless the change processes to break down the paradigm are already in process. It may be a fundamental error to assume that strategic change can come about as a result of the analysis and evaluation traditionally associated with strategic management. Rather, such techniques may be more usefully regarded as essentially dependent for success on the ability of managers to promote the processes of strategic change. To do this managers must understand that they have available to them many different approaches and mechanisms. These have been touched upon as we have moved through this book and they will now be elaborated on more specifically.

THE GENERALIZABILITY OF FINDINGS

It was said in the introductory chapter that this is not a comparative study. That is not to say that no comparisons were made between the findings and other research or empirical studies of strategic management, and many of these have been noted as the book has progressed. Whilst it has not been the intention to base this study upon such comparisons, the question does arise as to what extent the findings here are context-bound; to what extent they relate only to the circumstances in Fosters.

To some extent the answer to this question must be that the very nature of the propositions being made suggests that many of the observations must be context-bound. The way in which Fosters responded to its developing competitive environment in the 1970s, for example, was largely governed by its particular organizational paradigm and its specific political and cultural context. There is certainly no attempt to suggest that other firms faced with similar environments would have behaved in the same way, or that their paradigm or their cultural context, different as it must be, would have exerted the same influences; so at a very specific level the descriptions of strategic responses in this study must be context-bound.

It may also be so at a more general level. Schein (1985) argues that problems and processes of change differ according to different stages in an organization's life cycle. The problems of early growth are not the same as those of mid-life or decline; nor are the appropriate mechanisms for change the same in these different stages. In these terms, Fosters must be seen as an example of an organization in mid-life. It can also be argued that Fosters is an example of a particular type of management culture; what Miles and Snow (1978) might call a 'defender', with a low perceived environmental uncertainty and low perceived need for internal change (Anderson and Paine, 1975) in the 1970s and what Ouchi (1980) would call a 'clannish' organization. It had been convinced of its own strategy for success, concerned to become more and more efficient at developing that formula for success, with little desire to break away from what it knew what to do well, and with a strong binding, homogeneous set of beliefs. Certainly not all organizations are like this and it can be argued that the way in which Fosters responded in strategic terms, whilst perhaps typical of cultures such as theirs, would not be typical of other more aggressive or less homogeneous organizational cultures. This is a point with which I would not wish to argue. The intention is not to suggest that the lessons gleaned from the Fosters study are generalizable to all contexts. On the other hand, the situation in Fosters is not unusual and it is suggested that some of the lessons that can be learned from this study inform practitioners, teachers and researchers of problems and processes that can occur in many organizations.

Notwithstanding these caveats, the development of the arguments and propositions in this study have built on a raft of research carried out in many other organizations by many other researchers. The findings, whilst building on such research and hopefully developing it, do not contradict much of that evidence. Moreover, whilst this is not intended to be an exhaustive comparative study, such comparisons as can be made with the relatively limited number of longitudinal and contextual studies of strategic management in organizations do show that many of our findings bear close resemblance to them.

For example, my own comparative studies within the clothing retail industry (Johnson 1984; 1986) show that other major businesses competing with Fosters, such as Hepworths and Burtons, showed many similar processual characteristics through the same sort of period. The companies may have made different strategic responses, but it was clear that their own paradigms for much of their history governed the interpretation that management placed on the business environment, led to major strategic drift and, in both cases, that fundamental strategic change came about through the arrival of outsiders, who managed the political, cultural and social processes of change through essentially political and symbolic mechanisms. Further, and coincidentally, a study of a fourth competitor in the industry conducted by Green (1987) shows how John Collier remained largely the prisoner of its historical paradigm well into the 1980s.

Nor can it be argued that many of the findings are bound by the context of retailing. The central dominance of cognitive structures was demonstrated forcefully by Spender (1980) in his study of three quite different industry settings – the forklift truck industry, milk distribution and the foundry industry in the UK. He also demonstrated that the constructs within what he called a 'recipe' were largely operational in nature – beliefs and assumptions about centrally important routines of operation, bestowing beneficial competences upon the organization – and that these firmly held beliefs served as interpretative devices and as a repertoire for organizational action. He also pointed out that it was very rare for organizations to be able to challenge or change that recipe and that strategies were typically configured within it.

However, perhaps the fullest account of strategic change over time in an organization is the study by Pettigrew (1985b) of the industrial giant ICI, in which he studied, in context, the process of change over many years. Here we see many parallels with this study in a totally different industrial environment. Pettigrew shows the historical dominance of the ICI culture:

> Many of the people interviewed talked of ICI as a traditional, a conservative organisation, images of the 'great ship ploughing through waters' and not needing to change. (1985, p. 387)

Also, again, another ICI manager being self-critical:

> If you have an organisation which has been by-and-large successful, it's fifty years old, it's hierarchical, it's almost totally inbred, it advances layer by layer, rank by rank, it has to be very very conservative. And unless it falls off a cliff as it did in 1980, then people feel just as they would in a plant control room on a Friday afternoon, 'keep your hands in your pockets, don't touch

anything, its Friday, the plant's running well isn't it' (Pettigrew, 1985b, p. 388)

That manager could be describing Fosters in the 1970s, almost word for word, and the observations of process that Pettigrew goes on to note are also very similar. He notes the phenomenon of what has here been called 'strategic drift', for example in the plastics division; he observes that managers themselves learned that 'it takes the unambiguity of crisis to produce real learning, the desire to listen and the willingness to act' (p. 270). He shows how the intervention of what has here been called an 'outsider' in cultural and ideological terms, in the person of John Harvey-Jones, was required to effect the sort of fundamental change that came about in ICI in the 1980s. Moreover, he shows that similar processes of change were used by Harvey-Jones and included conscious political manipulation and posturing, the encouragement of subordinates to surface bad news and put pressure on senior executives and the symbolic positioning of himself by, for example, 'never missing a chance to make the point that I'm basically an operator' (p. 396).

It can also be observed through Pettigrew's study that significant changes occur because of the surfacing, in one case purely unintentionally, of key constructs within the historical paradigm. Moreover, change was directly linked to the re-configuration of power in the organization and the advent of 'young Turks [who] were by no means uniform in their perspectives or priorities for change' (p. 403). In other words the process for change was underway before any clear definition had been given of what new strategies should be pursued – processes fostered by political upheaval, questioning, the introduction of outsiders, and accelerated, for example, by working parties set up to legitimize change and symbolic acts – changes in structure or titles of divisions, financial reporting systems and the like.

In summary many of the processes observed within the context of Fosters are also observable, coincidentally within the same sort of time period, within a major multinational heavy chemicals industry. Similar mechanisms for change are also recorded in the studies of Schein (1985): in particular the role of outsiders as change agents; planned and unplanned events which have the effect of surfacing traditional assumptions and beliefs and exploding organizational myths; symbolic activity that activates organization members' strategic thinking; and changes in routines of operating that demand different patterns of organizational interaction. Nor do the findings bear comparison only with those of academic researchers. The practical experience of consultants who have been widely involved in processes of managing strategic change bear out many of the propositions. For example Julien Phillips (1986), a Principal Consultant with McKinsey's, has outlined his observations of how successful 'change managers' worked and concluded that they:

- Made clear the broad objectives of, and the key issues relating to, required change.
- Explicitly contrasted the old and the new, and in so doing surfaced tacit assumptions about the old.
- Dramatized change 'in order to increase the probability of emotional as well as intellectual understanding' (Phillips, 1986, p. 25).
- Effected substantial changes in power structures.
- Made sure key employees, 'way beyond top management', were involved in change decisions and implementation, often by use of working groups or project teams.
- Demonstrated the reality of change to managers through deeds, through changes in operating procedures and routines, and through top management's visible association with change advocacy.
- Employed symbolic mechanisms such as publicizing change heroes or stories of success or stage-managing events to dramatize the need for or advent of change.

It is not suggested that such comparisons prove that the processes observed in this study are in all cases generalizable. However, they are certainly not unique and the similarity with other studies does suggest that the developing explanations of change processes rooted in empirical research of this sort does help yield useful conclusions for both practitioners and other researchers.

IMPLICATIONS FOR PRACTITIONERS

Managers themselves, faced with the complexity and dramas of their organizational life, will also argue that they really should be more objective, or analytical or scientific in their approach to their job, that they take too little time out for planning, set too few or too imprecise objectives, do not think far enough ahead and so on. This sort of apology may have some validity in its self-criticism; there is no argument here that analysis or planning is not important. However, it is rarer to hear managers as self-critical about their lack of skills in knowing how to manage the social, political and cultural processes of change – the sorts of processes that have been shown to be so vitally important if strategies in businesses are to be managed. It is not enough for managers, faced with the complexity of strategic decision-making, to fall back on apparently analytical and planning modes of behaviour without knowing how to deal with the forces for inertia and the processes of change that will determine whether new ideas and new strategies might or might not be accepted. To do this managers need to understand how decisions are made in organizations, why and how decisions come about, and what skills and techniques can be employed to galvanize the sorts of changes that may be necessary. When it comes to the management of those most important decisions in business that we label 'strategic', managers should not pretend that the behaviour that typifies their organizational life is no longer relevant or important; on the contrary, managers should learn to manage more effectively within these realities of organizational life.

Loose/Tight Systems

In exploring these ideas more specifically we can begin with the notion of incrementalism. The recent advocacy of incrementalism in the management literature in effect argues that, whereas hitherto management theorists have implied that managers too often behave irrationally, this is not the case; indeed, the way managers manage strategy is 'logically' incremental. The criticism made in this book is that such advocacy appears to be based on the espoused theories of managers, like those of the Fosters managers in 1980, rather than a study of the management processes of strategy within the firm. It is not argued here that incrementalism is in some way 'wrong'; it is accepted that incrementalism, as a mode of management, is a natural outcome of the way in which organizations, as collectivities of individuals, order their world through the cognitive device we have here called the paradigm, lodged as it is in its cultural web. It is not a question of the extent to which incrementalism is 'wrong' or 'right'; what is important is what can be learned about managing in organizational systems, which naturally are likely to develop incrementally, so as to minimize the inherent dangers of these processes and ensure that the organization is capable of responding to the changes taking place around it. Many of the dangers, summarized in the notion of strategic drift, have already been discussed. The question remains of how it is possible to avoid them.

There is a need in all organizations for some homogeneity of beliefs and expectations about the competitive environment and modes of operation. Individuals operate on the basis of cognitive maps and it is not possible for them to re-invent their cognitive world every time they face a new situation. It follows that in a social setting there is need for some conformity of approach to interpreting new situations; without it there would be no organizational action, merely as many responses as there are individuals. The paradigm is the set of beliefs and assumptions that is held in a relative commonality and that achieves such conformity. However, if homogeneity around the paradigm is essential for the preservation of order, so is heterogeneity for the ability of the organization to change (Burgelman, 1983). Friedlander makes a similar point: 'A strong sense of identity involves investment, commitment, momentum – and paradox-ically, rigidity. These all preclude learning because their existence depends on limiting knowledge to that which will reinforce and applaud investment in . . . the established mission' (Friedlander, 1983, p. 210). He also quotes Maier as follows: 'For an organism to learn, it must be sufficiently heterogeneous to contain differences' (Maier, 1970, from Friedlander, 1983, p. 196). It is the same sort of argument as is made by those researchers who have examined 'excellent' corporations over the last decade: for example Peters and Waterman write about 'simultaneous loose–tight properties' in an organization: 'Organisations that live by the loose–tight principle are on the one hand rigidly controlled, yet at the same time allow (indeed insist on) autonomy, entrepreneurship, and innovation from the rank and file' (Peters and Waterman, 1982, p. 318). Or again as Kanter argues: 'The key is to allow a continual creative tension between grass roots innovation in a free-wheeling environment and periodic strategic decisions by strong central leaders' (Kanter, 1984, p. 296). These writers are arguing that organizations at one and the same time require belief and value systems with which those in the organization can strongly identify, but also require the sort of 'creative tension' in which differences of approaches, of attitudes, of beliefs and of action can maintain the sensitivity to a changing environment and the innovation for change that is necessary to avoid the risk of strategic drift.

This is a problem for managers. Conceptually we may regard the problem much as shown in figure 9.1. As Wilkins and Ouchi (1983) argue, those organizations that are 'clannish' in nature, that are largely homogeneous in their belief systems, are quite likely to demonstrate a high ability and willingness to adapt; but as they argue: 'The change problems come when organisational conditions are so radically altered that clan members must clearly violate their basic assumptions' (Wilkins and Ouchi, 1983, p. 479).

In other words the efficiency of change for an organization with an essentially homogeneous system of beliefs and assumptions is likely to be high provided the level of change being undertaken is relatively low; so the ability of a 'clannish' organization to change incrementally may be very great indeed. Where such systems fail is when they have to cope with much

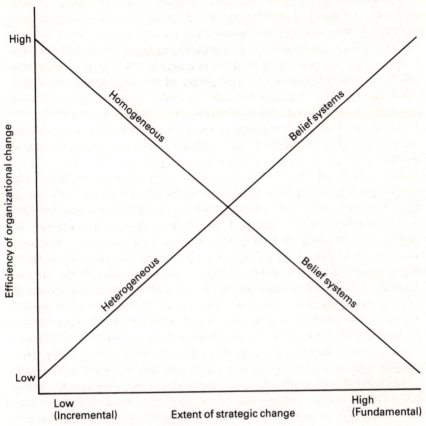

FIGURE 9.1 Change efficiency and belief systems

more fundamental strategic change. It is an argument well borne out in this study. However, conversely it can be argued that, whereas organizations with much more heterogeneous belief systems are more efficient at coping with high levels of change – what we have here called fundamental strategic change – such heterogeneous belief systems can be highly inefficient, markedly disruptive and wasteful of energy if low levels of change are required. The problem is that if the system is geared to low levels of change with homogeneous belief systems, there is a high likelihood in time of strategic drift; whereas if it is geared to high levels of change it is unlikely to cope efficiently with the more typically adaptive needs of the organization. What is required at one and the same time are clear belief and value systems with which those in the organization can strongly identify, but also the sort of 'creative tension' in which differences of approaches, of attitudes, of beliefs and of action can maintain the sensitivity to a changing environment and the innovation for change that is necessary to avoid the risk of strategic drift.

How is this combination of necessary bonding values and beliefs yet adequate heterogeneity to be achieved? The problem is to create a system that can handle the sort of change that organizations have to face over time, which requires a heterogeneous belief set, yet also retains a corporate thrust and identity. We can usefully draw on other studies to help here. In particular the studies of so-called 'excellent' companies by, for example, Quinn (1980), Peters and Waterman (1982) and Kanter (1983) yield useful findings.

The common ground in these studies is that 'excellent' organizations demonstrate a system of management in which there is a combined bonding set of beliefs of values – what Kanter calls a 'clear culture' – combined with the facility within the organization for the challenge of assumptions; the identity of individuals or groups with problems rather than ready-made solutions; and their willingness to progress in the management of those problems. In our terms what emerges is controlled challenge to the paradigm. Such organizations have an identity that is clear, understood both within the company and outside, yet with enough creative tension within the organization to carry it forward in terms of innovation and change. Argyris and Schon (1978) have argued that individuals in organizations must learn to accept and operate according to the notion of double-loop learning if organizations are to be able to cope with change. The argument is that managers must learn to live with ambiguity and be self-challenging, rather than seek conformity. Argyris and Schon, however, also found that it was remarkably difficult to achieve double-loop learning for individuals. Indeed it is argued that individuals may not wish to live with constant change, may become cynical of organizational change as 'the wisdom of the day before yesterday gives way to new truth, which in turn is replaced by a still more radiant one' (Wildavsky, 1972, p. 513) and that in any case constant change is very costly to bear. Yet, if we are to believe these studies of 'excellent' companies, it is just this sort of double-loop learning that takes place.

How can this be so? The general point is that such readiness to change in organizations is not dependent on the willingness of individuals alone, but on the organizational system that prevails. Double-loop learning in an organizational sense is a matter of culture, not simply a matter of individual cognition. To use Wildavsky's own terms, it is precisely that individuals, within an organizational setting of excellence, do wish to live with constant change but also do not see that as something imposed upon them, but something that they, themselves, are forging as a group. There appear to be some distinct lessons that can be learnt.

First, it is important that the organization has a clarity of purpose, some would say mission. It is difficult to be exact as to what form this might take. It could take the form of some set of overarching values that prevail in the organization, which everybody understands and can identify with. Quinn argues that organizations typically spend a great deal of effort trying to be very precise about their organizational goals yet such precision, often in the form of quantified aims, fails to provide any sort of organizational identity to which people can commit themselves. He argues that:

> Broad goals can create identity and elan. Effective organisational goals satisfy a basic human need. They enable people to develop an identity larger than themselves, to participate in greater challenges, and to have influence or seek rewards they could not achieve alone. Interestingly enough many employees can identify better with broad goals like being the best or the first in an area than they can with more specific numerical goals. (Quinn, 1980, p. 74)

He goes on to argue:

> More thoughtful top managers also carefully analyse whether one strategic goal or another will better attract the skilled people and personal commitments they want. (p. 75)

In other words these managers seek to encapsulate the core, underlying strategies of their organization into goals or values that form a coherent philosophy for that organization. Peters and Waterman provide an excellent example of this when they discuss Walt Disney Productions. Here we have a company in which its strategy of an all-embracing entertainment event for the family is translated into a set of values and messages to employees that are, at one and the same time, simple in general terms to understand, but require total commitment and intensive training to carry out, and are self-selecting in terms of recruitment. Customers are 'guests' who form an audience and the mission of the organization is to provide happiness through entertainment. This basic message is translated into the fabric of everyday life in the organization:

> The service through people theme at Disney starts, as it does in many of the excellent companies, with a special language. There is no such thing as a worker at Disney. The employees out front are 'cast members' and the personnel department is 'casting'. Whenever you are working with the public you are 'on stage'. (Peters and Waterman, 1982, p. 167)

The point is that there is a need for a clarity of mission, which needs to permeate the organization and be expressed in terms of values that people understand, goals that are of practical consequence to them and can be translated into behaviour that is of meaning to them. It is a theme that has recurred throughout our discussions; strategy must be meaningful to those in the organizations, and that means meaningful in terms of their everyday life, what they do, how they do it and even the language they use. The example from Fosters of the requirement for shop staff to wear clothes bought from within the shop is by no means as powerful an instance of this as we see at Disney; but it does show the extent to which the 'mundane' translation of strategy into action can demonstrate, at one and the same time, the meaning of the strategy and the values required by those in the organization to implement it.

However, it is not enough for goals and values to be clear – they must also be supported by the everyday expectations, beliefs and assumptions of those in the organization; in short the ideational culture must be supportive of the core values. Moreover, the danger we saw in Fosters of the managers becoming wedded over time to the taken-for-granted set of assumptions about 'how we do things around here', linked to the routines in the organization, must be avoided at all costs. If the organization is to be responsive to change and manage change effectively, the beliefs and assumptions that bond the managers must be at the strategic level and to do with the core values we have discussed. Bonding values and beliefs need to be of a higher order. When it comes to how to operate, managers should not believe that they know the solutions to problems; rather, they must be ready to accept that, maybe, there are new ways of doing things and the views that they hold may need to be changed, and changed frequently. Change in this sense needs to become 'normal'. Burtons is one of the most successful fashion retailers in the world; it has shown continued growth in profits and turnover from 1977 to the time of writing, and in doing so has continually innovated and responded to a changing retail environment. Ralph Halpern, its Chairman, talks about 'institutionalizing change':

> Change is always on the agenda; we don't just expect our executives to run the show, we expect them to change the show as well . . . . Our management philosophy is that people are trained and motivated to plan for change. We believe this is crucial to our continued profitable growth . . . . No store is allowed to go more than four–five years without complete modernisation . . . Only the most visionary retailers recognise the need to change a successful formula while it is still working. (Johnson, 1986 pp 21–22)

It is a system that also builds in challenges; challenges from outsiders as consultants, for example, to each of the main board members; and challenges from peers, for the expectation is that each manager will challenge his or her colleagues and 'argue their corner'. Indeed a common theme that recurs in these organizations is the challenging of taken-for-granted assumptions. Other writers have advocated other systems for dealing with this; Townsend (1970) advocates a 'court jester' role for an individual or group, close to the senior executives or chairman, with the specific brief of continually challenging that which he or she perceives to be assumed and with the protection and patronage of that senior executive. Similarly, and more formally stated, there are systems of devils advocacy as proposed by Janis (1972), Janis and Mann (1977), Cosier (1981) and Schwenk (1982) in which group assumptions are surfaced and systematically challenged within groups. Such systems may well be useful; however, as Beyer (1981, p. 194) notes, such systems may be ineffective if they assume that 'no difficulties arise from the unwillingness of organizational members to yield on matters of self-interest'. The point is that such systems can be effective in situations where organizational members identify and welcome such challenges. They are likely to be much more difficult to implement in cultures that are defensive, self-protecting of themselves and individuals, and without a culture of change.

Moreover, the expectation should be one of innovation and not just 'doing your job'. 3M has a high record of product innovation and, according to Peters and Waterman, senior executives explain that this is primarily because managers throughout the organization understand that the expectation is one of innovation, and that the responsibility for that lies with them all. So for example, if a manager gets an idea it is expected that time will be created outside the normal systems of working, to follow it through, that he or she will 'champion' it and persuade others to that way of thinking; that the manager will market the ideas internally and take on areas of resistance using lobbying systems to persuade others of the wisdom of the ideas. The innovations manager will use equipment or systems that he or she might not have authority over normally to experiment and test out ideas. The point is that in many organizations such behaviour would be frowned upon, would be seen as disruptive and would lead to the individual being seen as potentially dangerous. In 3M such behaviour is not only tolerated, but encouraged. If an organization is to change, be responsive and innovate the systems have to cope with the process of innovation; the process of innovation cannot be expected to cope with superimposed systems.

Organizational structure and systems also play a fundamental part in creating the context for change. We have already touched on this so far as it has been pointed out that over rigid systems can severely restrict the ability of individuals to innovate or challenge. There are further dangers and further lessons.

Kanter argues that organizations must avoid 'segmentalist structures' and adopt 'integrative' approaches. She explains:

> Companies with segmentalist cultures are likely to have segmented structures; a large number of compartments walled off from one another – department from department, level above from level below, field office from headquarters, labour from management or men from women. Only the minimum number of exchanges takes place at the boundaries of segments; each slice is assumed to stand or fall rather independently of any other anyway, so why should they need to co-operate? Segmentalism assumes that problems can be solved when they are carved into pieces and the pieces assigned to specialists who work in isolation. (Kanter, 1983, p. 28)

It is an argument that squares with that argued for the danger of the dominant paradigm. The paradigm at Fosters was essentially functional and operational; it encapsulated beliefs about the wisdom of operating in particular ways and dependencies on particular functions; problems were seen as capable of being dealt with essentially through mechanisms of buying or cost control. We have seen how such beliefs and assumptions were welded into the power structures in the organization. Those organizations that expect to innovate, that expect to change, need rather to adopt systems and structures that encourage the exchange and challenging of ideas across groups and between levels, and that minimize the extent to which powerful groups can isolate themselves from others or force their views and ways of doing things upon others.

Peters and Waterman and also Kanter note the predominance of task force or project groupings around particular issues that prevail in their 'excellent companies'. In 3M, for example, an innovating champion will be encouraged to build up a team of supporters around his or her interests, a team that might cross functional boundaries or draw on expertise from different parts of the diversified conglomerate. Such groups might not be long-lasting, or might eventually form themselves into new businesses completely. Hand in hand with such an approach is the avoidance of watertight job definitions, the breakdown of rigid organizational structures and the adoption of organic systems of management. Mintzberg (1979a) has pointed out that, whereas relatively rigid cultures and organizations – he calls them 'machine bureaucracies' – may be suited to simple and relatively stable business environments, it is unlikely that they will cope with situations of change. In such circumstances it is necessary to raise the level of tolerance to debate and dissent and this is likely to mean that more organic systems of management are required. One micro-electronics company in the UK, which demonstrated a growth, profit and innovation record in the UK over a ten-year period against apparently daunting competition from multinationals, prided itself on its 'lack of organization'. Managers had little concept of job descriptions or hierarchies; they might nominally know who was their 'boss', but this did not signify a statutory reporting relationship, and might well not be discerned by the outsider. They communicated with each other as the problems and issues dictated; they created their own tasks and responsibilities, and changed them when the problems changed. It was a system that was severely self-selecting. Individuals were rarely fired; if they could not cope with that way of working, they very soon left, usually in total bewilderment – but those who stayed tended to remain over a long period, contributed energetically with the minimum of direction, and were always ready to question and challenge current approaches to situations.

If the imposition of the will of powerful hierarchies is to be avoided it may be necessary to take specific steps to minimize such power. This may already be achieved if the sorts of systems described above are in operation. It is difficult to wield formal, hierarchical power in an organic system of management. However, it may be that such organic systems are not best suited to the organization; that some more formal sort of structure is required. There may, however, still be ways of minimizing the extent to which such formal structures can impose themselves so as to reduce innovation. One way may simply be to reduce the levels of management in the organization. We need to remember that most organizational forms that are traditional have derived from schools of thought rooted in views of the scientific manager of the early twentieth century. They are views that see the manager as analyst, the manager as instructor and planner and organizations as hierarchies with defined capabilities in terms of spans of controls in which each level has defined authority limits and can sanction particular sorts of expenditure or decisions. These are not organizations built around change; they are rather built about the confidence and stability of earlier decades. Moreover, such hierarchies are self-protecting both of the routines that exist and of mistakes and errors that might occur. In helping to make this point I have often asked managers what they would do if they made an important error of judgement in the organization; a typical response is that they would talk to their boss about it. The expectation is that 'a good boss would back me up'; the implication is that the different levels of management would dilute the problem as it proceeded upwards. The system in Burtons over its period of change and growth was quite different; there was the minimum of hierarchical structure; a main board with a chief executive and six functional 'managing directors' had up to 13 business units reporting to it. Each business unit had a main board with a replicated set of functional directors on it reporting to the functional directors on the main board. There were no divisional managing directors. As Ralph Halpern explained:

> If you have a series of managing directors in the divisions and you sit on top of that you are more likely to get out of touch. If you filter all knowledge through an individual it is very much filtered, so you only hear what he wants you to hear. It's really an explanation of his good performance or poor performance as filtered by him. I know because I've done it myself. What we wanted to happen was that central management should keep in touch with every facet of the business. They can see what's happening down to the market place. (Johnson, 1986 p. 23)

Of course, it also meant that executives in the businesses were able, like it or note, to communicate directly with the main board. As one executive explained:

> It's a very open system; it has to be; you can't hide anything.

It also supported the Burtons philosophy of mutual challenge of ideas within the organization, and meant that it was almost impossible to build up powerful elites within any one part of the organization.

A further point, again well illustrated by the Burtons example above, is the extent to which top management sees its role as 'hands-on' within the business. The idea of senior executives as somehow removed from the action, thinking strategically or working in remote committees about problems of quite different dimensions to those within the organization, receives little support from any of the studies of 'excellence'. Top management may be strategists, but they are also involved in the organizations, continually prompting the sort of change and innovation that they expect to see demonstrated. Kanter argues that: 'The key is to allow a continual creative tension between grass roots innovation in a free-wheeling environment in periodic strategic decisions by strong central leaders' (Kanter, 1984, p. 296). It is the same sort of 'loose/tight' operation that Peters and Waterman describe in which top management are able both to understand and identify with everyday problems, encourage the creative ability of individuals to deal with them in a way in which they take responsibility for them, themselves, and yet retain a tight hold on the central thrust and strategy of the organization as a whole. In a sense the organization is both centralized and de-centralized. Kanter explains this apparent contradiction as follows:

> Participation in a team with responsibility for a joint output is not always a preferable process for carrying out tasks; there are circumstances under which authoritative, unilateral decisions or delegation to a single individual makes

more sense. Several decades of social-psychological research and the accumulated wisdom of the companies struggling with participation make clear that the use of teams is most appropriate for purposes closely related to staying ahead of change: to gain new sources of expertise and experience; to get collaboration that multiplies a person's effort by providing assistance, backup, or stimulation of better performance; to allow all of those who feel they know something about the subject to get involved; to build consensus on a controversial issue; to allow representatives of those affected by an issue to influence decisions and build commitment to them; to tackle a problem which no one 'owns' by virtue of organisational assignment; to allow more wide ranging or creative discussions/solutions than available by normal means (e.g., to get an unusual group together); to balance or confront vested interests in the face of the need to change; to address conflicting approaches or views; to avoid precipitate action and explore a variety of effects; to create an opportunity and enough time to study a problem in depth; to develop and educate people through their participation; new skills, new information, new contacts.

In short, a great deal of innovation seems to demand participation, especially at the action or implementation stage.

Simply reverse these conditions, and it is clear that there are also times when participation or employee involvement is not appropriate: when one person clearly has greater expertise on the subject than all others; when those affected by the decision acknowledge and accept that expertise; when there is a 'hip-pocket solution' – the manager or company already knows the 'right answer'; when someone has the subject as part of his/her regular job assignment, and it was not his/her idea to form the team; when no one really cares all that much about the issues; when no development or learning important to others would be served by their involvement; when there is no time for discussion; when people work more happily and productively alone. (Kanter, 1984, pp. 242–3)

The Symbolic Support of Change

This study has also shown that the creation and maintenance of appropriate ideational culture, the communication of clear strategy and values, and the support for the sorts of systems and structures in the organization that provide an environment conducive to change, can be significantly supported and fostered by largely symbolic systems. Other writers would, in any case, argue that many of the structural variables we have discussed are essentially symbolic anyway. Task forces and project teams are ritualized identity-creating devices in organizations as well as problem-solving mechanisms; the form in which a job description or organizational chart is drawn up or explained symbolizes the nature of the organization and the expectations of the managers and staff within it.

Certainly if we move further into other mechanisms of control within the organization, their symbolic values become quite evident. The sorts of reward systems that operate within firms vary from the highly mechanistic rewarding of only pre-set numerical targets, through to those that are translated into theatre, that become events of applause for the 'heroes' of the organization who most symbolize the pursuit of organizational ideals. Apparently formal control mechanisms may take on a whole new set of meanings; for example, computerized stock control methods with the mechanistic aim of keeping stocks to a sensible minimum may also be used in retailers to challenge managers' assumptions about what can and cannot sell in the shops. Rates of depreciation clearly encapsulate assumptions about degrees and rates of change; one of the first acts of Ralph Halpern when he took over Burtons was to reduce the rates of depreciation; he could not espouse the need for rapid change and yet maintain the historical rates of depreciation. Targets set for managers may demand that they think outside their current horizons and invent new ways of approaching old problems.

Other writers (e.g. Peters, 1978; Dandridge et al., 1980; Boje et al., 1982; Smircich, 1983a; Wilkins, 1983; Trice and Beyer, 1984), also point to the way in which the stories, myths, rituals and other symbols that surround organizational life define reality for those in that organization. For example, if the espoused values are to do with change but the language and signs that exist within the organization are to do with history or the *status quo*, then it is likely that the more powerful signals within that organization will be from the more symbolic actions and language rather than that which is espoused. Whether or not that means that, by changing myths or introducing new myths, change can be itself introduced or speeded up, as some writers (e.g. Boje et al., 1982) claim is perhaps more questionable or at least worthy of further investigation. What is more likely is that these symbolic aspects of the organization need to be consonant with all the other devices for managing change in the organization.

Managing Fundamental Strategic Change

We have drawn here on studies of 'excellence'. In a sense success breeds success; 3M's ability to innovate successfully breeds more success at innovation; Burtons' success at adapting rapidly to a changing environment means that they are more confident in their experiments with new retail ideas; the micro-electronic company characterized by its looseness of structure can afford its inevitable dis-economies so long as the benefits of the system provide success. However, it is an uncomfortable fact that many of the organizations, for example studied by Peters and Waterman, have subsequent to the study become less successful, less able to innovate, more susceptible to the incursions of competition. In some cases this has been because the very confidence of managers has led them to over-stretch themselves and take on ventures that more conservative management teams would shun. In other cases, over time, the 'creative tension' has somehow atrophied into a set of apparently self-fulfilling assumptions that we have here termed the paradigm and led to strategic drift. As we have seen, it is also the case that many organizations do not start from a position of flexibility and innovation. They need to break down a history of inflexible, pre-ordained approaches to what managers see as well defined problems. It is in these states that more fundamental strategic change is required; it is here that the mechanisms for strategy re-formulation become the more important. The argument here is that the achievement of fundamental strategic change requires a change in the paradigm – a change in those taken-for-granted assumptions about how things are done and why the organization is successful – yet, as we have seen, because these *are* taken for granted, this is not the sort of change that is susceptible to intellectual, logical, rational debate. Moreover, it is not as straightforward as introducing new personnel into the firm since they will find, very likely, that the ideas that they introduce are politically threatening. The change process must be essentially cognitive, cultural and political since it is through these mechanisms that the paradigm is preserved or changed.

It is undoubtedly the case, as shown by many studies, that the need will be for outside influence in terms of the introduction of new values, beliefs and strategies. However, the problem is not so much the need for the outsider, as the means by which those ideas can be introduced and supported so as to achieve change. This study has suggested several such mechanisms.

A first step appears to be steps to 'unfreeze' the paradigm. Several mechanisms for such unfreezing have been identified and discussed fully previously. This discussion will not be repeated, but the points may usefully be summarized to show that they provide the context for intervention in order to achieve change. Such mechanisms include the following.

(1) Given the identification of potentially divergent forces in the organization, the fostering of the momentum for change that such divergence provides; this may not entail the overt support for specific views or advocated strategies, so much as the protection and support of individuals advocating them.

(2) One way in which such momentum may be fostered is through making public the debate about the need for change and the problems

facing the organization. In so doing, the constructs of the paradigm, normally hidden in the systems and rituals of the organization, are likely to be made more explicit and the bases of divergence more clear.

(3) It may be possible to heighten or create some trigger for change at an organizational level. In some of the organizations studied these have included such devices as external bank or city pressure, pressure from shareholders or non-executive directors, market research findings or projections of financial decline.

(4) Other means of challenging the paradigm are also possible. These include mainly symbolic challenges that have the role of demonstrating that there is a momentum for change and that the old ways of doing things cannot be considered as sacrosanct. Such symbolic challenges may be relatively slight in themselves, such as changes in operating procedures, forms of behaviour or rituals, but their effect may be highly significant. Senior executives in one rather traditional major manufacturing company in the UK recalled that in the period when they strove to change strategy fundamentally and to get management attitudes to change, the single most powerful public declaration of the significance of the changes required was the closure of the executive dining suite: 'everyone knew nothing would be the same again then'.

(5) The effects of these actions will be to increase tension and disunity in the organization. This has two effects; first, it allows divergent views to grow in significance, because the mechanisms for subjugating them are reduced; second, it breaks down the alliances of powerful individuals or groups that have resisted change.

(6) In the event of the disunity that has been promoted not breaking resistant alliances and leading naturally to compliance, then there may, again, be symbolic mechanisms open to the change agent. For example, the participation of 'converted' respected managers in symbolic acts of support for change, and the 'language of applause' for change may help induce compliance by identification or persuasion.

(7) It may be possible to involve managers in what amounts to partial implementation of, or adoption of, new strategies in such a way that they identify with and own them. This may be achieved, for example, by a manager's involvement in project planning or trials associated with the work of the outsider introducing new ideas, or by a manager being placed in a role as a counsellor to such an outsider.

(8) The most effective means of achieving the breakdown of the paradigm is to demonstrate, not by words and plans, but through action and results, the benefits of new strategies. However, the evidence is that the mechanisms for change will not be successful unless there is support for change agents from a recognized power base within the organization. The

difficulty here is that the power base – typically the chief executive – may be the most reluctant to accept the need for fundamental change, since his or her own position of power may be derived from association with the very paradigm that is the subject of attack. It is also likely that chief executives *in situ* typically see their role as that of problem solvers. The idea that they have a role play in a catalytic sense, politically, not so much in solving strategic problems as in supporting mechanisms for change, including very likely the work of a potentially disruptive change agent, would probably be foreign to many chief executives. Such a role supposes that the chief executive will be prepared to recognize that he or she does not know 'answers' to problems facing the organization; that in itself may well be seen as an admission of failure. Such a role also supposes a recognition that the existing strategy is in need of fundamental change, not marginal adjustment; and that is likely to imply an admission that the strategies previously advocated perhaps by that chief executive were misplaced, or inadequate. The advocacy of fundamental change, therefore, demands that the chief executive takes a different and difficult role; yet it is a role that is crucial to the change process and without which it is likely that the process will not succeed. It is for these reasons that fundamental change is often accompanied by a change in chief executive; it is not necessarily because the new chief executive has the 'answers' to the problems facing the business, but because he or she will be prepared to support and foster the mechansisms for change.

Analysis, Planning and the Role of Pre-history

The introduction of new ideas by outsiders does nothing in itself to guarantee the acceptance of those new ideas, or indeed their success in practice. The success of new strategies is dependent on the capabilities of the organization to put them into effect; there is therefore the need to understand and build upon, or adapt, the resources and skills of the organization. This need for understanding 'pre-history' becomes vital if the introduction of new ideas is to be effectively managed, and may crucially depend on the ability of the outsider to forge an alliance with those within the organization capable of constructive critical assessment of such pre-history. The extent to which such allies exist is likely to depend on the degree of flexibility and fluidity of the system internally; so, for example, organizations in which there is a high degree of heterogeneity of beliefs are more likely to yield such critical allies, whereas those with essentially homogeneous belief systems may yield few, if any, at all. In such circumstances the outsider has the difficult job of fostering the sort of heterogeneity that will facilitate strategic change, whilst building alliances which allow change to be managed and developing strategies to be refined.

In forging strategic change, it is this crucial role of understanding the constraints upon the organization and its capabilities that leads us to consider the place and role of analysis and planning in the process of strategic management. The proposition is that there is need for the process of strategic change to be under way before such planning can take effect. The likelihood of either new external ideas, more formal analysis or planned strategies giving rise to actual strategic change is unlikely if the sorts of processes of change that we have been discussing are not already under way. It is a mistake, and one of some considerable consequence, for managers or consultants to believe that formalized processes of strategic planning can give rise to strategic change without the context of change already being present. However, if processes of unfreezing the influence of the dominant paradigm and its protecting 'cultural web' are under way, with fresh ideas coming into the organization, and if there are allies within, critical of the past, then there is a momentum on which an analysed knowledge of pre-history and a planned refinement of new ideas can be built. In many firms this situation does not prevail. Such 'planning' as does go on does so in a situation where managers are likely to act and conceive of problems and opportunities within the current paradigm. The effect is to achieve a definition of strategy within that paradigm.

'Planning' as a term is much misunderstood and confused. Mintzberg (1981) has pointed out that 'strategic planning' has many different meanings. For some 'strategic planning' means the whole process of strategic management, both formal and informal; at the other extreme, for some it means the constrained activities of operational planning or budgeting. In between there are a whole variety of meanings. What is meant here by 'strategic planning' is those activities by which strategies are refined and defined, which include processes of analysis and evaluation; such processes occur but should be distinguished from a more general process of strategic management. It is a distinction of some consequence. We have seen that strategic management processes may take quite different forms in different organizations, so the impact of similar sorts of strategic planning mechanisms might well be quite different within different modes of strategic management.

In the event of the sorts of processes of strategic change we have discussed here being under way, then the need for strategic planning is consideable. There is certainly a need for analysis in at least two respects.

First, it can contribute to an understanding about the constraints placed upon the organization and the opportunities facing it, including the resources the organization can draw upon and the environmental forces it faces. This is what might be conventionally thought of as 'strategic analysis' but which, less conventionally, we have here termed the learning of pre-history. It is essentially to do with identifying the constraints on the organization and how they might be removed. Such analysis does not in itself provide a basis for the design of strategy but it does provide essential information that informs that strategy. Moreover, if the climate for change exists and the outside influence is credible and powerful enough then there is hope that such information will not be filtered through a pervasive paradigm as might otherwise happen.

A case can also be made for just as thorough an analysis of the assumptions and beliefs that go to make up what has here been called the paradigm in the organization and the mechansisms for its preservation, both political and cultural. Since such constructs are unwritten, tacit and difficult to detect, such analysis is difficult, but so too is the analysis of the uncertainty and complexity that we call the organizational environment. The analysis of political, cultural and cognitive systems is at least as important if strategic change is to be managed. The techniques for such analysis are as yet embryonic but they do exist in part (see, e.g., Mason and Mitroff, 1981; Johnson and Scholes, 1984; Davis, 1984; Sathe 1985). It is possible to surface some of the key assumptions that managers hold, identify the systems, symbols and stories that legitimize these and plot bases of power within the organization. Indeed a simple but powerful model for doing this is the cultural web illustrated in Figure 7.2. This has been used for such purposes with change agents working with organizations in order to identify the constructs of that organization's paradigm, how adaptive change has been built around that paradigm, and how associated power bases and wider cultural systems act to preserve its integrity. Such analysis does not in itself yield specific strategies or tactics for change but is likely to inform the change agent on likely areas of constraints to change, the extent of resistance to change and likely areas in which change can be fostered through political and symbolic activity.

The second area of planning is concerned with definitional issues. If planning cannot be effective unless it is done from within a process of strategic change already under way, it is none the less likely that the strategic solutions being advocated are generalized and ill defined – we saw as much in the Fosters study. The need is to move from this generalized momentum for strategic change to a strategy that is clearly defined in terms of market and competitive positioning, that therefore has meaning in the market and to members of the organization alike, and that takes account of resources and constraints to achieve the implementation of a coherent strategy for the future. This is the traditional area of strategic planning, much maligned, because such techniques have apparently borne so little fruit in many organizations. The argument here is not that the techniques are at fault but rather that their proponents have taken too little heed of the need for more general processes of strategic change and their relevance to planned strategic change. Managers need to learn how to manage both processes of strategic change and the planning of strategy and recognize that they are different but inter-dependent.

Can the Paradigm be Managed?

A good deal of discussion has concentrated on unfreezing processes, by which is meant the breaking down of the dominant paradigm, and the introduction of new ideas and new strategies. The question must therefore be answered as to whether a paradigm can be 'done away with', or conceivably be replaced with one that lasts longer or is more efficient. In other words, can the paradigm be managed? This is to misunderstand the notion of the paradigm. It is not to be likened to a document or a formal control sytem, or indeed anything that can be directly manipulated in a specific way. To repeat, the paradigm is a set of beliefs and tacit assumptions, held relatively commonly, and persisting over time.

Implicitly all organizations are likely to have a paradigm; the question is, do all organizations have a paradigm that is similar in nature in terms of its content, the levels of its constructs or its uniformity? The argument developed . . . in this book is that a paradigm which has evolved based on implicit beliefs *in ways of operating or competing* is particularly dangerous in organizations. If such beliefs are held commonly at this operational level and are taken as self-evident – and the experience of this study and the observation of other companies (e.g. see Spender, 1980) would suggest this is quite typical – then this is particularly problematic. However, it may be that the sort of operational level paradigm as identified in Fosters is not inevitable. It can be argued that organizations exist in which a paradigm is much more difficult to define because beliefs and assumptions are much more diverse. The studies of so-called 'excellent' organizations would suggest that in some there is a great deal more heterogeneity around rather more global sets of core beliefs and values. In such organizations operational constructs within the paradigm may have been replaced by higher-level values, bonding members of the organization together, and permitting a great deal more disagreement and creative challenge at a more operational level. To the extent that managers can promote such higher-level beliefs and develop systems that minimize the risk of atrophy around more operational, specific assumptions about routines, then we can argue that there is managerial influence. However, the notion that one can manage or replace a paradigm is misleading. It may be capable of detection and identification more or less precisely. It may be possible to identify the extent of homogeneity or heterogeneity of the paradigm; but this is not the same as saying that the paradigm can be managed in any mechanistic way. It is not, therefore, a question of whether or not the implicit assumptions held by managers can somehow be removed and replaced with others. Such assumptions evolve and develop over time. Rather, managers and change agents need to understand that they may be able to affect the context in which such developments take place in terms of the systems, symbols and structures of the organization. It is this role of managing the context of ideational culture that is a matter for managerial action.

Managing Across Modes of Strategic Management

As a lead into a discussion of strategic management processes, I have often asked groups of managers to tell me what they mean by 'strategic management'. The responses remain typically traditional; strategic management is seen as tasks of setting objectives, analysing environments, evaluating strategies, monitoring performance and so on. There may also be occasionally managers who talk about experimentation, the encouragement of new ideas and other statements that signify an understanding of rather more adaptive or incremental approaches to the management of strategy. However, seldom does there emerge any perceived relevance of the other modes of strategic management that have been discussed in this book. Table 9.1 suggests that there are important questions and lessons to be understood about strategic management from these other modes. The terms used in table 9.1 are somewhat different to the headings given in chapter 2, but they equate roughly.

By *adaptive* strategic management is meant the process of well informed incrementalism in which managers seek to move and change strategies, keeping continually in touch with a changing environment. It is recognized here that, without other modes of management occurring, this may well be a delusion. Managers may be simply re-creating their own version of reality according to dominant paradigms. The argument is that whilst such adaptive forms of management characterize excellent companies and are worth aspiring to, they can only occur within more generalized processes of strategic change as represented by other modes of strategic management.

The *political* mode of management recognizes that organizations are power structures in which individuals and groups seek to obtain resources and influence over other individuals and groups; in which power is likely to be associated with the dominant paradigm and therefore give rise to great resistance to change. Therefore, for the change agent, the management of the political processes within the organization is crucial if change is to be achieved. It is highly unlikely that an adaptive, flexible, responsive system can exist with entrenched political elites seeking to preserve the basis of their power.

The *cognitive* mode of strategic management is concerned with those very beliefs and assumptions that we have argued are central to understanding why and how strategic change comes about in organizations. The change agent needs to understand what these are and how they are preserved. It is also necessary to understand what mechanisms exist for surfacing and challenging such beliefs and assumptions.

TABLE 9.1 *Changing strategies: five modes of managing*

Adaptive	Political	Cognitive	Symbolic	Planning
* What mechanisms exist for fostering a momentum for continual change (refer to cols. 2–4)?	* What is the power structure in the organization? From what does that power derive?	* Do organization members subscribe to any overarching values/beliefs?	* Are rituals, stories, routines about change or the *status quo*?	* Is there a clear, explicit strategy?
* What is the record of and current 'side-bet experimentation'?	* What are the links between powerful groups and the paradigm?	* What are the key constructs in the paradigm?	* What are the most significant symbolic mechanisms for protecting the paradigm?	* Is it clear within and outside the organization what the goals and components of strategy are?
* What systems exist for encouraging experimentation: do any discourage it?	* Is a re-configuration of the power structure required?	* What devices exist for exposing and challenging the dominant paradigm?	* What opportunity is there for symbolic activity to promote 'unfreezing' and change?	* Is strategy regularly reviewed and re-specified?
* Does involvement in strategy formulation and implementation pervade the organization?	* Are power groupings balanced?	* Are 'outsider' interventions encouraged?		* Do the systems of analysis address paradigm identification?
	* Are all existing levels of management necessary?	* Is a clear organizational strategy 'translated' in terms of everyday values, symbols and language?		* Will processes of change within cols. 1–4 facilitate the impact of analysis/plans?
* Are there crossboundary project groups/ task forces?	* Are 'destructive processes' needed as a precursor to change? * Are top managers visible as champions of change?			* Do the systems of structure and control reinforce or contradict the promotion of strategic change?

The *symbolic* mode of strategic management is primarily concerned with the symbols, stories and systems that legitimize the key beliefs and modes of management in the organization. Moreover, it is likely that it is through this route that a momentum for change and legitimizing of change may well take place.

The *planning* mode of strategic management equates roughly to the scientific or rationalistic views that have pervaded management theory over so many years. These ideas are not dismissed; they are merely placed in the context of other modes of management without which planning techniques are unlikely to succeed or be effective.

The exhibit sets out some of the sorts of questions managers might ask themselves about the processes of strategic management in their organization across different modes of strategic management we have discerned. Managers need to manage strategically across all these modes; they cannot expect to manage the complexity of strategy in any one way. The list is not intended to be comprehensive and the questions will not be reviewed in detail again for they build on the discussion in the book so far. The intention is to provide a checklist upon which managers can themselves build.

CONCLUSION

At the time of writing these concluding remarks, Gareth Morgan's book *'Images of Organisation'* was published. In it he discusses the management of organizations through the device of describing them according to eight quite different 'metaphors'; organizations as machines, as organisms, as brains, as cultures, as political systems, as psychic prisons, as flux and transformation and as instruments of domination. The point he makes is:

> . . . that our theories and explanations of organisational life are based on metaphors that lead us to see and understand organisations in distinctive yet partial ways. . . . For the use of metaphor implies a way of thinking and a way of seeing that pervade how we understand our world generally. (Morgan, 1986, p. 12)

His argument is that researchers, students and managers alike can profitably conceive of organizations in different ways, can deliberately analyse and understand problems by approaching them through these different metaphors and gain insights they otherwise would not gain through such analysis. He argues that because organizations are complex they should not be seen in any one way:

Though managers and organisation theorists often attempt to over-ride this complexity by assuming that organisations are ultimately rational phenomena, that must be understood with reference to their goals or objectives, this assumption often gets in the way of realistic analysis. If one truly wishes to understand an organisation it is much wiser to start with the premise that organisations are complex, ambiguous, and paradoxical. (Morgan, 1986, p. 322)

This book has argued similarly that in managing such complexity there is little to be gained by conceiving of the management task in essentially rationalistic terms. Rather, we need to develop further theories of strategic management based on social, political and cultural models that, at one and the same time, help explain the process and provide insights into the practice. The more rational, traditional approaches to strategic management are not, in this way, diminished in importance, but are rather placed in context and, arguably, made the more useful.

The aim here has been to show that essentially interpretative perspectives on strategic management as a cultural and cognitive process can yield useful insights and are worthy of the attention both of practitioners and researchers.

References

R. P. Abelson, 'The Structure of Belief Systems' in R. C. Schenk and K. M. Colley (eds) *Computer Models of Thought and Language*, W. H. Freeman, pp. 287–339. 1973.

R. P. Abelson, 'Psychological States of the Script Concept', *American Psychologist* vol. 36, pp. 715–29, 1981.

H. Abravanel, 'Mediating Myth in the Service of Organisational Ideology', in L. R. Pondy, P. J. Frost, G. Morgan and T. C. Danbridge (eds), *Organisational Symbolism*, JAI, 1983.

F. Aguilar, *Scanning the Business Environment*, Macmillan, 1967.

S. Al-Bazzaz and P. Grinyer, 'Corporate Planning in the UK: The State of the Art in the 70's', *Strategic Management Journal*, vol. 2, pp. 155–68, 1981.

G. T. Allison, *The Essence of Decision*, Little, Brown & Co., 1971.

C. R. Anderson and F. T. Paine, 'Managerial Perceptions and Strategic Behaviour', *Academy of Management Journal*, vol. 18, pp. 811–23, 1975.

H. I. Ansoff, *Corporate Strategy*, Penguin, 1968.

J. Argenti, *Corporate Planning*, George Allen and Unwin, 1968.

J. Argenti, *Systematic Corporate Planning*, Nelson, 1974.

C. Argyris and D. A. Schön, *Theory in Practice Increasing Professional Effectiveness*, Jossey-Bass, 1974.

C. Argyris and D. A. Schön, *Organisational Learning: A Theory of Action Perspective*, Addison-Wesley, 1978.

J. S. Armstrong, The Value of Formal Planning for Strategic Decisions: Review of Empirical Research, *Strategic Management Journal* vol. 3, pp. 197–211, 1982.

C. Barnard, *The Functions of the Executive*, Harvard University Press, 1938.

H. Bahrami, 'Design of Corporate Planning Systems', *PhD Thesis*, University of Aston in Birmingham, 1981.

J. M. Bartunek, 'Changing Interpretive Schemes and Organisational Restructuring: the Examples of a Religious Order', *Administrative Science Quarterly*, vol. 29, pp. 355–72, 1984.

J. Beattie, *Other Cultures*, Cohen and West, 1964.

J. M. Beyer, 'Ideologies, Values and Decision Making in Organisations' in P. C. Nystrom and W. H. Starbuck (eds), *Handbook of Organisational Design*, vol. 2, Oxford University Press, 1981.

R. Bhaskar, *The Possibility of Naturalism: A Philisophic Critique of the Contemporary Human Sciences*, Harvester, 1979.

N. W. Biggart, 'The Creative-Destructive Process of Organisational Change: The Case of the Post Office', *Administrative Science Quarterly*, vol. 22, pp. 410–26, 1977.

E. Bittner, 'The Concept of Organisation', *Social Research*, vol. 32, pp. 239–55, 1965.

H. Blumer, 'Society as a Symbolic Interaction', in J. G. Manis (ed.), *Symbolic Interaction: A Reader in Social Psychology*, Allyn and Bacon, 1967.

R. Bogdan and J. S. Taylor, *Introduction to Qualitative Research Methods*, John Wiley and Sons, 1975.

D. M. Boje, D. B. Fedor and K. M. Rowland, 'Myth Making: a Qualitative Step in O D Interventions', *Journal of Applied Behavioural Science*, vol. 18, no. 1, pp. 17–28, 1982.

J. S. Boswell, *Business Policies in the Making*, Allen and Unwin, 1983.

J. L. Bower, *Managing the Resource Allocation Process: a Study of Corporate Planning and Investment*, Irwin, 1972.

R. H. Brown, 'Bureaucracy as Praxis: Toward a Political Phenomenology of Formal Organisations', *Administrative Science Quarterly*, vol. 23, pp. 365–82, 1978.

R. A. Burgelman, 'Corporate Enterpreneurship and Strategic Management: Insights from a Process Study', *Management Science*, vol. 29, pp. 1349–64, 1983.

G. Burrell and G. Morgan, *Sociological Paradigms and Organisational Analysis*, Heinemann, 1979.

E. E. Chaffee, 'Three Models of Strategy', *Academy of Management Review*, vol. 10, no. 1, pp. 89–98, 1985.

A. D. Chandler, *Strategy and Structure*, MIT, 1962.

Y. N. Chang and F. Campo-Flores, *Business Policy and Strategy*, Goodyear, 1980.

D. F. Channon, *The Burton Group Ltd* Case Clearing House of Great Britain and Ireland, 1972.

D. F. Channon, *The Strategy and Structure of British Enterprise*, Macmillan, 1973.

D. F. Channon, *The Service Industries, Strategy Structure and Financial Performance*, MacMillan, 1973.

J. Child, 'Organisational Structure, Environment and Performance the Role of Strategic Choice', *Sociology*, vol. 6, pp. 1–22, 1972.

M. D. Cohen, J. C. March and J. P. Olsen, 'A Garbage Can Model of Organisation Choice', *Administrative Science Quarterly*, vol. 17, pp. 1–25, 1972.

R. Cohen, L. L. Langness, J. Middleton, V. C. Uhendu and J. W. Vanstone, 'Entry into the Field' in R. Narroll and R. Cohen (eds), *A Handbook of Method in Cultural Anthropolgy*, Columbia University Press, 1973.

R. A. Cosier, 'Dialectical Inquiry in Strategic Planning; a Case of Premature Acceptance', *Academy of Management Review*, vol. 6, pp. 643–8, 1981.

H. Crozier, *The Bureaucratic Phenomenon*, University of Chicago Press, 1964.

R. B. Cyert and J. G. March, *A Behavioural Theory of the Firm*, Prentice-Hall, 1963.

R. L. Daft, 'Symbols in Organisations A Dual-content Framework for Analysis' in L. R. Pondy, R. J. Frost, G. Morgan and T. C. Danbridge (eds), *Organisational Symbolism*, JAI, 1983.

R. L. Daft and K. E. Weick, 'Toward a Model of Organisations as Interpretation Systems', *Academy of Management Review*, vol. 9, no. 2, pp. 284–95, 1984.

G. W. Dalton, 'Influence and Organisational Change', in G. W. Dalton and P. R. Lawrence (eds), *Organisational Change and Development*, Irwin, 1970.

M. Dalton, *Men Who Manage: Fusions of Feelings and Theory in Administration*, John Wiley and Sons, 1959.

M. Dalton, 'Preconceptions and Methods in Men who Manage', in P. E. Hammond (ed.), *Sociologists at Work*, Basic Books, 1964.

T. C. Dandridge, I. Mitroff and W. F. Joyce, 'Organisational Symbolism: a Topic to Expand Organisational Analysis', *Academy of Management Review*, vol. 5, pp. 77–82, 1980.

S. M. Davis, *Managing Corporate Culture*, Ballinger/Harper and Row, 1984.

T. Deal and A. Kennedy, *Corporate Cultures: The Rites and Rituals of Corporate Life*, Addison-Wesley, 1982.

N. K. Denzin, *The Research Act*, McGraw–Hill, 1978.

L. Dighton, *Frogs and Paradigms*, Corporate Renewal Associates, 1980.

L. Donaldson, 'Divisionalisation and Diversification: a Longitudinal Study', *Academy of Management Journal*, vol 25, pp. 321–37, 1982.

P. Drucker, *The Practice of Management, Pan Management Series*, vol. 00, Pan, 1968.

E. E. Evans-Pritchard, *Social Anthropology*, Cohen and West, 1951.

R. M. Emerson, 'Power–Dependence Relations', *American Sociological Review*, vol. 27, pp. 31–41, 1962.

A. Etzioni, *A Comparative Analysis of Complex Organisations* The Free Press, 1961.

L. Fahey, 'On Strategic Management Decision Processes', *Strategic Management Journal*, vol. 2, pp. 43–60, 1981.

R. A. Feinberg, D. Koscica and S. J. Recobs, 'Strategic Planning: What the Top 100 Stores Say', *Retail Control*, October, 1983.

M. S. Feldman and J. G. March, Information in Organizations as Signal and Symbol, *Administrative Science Quarterly*, vol. 26, pp. 171–186, 1981.

G. A. Fine, 'Negotiated Orders and Organisational Cultures', *Annual Review of Sociology*, vol. 10, pp. 239–62, 1984.

F. V. Fox and B. M. Staw, 'The Trapped Administratory: Effects of Job Insecurity and Policy Resistance Upon Commitment to a Course of Action', *Administrative Science Quarterly*, vol. 24, pp. 449–71, 1979.

J. W. Frederickson, 'Strategic Process: Questions and Recommendations', *Academy of Management Review*, vol. 8, pp. 565–75, 1983.

F. Friedlander, 'Patterns of Individual and Organisational Learning', in S. Srivastva (ed.), *The Executive Mind*, Jossey-Bass, 1983.

R. C. Fuller and R. R. Myers, 'The States of a Social Problem', in E. Rubington and M. S. Weinberg (eds), *The Study of Social Problems*, Oxford University Press, 1977.

C. Gilligan and C. Sutton, 'Strategic Planning in Grocery and DIY Retailing', in G. N. Johnson (ed.), *Business Strategy and Retailing*, John Wiley and Sons, 1987.

D. A. Gioia and P. P. Poole, 'Scripts in Organisational Behaviour', *Academy of Management Review*, vol. 9, no. 3, pp. 449–59, 1984.

D. Gladstein and J. B. Quinn, 'Making Decisions and Producing Action: The Two Faces of Strategy', in J. Pennings, *Organisational Strategy and Change*, pp. 198–216, Jossey-Bass, 1985.

B. C. Glaser, *Theoretical Sensitivity*, The Sociology Press, 1978.

B. C. Glaser and A. L. Strauss, *The Discovery of Grounded Theory*, Weidenefeld and Nicholson, 1968.

W. F. Glueck, *Strategic Management and Business Policy*, McGraw-Hill, 1980.

S. Green, 'From Riches to Rags: The John Collier Story: An Interpretative Study of Strategic Change', in G. Johnson (ed.), *Business Strategy and Retailing*, John Wiley and Sons, 1987.

L. E. Greiner, 'Evolution and Revolution as Organisations Grow', *Harvard Business Review*, July/August, pp. 37–46, 1972.

P. H. Grinyer and D. Norburn, Planning for Existing Markets: Perceptions of Chief Executives and Financial Performance, *The Journal of the Royal Statistical Society*, vol. 138 Series A, pp. 70–97, 1975

P. H. Grinyer, S. Al-Bazzaz and M. Yasai-Ardekani, 'Strategy, Structure, the Environment and Financial Performance in 48 UK Companies', *Academy of Management Journal*, vol. 23, pp. 193–220, 1980.

P. H. Grinyer and J. C. Spender, 'Recipes, Crises and Adaptation in Mature Businesses', *International Studies of Management and Organisation*, vol. 9, pp. 113–23, 1979a.

P. H. Grinyer and J. C. Spender, 'Turnaround: Managerial Receipes for Strategic Success: The Fall and Rise of the Newton Chambers Group', *Associated Business*, 1979b.

W. K. Hall, 'Strategic Planning Models: Are Top Managers Really Finding Them Useful', *Journal of Business Policy*, vol. 3, pp. 19–27, 1973.

D. C. Hambrick, 'Environment, Strategy and Power Within Top Management Teams', *Administrative Science Quarterly*, vol. 26, pp. 253–76, 1981.

M. Hammersley and P. Atkinson, *Ethnography: Principles in Practice*, Tavistock, 1983.

D. Harvey, *Business Policy and Strategic Management*, Charles E. Merril, 1982.

E. Harvey and R. Mills, Patterns of Organizational Adaptation: a Political Perspective, in M. N. Zald, *Power in Organizations*, Vanderbilt University Press, 1979.

B. L. T. Hedberg and S. Jönsson, 'Strategy Making as a Discontinuous Process', *International Studies of Management and Organisation*, vol. 7, pp. 88–109, 1977.

B. L. T. Hedberg, P. C. Nystrom and W. H. Starbuck, 'Camping on Seesaws: Prescriptions for a Self Designing Organisation', *Administrative Science Quarterly*, vol. 21, pp. 41–65, 1976

R. P. Herden and M. A. Lyles, Individual Attributes and the Problem Conceptualization Process, *Human Systems Management*, Vol. 2, pp. 275–284. 1981.

D. J. Hickson, R. J. Butler, D. Cray, G. R. Mallory and D. C. Wilson, 'Comparing 150 Decision Processes', in H. Pennings (ed.), *Organisational Strategy and Change*, Jossey–Bass, pp. 114–42, 1985.

D. J. Hickson, R. J. Butler, D. Cray, G. R. Mallory and D. C. Wilson, *Top Decisions: Strategic Decision Making in Organisations*, Basil Blackwell, 1986.

D. J. Hickson, G. R. Hinings, C. A. Lee, R. E. Schneck and J. M. Dennings, 'A Strategic Contingencies Theory of Intraorganisational Power', *Administrative Science Quarterly*, vol. 16, no. 2, pp. 216–29, 1971.

C. W. Hofer and D. Schendel, *Strategy Formulation: Analytical Concepts*, West, 1978.

O. R. Holsti, *Content Analysis for the Social Sciences and Humanities*, Addison–Wesley, 1969.

G. C. Homans, 'Contemporary Theory in Sociology', in R. E. L. Ferris (ed.), *Handbook of Modern Sociology*, Rand, McNally and Co., 1964.

A. S. Huff, 'Industrial Influences on Strategy Reformation', *Strategic Management Journal*, vol. 3, pp. 119–31, 1983.

A. S. Huff, 'A Rehetorical Examination of Strategic Change', in L. R. Pondy, P. J. Frost, G. Morgan and T. C. Dandridge (eds), *Organisational Symbolism*, JAI, 1983.

A. S. Huff and K. E. Fletcher, 'Strategic Argument Mapping', presented at the *Strategic Management Society Conference, Philadelphia, October 1984*.

E. Hunt, 'What Kind of Computer is Man', *Cognitive Psychology*, vol. 2, pp. 57–98, 1971.

E. Huse and J. L. Bowditch, *Behaviour in Organisations*, Addison–Wesley, 1977.

R. Hyman and B. Anderson, 'Solving Problems', in D. A. Kolb, I. M. Rubin, J. M. McIntyre (eds), *Organisational Psychology*, Prentice–Hall, 1974.

I. L. Janis, *Victims of Groupthink*, Houghton–Mifflin, 1972.

I. L. Janis, *Groupthink: Psychological Studies of Policy Decisions and Fiascoes*, Houghton-Mifflin, 1982.

I. L. Janis, 'Sources of Error in Strategic Decision Making', in J. M. Pennings (ed.), *Organisational Strategy and Change*, Jossey–Bass, pp. 157–97, 1985.

I. L. Janis and L. Mann, *Decision Making*, The Free Press, 1977.

E. Jaques, *The Changing Culture of a Factory*, Tavistock, 1951.

T. D. Jick, 'Mixing Qualitative and Quantitative Methods: Triangulation in Action', *Administration Science Quarterly*, vol, 24, pp. 601–11, 1979.

G. Johnson, 'The Process of Strategic Management – A Management Perspective', *PhD Thesis*, University of Aston in Birmingham, 1984.

G. Johnson, 'Strategic Management in Action', in V. Hammond (ed.), *Current Research in Management*, Francis Pinter, 1985.

G. Johnson, *The Burton Group (A & B)*, Manchester Business School, 1986.

G. Johnson and K. Scholes, *Exploring Corporate Strategy*, Prentice–Hall, 1984.

M. Kanter, *The Change Masters: Innovation for Productivity in the American Corporation*, George Allen and Unwin, 1984.

M. Keesing, 'Theories of Culture', *Annual Review of Anthropology*, vol. 3, pp. 73–9, 1974.

G. Kelly, *The Psychology of Personal Constructs*, W. W. Norton and Co., 1955.

H. C. Kelman, 'Compliance, Identification and Internalisation: Three Process of Attitude Change', *Conflict Resolution*, vol. 2, pp. 51–60, 1958.

S. Kiesler and L. Sproull, Managerial Response to Changing Environments:

Perspectives on Problem Sensing from Social Cognition, *Administrative Science Quarterly*, vol. 27 pp. 548–579, 1982.

D. A. Kolb, 'On Management and Learning Process, in D. A. Kolb, I. M. Rubin, J. M. McIntyre (eds.), *Organisational Psychology*, Prentice–Hall, 1974.

J. P. Kotter, 'The Psychological Contract; Managing the Joining-Up Process', *California Management Review*, pp. 91–9, 1973.

J. P. Kotter, *The General Managers*, The Free Press, 1982.

J. P. Kotter and P. Lawrence, *Mayors in Action*, John Wiley and Sons, 1974.

J. Kozielecki, *Psychological Design Theory*, D. Reidel and Co., 1981.

R. J. Kudla, The Effects of Strategic Planning Common Stock Returns, *Academy of Management Journal*, vol. 23 pp. 5–20, 1980.

D. Laynder, 'Grounded Theory: A Constructive Critique', *Journal for the Theory of Social Behaviour*, vol. 12, pp. 103–23, 1982.

E. P. Learned, C. R. Christensen, K. R. Andrews and W. D. Guth, *Business Policy: Text and Cases*, Irwin, 1965.

M. Leontiades and A. Tezel, Planning Perceptions and Planning Results, *Strategic Management Journal*, vol. 1, pp. 65–76, 1980.

K. Lewin, *Field Theory in Social Sciences*, Tavistock, 1952.

C. E. Lindblom, 'The Science of Muddling Through', *Public Administration Review*, vol. 19, pp. 79–88, 1959.

C. E. Lindblom and D. Braybrooke, *A Strategy of Decision*, The Free Press, 1963.

A. R. Lindesmith, *Opiate Addiction*, Principia, 1947.

A. R. Lindesmith, A. L. Strauss and N. K. Denzin, *Social Psychology*, Holt, Reinhart and Winston, 1977.

S. A. Lippman and R. P. Rumelt, 'Uncertain Imitability: An Analysis of Inter-firm Differences in Efficiency under Competition', *Bell Journal of Economics*, vol. 13, no. 2, pp. 418–38, 1982.

M. R. Louis, 'Organisations as Culture Bearing Milieux', in L. R. Pondy, P. J. Frost, G. Morgan and T. C. Dandridge (eds), *Organisational Symbolism*, JAI, 1983.

M. A. Lyles, 'Formulating Strategic Problems – Empirical Analysis and Model Development', *Stategic Management Journal*, vol. 2, pp. 61–75, 1981.

K. Mannheim, *Ideology and Utopia*, Routledge and Kegan Paul, 1936.

J. G. March and H. A. Simon, *Organisations*, John Wiley and Sons, 1958.

J. Marshall and A. McLean, 'Exploring Organisation Culture as a Route to Organisation Change', in V. Hammond (ed.), *Current Research in Management*, Francis Pinter, 1985.

J. Martin, 'Stories and Scripts in Organisational Settings', in A. H. Hastorf and A. M. Isen (eds), *Cognitive Social Psychology*, Elsevier, pp. 255–305, 1982.

J. Martin and M. E. Powers, 'Organisational Stories: More Vivid and Persuasive than Quantitative Data', in B. Staw (ed.), *Psychological Foundations of Organisational Behaviour*, Scott, Foresman & Co., pp. 161–8, 1983.

R. O. Mason and I. I. Mitroff, *Challenging Strategic Planning Assumptions*, John Wiley and Sons, 1981.

B. N. Meltzer, J. W. Petras and L. T. Reynolds, *Symbolic Interactionism: Genesis, Varieties and Criticism*, Routledge and Kegan Paul, 1975.

A. D. Meyer, 'How Ideologies Supplement Formal Structures and Shape Responses to Environments', *Journal of Management Studies*, vol. 19, no. 1, pp. 45–61, 1982.

J. W. Meyer and B. Rowan, 'Institutional Organisations: Formal Structures as Myth and Ceremony' *American Journal of Sociology* vol. 83, pp. 340–63, 1977.

M. B. Miles, 'Qualitative Data as an Attractive Nuisance: The Problem of Analysis', *Administrative Science Quarterly*, vol. 24, pp. 590–601, 1979.

R. E. Miles and C. C. Snow, *Organistional Strategy, Structure and Process*, McGraw-Hill, 1978.

D. Miller and P. Friesen, 'Archetypes of Strategy Formulation', *Management Science*, vol. 24, pp. 921–33, 1978.

D. Miller and P. Friesen, 'Momentum and Revolution in Organisational Adaptation', *Academy of Management Journal*, vol. 23, no. 4, pp. 591–614, 1980.

H. Mintzberg, *The Nature of Managerial Work*, Harper and Row, 1973a.

H. Mintzberg, 'Strategy Making in Three Modes', *California Management Review*, vol. 16, no. 2, 1973b.

H. Mintzberg, 'Patterns in Strategy Formation', *Management Science*, May, pp. 934–48, 1978.

H. Mintzberg, *The Structuring of Organisations*, Prentice–Hall, 1979a.

H. Mintzberg, 'An Emerging Strategy of "Direct" Research', *Administrative Science Quarterly*, vol. 24, pp. 582–9, 1979b.

H. Mintzberg, 'What is Planning Anyway?', *Strategic Management Journal*, vol. 2, pp. 319–24, 1981.

H. Mintzberg, O. Raisinghani and A. Theoret. 'The Structure of Unstructured Decision Processes', *Administrative Science Quarterly*, vol. 21, pp. 246–75, 1976.

H. Mintzberg and J. A. Waters, 'The Mind of the Strategist(s)', in S. Srivastva (ed.), *The Executive Mind*, Jossey–Bass, 1983.

G. Morgan, *Images of Organisation*, Sage, 1986.

G. Morgan, P. J. Frost and L. R. Pondy, 'Organisational Symbolism', in L. R. Pondy, P. J. Frost, G. Morgan and T. C. Dandridge (eds), *Organisational Symbolism*, JAI, 1983.

R. R. Nelson and S. G. Winter, *An Evolutionary Theory of Economic Change*, Harvard University Press, 1982.

D. Norburn and P. Grinyer, 'Directors without Direction', *Journal of General Management*, vol. 1, pp. 37–48, 1973/74.

R. O'Day, 'Intimidation Rituals: Reaction to Reform', *Journal of Applied Behavioural Science*, vol. 10, pp. 373–86, 1974.

W. G. Ouchi, 'Markets, Bureaucracies and Clans', *Administrative Science Quarterly*, vol. 25, pp. 129–41, 1980.

J. A. Pearce and R. B. Robinson, *Strategic Management*, Irwin, 1982.

C. Perrow, *Complex Organisations: A Critical Essay*, Scott, Foreman and Co., 1979.

T. J. Peters, 'Symbols, Patterns and Settings: an Optimistic Case for Getting Things Done', *Organisational Dynamics*, 1978.

T. J. Peters and R. H. Waterman (Jr), *In Search of Excellence*, Harper and Row, 1982.

A. M. Pettigrew, 'Information Control as a Power Resource', *Sociology*, vol. 6, no. 2, pp. 187–204, 1972.

A. M. Pettigrew, *The Politics of Organisational Decision Making*, Tavistock, 1973.

A. M. Pettigrew, 'Towards a Political Theory of Organisational Intervention', *Human Relations*, vol. 28, no. 3, pp. 191–208, 1975.

A. M. Pettigrew, 'Strategy Formulation as a Political Process', *International Studies of Management and Organisation*, vol. 7, no. 2, pp. 78–87, 1977.

A. M. Pettigrew, 'On Studying Organisational Cultures', *Administrative Science Quarterly*, vol. 24, pp. 570–81, 1979.

A. M. Pettigrew, 'Contextual Research: A Natural Way to Link Theory and Practice', presented to the *Conference on Conducting Research with Theory and Practice in Mind,* University of Southern California, November 1983.

A. M. Pettigrew, 'Examining Change in the Long Term Context of Culture and Politics', in J. M. Pennings (ed.), *Organisational Strategy and Change*, pp. 269–318, Jossey–Bass, 1985a.

A. M. Pettigrew, *The Awakening Giant*, Basil Blackwell, 1985b.

J. Pfeffer, *Power in Organisations*, Pitman, 1981a.

J. Pfeffer, 'Management as Symbolic Action: The Creation and Maintenance of Organisational Paradigms', in L. L. Cummings and B. M. Staw (eds.), *Research in Organisational Behaviour*, vol. 3, JAI, pp. 1–15, 1981b.

J. Pfeffer and G. R. Salancik, 'Organisational Decision Making as a Political Process: The Case of a University Budget', *Administrative Science Quarterly*, vol. 19, pp. 135–51, 1974.

J. Pfeffer and G. R. Salancik, *The External Control of Organisations: A Resource Dependence Perspective*, Harper and Row, 1978.

J. R. Phillips, 'When Good Management is not Enough', *The McKinsey Quarterly*, Summer, 1986.

M. Pitt and G. Johnson, 'Managing Strategic Change: A Chief Executive's Perspective', in G. Johnson (ed.), *Business Strategy and Retailing'*, John Wiley and Sons, 1987.

L. R. Pondy, 'Union of Rationality and Intuition in Management Action', in S. Srivastva (ed.), *The Executive Mind*, Jossey–Bass, 1983.

M. E. Porter, *Competitive Strategy*, The Free Press/Collier–Macmillan, 1980.

C. Pumpin, *Management Strategischer Erfolgs-positionen*, Haupt, 1983.

J. B. Quinn, *Strategies for Change*, Irwin, 1980.

B. D. Reed and B. W. Palmer, *An Introduction to Organisational Behaviour*, The Grubb Institute, 1972.

E. Rhenman, *Organisation Theory for Long Range Planning*, John Wiley and Sons, 1973.

A. J. Rowe, R. O. Mason and K. E. Dickel, *Strategic Management and Business Policy: A Methodological Approach*, Addison–Wesley, 1982.

R. P. Rumelt, *Strategy, Structure and Economic Performance*, Harvard University Press, 1974.

G. R. Salancik, J. Pfeffer and J. P. Kelly, 'A Contingency Model of Influence in Organisational Decision Making', *Pacific Sociological Review*, vol. 21, pp. 239–56, 1978.

S. Salmans, 'New Vogue: Company Culture', *New York Times*, 9 January 1983.

V. Sathe, *Culture and Related Corporate Realities*, Irwin, 1985.

L. Schalzman and A. L. Strauss, *Field Research: Strategies for a Natural Sociology*, Prentice–Hall, 1973.

E. H. Schein, 'Personal Change Through Interpersonal Relationships', in W. G. Bennis, D. E. Barlow, E. H. Schein and F. L. Steel, *Interpersonal Dynamics*, Dorsey, 1973.

E. H. Schein, 'Organisational Socialization and the Profession of Management', in D. A. Kolb, I. M. Rubin and J. M. McIntyre (eds), *Organisational Psychology: A Book of Readings*, Prentice–Hall, 1974.

E. H. Schein, *Organisational Culture and Leadership*, Jossey–Bass, 1985.

D. Schön, *The Reflective Practitioner*, Basic Books, 1983.

R. Schrank and R. Abelson, *Scripts, Plans and Knowledge*, Erlbaum, 1977.

H. Schwartz and S. Davis, 'Matching Corporate Culture and Business Strategy', *Organisational Dynamics*, Summer, pp. 30–48, 1981.

C. R. Schwenk, 'Effects of Inquiry Methods and Ambiguity Tolerance on Prediction Performance', *Decision Sciences*, vol. 13, pp. 207–21, 1982.

W. R. Scott, 'Field Methods in the Study of Organisations', in J. G. March (ed.), *Handbook of Organisations*, Rand, McNally and Co., 1965.

C. B. Schrader, L. Taylor and D. R. Dalton, Strategic Planning and Organizational Performance: a Critical Appraisal, *Journal of Management*, vol. 10, pp. 149–71, 1984.

A. Sheldon, 'Organisational Paradigms: a Theory of Organisational Change' *Organisational Dynamics*, vol. 8, no. 3, pp. 61–71, 1980.

P. Shrivastava and I. Mitroff, 'Frames of Reference Managers Use: a Study in Applied Sociology of Knowledge', in R. Lamb (ed.), *Advances in Strategic Management*, vol. 1, JAI, 1983.

S. Slatter, *Corporate Recovery*, Penguin, 1984.

C. Smart and I. Vertinsky, 'Designs for Crisis Decision Units', *Administrative Science Quarterly*, vol. 22, pp. 640–57, 1977.

L. Smircich, 'Organisations as Shared Meanings', in L. R. Pondy, J. Frost, G. Morgan and T. C. Dandridge (eds), *Organisational Symbolism*, JAI, pp. 55–68, 1983a.

L. Smircich, 'Concepts of Culture and Organisational Analysis', *Administrative Science Quarterly*, vol. 28, pp. 339–58, 1983b.

P. Soelberg, 'Unprogrammed Decision-Making', *Industrial Management Review*, Spring, pp. 19–29, 1967.

J-C. Spender, 'Strategy Making in Business', *PhD Thesis*, School of Business, University of Manchester, 1980.

B. M. Staw, 'The Escalation of a Commitment to a Course of Action', *Academy of Management Review*, vol. 6, pp. 577–87, 1981.

B. M. Staw and J. Ross, 'Commitment to a Policy Decision a Multi-theoretical Perspective', *Administrative Science Quarterly*, vol. 23, pp. 40–64, 1978.

G. A. Steiner, *Strategic Planning: What Every Manger Must Know*, The Free Press, 1979

A. Strauss, L. Schatzman, D. Ehrlich, R. Bucher and M. Sabshin. 'The Hospital and its Negotiated Order', in E. Friedson (ed.), *The Hospital in Modern Society*, The Free Press, 1963.

D. J. Teece, 'Applying Concepts of Economic Analysis to Strategic Management' in J. M. Pennings (ed.), *Organisational Strategy and Change*, Jossey-Bass, 1985.

J. D. Thompson, *Organisations in Action*, McGraw–Hill, 1967.

N. M. Tichy, *Managing Strategic Chante, Technical, Political and Cultural Dynamics*, John Wiley and Sons, 1983.

E. C. Tolman, 'There is More Than One Kind of Learning', *Psychological Review*, vol. 56, pp. 144–55, 1949.

R. Townsend, *Up the Organisation*, Michael Joseph Ltd, 1970.

H. M. Trice and J. M. Beyer, 'Studying Organisational Cultures Through Rites and Ceremonials', *Academy of Management Review*, vol. 9, no. 4, pp. 653–69, 1984.

B. Turner, *Exploring the Industrial Sub-Culture*, Macmillan, 1971.

B. Turner, *Some Practical Aspects of Qualitative Data Analysis: One Way of Organising the Cognitive Process Associated with the Generation of Grounded Theory, Quality and Quantity*, vol. 15, pp. 225–47, 1981.

M. Tushman and E. Romanelli, 'Organisation Evolution: A Metamorphosis Model of Convergence and Reorientation', in B. Staw and L. Cummings (eds), *Research in Organisation Behaviour*, vol. 7, JAI, pp. 171–222, 1986.

A. T. Tversky and D. Kahneman, 'Judgements Under Uncertaintity Heuristics and Biases', *Science*, vol. 185, pp. 1124–31, 1975.

J. van Maanen, 'The Fact of Fiction in Organisational Ethnography', *Administrative Science Quarterly*, vol. 24, pp. 539–50, 1979.

P. Watzlawick, J. H. Weakland and R. Fisch, *Change: Principles of Problem Formulation and Problem Resolution*, Norton, 1974.

K. E. Weick, 'Enactment Processes in Organisations', in B. M. Staw and G. R. Salancik (eds), *New Directions in Organisational Behaviour*, St Clair, 1977.

K. E. Weick, *The Social Psychology of Organizing*, Addison–Wesley, 1979a.

K. E. Weick, 'Cognitive Processes in Organisation', in B. M. Staw (ed.), *Research in Organisational Behaviour*, vol. 1, JAI, 1979b.

K. E. Weick, 'Managerial Thought in the Context of Action', in S. Srivastva (ed.), *The Executive Mind*, Jossey–Bass, 1983.

T. L. Wheelan and J. D. Hunger, *Strategic Mangement and Business Policy*, Addison–Wesley, 1983.

R. Whipp, R. Rosenfeld and A. Pettigrew, 'Understanding Strategic Change Processes: Some Preliminary British Findings', presented to the ESRC/Coopers and Lybrand International Research Seminar on The Management of Strategic Change, University of Warwick, May 1986.

A. B. Wildavsky, 'The Self-Evaluation Organisation', *Public Administration Review*, vol. 32, pp. 509–20, 1972.

A. L. Wilkins, 'Organisational Stories as Symbols which Control the Organisation', in L. R. Pondy, P. J. Frost, G. Morgan and T. C. Dandridge (eds), *Organisational Symbolism*, JAI, 1983.

A. L. Wilkins and W. G. Ouchi, 'Effective Cultures: Exploring the Relation Between Culture and Organisational Performance', *Administration Science Quarterly*, vol. 28, pp. 468–81, 1983.

R. K. Yin, *Case Study Research: Design and Methods*, Sage, 1984.

Subject Index

Author Index